Genocide Perspe

Essays on Holocaust and Genocide

Editor: Colin Tatz

The Australian Institute for Holocaust & Genocide Studies

UTSePress
2012

2

National Library of Australia Cataloguing-in-Publication
    entry
Tatz, Colin
Genocide perspectives IV : essays on   holocaust and
    genocide/Colin Tatz.
ISBN: 9780987236975
Genocide.   Antisemitism.   Holocaust, Jewish (1939-1945)
304.663

ACKNOWLEDGMENTS

This volume owes much to Sandra Tatz. It was Sandra who initiated the collection, contacted the contributors, arranged the peer reviews, helped organise the framework, proofed the contents, and designed the layout of this volume. My thanks to Gabrielle Gardiner and Cornelia Cronje at the University of Technology Sydney for this e-book and Agata Mrva-Montoya and Susan Murray-Smith from Sydney University Press for hard copies. Thanks to Konrad Kwiet, Graeme Ward, Winton Higgins, and Rowan Savage for their assistance and to Torunn Higgins for her cover design.

Three of the essays are modified, extended and updated versions of articles that have appeared elsewhere, as indicated in their contributions here. We acknowledge Oxford University Press as the publishers of the Michael Dudley and Fran Gale essay; *Patterns of Prejudice* (UK) for the Ruth Balint paper; and *Interstitio* (Republic of Moldova) for Shannon Woodcock's essay.

Cover design: Torunn Higgins

The essays in this volume are refereed.

CONTENTS

THE MAGNITUDE OF GENOCIDE

COLIN TATZ

I began teaching comparative genocide studies at Macquarie University in Sydney almost a quarter of a century ago. Exploring with students the scale and dimensions of a dozen cases of this 'crime of crimes', I found myself muttering about the need for markers or symbols to distinguish the immensity and proportions of the events, in short, their magnitude. I got no further than suggesting we borrow terminology from criminal justice systems which distinguish between murder and manslaughter, between degrees of intent in those crimes, between murder in the first and second degree, or as between a principal in the first degree and an accessory in the second.

I left it at that until April 2012 when I addressed a conference on 'The Holocaust and Legacies of Race in the Post-Colonial World, 1945 to the Present', a joint enterprise between the Universities of Cape Town, Southampton and Sydney. My theme was that Holocaust and genocide studies need to develop a 'Richter-Scale', a set of criteria which measures, however broadly, the immensity of a genocide much in the way that seismologist Charles Richter's magnitude scale denotes the level of energy produced by an earthquake. I am hardly suggesting a logarithmic 10-number formula, or anything as literal as that, but rather a *generally recognisable order of magnitude* — assuredly not for the sake of claiming in some quantitative way which event is the first, second or third, or which the 'biggest', 'smallest' or 'worst' explosion. There should be no room for a victimhood competition, but there is certainly place for a clear indication of the sometimes great variations from a single (or, rather, a multifactor) norm; a way to find similarities and differences between cases and within cases; and a way of distilling the core of the events so that we can do better than simple categorisations like unique, or universal, or singular, or exceptional—the terms that are evoked by the Holocaust. Some genocides, like the Jewish and Armenian events, are those things, but we need to delve deeper, to take into account and then examine a variety of components, ingredients, causative factors and outcomes. Within the components there are further degrees or gradations to be examined, such as the hierarchies of perpetrators, the differences in bystander behaviour, the qualities and quantities of rescue efforts, variations in victim resistance, similarities and differences in long-term impacts on targeted victim groups, in post-genocidal justice, in reparations mechanisms and their results.

Briefly, for the sake of convenience, accessibility and coherence, I list six major clusters for the assessment of a case of genocide: (1) the prerequisites of, or *pre*-cedents or precursors to, the event; (2) the actual genocidal event; (3) the post-genocide analyses; (4) the immediate aftermath of the genocide; (5) the long-term legacies of the genocide; and (6) other significant contributing factors. At first blush this could appear to be an autopsy model—a quantitative inquest into events that have occurred. But when completed, this 'Richter-Scale' will have to be both multi-dimensional—retrospective, reflective, prospective—and driven by a process or technique. The process needed can well be something like the thematic approaches to medicine: (a) 'epidemiological', that is, looking at the distribution of cases, their patterns, incidence, prevalence, influences, and their determinants; (b) 'preventive', staving off rather than having to treat the behaviour; (c) 'diagnostic', identifying and confirming the 'disease' from its signs and symptoms; (d) 'prognostic' in the sense of describing and forecasting the likely outcomes of the warning signs; (e) 'curative', that is, intervening by treatment and remedy of a particular ongoing situation (f) 'post-mortem', in the autopsy sense; and (g) 'rehabilitative', the manner and nature of repair and recovery. Mixing metaphors from history, medicine, law and seismology may seem a formidable exercise, but it can be done.

Under (1) precursors, *history* is essential. I suggest examining material on the birth (and death) of nations, of failed states, as seedbeds for genocide, together with the *chronicle* of intolerance, *dehumanisation* of the victims, and violence towards them. The perpetrator's *intent*, which often varies, is crucial: criminal acts rest on both intent and action (sometimes inaction). Separate is the matter of *motive*, which often varies from one genocide to another. There is a seeming omnipresence of a *race factor* in these events. Here *race* includes antipathy to any group's physical characteristics, or ethnicity, religion, language or culture; race and racism are not confined, historically, to colour. Without these precursors we get what I call 'X-Files' history — where bad guys arrive suddenly from outer space, wreak their terrible evil, and are vanquished by the good guys in, at most, a decade.

In (2), the physical action, we have to assess the *scale* and *dimension* of the crime, its actual *duration* as well as the immediate antecedent factors, the *pace* of the event, the *methods* employed (which, as we know, range from deliberate starvation to the building of death factories), the role and nature of several variations of *bystanderism*, *rescue* and *resistance*.

The task of (3), the post-event analyses, involves looking at *complicity* and *companionship* in the genocide, *responsibility* and *agency*, the *participation of the professions* and the *participation of the public*. The two latter items are seriously under-researched.

The period of aftermath (4) includes determining *accountability*, addressing the problems of *punishment* and *justice*, and the vexed matter of both *apologies* and *reparations*. The consequent *denialism* is a key issue and as with so many of genocide's other ingredients, there are at least ten varieties of this phenomenon, one of which is the *appropriation* of victim history.

As to (5), the legacies, we need to look at the long-term *outcome* of the event and at the *victimhood of the entire targeted group*, in addition to that of individuals. Genocides not only scar victim peoples for generations, they sometimes tend to replace or displace the targeted group's earlier history and achievements, leading to the genocide becoming the sole or major fulcrum of their ethnic identification.

Finally, under (6), there are, inevitably, other significant factors, such as whether the events occurred in *wartime* or *peacetime*, the nature of the perpetrator's *form of governance*, the limitations on the perpetrators of *geography*, and the entire (vexed) question of *intervention*. There may well be additional considerations.

My recent monograph — *Genocide in Australia: By Accident or Design?*[1] — portrays a history of both physical killing and forcible removal of children, both clearly acts of genocide but behaviours that spanned well over 100 years and occurred in 'dribs and drabs'. Not only the small coterie of professional denialists, but many colleagues and students insist that this history is so clearly different from that 'other planet', Auschwitz, or the ghastly streets of Kigali, that it can't be considered in the same breath or in the same encyclopaedia of genocide. It can, and the 'Richter' proposal would locate that case in a wide canvas and show just how different but genocidal is Australia's past.

Each of these italicised aspects in the scale will need exposition, explanation and detailed critical analysis. For example, the issues of *complicity*, the *professions*, *dehumanisation*, *responsibility*, *aftermath* and *apology* can come together in two very different genocides. Australia began

---

[1] An online and hard copy essay, published in 2011 by the Monash Indigenous Centre and the Castan Centre for Human Rights Law, Monash University, Melbourne. The essay is accessible from either of their websites by clicking on the heading 'Indigenous human rights and history' in the Castan website, or under 'MIC Research' for the same heading on the Monash Indigenous Centre web.

physical killing of Aborigines in the very early 1800s and ceased doing so in the late 1920s; the forcible removal of Aboriginal children began in the 1840s and ended in the late 1980s. The national apology was only formalised in the Federal Parliament on 13 February 2008. The German doctors did what they did between 1933 and 1945 and the formal apology has only now come from the *Bundesärtztekammer* (German Medical Association) on 23 May 2012, exactly 67 years after the last medical killings in the 'T4' euthanasia program. 'Contrary to popular beliefs', the Physicians' Conference said, 'doctors were not forced by political authorities to kill and experiment on prisoners, but rather engaged in the Holocaust as leaders and enthusiastic Nazi supporters'.[2] In June 2012 the *Annals of Anatomy* (*Anatomischer Anzeiger*) published the results of a 2010 symposium on German anatomy in the Third Reich.[3] The editors rightly ask why it took 65 years to acknowledge what was done. 'Forgive and forget' is a common enough catchcry, but forgiveness and forgetting are not synonyms, and both issues still loom large for [all] victims and their descendants.

The American philosopher Henry Theriault of Worcester State University in Massachusetts is joining me in researching, revising, expanding and arguing the case for this 'Richter' proposal as a taxonomic and diagnostic tool. Hopefully, the publication, possibly in short book form, will assist not only students but also some colleagues who constantly agitate, and sometimes bicker, about the nature of events in Bosnia, Kosovo, Libya, Syria, Darfur, the Nubian Hills, the Democratic Republic of Congo, the treatment of Karen tribes in Burma, Indian communities in the Amazon, and San

---

[2] http://vitals.msnbc.msn.com/_news/2012/05/24/11867152-german-doctors-apologize-for-holocaust-horrors.

[3] http://www.sciencedirect.com/science/journal/09409602, published by Elsevier. See *Annals of Anatomy*, vol 194 (3), June 2012, 225–314. The journal is a free download for one year.

Bushmen in Botswana. The H–Genocide list-serv is an acute indicator of these arguments and contentions. This scale could well be useful (and used) in the policy areas of governments.

Coincidentally, the need for clearer differentiation emerged with the two most recent volumes of *Genocide Studies and Prevention*. In this official journal of the International Association of Genocide Scholars (IAGS), the last two volumes[4] were dedicated to critical reflections on the state and future of genocide studies. In one of the 18 essays, my friend and colleague Robert Melson made a significant comment: '(1) that there are significant differences between modern or contemporary genocides and the mass murders of the past; (2) that there is no single explanation for genocide since there are different types of genocide that require separate explanations; and (3) that the testimonies of victims and survivors must be taken into account in order to better understand the motives of the perpetrators and bystanders and give victims and survivors a voice in the narrative of destruction.' This is not the place to analyse his analysis, but significant here is the (correct) assertion that there are different types of genocide that require different explanations.

The contributions

The essays in *Genocide Perspectives IV* were submitted before this 'Richter' proposal was articulated. Those accepted (after peer-review) were not included because of their illustration of such a scale, but in most instances they *do* illustrate and further define several of the components of that framework.

Seven of the essays deal directly with one or other form of *complicity*, perhaps the most under-researched aspect of genocide as legally defined. Complicity, according to Article III of the 1948 Genocide Convention, is a crime, and

---

[4] Vol 6, no 3, December 2011, and vol 7, no 1, April 2012.

punishable. Complicity is not really that difficult to comprehend: among other things, it can mean collusion, connivance, collaboration, involvement, abetment or, in popular parlance, being in cahoots. It also means being a *companion* to events in the sense of 'going along with' a system — knowing, nodding, shrugging but still either aware, accepting or benefitting in some way. Two of the essays here analyse the specific involvement of the healing professions, and another the complicity of the silent churches during the events. Complicity is also a major factor in various forms of *denialism*, such as the appropriation of the victims' experience, in the open acceptance of perpetrators as desirable immigrants, in 'closing chapters of history' that are, in fact, not closed at all.

Most contributions treat the issue of *dehumanisation*, the worthiness and unworthiness of targeted groups, including children. Two essays consider the quest for justice and the punishment of *genocidaires*; others deal with efforts at victim rescue and relief, rehabilitative therapies for victims, the prevention of genocide, and the search for some optimism in a world of utter darkness. Several contributions provide what Melson insists on — the voices of victims, even the mute ones exhumed from archives.

Many still believe that genocide is the result of a megalomaniacal despot wreaking evil or vengeance, and if not one man, then a group of 'true believers' dedicated to the annihilation of a real or imagined enemy, or the acquisition of its land and assets. Yehuda Bauer and Raul Hilberg, two great Holocaust historians, have always insisted on the role of a 'compliant bureaucracy', without which neither one man, nor his true-believing cohorts, nor his specially trained death squads, can achieve his or their purpose. Bureaucracy inevitably involves *the professions*, and apart from medical men, too little has focused on them. We know a great deal about the Nazi doctors, from their trial at Nuremberg to the books by, among others, A Mitscherlich and F Mielke (1949), Robert J Lifton (1986), Robert Proctor (1988), Michael Burleigh

(1997), Benno Müller-Hill (1998), Götz Aly (1994, 1999) and Paul Weindling (2005).[5] More works by men like Max Weinreich and Konrad Jarausch are needed to address the other professionals who have engaged in genocidal ideology and implementation. Weinreich addressed the matter of 'Hitler's professors' way back in 1946, and Jarausch (1990) has dealt with lawyers, teachers and engineers.[6] Among others, Susan Benedict[7] has assessed the role of nurses during the 'T4' euthanasia programs; and Edwin Black has truly audited the IBM corporation and its complicity in the Holocaust, providing the mechanical means of counting (victims) by Hollerith tabulating machines.[8] But there is need to examine

---

[5] Mitscherlich, A and Mielke, F (1949), *The Death Doctors*, London, Elek Books; Lifton, Robert J (1986), *The Nazi Doctors: Medical killing and the psychology of genocide*, London, Macmillan; Proctor, Robert (1988), *Racial Hygiene: Medicine under the Nazis*, Cambridge MA, Harvard University Press; Burleigh, Michael (1997), *Ethics and Extermination: Reflections on Nazi genocide*, Cambridge UK, Cambridge University Press; Müller-Hill, Benno (1998), *Murderous Science: Elimination by scientific selection of Jews, Gypsies and Others, 1933–1945*, Cold Spring, Harbor Laboratory Press; Aly, Götz, Chroust, Peter and Pross, Christian (1994), *Cleansing the Fatherland: Nazi medicine and racial hygiene*, Baltimore, The Johns Hopkins University Press; Aly, Götz (1999), *'Final Solution': Nazi population policy and the murder of the European Jews*, New York, Oxford University Press; Weindling, Paul (2006), *Nazi Medicine and the Nuremberg Trials: From medical war crimes to informed consent*, New York, Palgrave Macmillan.

[6] Weinreich, Max (1946), *Hitler's Professors: The part of scholarship in Germany's crimes against the Jewish people*, 1999 edition, New Haven, Yale University Press; Jarausch, Konrad (1990), *The Unfree Professions: German lawyers, teachers and engineers, 1900–1950*, New York, Oxford University Press.

[7] Benedict, Susan (2003), 'Killing while Caring: The nurses of Hadamar', *Issues in Mental Health Nursing*, 24, 5, January, 59–79.

[8] Black, Edwin (2001), *IBM and the Holocaust: The strategic alliance*

the many others — the accountants, architects, chemists, dentists, economists, journalists, pharmacists, physicists, surveyors, writers — who were either complicit as accessories or companions.

Michael Dudley and Fran Gale offer sharp insights into not only doctors but psychiatrists and other helping professions in a state bureaucracy. They have chosen the Judeocide as their framework — because it offers the starkest model yet of how the educated professions ought not to behave and because this case is so well documented and researched. Above all, they demonstrate the degrees of complicity in the collective abandonment of the ethics and codes of conduct both inherent and patent in their professions. They address the matter, however briefly, of professional associations and the manner in which they do not disassociate from members' behaviour — and in that sense, condone it. They treat the phenomenon of evil, obedience, conformity, the significant issues of *bystanderism*, the matter of 'knowing' yet denying, and the possible reasons for 'good' behaviour in rescue efforts. Paul Bartrop's examination of instances where 'good breaks out during genocide' is a significant companion to this discussion, particularly as he has chosen case studies outside of the Holocaust.

A significant adjunct to the Dudley-Gale analysis is the Robert Kaplan and Garry Walter essay which explores the continuity of some appalling psychiatric notions and practices that have assailed genocide from the precursor era to the Nazis, through to the Nazi ideologies, and beyond to the more recent genocidal events in Bosnia. Importantly, the authors take us back to the forerunners of much of Nazi medicine, the Turkish doctors and their role in the genocide of Turkey's three Christian minorities. The Serbian era is not closed, with Karadzic and Mladic on trial at The Hague (at

between the Nazis and America's most powerful corporation, New York, Crown Books.

this time of writing). Hitler apart, we have little in the genocide literature on the socialisation, mindsets and personalities of perpetrators, and this essay 'humanises' these inhumane destroyers of people. While they touch on the Soviet era of psychiatry, we should remember that profession's role in that despotic, erratic, brutal slice of the twentieth century's genocidal history.

Most scholars are interested in what the eminent historian Saul Friedländer called the 'transmission belts' of genocide. Obeying orders is generally considered significant, and in several essays here we have references to Stanley Milgram's obedience experiments in the United States. *Dehumanisation* of the victims is considered essential if 'ordinary people' are expected to participate in the genocidal processes. And it is in bureaucracies that we find the essence of that de- or non-humanising, the depersonalising and 'de-biologising' of those who are human. Bureaucracies are rarely places of innovation. Traditionally they are places of inertia. But once they develop a theme and a rhythm, they gather a momentum difficult to stop. They also develop a special language and lexicon for specific domains of administration. Rowan Savage sets the tone in his insightful analysis of what Philip Zimbardo has called 'administrative evil' — of *how* the dehumanising processes of bureaucracies facilitates genocide. Savage cites George Orwell's observation that special phraseology is needed if one wants to name things without calling up mental images of them. Thus genocide almost always involves a new vocabulary for victims, words needed to turn them into something other than one's kindly general practitioner, lawyer or accountant, other than one's friendly neighbour or old school mate. The Nazis were not alone in devising a new lexicon for their actions, executions and victims.[9]

---

[9] Esh, Shaul (1963), 'Words and Their Meanings: Twenty-Five

Animalisation and insectification are the keys to dehumanisation (both in the language of bureaucracy and in the physical actions in the killing fields), and dehumanisation in turn is a 'legitimation' of bureaucratic behaviour before, during and often enough, after the genocide. The Savage, Kaplan and Walter, and the Woodcock essays provide keys to comprehending this dimension of genocide in the Jewish, Rwandan, Bosnian, Romani and other cases.

Collusion and involvement don't have to be by way of physical acts of commission. Complicit passivity, negativity and omission are nowhere better illustrated than in the case of the churches during the Holocaust. My essay deals with the simple mechanics of *wanting* and *not wanting*, that is, a state of mind — whether individual, collective, corporate, or national — that is unwilling to act, or that doesn't want to act, even when it has the capacity to do so. *Not wanting* to act often involves what Yehuda Bauer calls 'hostile indifference' — and such was the story of both Protestant and Catholic churches, certainly in Germany, during the Nazi era. My view is that there is a much richer field of research here than spending more time examining psychological experiments on obedience, or more pointedly, conformity. It is also a plea for looking at the simpler questions and the simpler answers about human behaviour. We don't always have to resort to the concepts, high theories, new models and methodologic obsessions that now beset so much of the social sciences and humanities. Paul O'Shea, an internationally recognised authority on the Pius XII era, examines the Vatican archival records available to see some of the things that were *wanted, not wanted*, what was done and not done, in the case of Slovakia and its head, the priest Jozef Tiso, the willing and

---

Examples of Nazi Idiom', *Yad Vashem Studies*, 5, 133–67; Friedlander, Henry (1980), 'The Manipulation of Language', in Friedlander, Henry and Milton, Sybil (eds), *The Holocaust: Ideology, bureaucracy, and genocide*, Millwood NY, Kraus International, 103–13.

compliant assistant of Berlin. As terse as is some of his archival material, it is extraordinarily revealing. In one short column, and in the same breath so to speak, we have a Vatican lament about the death of two Vincentian priests in Auschwitz, the deportation of 70,000 Slovakian Jews, and a letter from the Chief Rabbi of the British Empire, Joseph Herman Hertz, begging the Pope for help — the terse reply to which was that 'the Holy Father is doing all he can'.

All genocide analyses look hard, and often unavailingly, for *accountability* and adequate *punishment* for the very few who are believed responsible for a genocide. The matter of *justice, reparations* and *apologies* for the many individual victims and for the targeted group as a whole are matters akin to quicksilver — visible but difficult to grasp, to apply, to appease or assuage the legacies of anguish. Winton Higgins examines the whole question of historical justice following the Nuremberg trials, and the way in which those innovative trials helped develop a new and invigorated sense of the rule of law and its implementation. His account of the context of the Nuremberg trial is fascinating and alive, yet ends in pessimism because of the way the United States, the driving force in this new post-war jurisprudence, has turned its back on the Nuremberg achievements by abjuring the new International Criminal Court. Where indeed is the saga of punity for genocide heading, even as we watch the tedious and tendentious trials of Slobodan Milosevic, deceased midstream, and now Radovan Karadzic and Ratko Mladic, both ailing at The Hague? A particularly fitting companion piece is Ruth Balint's tale of Károly Zantai, accused of a Jewish murder in Hungary, who is still, at this moment of writing in June 2012, contesting his extradition to Hungary. She demonstrates what tenacious field and library research can produce even on one 'nice old man', unblemished in his Australian life, whose days are ending in ignominy thousands of kilometres from the scene of his actions. As Michael Dudley and Fran Gale write in their opening lines, 'Nazism is not a closed episode'.

One of the major puzzles about the Genocide Convention of 1948 is how the fifth act of genocide in Article II, 'forcibly transferring children of the group to another group', came to be included. The first three acts defined in Article II clearly derive from the immediate vortices of the Armenian, Pontian Greek and Assyrian genocides and the Holocaust, and are indicative of a recent, short, sharp physical attack on the victims. But the fourth act, sterilisation, and the fifth on child removals, are suggestive of a much longer-term aim, a much longer time frame, than the acutely physical. Panayiotis Diamadis illuminates the appalling dynamic of children as victims of genocide in Canada, Australia, Turkey, Nazi Germany and Greece. Scholars tend to mention only one case of 'auto-genocide', the destruction of a *genocidaire's* very own people, namely, Cambodia. But Greeks forcibly removed their own children during an ideological and political battle after World War II — and that tale is both illuminating and frightful.

Shannon Woodcock takes us into the world of the 'Tigani', the Romani people of Romania — the ultimate victims of social pariahdom and *unworthiness*. 'The Tigan is not a man' is the title of her (2005) doctoral thesis and here she shows how these Romani people — stereotyped as uneducable, lazy, convicted, 'morally dangerous' and nomadic — were deported to Transnistria [an artificial geographic term created in World War II] and often to death. Her account includes first-hand testimony of people wrongly 'categorised' and here we find something of what Robert Melson insists is essential — the voice of the surviving victims in the chronicle of their negation as citizens and their destruction as humans. She also admonishes Western scholars for persisting with the use of the word 'Gypsy/Gypsies' in their writing. The Balint essay allows us to hear some of the voices of victims, perpetrators and witnesses *then* — rather than the post-event analyses by those who were not there. The voices of those involved are audible, even as they reside in archive drawers. David Denborough and Cheryl White examine the technique of narrative therapy for victims of the Rwandan, Jewish and Aboriginal genocides. Their essay gives us a remarkable connection between these three victim groups. In reality, narrative therapy embodies the direct voices of survivors, evocative, poignant, yet optimistic about having to live each day in the shadow of their disaster, each day with tears and memory, each day having to live next door to the perpetrators who wanted to kill them. [Woodcock appeals for just such a post-genocidal narrative therapy for the Tigani in Romania.] The voices here are mostly communal, dramatically showing both the pain endured during the genocide as well as the short- and longer-term *legacies* and *outcomes* of that catastrophe.

Genocide intervention and prevention have become (only relatively recently) major topics in contemporary scholarship. Isabelle Macgregor and Devin Bowles analyse some of the key issues and make a strong and eloquent plea for looking at what my 'Richter-Scale' proposes at the outset, namely, the 'upstream' factors that underlie an incipient genocide, with the obvious premise that addressing some of the *pre*-cedent features of an at-risk community can prevent an actual genocide, and if not prevent entirely, then at least mitigate it in some way. In today's technological age, there is no shortage of instruments to detect these early warning factors. The prevention aspect of genocide is now, somewhat belatedly, coming more fully into focus.

Paul Bartrop's account of 'good' amid the 'evil' is not, and doesn't pretend to be, a definitive analysis or a finite understanding of altruism, a topic of some weight in the literature but one which has produced no definite answers as to why people, sometimes 'unlikely' people, behave the way they did. His short cameos give us a glimpse into the kind of people who were prepared to take inordinate risks to *rescue* those destined for death. Amid the gloom that is genocide, we need to find a small ray of optimism. If we don't, then all is darkness, as in Jerzy Kosinski's nihilistic novel, *The Painted Bird*.[10] Vicken Babkenian explores the dimensions of both awareness of the Turkish onslaughts on Christian minorities from 1915, and the *rescue* and relief attempts in places as far away as Australia. From him we learn two things. First, that in genocide there can be a good sense of *wanting*, a willingness to act when you have the capacity to do so. Second, how to engage in 'double-think', the term George Orwell used to describe the capacity to hold two contradictory ideas in one's head simultaneously and not see the dissonance — in this case, Australian help, including official help, for victims of the Turks while engaging in a 'love affair' with the perpetrators, the arch-enemy Turks.

In the *Genocide Perspectives* series to date, some contributions have been commissioned and some volunteered. Some of the authors have been internationally recognised authorities;[11] others have been Australian scholars, many of them of the 'young brigade'. The growth of genocide scholarship here has been quite spectacular since the mid- to late-1980s. University courses are not 'thick on the ground' but several universities have specific courses or teach aspects of genocide. The secondary school curricula offer some case studies and a new national curriculum in the offing will allow teachers more room for the subject. While Australian insularity is evident in political and judicial comments that it was 'all a long time ago and far away', genocide is pretty much in the daily lexicon, and the dreaded 'G' word is now much more commonly discussed in relation to Aboriginal

---

[10] A novel published in 1965. It is the story of either a Romani or a Jewish boy wandering alone and helpless around Europe during World War II. There is no rescue, no salvation or redemption.

[11] Including Kurt Jonassohn, Zdzislaw Jan Ryn, Jürgen Matthäus, Richard Breitman, Vahakn Dadrian, Eric Markusen, Damir Mirkovic, Rubina Peroomian, Steven Jacobs, Christopher Saunders, Alan Kuperman, Henryk Swiebocki and Gregory Stanton.

Australians.

For me, the most significant emergence has been the way scholars have moved to a broader approach in their thinking and writing, comparing and contrasting, moving away from micro-analyses of one case and looking at a broader spectrum of concepts and cases. And while the 20th century was, indeed, the century of genocide, giving rise to literally thousands of works on the events of that time, there is still a need for more study of the 'cold cases' of genocide in antiquity, the Middle Ages, and the beginnings of modernity.

'WITH SCORN AND BIAS': GENOCIDAL DEHUMANISATION IN BUREAUCRATIC DISCOURSE

ROWAN SAVAGE

The quantification of nature, which led to its explication in terms of mathematical structures, separated reality from all inherent ends and, consequently, separated the true from the good, science from ethics. —*Herbert Marcuse*[1]

...political language has to consist largely of euphemism, question-begging and sheer cloudy vagueness. Defenceless villages are bombarded from the air, the inhabitants driven out into the countryside, the cattle machine-gunned, the huts set on fire with incendiary bullets: this is called pacification. Millions of peasants are robbed of their farms and sent trudging along the roads with no more than they can carry: this is called transfer of population or rectification of frontiers. People are imprisoned for years without trial, or shot in the back of the neck or sent to die of scurvy in Arctic lumber camps: this is called elimination of unreliable elements. Such phraseology is needed if one wants to name things without calling up mental pictures of them. —*George Orwell*[2]

Orwell is, of course, the dean of investigators into the political use of bureaucratic and euphemistic language to conceal the reality to which it refers, and which it constructs. This essay examines this set of utterances in episodes of genocide and mass killing: it is an analysis of the 'regimes of practices' — to use Michel Foucault's term — contingent upon the emergence of modernity. These regimes spawned a discursive strategy of bureaucratic dehumanisation that legitimised the mass killing of collectivities categorised according to demography, and

---

[1] Marcuse, H (1972), *One Dimensional Man*, London, Abacus, 121.

[2] Orwell, G (1961), 'Politics and the English Language' in George Orwell, *Collected Essays* London, Mercury, 347.

dealt with these collectivities — that is, oppressed and killed them — in rational-instrumental fashion.

My intent is both simple and specific: to examine the *role of bureaucratic discourse and structure as a form of dehumanisation in genocide and genocidal killing.* I do not intend to mount a general critique of bureaucratic centralisation as a system of power, though I draw upon such critiques to inform my argument. Nor will I present a more general case concerning bureaucracy as a functional aspect of state governance which makes genocide possible, though many aspects of such an argument have points of relevance to my subject matter. Both of these arguments — that is, general critiques of bureaucracy as a system of domination, and a claim concerning the centrality of bureaucracy *in toto* as an aspect of modernity which is deeply implicated in the practice of genocide — have been well outlined in the literature. My purpose, and the originality of my contribution, is not to recover this ground, but rather to use it as a point of departure to examine bureaucratic dehumanisation as a discursive strategy.[3] I look at the way in which this strategy came to be constituted, how it is internalised and enacted by perpetrators within bureaucratic systems, and how it may discursively construct its objects in ways which legitimise genocidal action to-ward them.

'Bureaucracy'

How are we to define 'bureaucracy'? While both bureaucratic practice and modern society have changed a great deal since the time of his writing, Max Weber's definition of bureaucracy

---

[3] For full discussion of the conceptualisation of genocidal dehumanisation as a discursive strategy, see Rowan Savage (2009), 'Genocidal Dehumanisation as a Discursive Strategy in the Modern Era', PhD thesis, University of Sydney.

is still a good 'shorthand' to identify what is meant. Weber's bureaucracy is an 'ideal type', one which is not fully manifest in any (or every) given situation.[4] In principle, bureaucracy is understood as a system of domination which is centralised, hierarchical, governed by a set of general, rational(ised) rules and based upon written documents, in which authority is graded in levels, particular bodies have fixed jurisdiction, and the (appointed) office of the individual is separate from her or his person (in terms of private life and domicile).[5] In analysing bureaucracy, it is important to distinguish between its aspect as a delegated structure of responsibility, and as a record-keeping exercise. Both of these aspects have roles to play in dehumanisation, roles which will become clear. The critiques of bureaucracy which we encounter here will show, first, how *contra* Weber, the necessity, neutrality, and rationality of modern bureaucracy as a system have been challenged; and second, the way in which this system, as a system, is deeply implicated in the enactment of death and destruction, what Philip Zimbardo terms 'administrative evil'.[6]

Bureaucratic management can be considered both a technique and a technology. Kathy Ferguson writes that '[t]he term "bureaucratization" refers to the invasion of disciplinary technique into both the discursive and the institutional

---

[4] For a problematisation of Weber via Bauman's argument on bureaucracy and genocide, see Bloxham, D (2008), 'Organized Mass Murder: Structure, Participation, and Motivation in Comparative Perspective', *Holocaust and Genocide Studies*, vol 22, no 2.

[5] Weber, M (1948), *From Max Weber: Essays in Sociology* (ed and trans H H Gerth and C Wright Mills), London, Routledge and Kegan Paul, 196–200.

[6] Zimbardo, P (2007), *The Lucifer Effect: Understanding how good people turn evil*, New York, Random House, 381; Zimbardo's analysis is useful despite my major misgivings about the use of the term and concept 'evil'.

practices of a particular realm of human relations...reshaping both the roles and the events available to people, and the language commonly used to describe those events, along bureaucratic lines.'[7] With regard to the human, it has been argued — most notably by Weber — that bureaucracy's 'specific nature...develops the more perfectly the more [it] is "dehumanised"', that is (according to this logic), the more it operates under the principle of *sine ira ac studio*, 'without scorn or bias'.[8] The material presented here will not analyse this claim regarding the function of bureaucracies in completing tasks, but it will be shown to be utterly false in the relationship it posits between dehumanisation and equal or respectful treatment.

I deal here with the 'realm of human relations' which pertains to bureaucratic mass killing. I examine, first, the inherently dehumanising tendencies of bureaucracy as a system and their specific implication in mass killing; and second, bureaucratic and euphemistic language which names victims as non-sentient objects. This most often occurs in bureaucratic utterances in which individuals are referred to as 'pieces', 'units' and so forth, but it may also occur in more direct metaphors in which victims are thought of or referred to as, for example, 'logs'. The salient feature here is that victims are 'de-biologised'; they are entirely denied agency and individuality; they are removed from the question of the moral order in regard to their status as objects of action; and they are turned into units of production (though 'destruction' might be the more appropriate term[9]). It will become apparent

---

[7] Ferguson, K E (1984), *The Feminist Case Against Bureaucracy*, Philadelphia, Temple University Press, 37.

[8] Weber, *From Max Weber*, 215–16.

[9] On the efficiency of organisational processes of destruction in the Holocaust, see Clegg, S (2009), 'Bureaucracy, the Holocaust and

that even non-bureaucratic de-biologising utterances tend to follow and emerge from the patterns created by modern bureaucratic discourse, and that such utterances are intimately connected with overtly bureaucratic dehumanisation.

Structure and subject

I outline the historical developments which created the system and the discourse of bureaucratic management, and the inherent ideological tendencies which were 'built in' to this system from its inception. I trace the ways in which bureaucratic-genocidal dehumanisation emerges, first, from the centralising project of modernity and the (nation-)state; second, from the mass scale on which ideology thus became able to be realistically conceived and action logistically executed; and third, from the tendency, not to ignore the existence of the individual as such, but to perceive, categorise and act upon the individual as an idealised type, and only as a representative of that idealised type. I show the way in which bureaucratic and euphemistic construction creates social, moral, physical and psychological distance which makes invisible the victims' humanity and the meaning or reality of involvement in action taken against them. I analyse the way in which the logic of bureaucratic discourse and practice is weighted against the humanisation of victims, before turning to the differences between the nature and use of bureaucratic and euphemistic discourse on the part of bureaucratic 'middlemen' in the killing process, and on the part of direct killers.

The purported nature of the ideal bureaucratic-rational system is that it is free from affect, and that its very purpose is to deal with, and to make comprehensible, processes concerning concrete physical reality. In contrast to this aspect

---

Techniques of Power at Work', *management revue*, vol 20, no 4, 336–40.

of its own ideological self-representation, the bureaucratic style tends to be heavily euphemistic in its *reduction of every item to a unit* which is interchangeable with other units in the same category, the specific nature of which is not important to the process. Bureaucratic discourse therefore produces euphemistic language including (as we will see) the classification of humans as 'units'. Bureaucratic management also produces non-verbal dehumanisation—for instance, the tattooing of numbers onto some of the Nazi camp prisoners at Auschwitz. I also deal with non-bureaucratic euphemistic language which names victims as inanimate objects—but may nonetheless relate to production, the better to associate killing with activities which do not produce equal psychic or cognitive dissonance. The connections between these forms, which at times seem unrelated, should become clear later. At this point, it suffices to say that bureaucratic and non-bureaucratic euphemism often work hand-in-hand, as in the Nazi case, where euphemisms which were not strictly bureaucratic, such as *Endlösung* (final solution), were used within official circles (indeed, euphemistic language, or lying, was itself specifically known as the 'language rule') along with strictly bureaucratic euphemisms relating to units, numbers, and so forth. These two related types of utterance, while not always present in the same situation, are mutually reinforcing.

Modernity, bureaucracy and the State: the creation of distance

'I am not a number, I am a free man!' ran the memorable catchphrase from the 1960s television series *The Prisoner*. While most people accept, grudgingly or otherwise, that modern mass society must be run on centralised bureaucratic principles in which statistics are the method by which policy decisions affecting individuals are made, this does not mean that being treated as a statistic does not cause fear and resentment, as in the case of 'Number Six'. And rightly so, given that this discursive strategy objectifies the individual and denies her/him agency in the construction of the nature of his/her own identity. The conceptualisation of the individual as one 'unit' among other identical units of the same kind (whatever the category chosen) allows the making of decisions which impact on individuals, without reference to their humanity—as Weber puts it, '[t]he "objective" discharge of business primarily means a discharge of business..."without regard for persons"'[10] —and therefore without reference to the human impact of such decisions. In modern bureaucratic society, emotional distance is created between the decision-maker or facilitator in a centralised position of power, and the object of her or his decision. In the words of James Waller, '[r]educed to data, dehumanised victims lose their moral standing and become objects requiring disposal'.[11] The most famous example of the murderous bureaucrat who manages to disavow connection with the consequence of his or her actions is, of course, Adolf Eichmann; but as we will see, *Schreibtischtäter* ('desk murderers') are not confined to the Nazi genocide.

According to Zygmunt Bauman (to whom, with Weber and Herbert Marcuse, this essay is indebted), 'the essence of bureaucratic structure and process' is the sole focus on instrumental-rational criteria for means, and the consequent dissociation of ends from moral evaluation.[12] This occurs through 'the meticulous functional division of labour', and

---

[10] Weber, *From Max Weber*, 215.

[11] Waller, J (2007), *Becoming Evil: How ordinary people commit genocide and mass killing* (2nd revised edn), Oxford, Oxford University Press, 208. On bureaucratic distance and psychological impact, see also Bloxham, 'Organized Mass Murder', 218.

[12] Bauman, Z (1989), *Modernity and the Holocaust*, New York, Cornell University Press, Ithaca, 98. See also Opotow, S (1990), 'Deterring Moral Exclusion,' *Journal of Social Issues*, vol 40, no 1, 175.

'the substitution of technical for a moral responsibility'.[13] How has this discursive formation emerged? We can begin to answer through the examination of a number of characteristics of the modern bureaucratic society—namely, the physical size and internal distances of units of governance, along with new technologies of communication; the psychological distance which accompanied its physical counterpart; the assumption of ethical authority by the state; and discourse emerging from Enlightenment ideology valorising 'reason' and 'rationality' as ends and as moral good in themselves.

In the modern era the (nation-) state model, along with the rise of mass society, involved, as the standard method of governance, the centralisation of power and the implementation of demographic techniques of population conceived and enacted from the centre[14] (made possible by modern technologies of speedy communication over long distances, technologies Weber calls 'the pacemakers of bureaucratization'[15]). The physically-distanced nature of modern society in itself has repercussions; as Bauman observes, 'responsibility is silenced once proximity is eroded; it may eventually be replaced with resentment once the fellow

---

[13] See also Betton, J and Hench, T J (2000), '"Any color as long as it's black": Henry Ford and the ethics of business', *Journal of Genocide Research*, vol 4, no 4, 539, on technical responsibility. See also Huggins, M K, Haritos-Fatouros, M and Zimbardo, P G (2002), *Violence Workers: Police torturers and murderers reconstruct Brazilian atrocities*, Los Angeles and London, University of California Press, Berkeley, 170–72.

[14] On the techniques of population in the context of mass killing, see Semelin, J (2007), *Purify and Destroy: The political uses of massacre and genocide*, New York, Columbia University Press, 338–39.

[15] Weber, *From Max Weber*, 213.

human subject is transformed into an Other', a process which may be all the easier considering the lack of intimate knowledge of the other occasioned by physical distance.[16] In this society, 'the distance at which human action may be effective and consequential...grow[s] rapidly'; but the capacity of the moral drive remains limited to the proximity of the individual.[17]

The distance created by modern bureaucratic systems is both physical and psychological.[18] Bureaucratic organisation creates a class of 'middlemen' (bureaucrats) who are vital to the enacting of power, but who do not feel a connection with these actions inasmuch as they neither order action (in the sense of deciding what action will be taken), nor physically carry it out.[19] Bauman writes that, as opposed to the conditions inhering in the pre-modern order, in the bureaucratic division of labour 'most functionaries of the bureaucratic hierarchy may give commands without full knowledge of their effects'.[20] It thus becomes possible for action to be disavowed by every party involved: '[f]or the person on whose behalf they are done, they exist verbally or in the imagination ...The man who has actually done them, on the other hand, will always view them as someone else's and

---

[16] Bauman, *Modernity and the Holocaust*, 193. This is not to say that familiar proximity always inhibits violence, as we see in episodes like the Rwandan genocide.

[17] Bauman, *Modernity and the Holocaust*, 193.

[18] For a discussion from a psychoanalytic perspective of the satisfactions and fulfilments for the individual of involvement in bureaucratic destructiveness, see Alford, C F (1990), 'The Organization of Evil', *Political Psychology*, vol 11, no 1, 18–20.

[19] Bandura, A (1999), 'Moral Disengagement in the Perpetration of Inhumanities', *Personality and Social Psychology Review*, vol 3, no 3, 199.

[20] Bauman, *Modernity and the Holocaust*, 99; Waller, *Becoming Evil*, 249.

himself as but the blameless instrument of an alien will'.[21] The division of any action into minute, functional, separate tasks spreads responsibility so thinly that no individual need feel it in regard to the final action:[22] 'the organization as a whole is an instrument to obliterate responsibility'.[23] As Waller notes, the larger the group is, the less responsibility is felt by any individual.[24] The acceptance of personal responsibility is also inhibited by the fact that '[t]he bureaucratic division of labor...creates an ethos in which refusing to kill would only alienate — in a condemnatory fashion — one's friends and colleagues and, in the end, not deter in the least bit the killing operations' (a subject to which we will return).[25] Ultimately, responsibility is both displaced onto the agency of others, and diffused to the point of non-existence.[26]

Furthermore, bureaucratic language (similar to that often used by perpetrators reporting their own participation in

---

[21] In Bauman, *Modernity and the Holocaust*, 25; see also Milgram, S (2005), *Obedience To Authority: An experimental view*, London, Pinter and Martin, (1st edn 1974), 9–10; Bandura, A (2002), 'Selective Moral Disengagement in the Exercise of Moral Agency', *Journal of Moral Education*, vol 31, no 2, 106–08.

[22] Bauman, *Modernity and the Holocaust*, 100; see also Waller, *Becoming Evil*, 247–50; Milgram, 12–13; Bandura, A, Barbaranelli, C, Caprara, G V, and Pastorelli, C (1996), 'Mechanisms of Moral Disengagement in the Exercise of Moral Agency', *Journal of Personality and Social Psychology*, vol 71, no 2, 365.

[23] Bauman, *Modernity and the Holocaust*, 163.

[24] Waller, *Becoming Evil*, 248.

[25] Waller, *Becoming Evil*, 250.

[26] Bandura, Barbaranelli, Caprara and Pastorelli, 365; Bandura, 'Moral Disengagement in the Perpetration of Inhumanities', 196–98; Bandura (1990), 'Selective Activation and Disengagement of Moral Control', *Journal of Social Issues*, vol 40, no 1, 34–37.

brutality) can be characterised as an 'agentless, passive style' which serves as a linguistic tool to create the appearance that action (in this case, action which might on other interpretations appear immoral) is 'the work of nameless forces rather than people':[27] Stanley Milgram calls this 'counteranthropomorphism', the attribution of an impersonal quality to forces which are human in origin and maintenance.[28] Bureaucratic processes thereby not only allow the evasion of responsibility, but create their own momentum, both actual and psychological, and, as we will see, ultimately *become their own end.*

Another aspect of the rational, centralised and bureaucratic nation-state (and nationalist) model of governance is the usurpation of supreme ethical authority by state powers on behalf of the societies which they rule.[29] 'The good of the nation-state' (or, as Weber put it, 'reasons of state') becomes the ultimate ethical authority, and technical experts are in turn employed to advise on action which in itself becomes a foregone, unquestionable conclusion.[30] Following from this, Milgram notes that a specific characteristic of modern society is the way in which it teaches individuals to respond to *impersonal* authorities.[31] In Rwanda, according to Alison Des Forges, the claim by perpetrators that

---

[27] Waller, *Becoming Evil*, 12; see also Bandura, 'Selective Moral Disengagement', 105; Bandura, 'Moral Disengagement in the Perpetration of Inhumanities', 195; Bandura, 'Selective Activation and Disengagement', 32.

[28] Milgram, 10.

[29] Bauman, *Modernity and the Holocaust*, 199. See Bloxham, 'Organized Mass Murder', 203.

[30] For a case study from Nazi Germany, see Mierzejewski, A C (2001), 'A Public Enterprise in the Service of Mass Murder: The Deutsche Reichsbahn and the Holocaust', *Holocaust and Genocide Studies*, vol 15, no 1, 33–46.

[31] Milgram, 139.

they killed because authorities told them to kill, reflects not a predisposition to obey orders but a recognition that the moral authority of 'the state' made 'the unthinkable' both thinkable and do-able.[32]

The rise of the distance society, operating in the framework of the model of the state, was necessarily accompanied by a massive expansion both of the techniques and discourse of bureaucracy, and of the bureaucratic classes. Bureaucratic demography was intimately informed by Enlightenment ideals which made 'rationality', placed in opposition to a devalued 'emotionality', a guiding principle and ideology of management and governance — the ideal, as Weber puts it, is '[t]he "objective" discharge of business ...according to *calculable rules* and "without regard for persons"'.[33] Ideology that depicts bureaucracy as a rational and pragmatic system dealing with concrete reality also conceals the value-laden metaphorical nature of the language which it employs. Marcuse, following Weber, calls this ideology 'technical rationality' and views it, at least in the Nazi case, as the 'legalized terror of bureaucratisation', an all-embracing instrument and apparatus of mass domination.[34] Logic, in Marcuse's view, emerges from and must pay tribute to systems of domination; rationality, expressed as an hypothetical system of forms and functions, is dependent on a pre-established universe of ends (ends which, as part of this process, conceal their pre-established nature); and rationality

---

[32] Des Forges, A (1999), *'Leave None To Tell The Story': Genocide in Rwanda*, New York, Human Rights Watch, 12.

[33] Weber, *From Max Weber*, 215 (original italics).

[34] Marcuse, H (1998), *Technology, War and Fascism: Collected papers of Herbert Marcuse*, (vol 1, ed Douglas Kellner), London and New York, Routledge, 77–78.

develops not only in, but *for* this system of ends.[35] Within this discursive-ideational system, the individual is literally reified — turned into a *res*, a thing, whose only pertinent qualities are those which are quantifiable.[36] Ultimately, in modern society the 'rational' is inherently political, and — rather than the irrational, as in some commonly held theories about oppressive social domination — it becomes the most effective vehicle of mystification.[37] In this process, 'the object world (including the subjects) is experienced as a world of *instrumentalities*' in which '[t]he technological context predefines the form in which objects appear'.[38] 'Rationality' (a means) comes to be seen as an end in itself, and as such conceals the actual purpose, or end, for which action is taken (as, for example, genocide and genocidal killing).

We have examined the characteristics of modern bureaucracy and their relationship to dehumanisation; what, we now ask, is the relationship between the system itself, and the individual within this system?

The individual within the bureaucratic system

How are individuals subsumed into a bureaucratic system?

---

[35] Marcuse, *One Dimensional Man*, 137.

[36] Marcuse, *One Dimensional Man*, 138.

[37] Marcuse, *One Dimensional Man*, 153.

[38] Marcuse, *One Dimensional Man*, 173 (original italics). We might also be reminded here of the way in which 'rationality' or 'reason' has been used as a justification for the oppression and destruction of humans who were claimed not to possess these qualities, and therefore to be in a 'lower', 'subhuman', or 'animal' condition — and speaking of the disempowered, it has also been argued that inherent in bureaucracy is a structural inequality in which the socially weakest are sacrificed in a form of 'triage' of the rationalising process (Sjoberg, G, Vaughan, T R and Williams, N (1982), 'Bureaucracy as a Moral Issue', *Journal of Applied Behavioral Science*, vol 20, no 4, 446–47).

The characteristics of bureaucracy outlined in the introduction tell us something about the way in which this process occurs. As Marcuse contends:

> bureaucracy...emerges on an apparently objective and impersonal ground, provided by the rational specialization of functions, and this rationality in turn serves to increase the rationality of submission. For, the more the individual functions are divided, fixated and synchronized according to objective and impersonal patterns, the less reasonable it is for the individual to withdraw or withstand...The rationality embodied in the giant enterprises makes it appear as if men, in obeying them, obey the dictum of an objective rationality...Private power relationships appear not only as relationships between objective things but also as the rule of rationality itself.[39]

This ideological representation of harmony between the special and the common interest is delusive.[40] Marcuse also suggests that the creation or expansion of an ideologised bureaucracy (as in Nazi Germany) offers numerous novel opportunities and creates a new elite, factors which in themselves bind individuals to bureaucracies and to the organisations which created them.[41] As we have seen, the end to which the apparatus of bureaucracy works is its own maintenance on an increasingly efficient scale;[42] therefore,

---

[39] Marcuse, *Technology, War and Fascism*, 57–58. Marcuse draws a value-distinction between private bureaucracy, and effectively democratic public bureaucracy which the argument of this essay would challenge; however, his insights into the functions of private bureaucracy may be generalised.

[40] Marcuse, *Technology, War and Fascism*, 57.

[41] Marcuse, *Technology, War and Fascism*, 75–76.

[42] Marcuse, *Technology, War and Fascism*, 78. For a contrasting position discussing the way in which entrepreneurial competition

every individual within the apparatus has an incentive to work toward this end. In Marcuse's words, 'morale has become a part of technology'.[43]

As well as this, bureaucracies are mass groups which are large enough that the individual is not personalised or known to all other members, but small enough to maintain the characteristic of being a group. Thus the moral obligation of individuals comes to be owed to the organisation to which they belong, and to individuals within that organisation, not to the objects on which they act.[44] In sum, moral concerns do not relate to the action one performs, but rather to how well one lives up to the expectations of authority and/or to those of one's (organisational) peers.[45] This, furthermore, is a self-reinforcing process: individual bureaucrats, observes Weber, have 'a common interest in seeing that the mechanism continues its functions and that the societally exercised authority carries on'.[46] In the bureaucratic situation, that is, a group identification occurs on the part of the individual

---

over efficiency within bureaucracies contributed to the Holocaust, see Mixon, F G Jr, Sawyer, C and Trevino, L J (2004), 'The bureaucracy of murder: empirical evidence', *International Journal of Social Economics*, vol 31, no 9, 855–67.

[43] Marcuse, *Technology, War and Fascism*, 161.

[44] Bauman, *Modernity and the Holocaust*, 99, 195; Bandura, 'Moral Disengagement in the Perpetration of Inhumanities', 196.

[45] Milgram, 10, 147–48; this phenomenon has also been documented in detail by Zygmunt Bauman, *Modernity and the Holocaust*, 159–66, by Hannah Arendt in her study of Adolf Eichmann (1983), *Eichmann in Jerusalem: A report on the banality of evil* [revised and enlarged edition], New York, Penguin, 22, 92, and, in regard to the expectations and judgements of one's equals rather than one's superiors, by Christopher Browning (2001), *Ordinary Men: Reserve Police Battalion 101 and the Final Solution in Poland*, London, Penguin, 174–75).

[46] Weber, *From Max Weber*, 228–29.

which 'carries with it a *repression of conscience* where "outside values" are excluded and locally generated values dominate'.[47]

Bureaucracy and individual morality

What exactly *are* these 'locally generated values'? Bureaucratic language charts the progress of labour, best expressed in statistics, which 'say nothing about the nature of the operation or its objects'.[48] In other words, bureaucratic discourse diverts any question of morality from the object, while concealing its human nature. What occurs as a result of these processes is, in Bauman's words, a state in which every action is *multifinal*: it 'can be combined and integrated into more than one meaning-determining totality. By itself, the function is devoid of meaning, and the meaning which will be eventually bestowed on it is in no way pre-empted by the actions of its perpetrators'.[49] In short, 'technical responsibility…forgets that the action is a means to something other than itself'.[50] It is only the *performance* of the act which is in question: Milgram calls this process a 'narrowing of moral concern'.[51] Further-more, the euphemistic terminology of modern bureaucracy, which over time seeps increasingly into everyday language, in itself distorts meaning regarding action. Marcuse identifies this as 'functional language', 'the language of one-dimensional thought', which identifies *things* and their *functions*. We may more specifically state here that, in terms of people, the individual is identified, firstly, with the collective, and secondly, with the effect that collective is said to have on

---

[47] Waller, *Becoming Evil*, 243, original italics; see also Milgram, 10–11.

[48] Bauman, *Modernity and the Holocaust*, 99.

[49] Bauman, *Modernity and the Holocaust*, 100.

[50] Bauman, *Modernity and the Holocaust*, 101.

[51] Milgram, 9.

'society'. Not only the non-human world considered as such, but also human beings and actions themselves, become Heideggerian 'standing-reserve'. Such language, by its internally constructed terms of reference, validates itself and grants itself immunity against contradiction, and denies possibilities of distinction and complexity.[52] This characterisation holds even (or perhaps particularly) when language 'does not transmit orders but information'.[53]

In itself, this aspect of bureaucracy may not *seem* directly related to dehumanisation. It is the dehumanising discursive strategy which constructs humans as objects that allows calculation to take place with the least possibility of 'moral calculus' regarding ends intruding: 'the language in which things that happen to [humans] (or are done to them) are narrated, safeguards its referents from ethical evaluation'.[54] This discourse of technical *expertise* assures the psychological distance of both 'desk-murderers' and 'hands-on' perpetrators from their victims.[55] Bauman offers the example of Willy Just, a German technical expert who gave advice on improvements to Nazi gas vans so that 'fluids' would flow to the middle, allowing 'thin fluids' to exit the van and 'thicker fluids' to be hosed out afterwards.[56] The 'personality type of the technical expert', writes Weber, is strongly furthered by the bureaucratisation of all domination.[57] The fact that feelings of moral responsibility continue to exist—but oriented toward

---

[52] Marcuse, *One Dimensional Man*, 80–88.

[53] Marcuse, *Technology, War and Fascism*, 91.

[54] Bauman, *Modernity and the Holocaust*, 103.

[55] Bauman, *Modernity and the Holocaust*, 196.

[56] Bauman, *Modernity and the Holocaust*, 197. For further examples of the role of technicians see also Katz, E (2005), 'On the neutrality of technology: the Holocaust death camps as a counter-example', *Journal of Genocide Research*, vol 7, no 3, 414–17.

[57] Weber, *From Max Weber*, 240.

fulfilling a technical role, rather than toward the ends or consequences of action — means that, in perpetrators' own eyes, their essential goodness is endorsed, allowing them to feel more 'human' and to return to society after the commission of their deeds.[58] Indeed, this situation, in which a perpetrator has entered into the realm of authority of their own free will, and recognises the justifying ideology of the actions demanded, secures not only obedience, but *willing* obedience, 'accompanied by a strong sense of doing the right thing'.[59] Finally, a bureaucratic structure which rewards loyalty and performance creates a situation in which professional self-interest can play a role in perpetrator attitudes to the task to which they have been assigned;[60] this includes their understanding of the meaning of victims' existence and of their actions toward victims.

Many examples can be found of the way in which the system outlined above binds willing perpetrators to systems of mass killing. Hannah Arendt argued that the 'horribly painstaking thoroughness' of Nazi genocide could be traced to the notion (very common in Germany, she added) that to be law-abiding is not only to obey laws, but to identify one's own will with the principle behind the laws.[61] In pre-colonial Rwanda, there was a well-developed system of hierarchical organisation and structure of authority, a fact that the Belgian

---

[58] Waller, *Becoming Evil*, 250.

[59] Milgram, 143–44.

[60] Waller, *Becoming Evil*, 253–54; see also Milgram, 139–40.

[61] Arendt, 136–37; it should be noted, however, that characterisations of cultures as more or less inherently 'law-abiding' are highly problematic, and are often self-comforting rationalisations on the part of external bystanders, rather than theoretically-considered explanations.

colonisers considered 'a major factor for progress'.[62] Also well-developed were institutions of labour mobilisation and requisition, a practice which would continue in colonial, and post-colonial, systems such as the *umuganda* (obligatory communal work).[63] It is worth noting here that Rwandan genocide was often characterised as 'communal work' — that is, both as familiar and morally unambiguous 'work' rather than 'killing' as such, and as an activity authorised by, ordered by, and for the good of the community — meaning that to reject such work was to betray the community.[64] Indeed, Philip Verwimp proposes as a representative example of this narrative the similarity between a 1979 exhortation of President Juvénal Habyarimana's to communal work in order to 'attack' the problem and 'destroy the forces of evil', and the

---

[62] Straus, S (2006), *The Order of Genocide: Race, power, and war in Rwanda*, Ithaca and London, Cornell University Press, 209–11.

[63] Straus, *The Order of Genocide*, 211–14, 217–18. The literal meaning of *umuganda* is the wood used to construct a house: Verwimp, P (2000), 'Development ideology, the peasantry and genocide: Rwanda represented in Habyarimana's speeches', *Journal of Genocide Research*, vol 2, no 3, 344; an interesting connection may be seen here with the genocidal exhortation, mentioned elsewhere in this essay, to 'cut the tall trees' (that is, kill Tutsi).

[64] Philip Verwimp suggests (in a controversial and somewhat eccentric article) that the ideology of development, combined with a valorisation of agricultural work (which was discursively constructed as excluding Tutsi) was the chief ideological motivating factor in the Rwandan genocide; an argument concerning the importance of this factor in discourse is put in Li, D (2004), 'Echoes of violence: considerations on radio and genocide in Rwanda', *Journal of Genocide Research*, vol 6, no 1, 15. Li suggests that as well as *umuganda*, '[t]he value of work was also tied to the virtues espoused by the Catholic Church (Prunier (1995), 77; Verwimp (2000), 338) and to the dignity of being associated with the activities of the state (Taylor (1999), 141)'.

language used in 1994 to refer to the killing of Tutsi.[65] Furthermore, the agricultural nature of much *umuganda* worked in tandem with the euphemistic framing of killing as 'chopping down the tall trees' (a theme to which we will return). After the genocide, many perpetrators explained their actions by reference to the importance of obeying 'the law' (*igeteko*) or 'the authorities'.[66]

We can conclude with Marcuse that in the modern society, domination and administration have ceased to be separate and independent functions.[67] The system is designed such that the individual comes to self-identify with that system; if not on all levels, certainly to the extent that the incentive to perform binds him/her to the system and seriously obstructs not only possibilities, but also the conceivability, of meaningful resistance.

In speaking of tendencies which support oppressive domination, two other properties of modern bureaucracy must also be noted. First, Weber argues that the chief influence on 'the bureaucratic tendency' was the need created by standing armies and by the connection of public finance with the military establishment, developments of the modern era; [68] this itself should tell us something about the nature of bureaucracy. Indeed, the military metaphor is frequently seen in genocide, and all the more so given that genocide is often carried out in periods of warfare. In Rwanda, for example, Tutsi were often depicted in an essentialised fashion as 'accomplices' of the rebel RPF, or as the generalised 'Tutsi enemy' or *Inkotanyi*: Scott Straus concludes that 'killing Tutsi

---

[65] Verwimp, 350.

[66] Straus, *The Order of Genocide*, 137, 159–60, 173, 219–21.

[67] Marcuse, *One Dimensional Man*, 92.

[68] Weber, *From Max Weber*, 212.

was inseparable from the language of war'.[69] Second, bureaucracy innately lends itself to concealment and (public) euphemism.[70] As Weber notes, for those within the system superiority is enhanced by keeping secret their knowledge and intentions, meaning that this tendency is built into the system: '[t]he concept of the "official secret" is the specific invention of bureaucracy, and nothing is so fanatically defended by the bureaucracy as this attitude, which cannot be substantially justified beyond these specifically qualified areas'.[71]

Some of the psychological states mentioned above are not innovations of the modern age — for example, the displacement of moral responsibility of those 'acting on orders'. This should not blind us to the fact that in the modern system as it was created in the West and then imposed, more or less thoroughly, on a global scale, these common psychological processes were employed in the creation of a new model of governance, and a new society. Physical, psychological, emotional and moral distance was created between those who enacted or supported power, and the objects of such action. Modern bureaucratic management was not and is not a neutral tool which can be put to any ends; it contains various propensities and tendencies, outlined above, which in some circumstances may be considered to be offset by other benefits, but in other contexts contribute immeasurably to the existence and operation of systems of destruction.[72]

---

[69] Straus, *The Order of Genocide*, 29, 50, 58.

[70] On bureaucratic secrecy and its relationship to power and morality see Sjoberg, Vaughan and Williams, 443–46.

[71] Weber, *From Max Weber*, 233.

[72] As mentioned in the introduction, we may consider 'bureaucracy' in itself to be a technology; in this sense, Eric Katz's argument regarding the misconception of a perception of technology as 'value-neutral' is highly relevant. As Katz observes, 'technologies determine

Genocidal and non-genocidal bureaucracy

We have seen the way in which the rise of the modern bureaucratic state allowed the removal of 'moral calculus' from the enactment of violence, and the way in which this process takes place both on the level of executive or collective decision-making, and at the individual level. From this premise, it may be objected that there is nothing uncommon about the fact that genocidal states use this kind of language about their subjects; that this fact has nothing specific to tell us about *genocide*, and that bureaucratic centralisation and its impact on society has already been exhaustively explored. Bauman acknowledges this objection when he writes that 'the adverse impact of dehumanisation is much more common than the habit to identify it almost totally with its genocidal effects would suggest'.[73] Taking this train of thought a step further, Donald Bloxham criticises Bauman's reading thus:

> To some degree genocidal structures inevitably will resemble the political systems in which they are embedded, and so Zygmunt Bauman, who locates the character of the Holocaust within the bureaucratic mindset that he sees as central to its perpetration, may be saying only that Nazi Germany was a modern state, which is self-evident.[74]

---

the forms of human life, and thus the values that humans live by' (413).

[73] Bauman, *Modernity and the Holocaust*, 103.

[74] Bloxham, 'Organized Mass Murder', 206. Bloxham makes more detailed criticisms of Bauman's argument regarding modernity, but, given that they relate to the specificities of the German situation, they will not be addressed here. In a comparative sense, Bloxham's argument is directed not at the conditions of modernity *in toto*, but at the argument that genocide is normatively carried out by modern methods. Indeed, Bloxham's argument for a comparative approach, for the importance of ideology as a motivating factor, and for an understanding of bureaucracy as a common modern characteristic

Bauman has indeed located the murderous social reorganisation of the Holocaust, and, by extension, other genocides, within the realm of the massive, rational, *ordering* process of modernity in which 'everyone will be transported from their present, contingent site to the place where reason orders them to be' (including nowhere).[75] And it is true that a bureaucratic system is the practice of the modern capitalist state or institution, no matter what substance it is dealing in (oil, sugar or people) and, furthermore, that it *always* deals with people in this way. An example can be found in the fact that *every* modern, Western, human society already, on a massive scale, treats biological beings (namely, animals and plants) in exactly this fashion: as interchangeable items representing a class, and as units of production. Far from being a counter-example, this demonstrates, first, that the fact that this is the standard system of organisation in such societies is intimately involved in the expression of dominance over particular groups; and second, that an enabling aspect of the enactment of such dominance upon humans is that it is discursively related to other forms of the enactment of dominance which are conceived as less morally problematic. As Bauman writes, 'the civilizing process is, among other things, a process of divesting the use and deployment of violence from moral calculus, and of emancipating the desiderata of rationality from interference of ethical norms or moral inhibitions'.[76] The infliction of genocide involves prejudice, in the sense of an emotional feeling of the lesser worth of or the danger posed by another

---

rather than a specific aspect of the Holocaust, can be read as supporting the argument that I present here.

[75] Bauman, Z (2000), 'The Duty To Remember—But What?', in Kaye, James and Stråth, Bo (eds) *Enlightenment and Genocide, Contradictions of Modernity* (Series philosophy and politics; no 5), Brussels, P I E-Peter Lang, 50.

[76] Bauman, *Modernity and the Holocaust*, 28.

collective, but also 'the routine and unemotional function of modern society'.[77] And both of these practices involve dehumanisation.

Given that genocide and mass killing are the extremes of the expression of violent dominance, the following becomes clear. Such discourse functions constantly at a lower-key register on an everyday level (to allow one not to think about the rise in levels of domestic violence or homelessness, the treatment of refugees and minority groups, or the fate of the dead animal on one's plate). But this means that it can be used as a model to create similar psychological-emotional states toward other circumstances, ones to which there has been less time to become habituated, which have not yet become socialised as norms, or which are periodical or circumstantial rather than ongoing. The very fact that decisions regarding action in mass society are, at least in principle, always made on the basis of statistical research and demography (whether they involve cuts in tax or cuts in welfare) means that the use of such language can normalise genocide. It makes genocidal action into just another task among many in the running of a well-ordered society, rather than leaving the possibility that it will be seen by the perpetrator as an unprecedented, extraordinary or qualitatively different event within her or his universe of meaning and morality.[78] As Bauman puts it, '[t]his mode can be put to the service of a genocidal objective without major revision of its structure, mechanisms and

---

[77] Bauman, 'The Duty To Remember', 52.

[78] On the discursive and structural similarities between the genocidal situation and 'everyday' corporate organisational trends, see Stokes, P and Gabriel, Y (2010), 'Engaging with genocide: the challenge for organization and management studies', *Organization*, vol 17, no 4, 474–76.

behavioural norms'.[79] In Rwanda, according to Des Forges:

[a]dministrators broke the genocide down into a series of discrete tasks which they executed without consideration of the ultimate objective of the work. Cultivators turned out for the long-standing practice of communal labor although they knew that they were to cut down people as well as the brush in which they found them. Priests announced public meetings without consideration of the message to be delivered there. Businessmen contributed money to the 'self-defense' fund established by the government as they had contributed to similar collections in the past, even though the money was to buy 'refreshments' for the militia and fuel to transport them to their places of 'work'.[80]

Such a process is self-sustaining, and contains its own momentum. Once individuals have been transformed into units, their very humanity 'slows down the smooth flow of bureaucratic routine', creating a 'nuisance factor' which means that individuals are considered not only with indifference, but with disapprobation and censure.[81] To return to an earlier point, Bauman maintains that bureaucracy is not merely a tool, which can be used for good or bad ends; rather, 'the dice are loaded', inasmuch as bureaucracy 'has a logic and momentum of its own'; it is 'programmed to seek the optimal solution', and to measure that solution in a way which does 'not distinguish between one human object and another, or between human and inhuman objects'.[82] In genocide and genocidal killing, the rational sequence of the destruct-ion of victims (as outlined by Raul Hilberg), beginning with definition and ending with annihilation, is arranged, according to the logic of bureaucratic discourse,

---

[79] Bauman, *Modernity and the Holocaust*, 104.

[80] Des Forges, 12.

[81] Bauman, *Modernity and the Holocaust*, 103–04.

[82] Bauman, *Modernity and the Holocaust*, 104.

precisely to evict the 'object' from the realm of moral obligation, with each step putting further distance between the victim, and perpetrators and bystanders.[83] We may also consider Wolfgang Sofsky's comment on categorisation in the Nazi camps: *in itself*, this system 'created distances, intensified antagonisms and drew lines of social demarcation that none could cross...[it] guided social judgement by intensifying the perception of differences'.[84] In the following section, I outline the way in which such categorisation dehumanises its objects and legitimises mistreatment and killing.

Bureaucracy, categorisation and dominance

In the introduction, I mentioned the way in which, in the modern age, individuals are categorised as representative of an ideal type. This type is chosen from among a pre-constructed taxonomy of types which is itself in turn chosen from other taxonomies as relevant to the situation at hand:[85] that is, a situational ideological framework is created through which circumstance is comprehended and action taken. Paul Chilton, drawing on research in the cognitive sciences, argues that language which categorises in this way blends the cognitive domains or 'modes' of social intelligence with those of intuitive essentialism and technicality (tool-making). A naturalisation of the categories which are used takes place (categories which, though they may belong only to humans,

---

[83] Bauman, *Modernity and the Holocaust*, 190–92. On the genocidal creation of bureaucratic distance see also Clegg, 340–41; Stokes and Gabriel, 465.

[84] Sofsky, W (1999), *The Order of Terror: The concentration camp* (trans W Templer), Princeton, Princeton University Press, 123.

[85] On categorisation in the context of arguments regarding genocidal and non-genocidal prejudice, see Billig, M (2002), 'Henri Tajfel's "Cognitive aspects of prejudice" and psychology of bigotry', *The British Journal of Social Psychology*, vol 41, 175.

do not in themselves remind one of the humanity of their objects), and humans thus come to be classified as non-human things which can be instrumentally manipulated.[86] In the discursive terms of modern technologies of population, in any given situation, one property is taken to be the defining characteristic of the individual (as a woman, Jew, Communist, *et cetera*), and that individual as such is synecdochal, is only a representative of the group of people who have that property, and who are a group only because they have that property.[87]

---

[86] Chilton, P (2005), 'Manipulation, memes and metaphors: The case of *Mein Kampf* in de Saussure, L and Schulz, P (eds) *Manipulation and Ideologies in the Twentieth Century: Discourse, language, mind*, Amsterdam/Philadelphia, John Benjamins Publishing Company, 40.

[87] See Graumann, C F (1998), 'Verbal Discrimination: a Neglected Chapter in the Social Psychology of Aggression', *Journal for the Theory of Social Behaviour*, vol 28, no 1, 48. On 'the Jew' as 'one political actor' in Nazi propaganda see Herf, J (2006), *The Jewish Enemy: Nazi propaganda during World War II and the Holocaust*, Cambridge Mass and London, The Belknap Press of Harvard University Press, 37–38. Herf also provides numerous examples of the way in which the singular term *Juda* was used to characterise the alleged actions of Jews. On the way in which the process of quantifiable efficiency removes the possibility of 'the intangibles of life' and of lives, see Betton and Hench, 538–39. We might also consider such characterisation to be a particular aspect of metonym, 'the part for the whole'; George Lakoff and Mark Johnson argue that, like metaphor, metonymy is deeply grounded in human thought and action, to the point that we are not necessarily conscious that it occurs (Lakoff, G and Johnson, M (1980), *Metaphors We Live By*, Chicago and London, University of Chicago Press, 35–40). Finally, Victor Klemperer has noted the way in which, under the Third Reich, categorical identity came to be a defining characteristic, such that he was always referred to officially as 'Jud Klemperer' ([the] Jew Klemperer) (Klemperer, V (2000), *The Language of the Third Reich: LTI – Lingua Tertii Imperii: A philologist's notebook* [trans M Brady, 3rd edn], London and New Brunswick N J, The Athlone Press, [original German date of publication 1957], 78; see also 176–77 on the universe

Bauman suggests that this kind of categorical abstraction 'is one of modernity's principal powers…genocide differs from other murders in having a category for its object'.[88] In a possible endgame, the individual becomes representative *only* of that property itself: Jews come to be understood not just as likely to bear or spread disease, not just as a metaphorical disease which makes up part of a figure of speech, but as 'disease incarnate'[89] (the Nazis also depicted them, and justified much of their treatment, as 'criminals incarnate'). In Rwanda, Straus notes the way in which 'over and over again' Tutsi were spoken of by perpetrators as a unit, 'a single entity with identical – and permanent – intentions': the category 'the Tutsi' came to substitute for the individual.[90] For many perpetrators, *the* central phrase of the genocide was recalled as *'Umwanzi ni umwe ni umututsi'* (the enemy is one; it is the Tutsi).[91]

Many scholars have shown the paradoxical nature of modernity, the way in which it contains its own contradictions. Thus, often-claimed dehumanising characteristics of modern society have been associated both with the group (mass culture, bureaucracy, centralisation, standardisation, homogenisation) and with the individual (in the claim that social groups and the moral and social benefits they create, whatever they may be argued to be, are being destroyed due to capitalist-consumerist individualism). But

---

of meaning contained within the adjective *jüdisch* [Jewish]).

[88] Bauman, 'The Duty To Remember', 36.

[89] On the disease metaphor see Savage, R (2007), '"Disease Incarnate": Biopolitical Discourse and Genocidal Dehumanisation in the Age of Modernity', *Journal of Historical Sociology*, vol 20, no 3, 404–40.

[90] Straus, *The Order of Genocide*, 173.

[91] Straus, *The Order of Genocide*, 225.

these positions are not necessarily as contradictory as they might seem, and the contradiction may be resolved by asking to what use a process is put: what is this process of production in fact producing, and at whose behest? The (identity of) the human individual *must be* conceptualised in the 'gaze' of the bureaucratic institution *both* as a demographic, *and* as a (single) unit of production — this concept can be seen as similar to Foucault's definition of the two poles of development of modern bio-power: the anatomo-politics of the human body, and that of the 'species body'.[92] The fact of the individual's existence as an individual is the locus of a process which, in conception, execution and aim, determines that the individual remain within the relevant category, and represent that category through his/her actions. This applies to all modern citizens, not only to victims but to their persecutors — though it should be affirmed that these categories are highly malleable according to time and circumstance: they are determined and produced by the question which is asked.[93] In Bauman's words, '[d]ehu-manisation starts at the point when, thanks to the distantiation, the objects at which the bureaucratic action is aimed can, and are, reduced to a set of quantitative measures'.[94] The definition of victims in this way 'sets them apart as a *different* category, so that whatever applies to it does *not* apply to all the rest' — individuals become exemplars of a

---

[92] Foucault, M (1978), *The History of Sexuality: Volume I: An introduction* (trans R Hurley), New York, Pantheon Books, 139; On Foucault, the 'gaze' of the State, identity, *Modernity and the Holocaust* see Clegg, 326–47.

[93] For a case study of the development of genealogy and racial classification through bureaucracy in Nazi Germany, see Hertz, D (1997), 'The Genealogy Bureaucracy in the Third Reich', *Jewish History*, vol 11, no 2, 53–78.

[94] Bauman, *Modernity and the Holocaust*, 102.

type, and that type 'seep[s] into their individualized image'.[95]

Groups of people may often be divided, on paper, into various categories; but this is not usually done in order to physically *destroy* one group. In bureaucratic genocide, language already exists in which is inherent a certain categorisation of the object (to be dealt with as inanimate), accompanied by a certain moral-emotional state (apathy) with regard to that object; the use of such language is standard practice in mass situations. This allows the employer of such language to deny the fact of the victims as living individual humans who, under previous normativities, would have been owed at least a minimal amount of consideration and/or obligation as to the way in which they were treated. This language, then, is a self-fulfilling prophecy of genocide, one in which victims are named as inanimate matter before they are transformed into that state.

The example of the genocide of Tutsi in Rwanda in the mid-1990s casts some light on these processes. At first glance, discussion of this case in terms of modernity and the state may seem counter-intuitive. The genocide took place during a period of civil war and administrative chaos, in which the official Rwandan government had collapsed after the assassinations of the President, Juvénal Habyarimana, and the Prime Minister, Agathe Uwilingiyimana.[96] Rwandan society was anything but highly modernised or industrialised; Rwanda was chiefly a subsistence agriculture economy, and the genocide itself can be characterised as 'low-tech' (in comparison to, for example, Nazi genocide). Given this, what

---

[95] Bauman, *Modernity and the Holocaust*, 191 (original italics).

[96] The history of the lead-up to the genocide, the connection between the assassinations of Habyarimana and the commission and outbreak of genocide, and the role of politicians in the genocide, are complex topics which are not relevant to the subject at hand.

role can bureaucracy and bureaucratic discourse have played? In the first instance, Rwanda is a prime example of the way in which bureaucratic techniques of demography and population management generate a precondition for genocide by creating and shaping identity categories. While 'Hutu' and 'Tutsi' were certainly identity categories in pre-colonial Rwandan society, they were categories which were both flexible and permeable. Between 1927 and 1936, the colonising Belgians — employing a divide-and-rule strategy typical of colonialism — (re)organised administration in the areas of education, state administration, taxation, and Church around these identities, took a census classifying every Rwandan as Hutu, Tutsi, or Twa, and issued identity cards bearing this information.[97] Identity cards continued to be used in the post-colonial period, and were employed during the genocide as a marker of identity, and hence as one method of identifying victims.

As Mahmood Mamdani observes, colonial rule (and the transition from direct to indirect colonial rule) came to be premised upon the necessity for hierarchical structures of domination, not only between colonisers and colonised, but also between different colonised collectivities. Legally- and politically-constructed hierarchies were organised by essentialised identity categorisation.[98] The centralised and hierarchical system of domination which the Belgians instituted in Rwanda was premised upon rule through the Tutsi, who, according to racial-religious 'Hamitic' theories current at the time, were racially superior, considered to be taller, lighter-skinned, and more fine-featured than the Hutu.[99] Indeed, in 1902 the Church described Tutsi as

---

[97] Mamdani, M (2002), *When Victims Become Killers: Colonialism, nativism, and the genocide in Rwanda*, Princeton and Oxford, Princeton University Press, 88.

[98] Mamdani, 24–28.

[99] The 'Hamitic' thesis is the Biblically-based concept that Tutsi

'supreme humans' (leaving an obvious inference to be drawn as to the 'human nature' of the Hutu).[100] In the post-colonial period the power dynamic was reversed, leaving the Tutsi a minority subject to institutionalised oppression, massacre, and ultimately genocide in the context of civil war. This demography played itself out in the periodic massacres of Tutsi which took place in the period between independence and the genocide. In the 1973 violence, which began with purges of Tutsi, 'officials and government supporters called the actions [purges] "ethnic rebalancing", "clearing off" (*déguerpir*) and removing a Tutsi "surplus". The issue to which they referred was "ethnic proportionality"'.[101] 'Ethnic balancing' was carried out by 'Public Safety Committees'.[102] The role of bureaucratic discourse in genocide, mass killing and mass violence in Rwanda is evident both in general terms, and in the specific use of language by perpetrators.

I do not claim that we can draw a straight line between bureaucratic colonial governance in Rwanda, and genocide. But we may say that this governance, and in particular the characteristically bureaucratic features which it imposed on Rwandan society in terms of hierarchy and the categorisation of essentialised identity, were necessary conditions for the genocide which occurred there. Mamdani argues that the origin of violence in Rwanda is found not in the realms of biology and culture, but rather, in state constructions of political identity.[103] It was not only the creation of a race-

---

originated in Northern Africa and were therefore, firstly, not 'black' in the same way as the 'Bantu' Hutu, and secondly, not indigenous to Rwanda.

[100] Mamdani, 88.

[101] Straus, *The Order of Genocide*, 190.

[102] Straus, *The Order of Genocide*, 191.

[103] Mamdani, 34.

mythology regarding Rwandan peoples which led to violent ongoing conflict; similar mythologies were applied elsewhere without this consequence. Rather, in Rwanda this notion became a rationale for a set of *institutions* inspired by, embedded in, and reproduced by this ideology.[104] The ideology was incorporated into a *system* organised along bureaucratic lines: an institutional construct.[105] Ultimately, the bureaucratic dehumanisation of Hutu (under the colonial regime) and Tutsi (in the post-colonial period) was a vital factor in the Rwandan genocide. The role of bureaucracy and bureaucratic discourse in this and other genocides goes beyond the fact that bureaucratic organisation is necessary in order to attempt genocide in the age of the mass society. Although present in varying degrees in different cases, this discursive strategy is intimately involved with dehumanisation in general, and specifically, genocidal dehumanisation.

In bureaucracies, however, it is not only victims but also perpetrators who undergo a process of de-individuation. In a group situation, there is a decreased focus on personal identity, which becomes submerged in the nature of the group, and general social norms have their place taken by situation-specific group norms.[106] This process also takes place in 'hands-on' situations, in which a perpetrator group who identify as such are more likely to behave cruelly and aggress-ively.[107] A common example would be a particular military unit or militia group, who generally share some kind of visual signifier, such as a uniform. This brings us to the question of the different psychological states of those indirectly and directly involved in killing, and the different

---

104 Mamdani, 87.

105 Mamdani, 87.

106 Waller, *Becoming Evil*, 251.

107 Waller, *Becoming Evil*, 251–52.

psychological desires and needs which euphemistic and bureaucratic language fulfils in each case.

Schreibtischtäter and direct perpetrators: distinctions and similarities

While some have spoken of 'primeval moral drives' against killing, I have argued elsewhere that this is an overstatement of the case.[108] It should not be assumed that individuals have an innate propensity not to act violently, which must be overcome by external influences. Milgram writes that '[t]hough such prescriptions as "Thou shalt not kill" occupy a pre-eminent place in the moral order, they do not occupy a correspondingly intractable position in the human psychic structure'.[109] Milgram's experiments have demonstrated that the commonsense understanding that it is more difficult to harm someone directly, than to order harm done — that the closer the victim, the harder it is to act against them — *is* borne out in fact.[110]

The literal distance between bureaucratic perpetrators and victims plays a part in legitimising their actions; but how does bureaucratic discourse relate to direct or 'hands-on' perpetrators, the men and women 'on the ground', who cannot ignore the physical consequences of their actions? For the direct perpetrator, killing, when constructed as the processing of objects, can be understood as an unpleasant task, but one identical in kind to other tasks which must be carried out for the functioning (or even the survival) of society. Their actions, just like those of the 'desk-murderer', are 'nothing personal', and hence may be disconnected or

---

[108] Savage, 'Genocidal Dehumanisation', 126–33; Bauman, *Modernity and the Holocaust*, 188.

[109] Milgram, 8.

[110] Milgram, 33–44.

compartmentalised from their self-conception.[111]
Furthermore, the language, discourses and practice of
industrialisation, or, in less modernised societies, of everyday
work, can be applied to the killing process.[112] In each case,
euphemistic language provides a discursive strategy in which,
despite the fact that terminology is not literally believed to be
factual, the mean-ing of acts can be altered to produce less
cognitive dissonance: 'as they live within their euphemistic
labels, and use them with each other, perpetrators become
bound to a psychologically safe realm of dissociation,
disavowal, and emotional distance'.[113] Albert Bandura, whose
work has consistently provided empirical demonstrations of
the disinhibitory power of euphemistic language, comments
that:

[e]uphemistic language...provides a convenient tool for
masking reprehensible activities or even conferring a
respectable status upon them (Bolinger, 1982; Lutz, 1987).
Through sanitized and convoluted verbiage, destructive
conduct is made benign and those who engage in it are
relieved of a sense of personal agency.[114]

The bureaucratic routinisation of actions, their division
into separate tasks which are performed identically each time

---

[111] Huggins, Haritos-Fatouros and Zimbardo, 59–60.

[112] Betton and Hench draw a connection between the Enlightenment
discourse of 'value-neutrality', adopted by business from the realm
of science, with the 'physical manifestations of Taylorism' such as the
assembly-line (537–38). A similar argument regarding discourse
around technology, made with regard to Nazi death camps, can be
found in Katz, 411.

[113] Waller, *Becoming Evil*, 212.

[114] Bandura, Barbaranelli, Caprara and Pastorelli, 365; see also
Bandura, 'Selective Activation and Disengagement', 31–32. We might
note here the telling term 'sanitised' language; on this subject see also
Bandura, 'Moral Disengagement in the Perpetration of
Inhumanities', 195; 'Selective Activation and Disengagement', 32.

they occur, desensitises the direct perpetrator to her or his own actions, and, '[o]nce habituated, the prevailing mindset becomes how to do it better, not whether to do it at all'.[115] It may seem on the surface that an important difference is that strictly bureaucratic euphemism does not deal directly with motivatory questions of morality, with the issue of 'should', while non-bureaucratic euphemistic language often does so in regard to the terms with which it creates meaning, inasmuch as the terms used themselves imply and thus call for the 'correct' action in response. This difference may be considered superficial, as, in each case, action is premised on similar discursive thinking. In bureaucratic discourse, action is premised on (moral) responsibility to the bureaucracy and one's fellows, while in the case of non-bureaucratic discourse action is determined both by the previous factors, by direct exhortation, and by the way in which 'reality' is thus constructed. According to Bandura, euphemistic language, either as 'sanitisation' or as the 'agentless passive voice', both of which are in evidence in documentary material presented in this essay, can be seen as an 'injurious weapon'.[116] The following examples provide elucidating evidence of the existence and function of euphemism at bureaucratic and non-bureaucratic registers.

The paradigmatic case of bureaucratic euphemistic language is, of course, the Nazi destruction of the Jews (though their record-keeping practices were rivalled by the Khmer Rouge in Cambodia). To take a few examples from a list which could be multiplied virtually *ad infinitum*: in terms

---

[115] Waller, *Becoming Evil*, 244–45, 248.

[116] Indeed, Bandura cites evidence that 'people behave much more cruelly when assaultive actions are given a sanitised label than when they are called aggression'. Bandura, 'Selective Moral Disengagement', 104.

of euphemistic language, we see such phrases as the prefix *Sonder-*, that is, 'special', which was widely used to indicate physical destruction, as, for example, in *Sonderbehandlung* ('special treatment', that is, killing), or *Sonderkommando* (the Jewish units which disposed of corpses); strictly-maintained linguistic reference to camp inmates as *Häftlinge* (prisoners);[117] the listing by statisticians and public health authorities of corpses as *Figuren* (figures or pieces); and memo references to victims as 'the load', 'number of pieces', and 'merchandise'.[118] Trains carrying Jews to camps were referred to by Ostbahn bureaucrats as *Seifenzuteilung* ('soap allotment'), while the people being transported were termed *Umsiedler* ('resettlers').[119] Another notorious example is found in the tattooing of numbers on camp prisoners. This highly bureaucratic and centralised genocide provides perhaps the most extensive use of such discourse, and the clearest demonstration of its purposes; in the fact, for example, that victims in the camps, if they had not been selected for immediate killing, were identified both by a number, and by a coloured symbol indicating to which group they belonged. These indicated and constructed a place in a hierarchy of power and value defined by the perpetrators, a place which defined the way in which the individual would be treated within the camps. A similar process obtained in Khmer Rouge Cambodia, where, upon reaching co-operative farms, people were grouped into three classifications, with the blue scarves given to city dwellers used to identify and target them as *bannheu*, or 'deposed'.[120] As Sofsky puts it,

absolute power is the absolute power to label...defining a

---

[117] Waller, *Becoming Evil*, 208.

[118] Waller, *Becoming Evil*, 208.

[119] Mierzejewski, 39–40.

[120] Raszelenberg, P (1999), 'The Khmers Rouges and the Final Solution', *History and Memory*, vol 11, no 2, 68–69.

taxonomy of categories into which every prisoner was pigeonholed...the use of the class hierarchy was a strategy of graded discrimination, persecution, and annihilation. The ultimate value in this pecking order was the worth a person's life was accorded. This value sign was sewn to an individual's clothing, visible for all to see, a stigmatic patch...[w]ith the aid of categories, power implemented its model of society.[121]

As well as the German case, euphemistic utterance, and language which transforms victims into objects without subjectivity can be found in many other episodes of genocide and genocidal killing; the resemblance to the better-known Nazi language is often striking. In planning the Srebrenica massacre, 'Bosnian Serb political and military leaders used a code to communicate among themselves, referring to the groups of men to be executed as "parcels"' to be 'delivered'.[122] In occupied China, Japanese army personnel conducting cruel and lethal medical experiments referred to the civilian Chinese who were their victims as *maruta* ('logs').[123] These prisoners were identified by a number and a card describing their biomedical particulars:[124] as one perpetrator recalled, '[a]lthough, when [prisoners] arrived, they each had cards with their name, birthplace, reason for arrest and age, we simply gave them a number. A *maruta* was just a number, a piece of experimental material.'[125] Biomedical records gave a prisoner's case number only, along with textbook-style,

---

[121] Sofsky, *The Order of Terror*, 19.

[122] In Semelin, *Purify and Destroy*, 254.

[123] Barenblatt, D (2004), *A Plague Upon Humanity: The hidden history of Japan's biological warfare program*, New York, HarperCollins Perennial, 49, 126.

[124] Barenblatt, xix.

[125] Barenblatt, 63.

identical full-body illustrations.[126] People to be shipped to Pingfan, headquarters of the notorious Japanese Biological Warfare Unit 731, were called *Tokui-Atsukai* ('special consignments'), while Japanese forces responsible for rounding up Chinese victims were known as the 'Special Handling Forces', and the activity of spreading disease among the populace in person, generally through the distribution of contaminated food, was called 'field strategy'.[127] Even in the Australian colonial era, Aboriginal victims of special Native Police Forces were labelled as 'kangaroos' who had to be 'dispersed'.[128]

As we see from these examples, euphemistic utterances employing the language of officialdom and production, and carrying the moral and ideological imperatives of these domains, are available for use by both direct and indirect perpetrators of mass killing. The non-bureaucratic naming of victims as inanimate objects is not as common as either bureaucratic discourse which de-biologises victims, or utterances which name them as threatening animals and disease organisms;[129] however, it should not be ignored. Non-bureaucratic objectifying language could be seen as a kind of halfway point between these two, or more strictly, three types (that is, de-biologisation and binarised biologisation). In this case, while victims are named as metaphors for other things,

---

[126] Barenblatt, 118.

[127] Barenblatt, 58, 62–63, 146. Here we might think of another common vegetable metaphor in the concept of 'root and branch' extermination, where the killing of civilians, or the employment of genocide as opposed to oppression, is justified by the need to remove the 'roots' of the 'problem'. See for example Straus, *The Order of Genocide*, 193.

[128] Tatz, Colin (2011), *Genocide in Australia: By Accident or Design?*, Monash Indigenous Centre, 21.

[129] For this three-part typology of genocidal dehumanisation, see Savage, 'Genocidal Dehumanisation'.

rather than completely written out of existence except as units, they nonetheless continue to be placed within the framework of units of production, as in the case of *maruta*, or of the Hutu Power call to 'cut down the tall trees', that is, to kill Tutsi.[130] Such a discursive strategy is not intimately related to modernity in itself in the same way that bureaucratic discourse is, though the systematic logic of production is undoubtedly a modern innovation. But it is related to episodes which could only have taken place under the auspices of modernity.

In Rwanda, a highly agriculturalised economy where the machete was a near-ubiquitous tool, the naming of Tutsi as 'tall trees' to be 'chopped down' performed a number of functions. Firstly, as with all dehumanisation, it functioned strategically to remove the sanctions otherwise attaching to the killing of fellow human beings, and to remove empathy which might otherwise be felt, by naming victims as non-human. Secondly, this language equated the killing of Tutsi with communal agricultural work, thereby framing genocide both as a familiar and morally impeccable activity and as a duty to the community. Thirdly, it made physical reference to the supposed height of Tutsi in comparison to Hutu, pointing out and stigmatising their difference from the ingroup and, in a metaphor within a metaphor, referring to the 'high' roles of power and prestige they were alleged to unfairly occupy within Rwandan society. Fourthly and finally, it referred to the manner in which they could or should be killed, that is, with machetes.

Euphemistic language which names victims as inanimate objects and units of production is not solely the confine of

---

[130] It is interesting that the two chief examples here both relate victims to plant life — that is, to an object envisaged as somewhere between animals and inanimate objects.

bureaucrats who do not 'get their hands dirty' in the actual business of torture, theft and killing; it is also used by those who are personally involved with such actions on a day-to-day basis, and is not limited to killing in highly modernised, bureaucratised and industrialised societies such as Nazi Germany. While a distinction should be drawn between, for example, Nazi paperwork in which Jews are considered 'units', and Hutu Power radio announcers calling for Hutu to 'chop down the tall trees', in each case this language objectifies victims, categorises them in a way which denies them individuality, defines their inclusion in the victim group as their only salient characteristic, and allows the 'invisible-ising' of the human consequences of action taken toward them. This permits in turn the full or attempted suppression of any moral or emotional response on the part of perpetrators—that is, in Arendt's (perhaps over-universal) phrase, the overcoming of 'the animal pity by which all normal men are affected in the presence of physical suffering'.[131]

In his analysis of National Socialism, Marcuse provides a further insight into the connection between bureaucratic and non-bureaucratic discourse in violent oppression. It may seem from outward appearances that the 'irrational' or 'idealistic' language embodied in philosophy, ideology and propaganda is opposed to technical-rational discourse 'pertaining to the realm of administration organization and daily communi-cation'; but Marcuse argues that each type is *technical*, that is, 'its concepts aim at a definite pragmatic goal, and fixate all things, relations and institutions in their operational function

---

[131] Quoted in Bauman, *Modernity and the Holocaust*, 20. See also Savage, 'Genocidal Dehumanisation', ch 4. My quotation of this phrase is not intended to concur with the argument that a normative human position is to refuse to participate, directly or indirectly, in killing.

within the National Socialist system'.[132] In genocide, the value of supra-technical mythological and metaphysical language becomes exclusively operational, as they are made parts of particular techniques of domination.[133]

Having demonstrated both the role played by bureaucratic, and euphemistic, language in genocide, and the intimate connection between these two forms, in concluding we must return to a final question relating to the individual psyche and the role of this discourse within a broader examination of the work done by dehumanisation — determining whether the role played by this discourse is legitimatory, motivatory, or both.[134]

Conclusion

While the biological determinism of modern racism is rooted in Enlightenment rationalism, the logistics of modern genocide and mass killing are no less the fruit of the huge modern projects of population, reliant on centralised, bureaucratic technologies of surveillance and action; and both legitimise the mass killing of individual human beings. Unlike other forms of dehumanisation, the bureaucratic-euphemistic strategic discursive type is *purely* legitimatory. It does not provide a motivation for killing, except inasmuch as the bureaucratic process creates its own objects and is self-perpetuating, as every individual is motivated to excel at their

---

[132] Marcuse, *Technology, War and Fascism*, 148–49.

[133] Marcuse, *Technology, War and Fascism,* 149. More recent socio-cultural analysis has focussed on the fact that *all* political forms of domination employ these 'supra-technical' discourses for their own purposes; but this does not detract from Marcuse's valuable insight into the workings of the genocidal state.

[134] For a detailed discussion of this distinction see Savage, 'Genocidal Dehumanisation', 168–77.

assigned task;[135] in overall terms, we may consider this a secondary motivation. But this language functions to conceal the human nature of the objects of power, and the human consequences of action, as well as displacing responsibility from the individual perpetrator — whether a bureaucratic functionary or a 'hands-on' killer. Thus, as a discursive strategy, it helps to achieve what Bauman argues was *necessary* for the perpetration of the Holocaust (and, we might add, most if not all other genocides): not the mobilisation of attitudes toward victim peoples, but merely their neutralisation.[136] Language itself enacts 'a transformation of personal relations into impersonal things and events'.[137] Further, the more such language *depersonalises* victims, the more possible it becomes to construct motivatory characterisations around violence toward the victim.[138]

The language of bureaucratic euphemism and production is intimately related to other types of genocidal dehumanisation, in that it allows the depersonalisation of victims, the distancing of the victim from perpetrators and bystanders, and an erasure of individuality which makes of the victim a 'blank slate' onto which can be written motivatory characterisations. In *itself*, however, it dehumanises victims by presenting them as non-human objects in a process of production — or rather, destruction — in which moral responsibility is defined by the process (the means), rather than the ends. As the examples presented in this essay demonstrate, this set of utterances appears in extremely diverse episodes, from those in which more motivatory types of dehumanisation are present (Nazi genocide of the Jews), to cases of genocidal killing in which

---

[135] Bauman, *Modernity and the Holocaust*, 101–02.

[136] Bauman, *Modernity and the Holocaust*, 185.

[137] Marcuse, *Technology, War and Fascism*, 150.

[138] Kershaw quoted in Bauman, *Modernity and the Holocaust*, 189.

there is no intent for the complete disappearance of the entire victim people (Japanese mass killing in China); as well as episodes in which more extreme and nakedly hostile biomedical forms of dehumanisation are not in evidence (genocide in Rwanda).

In terms of the work of dehumanisation, bureaucratic and euphemistic discourse may be considered to be chiefly legitimatory. It is applied permeably to both non-genocidal and genocidal situations, and it seems universally to appear in concert with other, more overt and overtly hostile forms of dehumanisation: it may thus be considered a 'constant' which is necessary for the legitimisation of modern genocide and mass killing, but is not sufficient, either as a motivation, or as a form of dehumanisation in itself.[139] Both in its relationship to non-genocidal practice, and in the lack of any motivatory aspect, it can be considered a relatively less extreme type of genocidal dehumanisation. Given that legitimisation is a universal function of genocidal dehumanisation, despite these qualifiers this type has a vitally important role to play in the commission and enactment of genocide in the modern era.

---

[139] Dehumanisation or demonisation in itself is never a sufficient or sole source of motivation for genocide; see Savage, 'Genocidal Dehumanisation'.

Genocide and the HEALING Professions

Michael Dudley and Fran Gale[1]

Nazism is not a closed episode. Like nuclear war and environmental destruction, it warrants universal concern. The professions in general, and the mental health and helping professionals in particular, have played key roles in waging the 'war on terror'. In 2007, a British doctor attempted to bomb Glasgow airport. Dr Che Guevara, Dr Radovan Karadzic, and those supporting Hamas provide examples of doctors or psychiatrists allied to state violence, as shown below and by Kaplan and Walter in this volume. Though it is imperative that helping professionals ponder professional abuses and their origins, contemporary bioethics generally neglects this record.[2] Individual professionals may exploit patients in a manner universally regarded as criminal or in breach of codes, but may also follow political-institutional or state-based rules without necessarily knowing (or perhaps 'knowing' — that is, they are denying at some level) that their behaviours are abusive. Such systemic abuses frequently involve loyalties divided between patients and third parties — in this case, the state.

In this contemporary setting, we examine the actions of Nazi doctors and psychiatrists, the lasting outcomes of the Nuremberg medical and other trials for both human rights and mental health, and most significantly, the motives and reasons for three kinds of behaviour: harming, standing by,

---

[1] This is a revised version of the chapter 'Through a Glass, Darkly: Nazi era illuminations of psychiatry, human rights and rights violations' that appears in their book, Dudley, Michael, Silove, Derrick and Gale, Fran (eds) (2012), *Mental Health and Human Rights: Vision, praxis and courage*, Oxford, Oxford University Press.

[2] Caplan (2007), 70–71.

and rescuing.

We chose the Holocaust because of its historical significance for human rights, and because it is a 'pure case' of genocide that has been researched in immense detail. The Holocaust is instructive about the causes and remediation of human rights abuses. Two motivating questions arise: first, what prevents today's doctors, psychiatrists and helping professionals falling from grace in comparable ways?; second, given the Holocaust's interplay of individual, situational and social factors, where should the emphasis in prevention lie? The answers matter greatly for states, institutions, and professional and other communities that must safeguard against recurrence.

The contemporary setting: human rights abuses specific to mental health

The 'war on terror' has damaged the human rights achievements that followed World War II. America's Bush administration 'achieved' this through 'rendition' of suspects to places of torture, by undermining the International Criminal Court, and by using notorious centres like Guantanamo Bay and Abu Ghraib prison, the former site of Saddam Hussein's tortures, murders and experiments.[3]

Many investigations into Abu Ghraib demonstrate that it was overcrowded and unsewered, and its staff and prisoners frequently killed or traumatised by constant shelling. Sweeps and checkpoints collected blameless civilians and families, and fear of their joining the insurgency and absence of administrative authority foiled their release. Missing was leadership by its new, inexperienced commander and other principals; staff training, supervision, accountability and co-ordination; and any capacity to care for prisoner children and

---

[3] Ehrenfreund (2007), 209–13.

inmates with contagious diseases or mental illness (Zimbardo 2007).

Frustrated higher commanders determined to extract 'actionable intelligence' from suspected insurgents. Major General Geoffrey Miller, visiting from Guantanamo Bay, stated he wanted Abu Ghraib's prisoners 'treated like dogs' (Karpinski 2004; Karpinski 2005). Post-Korean war programs, developed to enable military personnel to survive interrogations, were modified. They included long-term isolation, threats, exploitation of phobias, inducement of fear (among others, through the use of dogs), severe humiliation, including demeaning and sometimes sexual assault, degrading 'trophy photography' and sleep deprivation[4] (Sontag, 2003; Bloche and Marks, 2005). Both military and civilian suspects were held indefinitely, and their Geneva Convention rights to fair trial and freedom from 'cruel, inhuman and degrading' treatment were brushed aside. Abu Ghraib's civilian interrogators were anonymous and lawless, sometimes killing with impunity.

Philip Zimbardo rejects the emphasis on individual character, inevitably the official explanations which blame the 'bad apples', a minority of low-ranking individuals. Instead, he highlights situational and wider social contexts – the 'bad barrel' and 'bad barrel-makers' respectively. His interviews with Sergeant Chip Frederick, a key operations manager whom he was asked to help defend, reveal that untrained army reservists, despised by fellow soldiers, committed the abuses. Lack of actionable intelligence led to further pressure to break prisoners. Frederick, who previously acted as a guard in a low security prison, had no record of violence or antisocial behaviour, and his personality testing was unremarkable. Yet he was responsible for attaching electrodes to a hooded prisoner who was forced to stand on a box and

---

[4] Zimbardo (2007), 362–65.

told that if he moved he would be electrocuted. While Frederick received a severe sentence, heads of state and senior 'architects' — politicians, lawyers, security chiefs, military leaders, and medical personnel — escaped prosecution.[5] US Department of Defense documents show that health professionals worked in behavioural science consultation teams to facilitate coercive interrogations. They formulated general and individual interrogation approaches, allowed interrogators to exploit detainees' medical records, certified detainees' fitness, monitored interrogations, falsified medical records and death certificates, failed to report abuses and to provide basic medical care (Miles 2004). Abu Ghraib's psychiatrist was employed not to meet the needs of staff or mentally ill detainees, but to help make interrogations more effective.[6]

Not only did the higher command *not* authorise and check tactics, but directives for health professionals diverged markedly from recognised human rights standards. Some argued that as they were not operating as clinicians, patient ethical codes did not apply. Ethical guidelines from the US Presidential Task Force on Psychological Ethics and National Security did not prohibit psychologists' participation, nor require their adherence to international human rights law regardless of interpretation by military authorities (Bloche and Marks 2005). The American Psychological Association initially endorsed interrogation up to a 'sub-torture threshold', and was accused of dispensing with traditional ethical standards outside the strictly therapeutic context by separating clinical from non-clinical duties. But such coercive, deceptive procedures depart from the doctor–patient relationship with its precondition of voluntary, informed

---

[5] Zimbardo (2007), 324–443.

[6] Zimbardo (2007), 362.

consent. Even if physicians did not participate directly, their presence legitimated and sanitised it. The American Psychiatric Association stated that not only should psychiatrists not participate in torture, but should not be part of interrogations; and that they have a responsibility to report situations of torture. Moreover, there is no indication that doctors have the kind of skills that are useful in interrogation.

Enduring legacies of the Holocaust

The Nazi era is the nadir of modern Western history. At its heart are six million Jewish victims, and 23 million others,[7] actions so enormous, cruel and intricate as to defy credulity. Surviving and remembering such unalloyed evil forever changes feeling, thinking, imagination and memory (see Levi 1987; Higgins 2003, 2006). The death camps were another universe, defying speech (Adorno 1955) and commanding, at least initially, only silence in the face of it all. SS militiamen taunted their prisoners with the prospect of denial and disbelief as they worked to destroy all traces of evidence. In Terrence Des Pres' book *The Survivor: An anatomy of life in the death camps* (1976), a guard says to an inmate that even if he survives to tell the tale, no one will believe him. Fortunately, if that be the word, the Holocaust is a thoroughly documented historical event, as well as a universal symbol for radical evil, and a yardstick for crimes against humanity (Alexander et al 2009). US Prosecutor Robert Jackson stated in his opening address at the first Nuremberg trial: 'The wrongs which we seek to condemn and punish have been so calculated, so malignant and so devastating that civilisation cannot tolerate their being ignored because it cannot survive their being repeated.'

---

[7] Among others, 8.2 Russian civilians, 5.9 million Ukrainian civilians, 3.5 to 5 million Russian prisoners of war, 3.5 million Poles, 220,000 Romani, 22,000 anti-fascists, 15,000 Serbian partisans, 15,000 homosexual men, and 5,000 Jehovah's Witnesses. The Nazi allies, the Croatian *Ustasa*, killed 200,000 Serbs.

Mirroring and harnessing Western modernity, Nazism used technology and bureaucracy to pursue its ideologically-driven, murderous racism (Bauman 1989; Bauer 2001). Its economic, environmental and public health emphases are familiar, captivating and confronting (Dudley and Gale 2002). Holocaust analysts divide populations by their responses: perpetrators (numbering around two million), bystanders (numbering hundreds of millions), and rescuers, maybe a few tens of thousands (Bauer 2001). These categories, while heuristically useful, are not watertight. Bavarian peasants, for example, traded with Jewish cattle dealers despite Nazi attempts to prevent this, yet often approved antisemitic laws.[8] In the camps' 'grey zone', victims sometimes were accomplices (*kapos*, for example) to perpetrators, though perpetrators were not victims (Levi 1987). Despite the Nazi state's genocide and criminality, the actors were neither angels nor demons, but ordinary people (Bauer 2001; Browning 1998). Holocaust remembrance continues for victims and survivors, and for nations, communities and professions to prevent amnesia and protect against recurrence.

Nazi doctors and psychiatrists: activities

A particular breach of trust occurs when physicians abandon their special responsibilities (Grodin and Annas 2007; Annas and Grodin 1992). That doctors act as architects, leaders, instruments and auxiliaries of mass murder, conducting lethal experiments on behalf of a transgressor state, may beggar belief: yet after World War II, prosecution investigators at the Nuremberg and other medical trials exposed and thoroughly documented such activities on a large scale (Alexander 1948, 1949). The transgressions of doctors, psychiatrists and other professionals under Nazism have been extensively examined

---

[8] Kershaw (2000), 193.

(see Grodin and Annas 2007, Schmidt 2007, Weindling 2006, Baum 2008, Dudley and Gale 2002 and Markusen 1997 for examples of recent bibliographies). Such a debacle was unprecedented. Education and professional status, rather than conferring immunity, generally facilitated the Nazi agenda. Medicine in particular was united to the Nazi state, with psychiatry the chief medical specialty represented in the killing programs, without whom the Holocaust may well have failed (Dudley and Gale 2002; Markusen 1997).

As the Nazis removed moral restraints, they quickly ceased to ratify advanced Weimar republic legislation on human experimentation (Hanauski-Abel 1996). Clinicians and scientists decisively abandoned medical and psychiatric ethics when they promoted and participated in compulsory sterilisation. Doctors, psychiatrists, welfare, church and community groups supported the 1933 law which required mandatory and widely-enforced reporting. Lawyers, doctors and psychiatrists manned courts which heard cases in secret and allowed few successful appeals. The law encompassed those suffering from schizophrenia, manic depressive insanity, hereditary epilepsy, alcoholism, and Huntingdon's chorea, as well as hereditary blindness, hereditary deafness, severe deformity (including *talipes*, club feet), and congenital feeble-mindedness. The last, a vague, flexible category, captured social deviance (such as prostitution under 'moral feeble-mindedness'), and accounted for three-quarters of cases, including many in poverty. Sterilisation also allowed asylum directors to discharge patients and cut costs. Many patients died of surgical complications.[9]

From 1939 in occupied Poland, adults with mental disabilities were killed by poison gas, the first trial of this method. In Germany, doctors, psychiatrists, nurses and other helping professionals and staff joined with administrators in

---

[9] Lifton (1986), 25; Bock (1997), 161–62; Evans (2006), 507–11.

the *Tiergartenstrasse* (T4) 'euthanasia' program for children. Gassing was extended to adults with mental disabilities. Hitler's signature appears on the T4 program on his private letterhead.[10] The criteria for killing were both 'eugenic' (including 'non-Aryan') and economic, related to potential productivity, but in practice the victims were sacrificed for quotas and administrative efficiency. As an open secret, which claimed 200,000 victims, 'euthanasia' had many accomplices: the myth of a small group of fanatical perpetrators hoodwinking a public who knew nothing is untenable[11] (Friedlander 1995; Bauer 2001). That these institutions of intentional killing bore the insignia of the Red Cross on their rooftops is an indictment of both the German Red Cross and the International Commission of the Red Cross — which never disavowed or disaffiliated its German colleagues.

This dress rehearsal provided senior expertise to killing centres in the occupied territories, for the so-called '14f13' program that claimed approximately 50,000 concentration camp victims (Lifton 1986).[12] From mid-1941, doctors and psychiatrists oversaw the 'Final Solution', manning camps, performing executions and selections and providing ideological justifications[13] (Lifton 1986). In all phases, they exploited the murdered and the living for medical research. Coerced inmates underwent at least 26 types of experiments, including ice-water immersion, high altitude decompression, high-dose radiation, and making seawater drinkable, and often died in the search for better killing methods or through

---

[10] Kershaw (2008), 40.

[11] Evans (2006), 507–11; Evans (2009), 72–101.

[12] Schmidt (2007), 271.

[13] Proctor (1992), 27.

callous disregard.[14] While most experiments were scientifically useless,[15] the possible exceptions (hypothermia and decompression) raised sharp ethical questions about using knowledge obtained by such means (Moreno 2007; Müller-Hill 1988). Professor Louis Waller, an esteemed Australian legal authority, raised this question in 1985 under the illuminating title of 'The Fruit of the Poisoned Tree'.[16]

The motives of perpetrators — among which peer pressure, duress, authoritarianism, careerism and ideology featured prominently — are explored below. Specifically, Nazi pseudo-science ('race hygiene', 'scientific racism' and eugenics) and its biomedical engineering project for a *judenrein* utopia, dovetailed perfectly with the experimental ambitions of scientists, doctors and psychiatrists, whose careers prospered. Few psychiatrists resisted and no letters survive from psychiatrists on behalf of their patients to the authorities (Dudley and Gale 2002). As noted, nurses (McFarland-Icke 1999) participated in killings, while psychologists (Mandler 2002) were also implicated in the Nazi debacle.

When the war ended, the ensuing trials and plethora of psychiatrist and physician suicides sullied the reputation of German medicine. An American denazification report estimated that about half of German physicians were 'proven Nazis' — about 24,000, against the profession's later view of only 350 criminal doctors.[17] What had gone wrong, and how, was too complex for a trial which piloted new international law.[18]

Doctors and medical scientists denied complicity by

---

[14] Caplan (2007), 67; Schmidt (2007), 160ff.

[15] Weindling (2006), 4.

[16] Halm (1985), 95–100.

[17] Weindling (2006), 38–39.

[18] Schmidt (2006), 3, 168.

representing themselves as victims of Nazism. Unrepentant Nazis, conservatives, and leading physicians disparaged the trials as 'victors' justice', and suppressed publications by the trial's medical observers.[19] German medical associations avoided examining their Nazi past (Pross 1992; Kater 1997) and exonerated individuals by blaming socialised medicine and excessive state powers, while insisting on professional autonomy.[20] Cold War priorities (strategic research and intelligence) also protected those who were implicated. (Contemporaneously, the United States gave Japanese Unit 731 — which also conducted biological warfare experiments accounting for 270,000 victims — immunity from prosecution).[21] In the 1980s, a research-granting agency which funded Robert Ritter's project (see below), refused to acknowledge that its precursor financed the genocide.[22] Medical institutes and researchers used materials from murdered victims before this was outlawed and the remains reburied in 1989[23] (Hanauski-Abel 1996). Nazi influence also affected the World Medical Association, which virtually ignored the Nuremberg Code (Kater 1997).[24]

Human rights outcomes of the Nuremberg trials

The post-war Nuremberg trials of the Nazi leadership (1945–1949) were landmark events, defining new standards of international justice with far-reaching significance for human rights. An International Military Tribunal defined crimes such as conspiring against peace, waging aggressive war, and a

---

[19] Weindling (2006) 5, 39, 43, 211–17.

[20] Weindling (2006), 6; Schmidt (2007), 266.

[21] Weindling (2006), 309, 342.

[22] Müller-Hill (2007), 59.

[23] Müller-Hill (2007), 61.

[24] Schmidt (2007), 266.

new category, crimes against humanity, and tried the former Nazi military leaders for these and for war crimes. The trials of Nazi doctors, the *Einsatzgruppen* (the four mobile killing squads), jurists and industrialists, the war crimes trials in the separate zones of occupation, and national prosecutions in various German-occupied countries followed (Ehrenfreund, 2007). All four occupying powers exercised sovereignty and tried the Germans accused for crimes against pre-Nazi German law.

The trials overthrew, at least partially, the principle of national sovereignty — established by the Treaty of Westphalia in 1648 — which bestowed immunity on state functionaries within state borders. States and other authorities could not wilfully disregard individuals' rights. The trials also demolished the defence of superior orders, and the *tu quoque* ('you did it too') defence, thus re-asserting the principle of individual moral responsibility that had been eroded by authoritarian leadership.[25] These trials affected the rules of war and treatment of prisoners, and in bridging gulfs of language, nationality, custom and procedure, they proved feasible. The principle of universal jurisdiction held that any country where grave crimes are committed, such actions could be judged and individuals punished. The trials of Nazi industrialists foreshadowed lawsuits against businesses accused of human rights abuses.[26]

Furthermore, the extensive, authoritative documentation of Nazi atrocities '[established] these perceived "incredible" events by clear and public proof, so that no one can ever doubt that they were fact not fable'.[27] These trials in effect inaugurated Holocaust history, belied future Holocaust denial, and shaped German democracy.

---

[25] Schmidt (2007), 250.

[26] Ehrenfreund (2007), 107–10, 215–19.

[27] US Prosecutor Telford Taylor, quoted by Schmidt (2007), 174.

Raphael Lemkin coined the word 'genocide' to describe the German authorities' systematic murder of ethnic and religious groups defined as degenerate. Arguing that genocide should denote the motivation to commit such crimes, he criticised the new category 'crimes against humanity' for neglecting this motivation. How much the medical trials applied this reasoning is a moot point.[28] Telford Taylor regarded the experiments as pilot studies for genocide.[29]

The Nuremberg trials — and for medicine, the Nuremberg Code — were three great contemporaneous reforms, together with the formation of the United Nations (1945) and the publication of the Universal Declaration of Human Rights (1948). Collectively, they helped to launch the international human rights movement and frameworks, including the Genocide Convention; to revise the Geneva Conventions on laws and customs of war; and to establish the European Court of Human Rights, the Bill of Rights and subsequent rights treaties and institutions. They are relevant not just for medicine and mental health, but civil society and planetary survival (Robertson 2006; Ehrenfreund 2007).

Notwithstanding, enforcement has been piecemeal. During and after the Cold War, no international machinery underwrote human rights protections. Genocide continued: today, perpetrators in East Timor, the Congo, and Darfur remain free. The United States circumvented international standards in its 'war on terror'. The charge of 'victors' justice' (made by Hermann Göring at Nuremberg) endures: the Allies were not tried for dropping the atom bomb, for example. Nevertheless, the Nuremberg legacy endures in the Pinochet,

---

[28] Weindling (2006), 3, 102;

[29] Weindling (2006), 5; Schmidt (2007), 161.

Milosevic, Tadic and Karadzic trials, the advent of the International Criminal Court in 2002, and recent international actions to address genocide — the Kosovo bombings, and the tribunals or special courts for the former Yugoslavia, Rwanda, Sierra Leone and Cambodia[30] (Robertson 2006).

Positive outcomes from the doctors' trials: the Nuremberg Code and its successors

While the patient's health and protection from harm date from Hippocrates, informed consent and non-therapeutic experimentation only emerged in 19th century codes of ethics and pre-Nazi (1900 and 1931) German documents that thoroughly discussed these issues (Grodin 1992; Winau 2007).

The Nuremberg doctors' trial ended with a declaration about permissible medical experiments. In Europe and the United States, however, frequent dangerous medical experiments continued. The Tuskegee (Alabama) syphilis experiment which 'examined' the natural progression of the untreated disease on poor, rural, Black men began in 1932 but only ended in 1972 (Reverby 2009). Rediscovery of the 'Nuremberg Code' in the 1960s as the first global, comprehensive reflection on the nature, purpose and limits of human experimentation was vital to identifying and addressing this area[31] (Perley et al 1992; Grodin 1992).

Pre-eminently, the Code[32] requires voluntary informed consent. It mandates qualified researchers, socially beneficial intent, scientific design and results unobtainable by other methods. Benefits must outweigh risks, harm must be minimised, and risk to life prevented (except when researchers experiment on themselves). Subjects must be

----

[30] Ehrenfreund (2007), 153–96.

[31] Weindling (2006), 340–43.

[32]

http://www.ushmm.org/research/doctors/Nuremberg_Code.htm

allowed to withdraw at any time. Researcher responsibility for participants' well-being is paramount.

The Code's successors, not comprehensively discussed here, assert the rights of health research participants. They include the World Medical Association's Declaration of Helsinki (DoH)[33] which has formed the cornerstone of human research ethics. For vulnerable populations like children, prisoners and military personnel, the DoH emphasised physician responsibility[34] and softened the Code's absolute requirement of voluntary informed consent, instead requiring consent by legal guardians ('responsible relatives' for children; minors should consent where possible). Nevertheless, the first DoH revision (1975) confirmed that the interests of science and society should never take precedence over the well-being of the subject (para III 4), and decreed that research ethics committees (or their equivalent) must oversee research, initiating what is now widespread practice (Williams 2008).

The Council for the International Organisation of Medical Sciences (CIOMS), formed by World Health Organisation (WHO) and UNESCO, also developed the International Ethical Guidelines for Biomedical Research Involving Human Subjects (1982; CIOMS–WHO 1993), which despite some inconsistencies with DoH (Macklin 1999), were also informed by the Code. In communal and non-Western research settings, they noted difficulties with informed consent, research knowledge, funding and governance (Perley et al 1992). Successive DoH revisions have fired controversies about principled versus pragmatic approaches to research ethics in the developing world (Lurie and Wolfe 1997; Lie et al 2004;

---

[33] (1964), revised (1975), (1983), (1989), (1996), (2000), (2008), with clarifications (2002), (2004).

[34] Schmidt (2007), 283.

Social Medicine Portal 2008; Rennie 2008; Sharma 2004).

Harming by individuals and groups: social, situational and individual contributions

Like other great evils, the Holocaust was inhuman, yet humans were responsible for systematic attacks on humans. The social science lexicon rarely discusses evil, and behavioural scientists and clinicians reluctantly examine it, thus magnifying its apparent incomprehensibility. Some consign evil to the province of philosophers and theologians, or alternatively (and positivistically) reduce it to behaviour, biology or mental illness. This dishonours those with a genuine mental illness and relieves culprits of responsibility (Rosen 2011). The political and military elite of the Third Reich rarely suffered overt mental illness, though the fact that these were 'ordinary men' does not mean they were mentally healthy. Clinical science cannot exclude (im)moral acts from its purview, nor reduce them to judgements about (ab)normality. Like morality, it assays not just events and causes, but who we are, should be, and take ourselves to be (Glas 2006). Patients may interpret professional neutrality on such matters as indifference.

Evil encompasses moral wrongness as an end (the intent to harm) or a means to an end, and extreme harm, through acts disproportionate to any instigation or provocation. Bandura (1975) refers to 'moral disengagement', which involves suspending proactive humane behaviour and abandoning restraints on harmful behaviour. Some note the persistence of such acts, victims' helplessness, levels of perpetrator responsibility, and sometimes the 'magnitude gap' between damage to victims and benefits accruing to perpetrators (Berkowitz 1999; Hamilton and Sanders 1999).[35] Omission may also be evil (as discussed in Colin Tatz's essay in this volume on the churches during the Holocaust). Card's

---

[35] Staub (2003), 47–51.

definition[36] of evils as 'foreseeable intolerable harms produced by culpable wrongdoing' leaves open the question of intent, which may be complex, even impenetrable.[37] Noting humanity's potential for good and evil, this perspective bypasses essentialist dichotomies.

Motives and reasons for harming, with particular reference to the Nazi example

As suggested above, recurring individual, socio-cultural and situational factors contribute to mass human rights violations. Holocaust history, other genocides (not considered in detail here), and experimental psychology reveal this. Theories about Nazi doctors and psychiatrists' actions must not only consider these levels of action, but the wider German national situation. In the following sections, the Nazi example and experimental evidence are reviewed to shed light on motives and reasons for harming, bystanding and helping. To direct prevention, it is also important to decide where the 'engine-room' is located.

Personality

Early researchers considered innate characteristics. In 1955, Adorno and colleagues described the 'authoritarian personality' — characterised by conventionalism, authority submission, aggression, projection and anti-introspection — self-selecting for the Party and the SS. Rather than one (authoritarian) Nazi personality, unsurprisingly a wide range exists. For example, Robert Lifton describes SS doctor Josef Mengele's scientific detachment, flamboyance and fanatical cruelty; chief Auschwitz doctor Eduard Wirths' meticulousness and obedience; gynaecologist and mass

---

[36] Card (2002), 3.

[37] Staub (2003), 49.

steriliser Carl Clauberg's arrogant ambition. A frequent theme, noted with Lifton's [anonymous] doctor Ernst B, and Gitta Sereny's 1974 study of Franz Stangl (the commandant of Treblinka) and her 1995 biography of Albert Speer (Hitler's architect and from 1942 munitions/armaments minister), is of people emotionally starved or abused as children, struggling to make human connections and seeking liveliness in movements of national regeneration. Stangl feared resistance and was intimidated. Despite Speer's burden of guilt, his wish for transformation and to make amends, his narcissism prevented him empathising with the humanity of his slave labourers or the Jews whom he saw deported from Berlin, and even reciprocating the love of those close to him (Sereny 1998; Kubarych 2005). Speer's problem with denial is treated below.

Adorno and colleagues, however, postulated a relationship between authoritarian personality and the group and/or social environment.[38] Studies of mass human rights violations highlight how cultures of obedience — whether populist, authoritarian, collectivist or fundamentalist — reject social diversity and dissent. Frequently male-dominated, they avoid critical thinking, prize loyalty, honour and death for the group, and identify and punish their enemies. Institutional and informational control, indoctrination, creating fear and agonising uncertainty, destruction of family and social bonds, and brainwashing children (for example, as soldiers) all enable radical, utopian actions: violence against family, intimates, and moral codes (Glover 1999; Cohen 2001; Pina e Cunha et al 2010). Women are often particularly vulnerable.[39] Adorno and colleagues' observations about the dynamic interaction between individuals and German culture are highly pertinent. While individual doctors and scientists were centrally responsible, sponsored by the Nazi state, the failure of German society and institutions and the force of situations

[38] Baum (1998), 2.
[39] Baum (2008), 29, 48–49

and social roles must also be understood.

Interplay between personality, group, situational and social determinants

In Nazism, personality and situational determinants both contributed to the outcome of racist ideology. Hitler is the most striking example in point. In the 'historians' debate' in the 1980s (Mason, 1989), intentionalists like Lucy Dawidowicz (1975) emphasised the importance of Hitler's master plan as expressed in *Mein Kampf*, while functionalists minimised Hitler's role. They stressed anarchic forces, such as opportunism from Nazism's lower ranks, and bureaucratic chaos and infighting which drove improvisation and increasingly radical agendas (for example, Browning 1998, 2004). A more nuanced synthesis of intentionalism and functionalism now prevails (Bauer, 2001). Thus, Hitler's charismatic authority, according to Kershaw (2008), backed actions, however radical or inhumane, which furthered his ideological obsessions. His non-intervention style permitted party bosses, bureaucrats and professionals full scope for initiative. Since opportunities abounded for expansion, power, status and enrichment, there was never any shortage of chaotic rival schemes or willing participants. One might denounce neighbours to the Gestapo, slur a business competitor's 'Aryan' credentials, or nominate patients for the euthanasia program: this was all 'working towards the Fuhrer' (Kershaw 2008; Bankier 1988; Michman 2010). Competitors for Hitler's favour were often not told of rivals' plans, many of which were deleterious to a 'united' purpose.

Adolf Eichmann's rise from obscurity to managing the 'Final Solution' follows this trajectory (Kershaw 2008). In 1963, Hannah Arendt diagnosed Eichmann's 'banality of evil'; his incapacity to introspect and lack of inner language inclined him to unquestioning obedience to his assigned task, like a cog in a machine. Eichmann was also not devoid of ideological drivers. Though not radically antisemitic as a young man, he joined the Party late as a bourgeois careerist and swiftly took on its program (Berkowitz 1999; Cesarani 2006).

Yet the influence of individuals like Hitler on groups and wider society was also inevitably mutual. As we will see, to further pursue their program, the Nazis depended on public adulation or inertia and lack of resistance.

Socio-cultural and national-historical factors

Socio-cultural and national-historical factors contribute significantly to mass human rights violations.[40] At a personal or cultural level, tribalism and ethnic nationalism can nurse old narratives that maintain enmity. Past victimisation, enduring wounds, even early childrearing may trigger reactive withdrawal or compensatory anger. Severe, persistent life conditions and struggle for resources may frustrate basic needs like security, attachment, positive identity and role, effective control, justice and meaning (Maslow 1987, Silove 2000). When an individual or group's self-concept is vulnerable, setbacks overwhelm collective and personal self-worth. Defensive superiority then forms a compensatory identity that diminishes and scapegoats others. Leaders who share the group's culture, life situations and often unhealed wounds,[41] may then propagate destructive ideologies to gain followers or consolidate a following (Allport 1954).

From its foundation in 1871, Germany was a weak (and ultimately a failed) state (Moore 1966; Steinmetz 1997; Kershaw 2008; Higgins 2006), and a non-existent state in the Third Reich period, as Franz Neumann (1967) pointed out contemporaneously. Its ideologies of 'race hygiene' and 'scientific racism', and the Great War's bitter legacies, were

---

[40] Zimbardo (2007), 273–75; Staub, (2003), 352–53, 358.

[41] Staub (2003), 302.

primers for eventual genocide. Defeat, revolution and the Versailles Treaty's war guilt clauses fed the myth that Jews, socialists, Communists and war profiteers stabbed Germany in the back. Colossal reparations, foreign occupation of the Ruhr and hyper-inflation fuelled economic depression and social chaos. Hitler promised to redeem Germany by modernisation, racial purification and imperial conquest.[42] In the earlier Nazi years, many Germans experienced mystical, exalted states associated with nationalism (Soelle 2001), expressed in the resurgent economy, the spectacle of the Nuremberg rallies, the victories of German athletes at the Berlin Olympics, and Hitler's achievements in foreign affairs (Friedländer 2007). Psychiatrist Carl Jung, who loved pagan symbolism and myth, valorised the German peoples' revitalisation under National Socialism.[43] With the coming of the Third Reich, however, state deliberative decision-making also completely disappeared, civilised standards collapsed, and barriers to state-sanctioned inhumanity were rapidly removed (Mommsen 1997; Kershaw 2008). Race hygiene replaced social and sexual health clinics. Waves of repression and violence descended on Jews and other minorities. Political opponents held in the new Dachau concentration camp were murdered (Evans 2004; and Lifton).[44] Most Germans were insulated from the experience of these groups.

The role of antisemitism is disputed. Earlier historians traced a lineage from Luther through Christian antisemitism to the Third Reich (for example, McGovern 1973). Several authorities suggest that antisemitism was weaker in Germany than in other western countries, like France, and certainly weaker than in eastern Europe. For instance, from

---

[42] Kershaw (2008), 20.

[43] Noll (1997), 264.

[44] Lifton (1986), 25.

emancipation in 1848 till the Weimar Republic, German Jews did not die of antisemitic violence. During the Weimar period, polarisation occurred between Jewish integration and intensifying antisemitism among various organisations and political parties, especially just after World War I and the years immediately preceding the Third Reich, but not the period in between. From 30 January 1933, a cascade of disastrous policy, legal and social developments overtook Jews (Abrahams-Sprod 2006). Hitler's antisemitism, 'calculation and fanaticism' inspired these developments, and institutions, bureaucracies and professions willingly implemented them. Daniel Goldhagen's controversial 1996 thesis that antisemitism among ordinary Germans was always 'eliminationist' and enabled Holocaust killing has been strongly contested. Some thought it massively simplified and demonised German popular motivations, while others noted the lack of comparison with Nazi-occupied countries,[45] and as the sole cause of popular participation in genocide it was widely discounted. While antisemitism permeated German national culture, some view Nazi propaganda (at least to 1941) as apparently failing to bolster public support for anti-Jewish policy and provoking concerns about the illegality of these measures and possible repercussions. Others, like Robert Ericksen (2012), have shown just how complicit the churches and universities were in bolstering the Nazi regime. Ultimately, there was a distancing, an alienation and (from 1941) a buffer between the regime and a war-weary populace, who wanted to know little and who because of their pre-existent antisemitic attitudes, did not protest. Thus popular antisemitism may have directly motivated murder but also indirectly and probably more frequently contributed to the radical Nazi program's success by promoting non-intervention, that is standing by in all matters related to Jews (Bankier 1988; Michman 2010; Kershaw 2008). The literature

[45] Baum (2008), 27.

on who knew what and when, on who was complicit or merely companions to this genocide, has been sparse, but is coming into sharp focus with the research of Eric Johnston (2006) and Robert Ericksen (2012).

Bauman (1989) also highlights the Holocaust's origins in modernity, and particularly its trademark: instrumental rationality, which is characterised by segmentation of labour, categorisation and procedures. Although modernity does not explain all genocides, for example Rwanda,[46] instrumental rationality plays a vital role.

Instrumental rationality, group dynamics and 'othering'

Thus Bauman notes that administrative or organisational evil depends on deficient ethical frameworks, with efficiency paramount, conscience captive to authority, information diffused, and responsibility fragmented. Attention to task, technique, rules and limited morality separates actions from emotion.[47] Harms are even easier to commit when one is an intermediary, neither giving orders nor carrying them out (Kilham and Mann 1974), when one is anonymous or disguised[48] (Staub 2003), and when one is removed from the consequences of one's actions, as modern technological warfare and the Milgram experiments (see below) demonstrate. Eichmann and other 'desk murderers', using the railway tourist fare schedule, could therefore organise 'removal transports' to effect a 'change of residence' of Jews — to Auschwitz.[49] Bureaucratisation and progressively sophisticated means of killing such as Zyklon-B gas chambers rather than shooting, maximised efficiency and psychological

---

[46] Kershaw (2008), 22.

[47] Cohen (2001), 95.

[48] Zimbardo (2007), 297–323.

[49] Glas (2006), 178–79.

insulation: perpetrators did not face their victims, who became non-human legitimate targets (Browning 1998; Glover;[50] Russell and Gregory 2005; Bauman 1989, and Rowan Savage in this volume). Each agent's task is plausibly deniable. As a good manager or employee, effective, efficient and legal, one can still (un)wittingly commit evil acts (Adams and Balfour 2004; Pina e Cunha et al 2010). Contemporary examples include international corporations that deal in destruction and death: international small arms traders, the tobacco lobby (Bandura 1999), multinational polluters, and the Hardie asbestos scandal in Australia (Peacock 2009).

Similarly, in overt war, terrorism and genocide, group allegiance and absolution facilitate killing; and situational and group roles, and cultural and organisational arrangements channel the emotions and proclivities of perpetrators. Fundamental needs to survive and belong mean accepting group norms and co-operation (Staub 2003; Zimbardo 2007). Promoting soldiers' connections with comrades also enhances their willingness to act for them and their operational effectiveness against enemies (Grossman 1996).

Interviewing Nazi killers, Lifton and psychiatrist Henry Dicks (1972) underscored their normality rather than pathology.[51] Collective, diffused or displaced responsibility allows people to behave more cruelly than if acting alone, to relinquish responsibility for victims' life and welfare, and makes bystander helping less probable.[52] Christopher Browning, studying the trial documents of Reserve Police Battalion 101, comprising 'ordinary' middle-aged working class men from the social democratic city of Hamburg, emphasised such variables: group and tribal loyalty, peer pressure, assigned roles and obedience to authority. Ordered

---

[50] Glover (1999), 64–68.

[51] Berkowitz (1999), 249.

[52] Bandura (1999), 198; Staub (2003), 330.

to murder Jews in a Polish village (Josefow), the group leader gave his men the choice to opt out, but less than 15 of 500 did so. Not initially heartless, they became progressively de-sensitised, eventually murdering 70,000–80,000 people (Browning 1998) sometimes bringing their wives and girlfriends to watch their weeks' 'work', and they became the most efficient killers in the Lublin district.

Dehumanisation involves stripping people of human qualities, thus denying likeness, empathy and obligation. Social group research demonstrates that in-groups rate themselves as more human than out-groups and strangers (Haslam et al 2005). Thus moral principles apply to 'us', but not 'them'.[53] 'Just-world' thinking assumes the world is just, therefore suffering people invited their fate by their actions or character: hence perpetrators devalue people they have harmed (Lerner 1980; Staub 2003). In wars and actions against 'undesirable' minorities, state propaganda portrays enemies as greedy, cruel, godless, raping, murdering, criminal, mindless savages or barbarians or 'gooks', demonic, or dangerous animals (Keen 2004; Glover, 1999; Zimbardo[54]).

As Primo Levi's Nazi camp commandant explained, rather than being pointlessly cruel to those who would die, dehumanising victims enabled perpetrators to kill (Levi, 1987). Nazism sought to influence public perception through propaganda films that portrayed Jews, Roma, homosexuals, and people with mental disabilities as vermin or as vicious, lascivious, sinister, grotesque or otherwise subhuman. Such films popularised 'natural selection', and promoted voluntary and involuntary 'euthanasia'.[55] Blaming victims by staging

---

[53] Staub (2003), 305.

[54] Zimbardo (2007), 313.

[55] Gallagher (1990), 92; Friedlander (1995), 88–93.

incidents where they stand accused as provocateurs (as the Nazis did to Jews on *'Kristallnacht'* or Hitler did to Poland at the outbreak of World War II) absolves the perpetrator and justifies further aggression and marginalisation. Zimbardo (2007) shows how institutional power without safeguards leads to abuse. Contagion of emotions may spread with mobs. For some, psychological mechanisms such as sadism, sensational thrill-seeking and threatened egotism may play into this (Baumeister and Campbell 1999). In short, dehumanising people enables torture and murder (see Rowan Savage in this volume).

Language, and the problem with and function of denial

Denial (specifically knowing yet not-knowing), which operates at personal, cultural and official levels (Cohen 2001), is the *sine qua non* of mass human rights violations. Denial is literal ('nothing is happening'), interpretative ('what is happening is not what it seems'), volitional ('it's got nothing to do with me'), 'relativist' ('yes, but look at what the Russians did to German civilians'), and so on.[56]

Exculpatory or neutralised language is intrinsic to rights violations. Harms are often justified by invoking higher moral principles (just war theories and rhetoric rationalise making war to resist oppression, save humanity, or secure peace), or by using euphemistic or non-agentic phrases (for example, 'collateral damage', 'surgical strikes', 'friendly fire') (Bandura 1999). Nazi deceptive or distancing language (for example, 'selection', 'special operation', 'resettlement', 'Final Solution') facilitated denial for observers and victims, enabling perpetrators to split off and disown personal acts (Arendt 1963; Cohen[57]). The term 'Final Solution' stood for mass murder without sounding like it, keeping the focus on

---

[56] Cohen (2001), 7–9.

[57] Cohen (2001), 79.

problem-solving.[58]

For Hitler, compartmentalisation was vital. Personally, he avoided physical and visual contact with the consequences of his murderous orders, and actively prevented others telling him the truth. Collectively, Hitler strictly separated his life with Himmler, Goebbels, his generals and staff from his intimate personal circle. He also required compartmentalisation by others. A notice on every wall read: 'Every man need only know what is going on in his own domain'. Compartmentalisation involved not only activities but also thinking. Speer observed that linked with his secrecy order, this meant much more than Hitler's wanting people to concentrate their minds — it meant it was dangerous not to[59] (Kubarych 2005).

Albert Speer exemplifies individual denial. While denying lifelong that he knew the Jews were being exterminated, Speer affirmed that he was blind by choice, not ignorant. Noticing the obvious destruction of 'Kristallnacht' and Jewish evictions, he avoided knowing the reasons. He eluded recognising the barbarous conditions of his slave labourers. A friend advised him never to visit Auschwitz: what he saw there he was not permitted to describe and could not describe. Speer avoided querying him or anyone, evading evidence that would confirm his suspicions that crimes had been committed. He admitted he was 'inescapably contaminated morally; from discovering something which might have made me turn from my course, I had closed my eyes' (Sereny 1996; Kubarych 2005). On tough questions, he generalised about specifics and admitted a little to deny a lot. It was not that Speer did not want to know, but (more strongly) that he wanted not to

---

[58] Zimbardo, (2007), 215; Lifton (1986), 420-55.

[59] Sereny (1996), 148.

know (Kubarych 2005).

German collective denial was expressed and examined after April 1945, when the widely publicised liberation of the Bergen–Belsen concentration camp shocked the world. As events unfolded, many Germans claimed 'We knew nothing about this' (*Davon haben wir nichts gewusst*). Though Germans knew of Nazi murderousness towards Jews through propaganda (Johnson 2005), awareness of genocide (which began after the invasion of Russia) had come gradually for the Allies and Germans. Except for civilians and soldiers in close proximity to the *Einsatzgruppen*, the concentration camps in German-occupied lands or extermination camps in Poland, there were rumours and guesses (Sereny 2000). German historian Peter Longerich comments that *Davon*, meaning 'about this', implies knowledge and unwillingness to openly address the subject further. The verb *gewusst*, implying knowledge, is carefully chosen, not excluding rumours and partial information that was uncertain. People accordingly employed this strategy to distance themselves from responsibility (Richards, 2006). The Holocaust therefore was an open secret in real time (Cohen 2001). The question of knowledge and accountability has been central to recent German history (see below). After the war, many asserted that Germans had been misled[60] or were uninformed. Defendants concealed, distorted or justified their roles, for example citing obedience and community loyalty during war[61] or were self-righteously indignant.[62] Neurologist Julius Hallervorden, who removed brains from murdered children with cerebral palsy, told Leo Alexander that 'there was wonderful material among those brains, beautiful mental defectives...[but] how they

---

[60] Schmidt (2007), 268.

[61] Schmidt (2007), 157.

[62] Weindling (2006), 161.

came to me was none of my business'.[63]

Gradualism

People and societies change for worse (or better) through stepwise actions (Zimbardo 2007; Staub[64]). Prefacing big requests with related smaller requests (the 'foot-in-the-door' tactic) is effective (Staub;[65] Milgram 1963; Zimbardo 2007). Learning through participation is critical—for harming, gradually inducting and capturing people in practices they normally find morally abhorrent. Thus exposure and step-wise change overcomes resistance, altering values, self-concept and behaviours. 'Teachers' who shock errant 'learners' increase shock intensity as learner performance declines (Bandura et al 1975). Some observe the role of learned perversity or unleashed sadism, based on an emerging culture of freedom from constraints that is associated with absolute power, or the removal or suppression of negative consequences for undertaking increasingly cruel acts upon others (Rosen 2011).

Under the Nazis, Jewish assimilation and the German–Jewish symbiosis was destroyed through progressive exclusion (dismissal from jobs, expropriation, disenfranchise-ment, prohibition of marriage and sexual relations), terrorisation (the *'Kristallnacht'* pogrom), stigmatisation (wearing yellow stars), and finally removal and extermination (Staub;[66] Abrahams-Sprod 2006). The 'euthanasia' programs pioneered Holocaust technologies, and effected psychological and institutional changes that facilitated it (Dudley and Gale

---

[63] Weindling (2006), 70; Alexander, (1949), 4.

[64] Staub (2003), 29, 303.

[65] Staub (2003), 326.

[66] Staub (2003), 291–324.

2002; Staub[67]). Eichmann acclimatised to genocide through ethnic cleansing of Poles in 1939. When first exposed to bodies of massacred Jews, he reacted with revulsion: however, Nazi ideology, Führer loyalty, his need to belong and careerism, made him continue and ignore his distress, which gradually extinguished (Arendt 1963). Stangl was also drawn into genocide in a stepwise fashion (Sereny 1974). For members of Police Battalion 101, police force career choice and training and increasing Jewish persecution may possibly have aided their desensitisation.[68] Greek torturers were not selected for sadism but non-deviancy, identification with the political regime, and obedience. Training bound them together through initiation rites, isolation, new values, and elitist language; de-individuation and prevention of thinking; and exposure to frequent, group controlled violence (Gibson and Haritos-Fatouros 1986). Forms of contractual obligation are created, meaningful roles are played, and apparently reasonable rules become binding. Preventing exit, and offering an (ideological) end to justify the means (Staub 2003) are also important. The induction of executioners (Haney et al 1997; Robertson 2006), the 'normalisation' of executions in various countries, and the evolution of terrorists (Bandura 1999) exemplify the same gradualism. In war, indoctrination, humiliation and distancing and the killing or wounding of comrades may provoke explosive retaliation and excitement, a wish to go on killing.[69] Glover (1999) convincingly documents a stepwise progression in the shift to killing at distance, from the British naval blockade in World War I to the use of the atomic bomb, and details the institutional momentum, moral inertia, diffused responsibility and moral sliding that made it possible. The role of miscommunication, Hobbesian fear and military drift should also not be

---

[67] Staub (2003), 304.

[68] Staub (2003), 18–19.

[69] Glover (1999), 47–57.

underestimated.

Nazi doctors and psychiatrists: motivations and reasons

Illich and Foucault chart the dangers inherent in medical power and biological knowledge.[70] (Technical knowledge can facilitate both healing and killing (Lafleur et al 2007)). Unsurprisingly, similar motives and reasons emerge in medical and helping contexts: as noted above, the criteria for 'euthanasia', for example, were ideological ('eugenic', antisemitic, and economic), practical (related to administrative efficiency), and achieved through bureaucratic routine, peer pressure, propaganda and inducements.[71]

At Nuremberg, Nazi doctors and psychiatrists multiplied excuses. These included: following orders, *tu quoque*, acting for public health or national security, total war demands extreme measures (Proctor 1992), the captives would be killed anyway, prisoners who volunteered for experiments were offered freedom (there was no evidence of this) or might expiate their 'crimes' (that is, minority group status or political beliefs), scientists lacked moral or 'values' expertise, or that the few could be sacrificed for the many (Caplan,[72] Schmidt 2007, Weindling 2006). The post-war medical trials admitted none of these justifications. Moreover, the claim that the Nazis enforced psychiatric co-operation is a half-truth at best. Despite pressure from peers and superiors, higher ranking and direct perpetrators were seldom simply coerced into transgression. Doctors were not coerced, insane, psychopathic, demonic or incompetent, but frequently pillars of the establishment.[73] German medicine affiliated to the Nazi

---

[70] Weindling (2006), 5.

[71] Evans (2009), 101.

[72] Caplan (2007), 66–70.

[73] Caplan (2007), 65.

party early[74] and enthusiastically – it actively welcomed the Nazis (Dudley and Gale 2002) – and in greater numbers than any other professional group (Proctor 1988). The SS was the chief perpetrator organisation, which recruited a high number of professional culprits, especially doctors. Antisemitic ideology, obedience and more authoritarian personality orientation distinguished SS members (Dicks 1972; Merkl 1980; Elms and Milgram 1966; Staub[75]). Scientists were not bystanders or pawns: many helped construct Nazi racial policies[76] which progressively subverted discussions of human experimentation in ethics journals.[77]

German psychiatry, which was somatically focused, state-dominated and objectified patients,[78] had aided the pursuit of compulsory sterilisation and 'euthanasia'. Eugenics and 'race hygiene' resulted in compulsory sterilisations in several countries. German authorities argued the war sacrificed the best genes, while medicine supported the weak, leaving the worst to proliferate. Purging such 'epidemics' would redeem and regenerate Germany. Many Nazis therefore endorsed medical 'counter-selection' of 'degenerate' individuals and 'useless eaters' (those with various physical, mental and intellectual disabilities, or belonging to certain cultural groups) for euthanasia (Zimbardo;[79] Weindling;[80] Gallagher 1990; Lifton 1986, Friedlander 1995; Dudley and Gale 2002). Hitler conceived the German nation as a body to which every true German was indissolubly joined but from which the Jewish 'bacillus', 'virus', 'gangrenous excrescence' were to be

---

[74] Weindling (2006), 5.

[75] Staub (2003), 300–01.

[76] Proctor (1992), 29.

[77] Frewer (2007), 30–45.

[78] Pross (1992), 38; Weindling (2007), 7.

[79] Zimbardo (2007), 313.

[80] Weindling (2006), 99, 158.

extirpated. Thus genocide was an immune response to illness in the body politic (Koenigsburg 2009). Robert Ritter, psychiatrist with the German National Institute of Health, also viewed 90 per cent of Romani as descendants of the lowest European criminal sub-proletariat, dispatching many for killing.[81] The supposed subhuman status of live subjects also facilitated coerced experiments. Commitment to public health and alternative medicine contrasted with denial of the social causes of poverty.[82]

Interviewing Nuremberg medical defendants and others, Alexander (1948, 1949) concluded that indoctrination, group seduction and sanctioning led to denial of individual responsibility and reality. He speculated that the Nazi regime's enforcement of *Blutkitt* ('blood putty'), the collective commission of crimes contrary to one's personal values, confirmed extraordinary service in the 'greater cause' or 'sacred mission', proving and reinforcing party allegiance and loyalty. Thus Himmler, famously addressing the SS perpetrators, pardoned them in discharging their 'heroic duty'. Doctors and psychiatrists were often committed Nazis, who 'selected' for national health. For doctors and psychiatrists, the language of eugenics, and the metaphor of surgical extirpation of the ulcer or gangrene of Jewry and other 'degenerates' from the body of German humanity, represented murder as a public service.[83] Ferocity and hardness replaced Judeo–Christian compassion (Gallagher;[84] Glover 1999). Among camp doctors, Lifton noted 'doubling', whereby a portion of the self becomes the whole (or 'Auschwitz self'), enabling self-deception and adaptation to

---

[81] Müller-Hill (2007), 59; Weindling (2006), 188–89; Pross (1992), 37.

[82] Pross (1992), 38.

[83] Friedlander (1995), 11; Graham (1977), 1138–39; Evans (1997), 73.

[84] Gallagher (1990), 198.

evil environments. Irrespective of this construct's validity (Burleigh 1994; Cohen 2001; Gaita[85]), the separation of roles characterised T4 psychiatrists.

In contrast to the notion of a 'duty to kill', embodied in medical writings of the time (Dudley and Gale 2002) is the motive of venality. As noted above, opportunism and careerism were rampant as the Nazis offered non-Jewish doctors, who did not demur, improved earnings, assets, research opportunities and status as Jewish colleagues were ousted (Proctor 1992). Self-interest — such as financial incentive, career advancement or expropriation — is a common motive in genocide and mass murder.[86] Zealots also participated eagerly in exterminations, others performed required duties more or less methodically, others again participated reluctantly.[87]

Holocaust bystanders

Standing by rarely receives sufficient attention, compared with perpetrators, victims and rescuers. Standing by encompasses a number of heterogeneous responses. Some bystanders may be guilt-ridden. Others may fear consequences, be in denial, suppressing uncomfortable knowledge (Speer fits this description), be morally indifferent, or tacitly approve or be complicit in what is occurring.[88]

In the Third Reich, many were passive bystanders or even active participants, boycotting Jewish businesses, benefiting from expropriations of Jewish property or firing Jewish employees, breaking off friendships (Abrahams-Sprod 2006). Deception and obfuscation determined the 'language rules' (Goldhagen 1996, Arendt 1963, Cohen 2001). As noted, Jewish

---

[85] Gaita (1999), 225–26.

[86] Staub (2003), 291–324; Baum (2008), 31.

[87] Lifton (1986), 194.

[88] Kershaw (2008), 11.

and non-Jewish doctors were pitted against each other. The Berlin Psychoanalytic Institute, renamed after Göring, accommodated psychoanalytic concepts to Nazi ideology.[89] Psychiatrists enhanced their lowly status by accepting the task of identifying and excluding inferior Germans.[90] German psychiatrist Oswald Bumke asserted in 1945 that though killing people with mental illness was meant to be top secret, 'the sparrows were whistling it from the rooftops'.[91]

Research on bystanders and rescuers, compared with perpetrators, is scant. Underpinning bystanding are situational risks that are judged insuperable, and the wish for normality, predictability and social acceptance. Numbing and avoidance of critical thinking are common. Depending on social conditions, bystanders may become temporary perpetrators or rescuers.[92]

Bystanders have power to influence events. To act against Jews, the Nazi leadership needed a reliable substrata of antisemitism. They were apprehensive about popular reactions, but surprised and emboldened by the lack of response, and also popular action against Jews (Hilberg 1961; Dawidowicz 1975; Staub[93]). Arendt (1994) spoke of 'the empty space' forming around friends and loved ones when the Nazis came to power, in the wave of co-ordination, not yet the pressure of terror. Thus bystanders — nice enough men and women whose moral sense was blunted — made the Holocaust possible (Gryn 1996).

---

[89] Staub (2003), 306–07.

[90] Müller-Hill (1988), 22; Friedlander (1995), 123–24.

[91] Schmidt (2007), 92.

[92] Baum (2008), 153–80.

[93] Staub (2003), 309.

As bystanders, many nations facilitated the Holocaust. Antisemitism existed in western nations. They supported the 1936 Berlin Olympics. American corporations traded with Germany throughout the 1930s (Wyman 1984). In May 1939, the *SS St Louis* carried 937 Jewish refugees from Hamburg to Cuba, which denied them entry. So, despite appeals, did the United States. Britain, France, Belgium and Holland finally admitted them but subsequently many died in Nazi gas chambers, a consequence of collective international indecision and policy failure regarding Jewish refugees (Thomas and Morgan-Witts, 1974). The Rwandan genocide,[94] and events in Darfur (among others) also exemplify the effects of standing by.

Motives and reasons for harming: experimental models

A number of experimental paradigms have modelled elements of perpetrator behaviour, shedding light on Holocaust events as well as later genocides. Stanley Milgram's famous experiments (1963, 1974) examined how obedience to authority and conformity might violate people's basic moral beliefs. Milgram was inspired by Asch's conformity experiments. These demonstrated that individual participants' visual comparisons of different line lengths with a reference line could be influenced by peers' false responses. Dissenting peer responses reduced the likelihood of conformity (Asch 1956), but collectivist cultures increased it (Bond and Smith 1996). The Holocaust and contemporaneous Eichmann trial primed Milgram's work.

In New Haven, Connecticut, 1,000 adults aged 20 to 50 years from numerous occupations and educational backgrounds, became unwitting subjects for Milgram's purported study of memory and learning. A white-coated, impassive experimenter ordered them to teach a pleasant volunteer stranger a series of word pairs, using a generator

---

[94] Staub (2003), 341–50.

that supposedly administered increasingly painful and hazardous shocks when errors were made. The learner, out of sight in another room, was the experimenter's confederate, and though increasingly distressed sounds were pre-recorded and played for each shock level, no shocks were actually given. The experimenter met participants' distress, questioning and wish to discontinue with reassurances that he would assume all responsibility and there was no permanent damage, but increasingly assertive demands that they continue.

Beforehand, Milgram polled professionals' predicted outcomes. All 14 Yale University senior psychology majors believed that very few (average 1.2 per cent) would inflict maximum voltage. Thirty-nine psychiatrists predicted that 0.1 per cent (the 'pathological fringe') would administer maximum voltage, only 4 per cent would reach 300 volts, and most would not exceed 150 volts. The actual results starkly discredited these predictions. Despite personal distress, when pressed, almost two-thirds of participants obeyed to the end (three administered 450 volts). Women and men were equally obedient. The experiment delivered similar results in Princeton, Rome, South Africa, Australia and Munich (where 85 per cent of subjects obeyed until the end) (Milgram 1974). High compliance (6 per cent) occurred when peers complied, the experimenter was adjacent, the learner was in another room, distress sounds were absent, and the warning was only written on the shock generator. Thus avoiding personal sensory awareness of the impact of harmful acts was crucial. Conversely, the experimenter's reduced physical proximity (for example, instructing via phone), the learner's distress sounds or increased proximity (for example, having to hold the learner's arm on a shock plate), conflicting authority (incompatible orders of equal status experimenters), and peer rebellion (observed disobedience of other teachers (actually actors)), reduced obedience. Perhaps non-strangers (family, friends) as learners reducing emotional distance would have decreased obedience, while the procedural impersonality of the shock generator facilitated it (Russell and Gregory 2005). Choosing to please rather than confront the experimenter, most participants relinquished personal responsibility and delegated: administering word-pair tests while another participant administered shocks ensured high (93 per cent) compliance. Milgram[95] associated this with modern bureaucracy, which absolves most from directly destructive actions, employing small numbers of 'the most callous and obtuse' for 'dirty work'. For those who resisted, personalities, feelings of competence, values and (sometimes) group cultures were important (Milgram 1974; Staub 2003).

Albert Bandura et al (1975), purporting to study the effects of punishment on decision-making, derived similar findings. 'Supervisors' who were told to administer electric shocks to unseen subjects who made faulty decisions, increased the intensity of 'shocking' behaviour if responsibility was collective rather than individual, and if recipients were negatively labelled. (No electric shocks were actually given). As performance declined, shock intensities increased, creating further failures that were taken as further evidence of culpability. Self-exonerating justifications prevailed.

The also famous Stanford Prison Experiment (SPE) (Zimbardo 2007; Haney et al 1973) explored the effects of situational variables (including duress and peer pressure) on individual behaviour. Role-playing life in a simulated prison, 24 white middle class young males selected for apparently normal psychological adjustment were randomly assigned to the parts of warders or prisoners. The experiment intentionally reproduced the worst features of prisons, including de-individuation (warders) and dehumanisation (prisoners). Warders received military uniforms, wooden batons and reflective glasses (minimising eye contact), and

---

[95] Milgram (1974), 121–22.

worked in shifts, returning home off hours. Prisoners donned smocks without underpants, thongs and ankle chains, were assigned identifying numbers, and booked in by actual police co-operating with the experiment at its inception. Loss of personal identity facilitated learned helplessness, with prisoners suffering and accepting sadistic and humiliating treatment from guards. Physical punishments and arbitrary controls included deprivation of privacy, food and sleep, and degrading practices, for example, enforced nudity, and cleaning toilets with bare hands. Some resisted, others became zealous models, many developed uncontrollable crying or disorganised thinking. As with the Nazi doctors (Lifton 1986), guards were zealous, methodical or reluctant, though even the latter failed to challenge the situation.[96] Inadequate supervision abetted prisoner abuse. The experiment had to be abandoned after six days of the projected fortnight.

Contrary to expectation that individuals facing moral dilemmas would follow their conscience, Milgram's experiment showed that directives from authorities overwhelmed the morality of most individuals who are in no way evil (Milgram 1974; Blass 2002). Zimbardo et al's experiment (and also that by Bandura et al) similarly revealed the importance of individual, situational and systemic factors, including de-individuation and dehumanisation, in understanding institutional abuses (Zimbardo,[97] Staub 2003).

Taken together, these experiments illustrate the influence of experimentally induced authority, peers, institutional ideology ('the slogan that legitimises the means to attain the goal'[98]) and onlookers, on individual behaviours. Ordinary

---

[96] Zimbardo (2007), 208.

[97] Zimbardo (2007), 297–323, 330.

[98] Zimbardo (2007), 226.

people, performing tasks without particular hostility, can act destructively even without physical coercion. Obedience to authority can lead to verbal abuse, sexual assault (strip-search scams provoked by anonymous 'police officers' in American fast-food restaurant chains) or death (for example, doctors' power over nurses in drug ordering, airline pilots' authority over first officers) (Zimbardo 2007, 278ff). Schoolteachers favouring students with blue eyes or brown eyes can transform classrooms into totalitarian, abusive and exclusive environments (Peters 1985). Ron Jones, a teacher in Palo Alto, produced his film 'The Third Wave' in 1967: it showed high school students just how easily fascist behaviour could be 'created' when hierarchies, dressed in appropriate uniforms and insignia, are introduced. This 'situational' paradigm, rather than formal mental illness, repeatedly supports torture and mass murder, as exemplified by the Third Reich's camp guards, Rwandan and former Yugoslavian genocides, terrorists and suicide bombers,[99] and destructive cults (Jim Jones' People's Temple, Aum Shinrikyo). Role identification and compartmentalisation can produce dire results, as the camp guards who played Bach while they murdered Jews illustrates.[100]

Milgram[101] believed his results confirmed Arendt's conception of 'the banality of evil'. However, direct authority does not fully explain the sanctioning of harms in everyday situations, where authority is often deliberately diffused, and where ideology is vital (Bandura 1999).

This is not to excuse individuals' reprehensible actions, or to minimise their accountability. But investigators differ in interpreting individual vulnerability to antisocial behaviours and 'moral disengagement'. Bandura (1999) cites parenting

---

[99] Zimbardo (2007), 293; Baum (2008), 76–78.

[100] Gaita (1999), 225–26.

[101] Milgram (1974), 6.

failures, abuse and neglect, early aggression, failure to recognise and cultivate pro-social behaviour, lack of guilt, rumination over personal injustices and retaliation, and lack of perceived efficacy to withstand peer pressure. Zimbardo (2007) argues that these experiments show the potential corruptibility of anyone (including our kin and ourselves) given the right situational and/or systemic (socio-cultural) forces, and difficulty predicting behaviours under stress even with prior knowledge of people's innate, apparently 'normal', dispositions. Baum[102] responds that this does not account for individual rescuing, and emphasises the predictive importance of personal emotional development.

Motives and reasons for helping

Social psychology emphasises the power of social situations: under conducive conditions, ordinary decent people can do appalling things. However, the situational paradigm begs the question about why some people behave well, heroically and sometimes repeatedly, in dire situations (Bernstein 2002; Baum 2008). Milgram found a sizeable minority resisted pressure, displaying moral courage and imagination (Bandura 1999). Against self-interest, without expectation of gain, and often in prolonged peril, rescuers of Jews in the Holocaust frequently acted for acquaintances or strangers. Such active behaviour (those honoured by Yad Vashem under-represent those who rescued) was often crucial to outcome in Nazi-occupied Europe. Typically, they minimised their contribution, rather than seeing it as heroic. Their actions and motives have been frequently described (for example, Tec 1986; Oliner and Oliner 1988; Paldiel 1988; Fogelman 1994; Gilbert 2002).

Helping can be situationally influenced. For example, the

---

[102] Baum (2008), 4–5, 44–45, 88.

more people who witness an emergency, the less likely they will help (Darley and Latane 1968). Diffusion of responsibility may explain this,[103] because helping is more likely when needs are clear, great, impactful and focused, costs are affordable and the behaviour required is socially acceptable.[104] Time pressure (Darley and Batson 1973) and the prior relationship are also relevant. In Milgram's experiments, as noted, situational determinants, like being personally responsible for and witnessing harms one causes (Milgram 1974; Bandura et al 1975), affected obedience.

But this is notwithstanding the importance of character, competencies in crises, and the capacity of situations to shape character. Crime interveners have a sense of capability founded on training and subjective personal strength (Hudson et al 1981). Steps in help include noticing, understanding the urgency, assuming responsibility, deciding how to help, and implementing one's decision. Like perpetrators and bystanders, rescuers evolve. Contact leads to identification, becoming aware of the human characteristics of those being killed or harmed converts bystanders from passivity to action, and gradual incremental involvement becomes an obsession to rescue. The stories of famous rescuers Oskar Schindler (Keneally 1983) and Raoul Wallenberg show this (Bandura 1999, Staub 2003).

Many Holocaust rescuers and Milgram experiment defiers were deeply connected to and identified with moral parents and families holding strong humanitarian values. Notably, they received less punitive rearing, with closer fathers and more reasoning and explanation (London 1970; Oliner and Oliner 1988; Blass 1991; Blass 1993,[105] Tec 1986; Staub,[106]

---

[103] Zimbardo (2007), 315.

[104] Staub (2003), 125, 131.

[105] Blass (1993), 40–41, cited in Berkowitz (1999), 249.

[106] Staub (2003), 314.

Baum[107]). While perpetrators have over-developed social identities, rescuers were far more often emotionally mature: independent-minded, emotionally intelligent, having higher self-esteem, subscribing to universal ideals and principles (Baum 2008), and socially responsible. Rescuers differed from bystanders on locus of control, autonomy, risk-taking, social responsibility, tolerance and authoritarianism, empathy, and altruistic moral reasoning (Midlarsky et al 2005). While trait adventurousness characterised some, all rescuers showed courage when confronted with daunting risks. Some belonged to resistance groups, church groups or nations that shaped their responses, though religion did not notably associate with rescuing. Such 'pro-social orientation' (Staub 1995) may be grounded in respect and moral standing, moral principles and identity, and in affective connections and sympathy (Staub 1995; Glover 1999).

The psychology of altruism is relevant here. Altruism is the motivation to help others or for others' welfare without regard to reward or the benefits of recognition. While the payoffs of altruism are hotly debated, helping has its own momentum: the great majority of helpers describe the experience as positive, while conversely people whose lives are more satisfying feel they have more to give others. Research shows that materialistic-competitive goals (wealth, career success, power) are inimical to helping, though not other personal goals (for example, support and security, personal growth, competence, control).[108]

Whole cultures of rescue confronted Nazism, as in Denmark and Bulgaria, and Italy and Hungary before German takeovers in 1943 and 1944 respectively. National

---

[107] Baum (2008), 90–91, 185.

[108] Staub (2003), 145–56.

leadership [and internal political struggles] prevented Bulgarian Jews being deported. Some members of the German Confessing Church, Holland's Antirevolutionary Church, and various Italian and French villages exemplify resistance (as discussed in Colin Tatz's chapter in this volume). In Le Chambon-sur-Lignon, descendants of persecuted Protestant Huguenots led by their pastor and his wife, hid thousands of Jews from the Nazis (Sauvage 1989; Baum[109]). Relatives and institutions that protested killing of people with mental, physical and intellectual disabilities acted similarly. Against German efficiency, incorruptibility and obedience, divergent civic traditions (of freedom and equal rights in Denmark, and unpunctuality and inefficiency in Italy) may also have contributed to this outcome (Glover, 1999). At a macro-political level, *realpolitik* may determine whether people or nations intervene in oppression or aggression (for example, European nations deciding whether to stop Hitler before World War II). However, membership and memory of minority group status, pro-social orientation, and leadership all contribute to outcomes in national and whole-cultural situations.

Preventing mass human rights violations: where is the engine-room?

The Holocaust contains individual, situational and social determinants, and (in)humanity arises from ordinary psychological, situational and socio-cultural processes and their evolution into extreme forms. Yet should preventive approaches to mass human rights violations target the level of individual frailty and transgression, or institutional, communal, socio-cultural and national influences? How to address situational factors in facilitating such abuses?

It is a paradox that individuals rather than groups are generally held legally accountable for mass human rights

---

[109] Baum (2008), 205–06.

violations, yet locating the prime cause of such violations in individual frailty and pathology seems misconceived. Moral actions while remaining the actor's personal responsibility presuppose wider influences (Bandura, 1999; Zimbardo, 2007; Staub, 2003). Research meta-analyses reveal the power of social situations on behaviour is robust, yet criminal justice systems rarely address this.[110] While individual perpetrators played key roles, the role of German society and nation was absolutely crucial, for example, in accepting Hitler and not resisting antisemitic policies. Virtually every German institution, occupational group or profession contributed voluntarily (usually enthusiastically) to the 'Final Solution', turning their own traditional ethical protocols upside down (Higgins 2006). The effect of this inertia on further Nazi programming has been noted.

Because humans are herd animals, most will do what the herd is doing. Most will manifest as 'saints' or 'sinners' according to the health or breakdown of those communal, societal and political forms of association with which they identify. This suggests there may be value intervening at a number of levels. Educational programs that seek to influence the moral awareness and development of individual children and adults about racism and social inclusion are of potentially great significance, as is the preservation of the moral resources — respect, sympathy and friendship — and cultivation of a moral identity and imagination, in promoting helping and resistance. Pre-eminently, paying attention to these wider determinants and preventing the decline of social and national institutions that preserve civility constitutes a crucial arena for genocide prevention (Higgins 2003; Higgins 2006).

Acknowledgements

[110] Zimbardo (2007), 321.

Michael Dudley and Fran Gale thank Winton Higgins, Alan Rosen, and Colin Tatz for suggestions about the argument, content and style.

References

Abrahams-Sprod, M (2006), 'Life Under Siege: The Jews of Magdeburg under Nazi rule', PhD thesis, University of Sydney, Sydney.

Adams, G, Balfour, D (2004), 'Human rights, the moral vacuum of modern organisations, and administrative evil', in Campbell, T and Miller, S (eds) *Human Rights and the Moral Responsibilities of Corporate and Public Sector Organisations*, chapter 11, 205–21, Alphen aan den Rijn, Kluwer Academic.

Adorno, T (1955, reprinted 1967), *Prisms*, London, MIT Press.

Alexander, J C, with Jay, M, Giesen, B, et al (2009), *Remembering the Holocaust: A debate*. Oxford, Oxford University Press.

Alexander, L (1948), 'War crimes: Their socio-psychological aspects', *American Journal of Psychiatry*, 105, 170–77.

Alexander, L (1949), 'Medical science under dictatorship', *New England Journal of Medicine*, 241 (2), 39–47.

Allport, G W (1954), *The Nature of Prejudice*, Reading MA, Addison-Wesley.

Amnesty International (1980), *Testimony on Secret Detention Camps in Argentina*, London, Amnesty International Publications.

Annas, G, Grodin, M (eds) (1992), *The Nazi Doctors and the Nuremberg Code*, New York, Oxford University Press.

Arendt, H (1963, revised edition 1968), *Eichmann in Jerusalem: A Report on the banality of evil*, New York, Viking, .

Arendt, Hannah, (1994), *Essays in Understanding, 1930–1954* (J Kohn, ed), New York, Harcourt, Brace and Co, 10–11.

Arendt, Hannah (1966), Introduction to Naumann, B, *Auschwitz*, New York, Praeger, xxiv.

Asch, S E (1956), 'Studies of independence and conformity: A minority of one against a unanimous majority', *Psychological Monographs, 70* (whole of no 416).

Baldwin, P (ed) (1990), *Reworking the Past: Hitler, the Holocaust and the historians' debate*, Boston, Beacon Press.

Bandura, A (1999), 'Moral Disengagement in the Perpetration of Inhumanities', *Personality and Social Psychology Review*, 3 (3), 193–209.

Bandura, A, Underwood, B, Fromson, M E (1975), 'Disinhibition of aggression through diffusion of responsibility and dehumanisation of the victims', *Journal of Research in Personality*, 9, 253–69.

Bankier, D (1992), *The Germans and the Final Solution: Public opinion under Nazism*, Oxford and Cambridge MA, Blackwell.

Bauer, Y (2001), *Rethinking the Holocaust*, New Haven, Yale University Press.

Baum, S K (2008), *The Psychology of Genocide: Perpetrators, bystanders and rescuers*, New York, Cambridge University Press.

Bauman, Z (1989), *Modernity and the Holocaust*, Ithaca NY, Cornell University Press.

Baumeister, R F, Campbell, W K (1999), 'The intrinsic appeal of evil: sadism, sensational thrills, and threatened egotism', *Personality and Social Psychology Review*, 3 (3), 210–21.

Berkowitz, L (1999), 'Evil is more than banal: situationism and the concept of evil'. *Personality and Social Psychology Review*, 3 (3), 246–53.

Bernard, V, Ottenberg, P, Redl, F (1965), 'Dehumanisation: a composite psychological defense in relation to modern war', in Schwebel, M (ed) *Behavioural Science and Human Survival*, Palo Alto CA, Science and Behavior Books, 64–82.

Bernstein, R (2002), *Radical Evil: A philosophical interrogation*, Cambridge UK, Polity Press.

Blass, T (1991), 'Understanding behavior in the Milgram obedience experiment: the role of personality, situations, and their interactions', *Journal of Personality and Social Psychology*, 60, 398–413.

Blass, T (1993), 'Psychological perspectives on perpetrators of the Holocaust: the role of situational pressures, personal dispositions, and their interactions', *Holocaust and Genocide Studies*, 7, 30–50.

Blass, T (2002), 'The man who shook the world', *Psychology Today*, March/April, 69–74.

Bloche, G, Marks, J (2005), 'When doctors go to war', *New England Journal of Medicine*, 352, 3–6.

Bock, G (1997), 'Sterilisation and "medical" massacres in National Socialist Germany: ethics, politics and the law', in Berg, M, Cocks, G (eds) *Medicine and Modernity: Public health and medical care in nineteenth and twentieth-century Germany*, German Historical Institute, Washington DC, and Cambridge University Press, 149–72.

Bond, R, Smith, P B (1996), 'Culture and Conformity: A Meta-Analysis of Studies Using Asch's (1952b, 1956) Line Judgment Task', *Psychological Bulletin*, 119 (1), 111–37.

Browning, C (1998), *Ordinary Men: Reserve Police Battalion 101 and the Final Solution in Poland*, [2nd edn], New York, Harper Collins.

Browning, C R (2004). *The Origins of the Final Solution: The evolution of Nazi Jewish policy, September 1939 – March 1942*, Lincoln, University of Nebraska Press.

Bullock, A (1992), *Fanaticism and Calculation, Hitler and Stalin: Parallel lives*, New York, Knopf.

Burleigh, M (1994), *Death and Deliverance: 'Euthanasia' in Germany ca. 1900–-1945*. Cambridge, Cambridge University Press.

Caplan, A (2005), 'Editorial: The misuse of the Nazi analogy', *Science*, 22 July, 535. DOI 10.1126/science 1115437.

Caplan, A (2007), 'The ethics of evil: the challenge and lessons of Nazi medical experiments', in Lafleur, W R, Böhme, G, Shimazono, S (eds), *Dark Medicine: Rationalising unethical medical research*, Bloomington, Indiana University Press, 63–72.

Card, C (2002), *The Atrocity Paradigm: A theory of evil*, New York/London, Oxford University Press.

Cesarani, D (2006), *Becoming Eichmann: Rethinking the life*, *crimes, and trial of a desk murderer,* Cambridge MA, Da Capo Press.

Cohen, S (2001), *In Denial: Knowing about atrocities and suffering* Cambridge UK, Polity/Blackwell.

Council for International Organizations of Medical Sciences and World Health Organization (1993), *International Ethical Guidelines for Biomedical Research Involving Human Subjects,* Geneva.

Darley, J M, Batson, C D (1973), 'From Jerusalem to Jericho: a study of situational variables in helping behavior', *Journal of Personality and Social Psychology,* 27, 100–08.

Darley, J M, Latane, B (1968), 'Bystander intervention in emergencies: diffusion of responsibilities', *Journal of Personality and Social Psychology,* 8, 377–83.

Dawidowicz, L S (1975), *The War Against the Jews: 1933–1945,* New York, Holt, Rinehart and Winston.

Des Pres, T (1976), *The Survivor: An anatomy of life in a death camp,* New York, Oxford University Press.

Dicks, H (1972), *Licensed Mass Murder: A socio-psychological study of some SS killers,* London, Sussex University Press.

Dudley, M, Gale, F (2002), 'Psychiatrists as a moral community? Psychiatry under the Nazis and its contemporary relevance', *Australian and New Zealand Journal of Psychiatry,* 36, 585–94.

Ehrenfreund, N (2007), *The Nuremberg Legacy: How the Nazi war crimes trials changed the course of history,* New York, Palgrave Macmillan.

Elms, A, Milgram, S (1966), 'Personality characteristics associated with obedience and defiance toward authoritative commands', *Journal of Experimental Research in Personality,* 2, 292–89.

Ericksen, Robert (2012), *Complicity in the Holocaust: Churches and universities in Nazi Germany,* New York, Cambridge University Press.

Evans, R J (2006), *The Third Reich in Power, 1933–1939.* Penguin, London.

113

Evans, R J (2009), *The Third Reich at War*, London, Penguin.

Evans, R J (1997), 'In search of German Social Darwinism', in Berg, M, Cocks, G (eds), *Medicine and Modernity: Public health and medical care in nineteenth and twentieth-century Germany*, Washington DC, Cambridge University Press and German Historical Institute, 55–80.

Evans, R J (2004), *The Coming of the Third Reich*, London Penguin.

Fiske, S T, Harris, L T, Cudy, A T C (2004), 'Why ordinary people torture enemy prisoners', *Science (Policy Forum)* 3006, 1482–83.

Fiske, S T (2003), *Social Beings*, New York. Wiley.

Fogelman, E (1994), *Conscience and Courage: Rescuers of Jews during the Holocaust*, New York, Doubleday.

Freedman, R (2010) (director), 'The Wrong Side of the Bus', a documentary film about Sid Bloch and Apartheid, 2010.

Frewer, A (2007), 'Medical research, morality, and history: The German journal 'Ethik' and the limits of human experimentation', in Lafleur, W R, Böhme, G, Shimazono, S, *Dark Medicine: Rationalising unethical medical research*, Bloomington, Indiana University Press, 30–45.

Friedlander, H (1995), *The Origins of Nazi Genocide: From euthanasia to the Final Solution*, Chapel Hill NC, University of North Carolina Press.

Friedländer, S (2007), *The Years of Persecution: Nazi Germany and the Jews 1933–1939*, Phoenix, Orion, London, (original edition, Weidenfeld and Nicolson, 1997).

Gaita, R (1999), *A Common Humanity*, Melbourne, Melbourne University Press.

Gallagher, H G (1990), *By Trust Betrayed: Patients, physicians and the licence to kill in the Third Reich*, revised ed, Arlington VA, Vandermere Press.

Gibson, J T, Haritos-Fatouros, M (1986), 'The Education of a Torturer', *Psychology Today*, November, 50–58.

Gilbert, M (2002), *The Righteous: The unsung heroes of the Holocaust*, Chatham, Kent, Doubleday.

Glas, G (2006), 'Elements of a phenomenology of evil and

forgiveness', in Potter, N N (ed), *Trauma, Truth and Reconciliation: Healing damaged relationships*, New York, Oxford University Press, 171–202.

Glover, J (1999), *Humanity: A moral history of the twentieth century*, New Haven, Yale University Press.

Goldhagen, D J (1996), *Hitler's Willing Executioners: Ordinary Germans and the Holocaust*, New York, Knopf.

Graham, L R (1977), 'Science and values: the eugenics movement in Germany and Russia in the 1920s', *American Historical Review*, 82, 1133–64.

Grodin, M (1992), 'Historical origins of the Nuremberg Code', in Annas, G, Grodin, M (eds), *The Nazi Doctors and the Nuremberg Code*,' New York, Oxford University Press, 121–48.

Grodin, M, Annas, G (2007), 'Physicians and torture: lessons from the Nazi doctors', *International Review of the Red Cross*, 89, September, 635–54.

Grossman, D (1996), *On Killing: The psychological cost of learning to kill in war and society*, Boston, Little, Brown and Co.

Gryn, H (2000), *Chasing Shadows: Memories of a vanished world*, London, Viking.

Halm, Albert (ed) (1985), *The Gift of Life*, Sydney, Australian Association of Jewish Holocaust Survivors, 95–100.

Hamilton, V L, Sanders, J (1999), 'The second face of evil: wrongdoing in and by the corporation', *Personality and Social Psychology Review*, 3 (3), 222–33.

Hanauski-Abel, H (1996), 'Not a slippery slope or sudden subversion: German medicine and national socialism in 1933', *British Medical Journal*, 7 December, 313, 1453–63.

Haney, C (1997), 'Violence and the capital jury: mechanisms of moral disengagement and the impulse to condemn to death', *Stanford Law Review*, 49, 1447–86.

Haney, C, Banks, W P, Zimbardo, P G (1973), 'Interpersonal dynamics in a simulated prison', *International Journal of Criminology and Penology*, 1, 69–97.

Haslam, N, Bain, P, Douge, L, Lee, M, Bastian, B (2005), 'More human than you: attributing humanness to self and others', *Journal of Personality and Social Psychology*, 89, 937–50.

Higgins, W (2003), *Journey into Darkness*, Sydney, Brandl & Schlesinger.

Higgins, W (2006), 'Could it happen again? The Holocaust and the national dimension', in Tatz, C et al, (eds.), *Genocide Perspectives III: Essays on the Holocaust and other genocides*, Sydney, Brandl & Schlesinger with the Australian Institute for Holocaust and Genocide Studies, 54–77.

Hilberg, R (1961), *The Destruction of the European Jews*, New York, Harper and Row.

Hudson, T L, Ruggiero, M, Conner, R, Geis, G (1981), 'Bystander intervention into crime: a study based on naturally occurring episodes', *Social Psychology Quarterly*, 44 (1), 14–23.

Johnson, E, Reuband, K H (2005), *What We Knew: Terror, mass murder, and everyday life of Nazi Germany*, New York, Basic Books.

Karpinski, J (2004), BBC Radio 4 interview with Brigadier General Janis Karpinski, 15 June 15.

Karpinski, J (with Strasser, S) (2005), *One Woman's Army: The commanding general at Abu Ghraib tells her story*, New York, Miramax Press.

Kater, M (1997), 'The Sewering scandal of 1993 and the German medical establishment', in Berg, M, Cocks, G (eds) *Medicine and Modernity: Public health and medical care in nineteenth and twentieth-century Germany*, Washington DC, Cambridge University Press and German Historical Institute, 213–34.

Keen, S (2004), *Faces of the Enemy: Reflections on the hostile imagination* (original edition, 1991), San Francisco CA, Harper San Francisco.

Kelman, H C, Hamilton, V L (1989), *Crimes of Obedience: Towards a social psychology of authority and responsibility*, New Haven CT, Yale University Press.

Keneally, T (1983), *Schindler's Ark*, UK, Coronet Books.

Kershaw, I (2000), *The Nazi Dictatorship Problems and*

Perspectives of Interpretation, London, Arnold Press.

Kershaw, I (2008) '"Working towards the Führer": Reflections on the nature of Hitler's dictatorship', in Kershaw, I, *Hitler, the Germans and the Final Solution*, Jerusalem, International Institute for Holocaust Research, Yad Vashem, and New Haven, Yale University Press, 29–48 (originally published 1997).

Kilham, W, Mann, L (1974), 'Level of destructive obedience as a function of transmitter and executant roles in the Milgram obedience paradigm', *Journal of Personality and Social Psychology*, 29, 696–702.

Koenigsburg, R (2009), *Hitler's ideology: embodied metaphor, fantasy and history*, Charlotte NC, Information Age Publishing.

Kubarych, T S (2004), 'Self-deception and Peck's analysis of evil', *Philosophy, Psychiatry, & Psychology*, 12.3, 247–55.

Lafleur, W R, Böhme, G, Shimazono, S (2007), *Dark Medicine: Rationalising unethical medical research*, Bloomington, Indiana University Press.

Lerner, M (1980), *The Belief in a Just World: A fundamental delusion*, New York, Plenum.

Levi, P (1987), *The Drowned and the Saved*, New York, Summit.

Lie, R K, Emanuel, E, Grady, C, Wendler, D (2004), 'The standard of care debate: the Declaration of Helsinki versus the international consensus opinion', *Journal of Medical Ethics* 30 (2), 190–93. doi:10.1136/jme.2003.006031. PMID 15082816

Lifton, R (1986), *The Nazi Doctors: Medical killing and the psychology of genocide*, New York, Basic Books.

London, P (1970), 'The rescuers: motivational hypothesis about Christians who saved Jews from the Nazis', in Macauley, J, Berkowitz, L (eds), *Altruism and helping behavior*, New York, Academic Press.

Lurie, P, Wolfe, S M (1997), 'Unethical trials of interventions to reduce perinatal transmission of the human immunodeficiency virus in developing countries', *New*

England Journal of Medicine, 337 (12), 18 September, 853–56.

Macklin, R (1999), *Against Relativism*, New York, Oxford University Press.

Mandler, G (2002), 'Psychologists and the Nazi socialist access to power', *History of Psychology*, 5 (2), 190–200.

Markusen, E (1997), 'Professions, professionals, and genocide', in Charny, I (ed) *Genocide: A critical bibliographic review*, vol 4, Facts on File, Institute on the Holocaust and Genocide, New York/Oxford, 264–98.

Maslow, A (1987), *Motivation and Personality*, (3rd edn, original published 1954), New York, Harper and Row.

Mason, T (1989), 'Intention and Explanation: A Current Controversy about the Interpretation of National Socialism', in Marris, M (ed), *The Nazi Holocaust Part 3, The 'Final Solution': The Implementation of Mass Murder*, vol 1, Westpoint CT, Mecler, 3–20.

McFarland-Icke, B R (1999), *Nurses in Nazi Germany: Moral choice in history*, New Jersey, Princeton University Press.

McGovern, W M (1973), *From Luther to Hitler*, New York, Houghton Mifflin.

Merkl, P (1980), *The Making of a Stormtrooper*, Princeton NJ, Princeton University Press.

Michman, D (2010), 'Despite the importance and centrality of antisemitism, it cannot serve as the exclusive explanation of murder and murderers': David Bankier's (1947–2010) path in Holocaust research'. Translated from the Hebrew by Stephanie Nakache, Jerusalem, *Yad Vashem Studies* 38, 1, 15–45, also at http://www1.yadvashem.org/yv/en/about/institute/studies/issues/38-1/michman.pdf accessed 18 July 2011.

Midlarsky, E, Jones, S E, Corley, R P (2005), 'Personality correlates of heroic rescue during the Holocaust', *Journal of Personality*, 73 (4), August, 907–34.

Miles, S H (2004), 'Abu Ghraib: its legacy for military medicine', *Lancet*, 364, 725–29.

Milgram, S (1963), 'Obedience to authority', *Journal of Abnormal and Social Psychology*, 67, 371–78.

Milgram, S (1974), *Obedience to Authority: An experimental view*, New York, Harper and Row.

Mommsen, H (1997), 'Cumulative radicalisation and progressive self-destruction as structural determinants of the Nazi dictatorship', in Kershaw, Ian and Lewin, Moshe (eds), *Stalinism and Nazism: Dictatorships in comparison*, Cambridge, Cambridge University Press.

Moore, B (1966), *Social Origins of Dictatorship and Democracy: Lord and peasant in the making of the modern world*, Boston, Beacon Press.

Moreno, J D (2007), 'Stumbling towards bioethics: human experiments policy and the early cold war', in Lafleur, W R, Böhme, G, Shimazono, S, *Dark Medicine: Rationalising unethical medical research*, Bloomington, Indiana University Press, 138–46.

Müller-Hill, B (1988), *Murderous Science: Elimination by scientific selection of Jews, Gypsies and others, Germany 1933–1945*, Oxford, Oxford University Press.

Müller-Hill, B (2007), 'The Silence of the Scholars', in Lafleur, W R, Böhme, G, Shimazono, S, *Dark Medicine: Rationalising unethical medical research,* Bloomington, Indiana University Press, 57–62.

Neumann, F (1967), *Behemoth: The structure and practice of National Socialism 1933–44*, (second ed), London, Frank Cass & Co.

Noll, R (1997), *The Aryan Christ: The secret life of Carl Jung*, London, Macmillan.

Novick, P (2000), *The Holocaust and Collective Memory: The American experience*, London, Bloomsbury.

Nuffield Council on Bioethics (2005), *The ethics of research related to healthcare in developing countries: A follow-up discussion paper,* accessed from http://www.nuffieldbioethics.org 26 Oct 2010. London: Nuffield Council on Bioethics.

Oliner, S P, Oliner, P M (1988), *The Altruistic Personality: Rescuers of Jews in Nazi Europe*, New York, Free Press.

Paldiel, M (1988), 'The altruism of Righteous Gentiles',
Holocaust and Genocide Studies, 3, 187–96.

Peacock, M (2009), *Killer Company*, Sydney, HarperCollins.

Peck, M S (1982), *People of the Lie: The hope of healing human evil*,
New York, Simon and Schuster.

Perley, S, Fluss, S S, Bankowski, Z, Simon, F (1992), 'The
Nuremberg Code: an international overview', in Annas, G,
Grodin, M (eds), *The Nazi Doctors and the Nuremberg Code*,
New York, Oxford University Press, 149–73.

Peters, W (1985), *A Class Divided Then and Now*, (expanded
edition, original 1971), New Haven CT, Yale University
Press. See also the PBS Frontline documentary 'A Class
Divided', available online at
www.pbs.org/wgbh/pages/frontline/shows/divided

Pina e Cunha, M, Rego, A, Clegg, S (2010), 'Obedience and
evil: From Milgram and Kampuchea to normal
organizations', *Journal of Business Ethics*, DOI
10.1007/s10551-010-0510-5.

Power, S (2002), *'A Problem from Hell': America and the age of
genocide*, New York, Basic Books.

Proctor, R (1992), 'Nazi doctors, Racial medicine and human
experimentation', in Annas, G, Grodin, M (eds), *The Nazi
Doctors and the Nuremberg Code*, New York, Oxford
University Press, 17–31.

Pross, C (1992), 'Nazi doctors, German medicine and
historical truth', in Annas, G, Grodin, M (eds), *The Nazi
Doctors and the Nuremberg Code*, New York, Oxford
University Press, 32–52.

Rennie, S (2008), 'The FDA ditches the Declaration of
Helsinki', *Global Bioethics Blog*, 6 May, at
http://globalbioethics.blogspot.com/2008_05_01_archive.
html accessed 24/11/10).

Reverby, S (2009), *Examining Tuskegee: The infamous syphilis
study and its legacy*, University of North Carolina Press.

Richard, F D, Bond, D F (Jnr), Stokes-Zoota, J J (2003), 'One
hundred years of social psychology quantitatively
described', *Review of General Psychology*, 7, 331–63.

Richards, H (2006), 'We knew nothing about this', *Times*

Higher Education, 8 September.,
http://www.timeshighereducation.co.uk/story.asp?story Code=205253&sectioncode=26 accessed 14 February 2010.

Robertson, G (2006), *Crimes against Humanity: The struggle for global justice*, 3rd ed, Melbourne, Penguin.

Rosen, A (2011), 'Are we letting bad guys like Gaddafi off the hook?', *National Times* (Fairfax Press, *Sydney Morning Herald, The Age*), 23 March.

Russell, N, Gregory, R (2005), 'Making the Undoable Doable: Milgram, the Holocaust, and Modern Government', *American Review of Public Administration*, 35 (4), December, 327–49. Doi 10.1177/0275074005278511.

Sauvage, P (1989), 'Weapons of the spirit: the astonishing story of a unique conspiracy of goodness' [film], Friends of the Le Chambon Foundation, Los Angeles.

Schlink, B (2009), *Guilt about the Past*, St Lucia, University of Queensland Press.

Schmidt, U (2004, second edn 2006), *Justice at Nuremberg: Leo Alexander and the Nazi doctors' trial*, Basingstoke UK, Palgrave Macmillan.

Sereny, G (1974), *Into That Darkness: From mercy killing to mass murder*, London, Pimlico.

Sereny, G (1996), *Albert Speer: His battle with truth*, London, Picador.

Sereny, G (2000), The German Trauma: Experiences and reflections 1938–2001, London, Penguin.

Sharma, D C (2004), 'India pressed to relax rules on clinical trials. Drug companies claim changes are essential, but critics fear Indian patients will become guinea pigs', *Lancet*, 8 May, 363 (9420), 1528–29.

Silove, D (2000), 'A conceptual framework for mass trauma: implications for adaptation, intervention and debriefing', in Raphael, B, Wilson, J (eds), *Psychological Debriefing: Theory, Practice and Evidence*, Cambridge, Cambridge University Press, 337–350.

Social Medicine Portal (2008), 'FDA abandons Declaration of

Helsinki for international clinical trials', 1 June, 2008, http://www.socialmedicine.org/2008/06/01/ethics/fda-abandons-declaration-of-helsinki-for-international-clinical-trials/ accessed 31/12/10.

Soelle, D (2001), *The Silent Cry: Mysticism and resistance*, Minneapolis, Fortress Press.

Sontag, S (2003), *Regarding the Pain of Others*, London, Penguin.

Staub, E (1989), *The Roots of Evil: The origins of genocide and other group violence*, New York, Cambridge University Press.

Staub, E (2003), *The Psychology of Good and Evil: Why children, adults and groups help and harm others*, Cambridge UK, Cambridge University Press.

Steinmetz, G (1997), 'German exceptionalism and the origins of Nazism: the career of a concept', in Kershaw, Ian and Lewin, Moshe (eds), *Stalinism and Nazism: Dictatorships in comparison*, Cambridge, Cambridge University Press, 251–84.

Tec, N (1986), *When Light Pierced the Darkness: Christian rescue of Jews in Nazi-occupied Poland*, New York, Oxford University Press.

Thomas, G, Morgan-Witts, M (1974), *Voyage of the Damned*, New York, Stein and Day; Weindling, P J (2006), *Nazi Medicine and Nuremberg Trials: From medical war crimes to informed consent*, Basingstoke UK, Palgrave Macmillan.

Williams, J R (2008), 'The Declaration of Helsinki and public health, *Bulletin of the World Health Organisation*, 86, August, 650–52.

Winau, R (2007), 'Experimentation on humans and informed consent: how we arrived where we are', in Lafleur, W R, Böhme, G, Shimazono, S, *Dark Medicine: Rationalising unethical medical research*, Bloomington, Indiana University Press, 46–56.

Wyman, D S (1984), *The Abandonment of the Jews: America and the Holocaust, 1941–1945*, New York, Pantheon.

Zimbardo, P (2007), *The Lucifer Effect: How good people turn evil*, London, Rider.

FROM KRAEPELIN TO KARADZIC: PSYCHIATRY'S LONG ROAD TO GENOCIDE

ROBERT M KAPLAN AND GARRY WALTER

...it is always a simple matter to drag people along whether it is a democracy, or a fascist dictatorship, or a parliament, or a communist dictatorship. Voice or no voice, the people can always be brought to the bidding of the leaders. All you have to do it tell them they are being attacked, and denounce the pacifists for lack of patriotism and exposing the country to danger. It works the same for every country. — *Herman Göring, Commander-in-Chief of the Luftwaffe, at Nuremberg*[1]

The twentieth was the century of mass murder, as Niall Ferguson,[2] Eric Hobsbawm,[3] [4] and others have pointed out. The rate of civilian deaths rose from less than 5 per cent before World War I to over 80 per cent by 1980, with women and children a significant majority. The death toll from genocide, mass murder, forced starvation, ethnic cleansing and expulsion exceeded 170 million. In 1990, Michael Burleigh could say that the chance of events such as the Holocaust occurring again were remote; after 11 September 2001, he stated that humankind faced an existential threat to its future.[5]

---

[1] Gilbert, G M (1947), *Nuremberg Diary*, New York, Signet.

[2] Ferguson, Niall (2006), *The War of the World: History's age of hatred*, London, Allen Lane.

[3] Hobsbawm, Eric (1994), *The Age of Extremes: The short twentieth century 1914–1991*, London, Penguin.

[4] Hobsbawm, Eric (1992), *Nations and Nationalism since 1780: Programme, myth, reality*, Cambridge, Cambridge University Press.

[5] Burleigh, Michael (2008), *Blood & Rage: A cultural history of terrorism*, New York, Harper Perennial. Also review by Stuttaford, Andrew (2008), 'Sacred monsters. On *Blood & Rage: A cultural history of*

In a Europe that had been [relatively] peaceful since 1945, the wars that followed the collapse of Yugoslavia in 1990 caused dismay at the rapid rise of extreme nationalism.[6] Images of gaunt prisoners in Serbian concentration camps between 1992 and 1995 raised the spectre of genocide. Between 150,000 and 250,000 people were killed and a million made homeless. By 1995, when hostilities came to an end following the Dayton Agreement, there were reports of atrocities on all sides — Serbian, Croatian and Muslim Bosnians — but the chief perpetrators were the Serbian Bosnians. Led by Dr Radovan Karadzic, and under the military command of General Ratko Mladic, the Serbs committed genocide to render 70 per cent of the territory of Bosnia free of non-Serbian inhabitants.[7]

Many aspects of the Bosnian genocide were deeply disturbing. But one startling feature emerged — the role of psychiatrists. They were leading figures in the Bosnian Serb political party, the Serb Democratic Reform (SDF). Serbian psychiatrists adopted a public role to promote their nationalist aims, justify the behaviour of the military forces, and denigrate the opposition in psychological terms. The unique spectacle was that of a practising psychiatrist, Dr Radovan Karadzic[8] — in his role as President of *Republika Srpska* — actively directing the military activities, notably the siege of his home town of Sarajevo.

---

terrorism by Michael Burleigh', *The New Criterion* 27, 68, republished 2009 on-line: www.newcriterion.com/articles.cfm/Sacred-monsters-3924, accessed 20 March 09.

[6] Niebuhr, Robert (2007), 'Yugoslavia: The final showdown', *Small Wars & Insurgencies*, September, 18, 3, 380–96.

[7] Cigar, Norman (1995), *Genocide in Bosnia: The policy of 'ethnic cleansing'*, College Station, Texas, Texas A&M University Press.

[8] Kaplan, Robert M (2003), 'Dr Radovan Karadzic: Psychiatrist, poet, soccer coach and genocidal leader', *Australasian Psychiatry*, 11, 74–78.

At this time of writing, Karadzic is on trial before the International Criminal Court in The Hague. His case should shed light on how he used his psychiatric training to devise terror tactics for dealing with the enemy. It may also answer a key question: how does the profession of psychiatry lend itself to such extraordinary state abuse? Decades earlier, in the Nuremberg Doctors' Trial,[9] it became apparent that the medical profession contained within itself the necessary ingredients for much of its own ruin. And in this regard the psychiatric profession, so often regarded as marginal to the medical mainstream, set the agenda for the rest of the profession [see the Dudley and Gale chapter in this volume].

The path from marginalisation to acceptance in mainstream medicine and the use of modern technology in psychiatry goes back to the early years of the nineteenth century. Psychiatry unerringly allied itself with the dominant social agendas of the day. That the model arose in Germany meant that eugenics, racism and nationalism were allied to an academic approach in which the individual was readily submerged by the doctrine of the greater good of the nation. From Sigmund Freud and Emil Kraepelin, reductionist or vulgarised psychological concepts were used as a tool for ideological pursuits. These tendencies surface recurrently whenever psychiatry becomes involved in abuse of human rights by the nation-state. The terminus of this path, the Bosnian genocide, illustrates this theme.

---

[9] 'The doctors' trial', Jewish Virtual library, http://www.jewishvirtuallibrary.org/jsource/Holocaust/doctorstoc.html. Accessed 26 November 2011.

The rise of psychiatry

Insanity...provides us with the proper scale for comprehending the numerous intellectual, moral, religious, and artistic currents and phenomena of our social life. *— Emil Kraepelin*[10]

Psychiatric illness has been recognised since antiquity. There are credible descriptions of schizophrenia in the Mesopotamian Assyrian Codex.[11] Until the nineteenth century, psychiatry — its practitioners often referred to as 'mad-doctors' or 'alienists' — was mostly a custodial business, looked down upon by the medical profession and feared by the public. The Enlightenment led to new attitudes. Phillipe Pinel (1745-1826), a fervid revolutionary, believed in an illness model of symptoms and treatment.[12] The belief that the root cause of mental illness lay in the environment led to more humane psycho-social methods of management in what was known as 'moral treatment'. Pinel's work led to the removal of chains and shackles for the ill, liberation from dungeons, and to the rise of the asylum. Thus began institutionalised psychiatry and the process of organising its practitioners into a professional discipline.

By the second half of the nineteenth century one condition came to dominate and define psychiatry: neurosyphilis,

---

[10] Decker, H S (2004), 'The psychiatric works of Emil Kraepelin: A many-faceted story of modern medicine', *Journal of the History of Neurosciences*, 13, 3, 248-76.

[11] Jeste, Dilip, del Carmen, R, Lohr, J B and R J (1985), 'Did schizophrenia exist before the eighteenth century?', *Comprehensive Psychiatry*, 26, 6, 493-503.

[12] Pinel, Phillipe (1806), *A Treatise on Insanity*, translated from French by D D Davis, Sheffield, Cadell and Davies.
http://books.google.com.au/books?id=4snWNO11ETAC&printsec=frontcover&source=gbs ge summary
r&cad=0#v=onepage&q&f=false

known as Generalised Paresis of the Insane, or GPI. Psychiatry had found its grand cause, its defining illness, and it was not until the middle of the twentieth century that GPI ceased to play a part in the daily life of doctors in psychiatric wards. GPI was a uniformly fatal disease that affected men more than women. A middle-class illness, it struck at the heart of the class interests — property. The patient would have a change in personality, a sense of self-importance and an expansive tendency leading to wild spending, investing and drinking. This wrecked the family business and distressed relatives. The victim could ruin the family fortunes, making it 'a disease that had everything to do with property and little to do with sex'.[13] Patients became demented and unable to care for themselves, often dying in lunatic asylums.

As the twentieth century loomed, the syphilis organism showed its adaptability. Neurosyphilis became, as it were, more egalitarian. Previously an illness of predominantly upper-class men, it went 'down market', affecting women as commonly as men.[14] Syphilis occupied such a dominating role in the pantheon of diseases that it was accorded 113 pages in the 1893 Index Catalogue of the Surgeon General; tuberculosis, a much more prevalent condition and one with a greater morbidity, was given a mere 55 pages.[15]

Prevalent in all this was an especially malignant idea, namely, hereditary syphilis. First raised in 1595, this was to become a *leitmotif* of the times. How could a third generation

---

[13] Shorter, Edward (1997), *A History of Psychiatry: From the era of the asylum to the age of Prozac*, New York, John Wiley and Sons.

[14] Hare, E H (1959), 'The origin and spread of dementia paralytica', *Journal of Mental Sciences*, 105, 594–626.

[15] Silverstein, Arthur M and Ruggere, Christine (2006), 'Dr Arthur Conan Doyle and the case of congenital syphilis', *Perspectives in Biology and Medicine*, 49, 2, 209–19.

of a family be so afflicted unless the disease was inherited? Arthur Conan Doyle, creator of the fictional Sherlock Holmes, graduated as a doctor in 1881, a period when the Lamarckian theory of acquired characteristics featured prominently in medical education. Doyle chose the topic of complications of tertiary syphilis for his MD thesis. In 1894, his short story 'The Third Generation', illustrated how syphilis could affect several generations of a family, leaving havoc in its wake.[16]

The idea of hereditary syphilis had remarkable persistence. Despite the discoveries of Louis Pasteur and Robert Koch, it endured, fitting perfectly into the theory of degeneration. It coursed through psychiatry like a septic stream into the twentieth century. It attracted an obscure youth living in Vienna. Coming from a rural background rife with intermarriage, mental handicap and ancestor confusion, Adolf Hitler was convinced that hereditary syphilis, 'spread by the Jews', would destroy the German race, his obsession fuelled by persistent rumours that he had a Jewish grandfather. Hitler did not understand the difference between congenital syphilis (the organism can cross the placental barrier, which distinguishes it from other sexually transmitted diseases) and hereditary syphilis. Years later, it was to surface in *Mein Kampf* where 13 pages were devoted to explaining how the syphilitic taint, (allegedly) spread by Jews, passed down the generations.[17]

In a Europe that was growing in wealth and creating a large bourgeoisie, nationalists seized on middle-class fears of being outbred and losing their privileged status to a surging proletariat. In response, an alliance arose between two

---

[16] Silverstein and Ruggere, op. cit.

[17] Hitler's obsession with syphilis led to inevitable accusations that he suffered the disease. Despite heroic efforts to prove this there is no evidence to support the claim. See Redlich, Fritz (1998), *Hitler: Diagnosis of a destructive prophet*, New York, Oxford University Press.

unlikely forces: nationalism (with the Catholic church in close association) and 'respectability'. Nationalism represented an unrepentant swing back to the past, but with significant differences. The cities, hotbeds of liberalism and modernism, encompassed everything that was wrong with the nation. Marginal groups like Jews, Romani and Slavs were perceived as a threat to the social order through their birth rates and their values. They were said to propagate anti-clerical philosophies like abortion, sexual perversion and breakdown of the traditional family unit. The countryside, including regions of appalling backwardness, poverty, ignorance, and devotion to the irrational, was idealised as the *völkisch* culture which represented a glorious and unsullied past.

The nation was divided along faultlines of race and an extraordinary dichotomy in the private and public life of the individual. State policy ensured a 'polite' society in which sexual activities were directed to childbirth within marriage. Sex began to be regulated for the wellbeing of the greater society. The medical profession duly stepped forward, providing a forensic basis for state regulation. The 'classification' of sex was initiated by psychiatrist Baron Richard von Krafft-Ebing. A believer in the theory of degeneration, he wrote *Psychopathia Sexualis*, probably the only medical book to have pornographic status. In the process, he gave the world the term 'sado-masochism', but he focused mainly on homosexuality. The state now had the legal basis to prosecute aberrant individuals. 'Perversions' such as masturbation, homosexuality and trans-sexualism were deemed precursors to moral insanity. Krafft-Ebing's book was published in 1886 and by 1871 the German Criminal Code (in its notorious Paragraph 175) had made homosexuality a criminal offence. These outlooks created a breach into which not only Freud but many others surged. The medical profession, including psychiatry through its desire to explain, classify and 'own' many different forms of behaviour, was now in a position to pass judgment on all of society, a role that was deeply antipathetic to the ancient and sacred role of treating the individual without fear or favour. To pass from healing the person to the role of healer of society was an opportunity that some could not resist.

Kraepelin and the German eugenics movement

There are two sorts of psychiatrists, those by inclination, and those by chance; those entering psychiatry by chance are sometimes reasonable. — *Emil Kraepelin*[18]

An indication of the age is that the three of the most important figures in twentieth century psychiatry were born almost simultaneously — Emil Kraepelin and Sigmund Freud in 1856 and Eugen Bleuler a year later. Compared to the rest of Europe, German psychiatry had a significant advantage. It was practised by academicians who perceived themselves as scientists and saw their patients as research material.[19]

Emil Kraepelin (1856-1926)[20] qualified in medicine at the University of Leipzig in 1878 and, unusually, wanted to study psychiatry from the start.[21] His intention was to establish a discipline based on findings that could be proved, abandoning speculative theories from romanticism. Like all psychiatrists of the day, Kraepelin learnt his craft through clinical encounters with syphilis, writing what is probably still the best book on its psychopathology and predicting

---

[18] Boroffka, Alexander (1990), 'Emil Kraepelin (1856-1926)', *Transcultural Psychiatry*, 27, 228-37.

[19] Engstrom, Eric (2003), *Clinical Psychiatry in Imperial Germany: A history of psychiatric practice*, Ithaca, New York, Cornell University Press.

[20] Shepherd, Michael (1995), 'Kraepelin and modern psychiatry', *European Archives of Psychiatry and Clinical Neuroscience*, July, 245, 4-5, 189-95.

[21] Meyer, A (1994), 'In memoriam, Emil Kraepelin. 1927', *American Journal of Psychiatry*, 151, 6 Supplement, 140-43.

(correctly) that GPI arose from *Treponema pallidum* infection.

Kraepelin was the organising principal in modern psychiatry. His findings became the paradigm for twentieth century psychiatry. He had deeply bureaucratic instincts, he developed training programs, and constantly lobbied the government for mandatory syphilis testing and alcohol control.[22] In 1917, he founded the German Institute for Psychiatric Research, a centre that came to dominate psychiatric research.

The eminent psychoanalyst and historian Gregory Zilboorg[23] described Kraepelin as an 'academic man' who lacked human interest in the individual. He was unreservedly antisemitic, describing Jews as 'a very great danger' to the German 'race' through a tendency to forge ahead. Among the races and classes, he believed that Romani, swindlers, poets and 'psychopathic Jews' were prone to hysteria.[24] [25] Kraepelin's psychiatry was dominated by a somatic or biological perspective in which biographical, social, cultural and psychological dimensions were marginalised. He was the first to apply these terms not solely to individuals but to social groups and institutions. Behaviour that did not correspond with his outlook was attributed to the theory of *degeneration*.[26]

---

[22] Jablensky, Assen (1995), 'Kraepelin's legacy, paradigm or pitfall for modern psychiatry?', *European Archives Psychiatry and Clinical Neuroscience*, 245, 4–5, 186–88.

[23] Zilboorg, Gregory (1957), 'Eugen Bleuler and present-day psychiatry', *American Journal of Psychiatry*, October, 114, 4, 289–98.

[24] Shepherd, op cit, 193.

[25] Decker H S (2004), 'The psychiatric works of Emil Kraepelin: a many-faceted story of modern medicine', *Journal of the History of the Neurosciences*, September, 13, 3, 248–76.

[26] Lomax, Elizabeth (1979), 'Infantile syphilis as an example of

Preoccupied with the 'will', Kraepelin appeared indifferent to the problems of shell-shocked soldiers or hysterics.[27]

In 1915, psychiatrist Professor Albert Hoche described the end of individualism and the transformation of the nation into a higher organism, the *Volk*.[28] Eugenics, arising from the practice of pedigree in veterinary science, became a dominant theme in German medicine and science. Prominent eugenicist Ludwig Woltmann, who drew on Charles Darwin and Comte Arthur de Gobineau for inspiration (with some Karl Marx thrown in for good measure), made race a central concern.[29] German eugenics was a vulgarised form of Social Darwinism, portraying the struggle for survival in simplistic racial terms, constantly raising the threat to the German people from 'other' groups. Preaching Germanic supremacy, he regarded the struggle for existence as a racial conflict in which Germany would eventually predominate. Three prominent disciples were anthropologists Otto Ammon and Eugen Fischer, the latter then based at the University of Freiburg, and Professor Ludwig Schemann.[30] Schemann translated and introduced into Germany the Frenchman Comte de Gobineau's four-volume essay on *The Inequality of the Human*

---

nineteenth century belief in the inheritance of acquired characteristics', *Journal of the History of Medicine and Allied Sciences*, January, 34, 1, 23–39.

[27] Kraepelin, Emil (1919), 'Psychiatric observations on contemporary issues', first published in *Süddeutsche Monastshefte*, June xvi, 2, 171–83. Translated by Eric J Engstrom (1992), *History of Psychiatry*, June, 3, 10, 253–69.

[28] Kaldjian, Lauris (2000), 'Eugenic sterilization and a qualified Nazi analogy: the United States and Germany, 1930–1945', *Annals of Internal Medicine*, February 15, 132, 4, 312–19.

[29] Weikart, Richard (2003), 'Progress through racial extermination: Social Darwinism, eugenics, and pacifism in Germany, 1860–1918', *German Studies Review*, May, 26, 2, 273–94.

[30] Weikart, op cit

Races, the doctrine of degeneration and decline and, above all to eager German ears, the 'science' of racial purity.

The trail from the gas chambers and ovens of Auschwitz can be followed back to the hitherto forgotten but first genocide of the century — the Herero and Nama slaughter in German South West Africa (now Namibia) between 1904 and 1906. The first demonstration of the malign consequences of biological racism resulted in the annihilation of over 80 per cent of the Herero nation, the effects of which are still being felt today.[31][32] This event was largely assisted by the efforts of Eugen Fischer. In 1908 he studied (or rather, he did a series of pseudo-scientific measurements) of 310 children of a mixed race group arising from cohabitation of the settlers and native women in German South West Africa, a people known as the Rehoboth Bastards or Basters. He argued that the physically strong and healthy Basters should initially be allowed to increase in numbers to provide labour to the settlers; thereafter, one should only grant them the minimum protection they needed 'as a race inferior to us' and for as long as these physically strong but mentally inferior mongrelised people were useful. Then nature should take its course through 'free competition, which in [Fischer's] opinion, means [their] demise'.

The Herero genocide was driven by the racial theories of such physical anthropologists. The influence of these men on German medicine, especially psychiatry, was considerable and set the tone for what was to follow. After Germany was defeated and excluded from the colony, the Herero genocide subsided into obscurity [until a decade ago], but its lessons

---

[31] Weikart, op cit, 288.

[32] Olusoga, David and Erichsen, Casper (2010), *The Kaiser's Holocaust: Germany's forgotten genocide and the colonial roots of Nazism*, London, Faber.

133

were well learned. The terms *Lebensraum* [need for living room] and *Konzentrationslager* [concentration camp] established the pattern of state organisation of genocide by biological means, largely run by doctors.[33] It is no coincidence that a number of leading Nazis had close connections with German South West Africa and acted as 'conduit' for these concepts. Of these, Herman Göring was the most notorious.[34]

Fisher's study, published in Germany in 1913, must be regarded as one of the precursors of the Holocaust. In 1919, Entente troops, mostly French, occupied the Rhineland. Children born out of wedlock (known as Rhineland Bastards) arose from relations between local women and the soldiers. After 1937, Fisher created a medical unit, Commission Number 3, to secretly sterilise 400 children of 'Rhineland Bastards'. In 1927, Fischer became Director of the new Kaiser Wilhelm Institute for Anthropology, Human Heredity, and Eugenics in Berlin, supervising academics who became leading figures in providing justification for Nazi antisemitism and developing laws which then excluded Jews, Rom people and other 'non-Aryans' from German citizenship. By training SS doctors and medical students in eugenics and racial hygiene, he supported physicians directly involved in mass murder and crimes against humanity. Fischer used his scientific authority to justify colonial exploitation and racial extermination. His disciples were equally influential in anthropology, sociology, medicine and eugenics. Fritz Lenz became the first professor of 'Race Hygiene' at the University of Munich in 1923. Setting the tone for the medical involvement in genocide, in a 1917 article Lenz, Fischer's close colleague, proposed putting the interests of one's race above

[33] Madley, Benjamin (2005), 'From Africa to Auschwitz: How German South West Africa incubated ideas and methods adopted and developed by the Nazis in Eastern Europe', *European History Quarterly*, 35, 3, 429–64.

[34] Madley, op cit, 450.

all ethical considerations.

To what extent psychiatrists were the driving force in devising biological solutions to racial 'problems', or were easily encouraged to do so,[35] may be debatable, but there can be little doubt about their enthusiasm to become involved. In the lead-up to World War I, eugenics as the dominant paradigm flourished in Germany, America, Great Britain, Sweden and elsewhere, with Fischer at one point hailed as heading an international eugenics organisation. Eugenics had a considerable influence on research, planning and the quest for effective treatments. Other influences were also beginning to establish themselves, notably the rise of psychoanalysis. Initially concerned with establishing his movement, Freud's testimony to the commission of inquiry on war neurosis led to growing interest. In the decades before his death, Freud began to stray from strictly technical issues, writing instead about the application of psychoanalysis to the condition of humanity as a whole. Reacting to the rise of fascism, Freud came to hold a pessimistic view of human nature as dominated by the death instinct. Religion was merely an illusion. He was not alone in this: Kraepelin wrote about Bismarck, describing Weimar republican society as hysterical and the socialist leaders as psychopathic. Yet soon the medical profession itself came to be caught up in horrific abuse and widespread death in the Armenian genocide. That genocide and its biological thrusts set the stage for what was to be the precursor to the Holocaust.

Doctors and the Armenian Genocide

If a physician presumes to take into consideration in his work

---

[35] Friedlander, Henry (1995), *The Origins of Nazi Genocide: From euthanasia to the final solution*, Chapel Hill, University of North Carolina Press.

whether a life has value or not, the consequences are boundless and the physician becomes the most dangerous man in the state. — *Christopher Willhelm Hufeland*[36]

The 1914–1923 Armenian, Pontian Greek and Assyrian genocide was in so many ways the template for the Holocaust: forced emigration, expulsions, property confiscations, forced labour, public torture and executions, medical experiments, elementary gassings, starvation, and death marches. It was largely directed and carried out by doctors, leading members of the Ittihadist Party who came to power in a coup in 1908.[37] Dr Behaeddin Sakir and Dr Mehmett Nazim, held responsible in part for the deaths of at least 1.5 million Armenians, 350,000 Pontian Greeks and perhaps 250,000 Assyrian Christians, played a pivotal role in the establishment and deployment of the Special Organisation units, extermination squads staffed by violent criminals released from prisons to undertake killings. Sakir had worked as chief physician of Soloniki Municipal Hospital and Nazim, described as 'a doctor by profession and not without promise', in what must be regarded as one of the most misguided appointments in the history of medicine, was designated Professor of Legal (Ethical) Medicine at Istanbul Medical School.

Many of their collaborators, mostly governors of the Anatolian provinces where the Armenians lived, were graduates of the Imperial Medical School. Medical personnel did not merely supervise proceedings but were directly involved in the killings, often participating in torture. Dr Mehmed Reşid, known as the 'Executioner Governor', was

---

[36] Haas, François (2008), 'German science and black racism — roots of the Nazi Holocaust', *Federation of American Societies for Experimental Biology Journal*, February, 22, 2, 332–37.

[37] Dadrian, Vahakn (1986), 'The role of Turkish physicians in the World War I genocide of Ottoman Armenians', *Holocaust and Genocide Studies*, 1, 2, 169–92.

extraordinarily brutal, smashing skulls, nailing red-hot horseshoes to victims' chests, and crucifying people on makeshift crosses. Sadistic cruelty was demonstrated by ophthalmologists who gave eye drops to children that made them blind and who performed unnecessary, deliberately disfiguring ophthalmological procedures, especially on young girls.[38] Other doctors, describing their victims as subhuman, used them as guinea pigs to infect a range of diseases. Hundreds of victims were injected with blood from typhus cases.

Dr Ali Said was accused of killing thousands of infants, adults and pregnant women by administering poison as liquid medicine. He ordered the drowning at sea of patients who refused the 'medicine' and directed the disposal of their corpses. Infant victims of Dr Tevfik Rusdü were taken to a purported steam bath and killed with a toxic gas, an ominous precursor to the later Judeocide.

The later Kemalist government turned its back on the issue and the collective (and aggressive) Turkish denial that the genocide had ever occurred took hold. In the years afterwards, looking at the issue from radically different moral standpoints, both Hitler and Churchill noted that everyone [wilfully] forgot the matter before long and Armenia was destined to slip into the West's historical amnesia [at least until the 1980s].

Dr Mehmed Reşid's suicide note summed up the attitude of these medical *genocidaires*:

> Even though I am a physician, I cannot ignore my nationhood. Armenian traitors…were dangerous microbes. Isn't it the duty of a doctor to destroy these microbes? My

---

[38] Dadrian, Vahakn (2003), 'Children as victims of genocide: the Armenian case', *Journal of Genocide Research*, 5, 3, 421–37.

Turkishness prevailed over my medical calling. Of course my conscience is bothering me, but I couldn't see my country disappearing. As to historical responsibility, I couldn't care less what historians of other nations write about me.[39]

The Armenian genocide set the groundwork for the most notorious examples of medical complicity in state abuses: the Nazi doctors who participated in euthanasia and genocide, and the Japanese doctors who practiced biological warfare. Included among the former were psychiatrists, who, in carrying out Hitler's euthanasia program on their patients, appear to have been in a state of complete moral disarray.

Racial psychiatry, sterilisation and the Holocaust

[Hitler] could, if need be, do without lawyers, engineers, and builders, but not without medical professionals, suggesting in an early speech before the National Socialists Physicians' League...'you, you Nationalist Socialist doctors, I cannot do without you for a single day, not a single hour. If ...you fail me, then all is lost. For what good are our struggles, if the health of our people is in danger?' --*Adolf Hitler*[40]

Many members of the German medical profession needed no pushing to accept Nazi ideology after Hitler came to power in 1933. Doctors were the first profession to join and embrace the Nazi party and had the largest representation of all occupational groups;[41] of 15,000 Nazi Party medical members, 3,000 were psychiatrists. Nazi racial theories were accepted without question. The profession acquiesced in the drive to expel all Jewish doctors. The Nazi physician was designated a 'selector' to improve the health of the nation by removing

---

[39] Baron, J H (1999), 'Genocidal doctors', *Journal of the Royal Society of Social Medicine*, 92, 11, 590–93.

[40] Haas, op cit, 332.

[41] Kater, Michael H (2000), *Doctors under Hitler*, Chapel Hill, NC, The University of North Carolina Press.

'inferiors'.[42] Eugenics and racial hygiene were compulsory subjects in medical schools. This enthusiasm was not restricted to Germany. Following the Anschluss, Austrian physicians forced Jewish doctors out of the Vienna Faculty of Medicine, which more than any other European university had a huge Jewish presence — 78 per cent of the staff, including some Nobel Prize winners.

The role of psychiatrists in mass murder began in 1938 with their prominent involvement in the sterilisation of patients said to have incurable physical or mental disease. The process soon accelerated with the move to exterminate psychiatric patients. In 1928, jurisprudence professor Karl Binding and psychiatrist Albert Hoche enunciated their concept of 'life unworthy of life', which quickly became the *raison d'etre* of the Nazi biological vision. The '*Aktion* T4 program' to kill 'unworthy' adults on eugenic grounds was based at six centres in Germany and Austria. Under the sign of the Red Cross, gas chambers were introduced to dispose of 'incurables' from the mental hospitals of the Reich. Psychiatrists experimented with killing by phenol injections and carbon monoxide gassing. *Tiergartenstrasse* 4 was the address at which the Auschwitz, Belzec, Treblinka, Majdanek and Sobibor gas chambers had their first trial run.

No coercion was involved. Resistance to participation in these activities was very limited. Opposition to the T4 philosophy came from men like Bishop Clemens von Galen, Karl Bonhoeffer, Oswald Bumke and Gottfried Ewald. John Rittmeister, a Swiss-trained psychoanalyst and Communist had been involved in underground activities to oppose the Nazis, ostensibly spying for America; he was the only

---

[42] Proctor, Robert (2000), 'Nazi science and Nazi medical ethics: some myths and misconceptions', *Perspectives in Biology and Medicine*, Spring, 43, 3, 335–46.

psychiatrist to be executed — by beheading in May 1943.[43] Ernst Kretzmer made the observation that whereas in the past they had treated psychopaths, they were now ruled by them — and was lucky to get away with his life. Paul-Gerhard Braune, who was arrested, wrote to Hitler condemning the very concept of 'life unworthy of life', warning that the moral foundations of the nation would be undermined.

There was no shortage of supporters of the euthanasia program. The leading figure, Ernest Rüdin, was followed by professors Heyde, Carl Schneider, de Crinis and Nitsche. Carl Jung's enthusiasm for Nazism went well beyond mere flirtation but he managed to cover his tracks after the war. There were at least 275,000 victims of this 'cleansing' program. Schneider's eagerness included grandiose plans for a vast research institute to study genetic aspects of idiocy and, while it never materialised, he did experimental work on brains from euthanased patients.[44]

German doctors unquestioningly shared the values of Wilhelmine Germany. The loss of World War I came as a shattering blow, followed by the Weimar Republic, a regime they rejected. There was also a practical issue: loss of income. Following the Depression, health funding was significantly reduced and medical schools were producing far more graduates than the system could absorb, a situation only remedied by Hitler's ascent to power in 1933. That the mass clearing of all Jewish doctors from practice would inevitably lead to an improvement also featured in the doctors' thinking.[45] From 1927 to 1932, the average annual income of

---

[43] Hunter, Ernest (1993), 'The snake on the caduceus: dimensions of medical and psychiatric responsibility in the Third Reich', *Australian and New Zealand Journal of Psychiatry*, March, 27, 1, 149–56.

[44] Lifton, Robert J (1986), *The Nazi Doctors: Medical killing and the psychology of genocide*, New York, Basic Books, 123.

[45] Biddiss, M (1997), 'Disease and dictatorship: the case of Hitler's

doctors fell by 27 per cent; by 1935 it had increased by 25 per cent.[46]

The central concept in Nazi ideology was the 'symbolisation of immortality'. Fritz Lenz (and later Rudolf Hess) would suggest that National Socialism was nothing but applied biology.[47] The German medical profession was designated the 'central intellectual resource' of the New Order.[48] In this grotesquely thaumaturgic vision, the doctor was the final agent in the Nazi myth of therapy by mass murder. Seduced by the power of utilitarian thought and arguments, German doctors allied their professional skills with the annihilating process of a despotic government. Echoing Turkey's Dr Mehmed Resid, Fritz Klein, a Nazi doctor, explained to author Robert Jay Lifton that he 'killed in order to cure'[49], and that made him a good doctor. Their statements at Nuremberg indicated how they lost their moral bearings in this grotesque Nazi political culture.[50]

During World War II, doctors made 'selections' at the death camps, dividing victims into those destined for immediate extermination in the gas chambers and those who

Reich', *Journal of the Royal Society of Medicine*, June, 90, 6, 342–46.

[46] Sofair and Kaldjian, op cit

[47] Baur, E, Fisher, E and Lenz, F (1931), *Menschliche Auslese und Rassenhygiene (Human Selection and Race Hygiene)*, Munich, Lehmanns, 417. Baur, E, Fischer, E and Lenz, F (1931), *On Human Heredity*, translated by Eden & Cedar Paul, New York, Macmillan Co.

[48] Proctor, Robert (2000), 'Nazi science and Nazi medical ethics: some myths and misconceptions', *Perspectives in Biology and Medicine*, Spring, 43, 3, 335–46.

[49] Lifton, op cit

[50] 'Extracts from final statements of defendants', in Spitz, Vivien (2005), *Doctors from Hell: Accounts of Nazi experiments on humans*, Boulder, CO, Sentient Publications, 258–62.

could do some useful work or could be used in experiments. The operation of the crematoria, determination of when the victims were dead and choice of means of killing were done under medical supervision.

Psychiatric euthanasia centres served as training institutions for SS doctors who went on to construct the death camps. These doctors had seven times the membership of the SS compared to other sectors of the German population.[51] No coercion was required to get doctors to work in experimental institutes or concentration camps and there was no shortage of volunteers. Large-scale experimental programs were conducted by leading medical research institutes using *untermenschen*, 'sub-human' subjects, from concentration camps. The only physician to command a death camp (Treblinka) was psychiatrist Dr Imfried Eberl.[52]

The Nuremberg Doctors Trials in 1946 proved every-thing — and nothing.[53] They revealed the role of doctors in experimenting on human subjects and in running death camps. The doctors, to a man, lacked any contrition, stating that they were doing no more than following state policy and their experiments were all done for 'the greater good'. It is perhaps problematic that the trial focus was arguably on details of warped experimentation rather than the doctors' role in industrialised mass murder.

The Nuremberg Code established criteria to ensure that the abuse of human beings for experimentation would not

---

[51] Zwi, Anthony (1987), 'The political abuse of medicine and the challenge of opposing it', *Social Science and Medicine*, 25, 6, 649–57.

[52] Strous, Rael D (2006), 'Nazi euthanasia of the mentally ill at Hadamar', *American Journal of Psychiatry*, January, 163, 1, 27.

[53] Marrus, Michael (1999), 'The Nuremberg Doctors' Trial in historical context', *Bulletin of the History of Medicine*, 73, 1, 106–23.

occur again.[54] Alone of German institutions, the medical profession escaped denazification. No attempt was made to acknowledge the abuses — let alone even atone for them — and this continued until well into the 1970s when intense (and foreign) exposure forced some concessions.

Medical abuse after 1945 — a growth industry

> There is nothing in the human being that which cannot be verbalised…What a person hides from himself, he hides from society. There is nothing in Soviet society that is not expressed in words. There are no naked thoughts. The unconscious does not exist because it is not available for the conscious control. — *Joseph Stalin*[55]

By the time of Hitler, the distinction between civilian and military combatants was blurred beyond recognition; atrocities against the civilian population were regarded as an essential means of waging war. Murder of civilians was a feature of World War II; in Yugoslavia, for example, more civilians had been killed by Chetnik and *Ustasa* resistance forces than by the Nazi invaders.

What happened in mid-Europe mid-century gave birth to the shibboleth 'Never Again!'. The Holocaust, the Nuremberg and 110,000 other trials that ensued, and the 1948 *Convention on the Prevention and Punishment of Genocide* led to this universal cry. But it wasn't long before we had to witness genocide yet again in most continents and in diverse domains: the Soviet deportations of whole nations, the Indonesian

---

[54] (1996), 'The Nuremberg Code (1947)', *British Medical Journal*, 3131448.1, DOI 10.1136/bmj.313.7070.1448. Available from http://www.bmj.com/content/313/7070/1448.1.full

[55] Korolenko, Caesar and Kensin, Dennis (2002), 'Reflections on the past and present state of Russian psychiatry', *Anthropology and Medicine*, 9, 51–64.

massacres, genocide in East Timor, Burundi, Rwanda, the Chittagong Hill Tribes, the massive death tolls in establishing first Pakistan, then Bangladesh. Amidst such carnage, there was the spectre of Soviet psychiatry distorting every ethical precept of the profession in its role as a slavish agent of the Soviet regime. If people began to think that postwar genocide was by now essentially the province of Africa and Asia, they were wrong. A nightmare in the Hitlerian mould was awaiting in what was Yugoslavia.

The origins of Yugoslavian medicine and psychiatry

At a time when Germany can expel tens of thousands of Jews and Russia can shift millions of people from one part of the continent to another, the shifting of a few hundred thousand Albanians will not lead to the outbreak of a world war. — *Vaso Cubrilovic, predicting ethnic cleansing*[56]

Information on the origin and development of Yugoslavian psychiatry and psychology is almost nonexistent in the English literature, and scarce enough in Serbo-Croatian journals,[57] [58] but certain conclusions can be drawn. Following the Enlightenment, Croatian and Latinist writers made contributions to psychology— Croatian philosopher Marko Marulic (1450-1542) is credited with first using the term 'psychology',[59] but it took until 1920 before psychology had an academic place in universities.

Yugoslavian psychiatry, like the rest of Europe, drew

---

[56] Weine, Stevan (1999), *When History is a Nightmare: Lives and memories of ethnic cleansing in Bosnia–Herzegovina*, Rutgers University Press, London, 87.

[57] Kline, Nathan S (1963), 'Psychiatry in Yugoslavia', *Psychiatric Quarterly*, April, 37, 245-52.

[58] Starjevic, V, personal communication.

[59] Marinkovic, Ksenja (1992), 'The history of psychology in former Yugoslavia: An overview', *Journal of the History of the Behavioral Sciences*, 28(4), 340-51.

heavily on the German School, with its emphasis on Kraepelinian dualism, biological factors and eugenics. Psychoanalysis had a natural attraction to some individuals when Vienna, where Freud was based, and the regions that became Yugoslavia, were still in the Austro –Hungarian Dual Monarchy. Following World War II, at least in the first few years, the Communist federated state that appeared under Marshall Tito was determined to be more ideologically pure than Stalinist Russia. Yugoslavian psychiatry changed when psychological testing and psychoanalysis were seen as politically unacceptable bourgeois indulgences. The emphasis was on Pavlovian behaviourism, with the addition of biological treatment. Within a decade, ideological restrictions were relaxed.

Despite rigid centralisation of control, psychiatric services varied between the component states and this tended to influence the approaches taken. The influence of Communism was regarded as stronger and lasted longer in Serbia than in Croatia and Slovenia. The result was a greater emphasis on a clinical and more 'person-orientated' psychology in Belgrade, while there was greater production of academic research-based work in Zagreb. Possibly because of its long-standing ties to the Germanic world, Zagreb was the most well-endowed centre, while Belgrade tended to attract those who were psychoanalytically orientated.[60] There was nothing unusual about this: even in Nazi Germany, where Freud was considered anathema, a form of analytic psychotherapy continued at the Göring Institute for the duration World War II. After 1970, Yugoslavian psychiatrists would regularly attend international conferences and train at other centres, such as the Tavistock Institute or the Maudsley Hospital in London.

---

[60] Kline, op cit

Psychiatrists and the Bosnian genocide

These are truly scenes from hell, written on the darkest pages
of human history. *—Judge Fouad Riad (1995), reviewing the
Srebrenica killings*[61]

The 1992–1995 Bosnian war arose from the break-up of the
nation state called Yugoslavia. Following the death of Tito
and the fall of Communism, multi-ethnic Yugoslavia was
doomed. Slovenia, after a brief clash with Croatia, was the
first to secede. Transforming seamlessly from their role as
Communist apparatchiks to nationalist leaders, Franjo
Tudjman (Croatia) and Slobodan Milosevic (Serbia) were
determined to expand their territories by expelling other
ethnic groups. Playing on ancient scores, the two states went
to war in 1991, with atrocities on both sides. While both made
gains, the outcome was less than satisfactory for Milosevic,
who then set his sights on the multi-ethnic state of Bosnia–
Herzegovina as his prime goal.[62] Milosevic used the Serbian
Democratic Party of Bosnia–Herzegovina (SDS) as a proxy for
his goal of creating a Greater Serbia.

An ominous phrase entered the lexicon: 'ethnic cleansing',
the use of brutal force to remove Muslims from territories
claimed by the Serbs. Harking back to the atrocities of the
Croatian *Ustasa* during World War II, it has the same meaning
and intent as clearing Europe of its Jews, *Judenrein*. Ethnic
cleansing involved individual and mass killing, arbitrary
extrajudicial killings, mass rape, starvation, destruction of
residences, property and religious institutions, and
population expulsion.[63] It was first used by Slobodan

61

http://www.guardian.co.uk/world/2005/jul/12/warcrimes.iantray
nor/print, retrieved 24 Nov 2011

[62] Markusen, Eric (2003), 'Genocide in former Yugoslavia, 1992–1995',
Journal of Genocide Research, December, 5, 4, 605–15.

[63] Blum, Rony, Stanton, G H, Sagi S, and Richter, E D (2008),' "Ethnic

Milosevic in April 1987 to describe Albanian violence towards the Kosovar Serbs. The term was then used by the media from July 1991 and by the United Nations in 1993; recent examples of the practice and its underpinnings have been thoroughly examined in Norman Naimark's book, *Fires of Hatred*.[64]

Serbian psychiatrists were prominent in nationalist politics. The SDS, including many of its medical members, was established in 1990 by Zagreb-based psychiatrist Dr Jovan Raskovic.[65] He was born in Knin in 1929. With the onset of war, his family moved to Zagreb. He studied medicine at the University of Zagreb, qualifying in 1956. He obtained his psychiatric degree in 1962 and worked in the neuropsychiatric ward at Sibenik Hospital. A well-known psychiatric figure in Yugoslavia, he published widely in international psychiatric journals. His early papers on social and cultural topics give little indication of his political views. Later books (*Narcissism* and *Depersonalisation*, 1990) were more explicit, and the most notorious was *Luda Zemlja* (*The Mad Country*, 1990).[66] Raskovic wrote that Catholics (Croats), Orthodox (Serbs) and Muslims experienced different neuroses: Serbs were strongly oedipal, Croats fearful of castration and Muslims anally fixated.[67] On this premise, Croats were psychologically driven to challenge the power of Serbs, the 'nation of tragic destiny'. The connection between heaven and national destiny created 'conditions for the religious destiny of an ethnical being'. As a

---

cleansing" bleaches the atrocities of genocide', *European Journal of Public Health*, April, 18, 2, 204–09.

[64] Naimark, Norman (2001), *Fires of Hatred: Ethnic cleansing in twentieth-century Europe*, Cambridge, Mass, Harvard University Press.

[65] Weine, op cit, 91–93.

[66] Weine, op cit, 92.

[67] Weine, op cit, 91.

result of 'laws regarding the hygiene of the anal channel', Muslims were disposed to gather property and behave aggressively. In this fashion, Raskovic used psychoanalytic jargon to justify Serbian aggression, while simultaneously dehumanising the Muslim opposition. He claimed[68] that his conclusions were derived from decades of psychiatric work at the borders of the three republics.

Raskovic addressed public meetings. He refused to join Tudjman's government because the latter would not acknowledge Serbian rights. Tudjman made public a tape-recording in which Raskovic derided Serbians, forcing Raskovic to stand down. He retired to Belgrade and from any further involvement in politics.

In 1989, an obscure Sarajevo-based psychiatrist, Dr Radovan Karadzic, became head of the Serbian Green Party (a grim irony in view of his later despoiling of large tracts of Bosnia). The following year he surprised many by replacing Raskovic as head of the SDS. He immediately adopted a posture of aggressive nationalism and vicious anti-Muslim rhetoric, confusing many who had regarded him as unscrupulous but apolitical until then. The SDS proclaimed a network of 'Serb Autonomous Regions' which[69] from 1992 orchestrated the removal of all Muslims and Croats in the Serbs' path. After a strong vote in the November 1990 elections, the SDS participated in a tri-national Bosnian government under President Alija Izetbegovic. As Yugoslavia moved toward dissolution in the following year, Karadzic warned that if Bosnia and Herzegovina declared independence, Bosnian Serbs would secede and seek union with Serbia. After the republic's electorate voted for independence, war erupted in April 1992.

---

[68] Weine, op cit, 99.

[69] Gow, James (2003), *The Serbian Project and its Adversaries: A strategy of war crimes*, London, C Hurst and Co.

Karadzic became president of the Bosnian Serb Republic (*Republika Srpska*) based in the self-proclaimed capital of Palé. By December 1992, Bosnian Serbs had seized about 70 per cent of Bosnia and Herzegovina. In the course of the conflict, Serb forces committed many atrocities, chiefly against Muslims. Tactics included mass execution, the establishment of rape centres, torture, and forcible removal of people. Concentration camps, not seen in Europe since the Nazi era, were re-established. Karadzic authorised the siege of Sarajevo, shelling the homes of his colleagues and killing patients in their beds at the hospital where he had worked until recently[70].

Sydney psychiatrist Dusan Kecmanovic, who had direct experience of the events that led to the post-Yugoslavia wars, described the behaviour of psychiatrists at the time as 'ethno-nationalism' — defined as the absolute precedence of loyalty to one's own ethno-national group.[71] This was characterised by preferential treatment of patients of the same ethnicity, the disproportionately high numbers of psychiatrists among the political leadership, and the involvement in ethno-nationalist studies or statements beyond usual professional interests. These criteria applied to the ethno-psychological writings of both the Croatian and Serbian psychiatrists of the period. Each side used psychoanalytic vocabulary to rationalise the defects of their enemies.

In 1993, Serbian psychiatrists published *The Stresses of War* — in collaboration with government departments —

---

[70] Kaplan, op cit

[71] Kecmanovic, Dunsan (1999), 'Psychiatrists in times of ethnonationalism', *Australian and New Zealand Journal of Psychiatry*, June, 33, 3, 309–15.

documenting the effects of the war on the Serbian people.[72] The book alleged that the international media 'satanised' the Serbian people, preparing the way for genocide against them. While condemning war crimes and genocide, the authors' bias was evident in their discussion of the rape of non-Serb women. First, they claimed that the number of victims was greatly understated; second, the tendentious allegation was posited that rapes could not have been ordered by officers because soldiers cannot get erections on command. In an ironic reversal of Dr Raskovic's writings, the psychiatrists alleged that psychiatry was being misused to 'spread hatred against the Serbian people', and in their subsequent book, *Sanctions* (1994),[73] it was suggested that growing international sanctions acted as a prelude to Serbian genocide.

Professor E Klein of Zagreb University wrote that Serbs were militant, had a warrior culture and tended to form groups around warrior-leaders. They often had an inferiority complex because of their 'lower level of civilisation and culture'.[74] Professor M Jakovljevic, at the same institution, said Serbs had a paranoid political culture manifesting in an 'almost erotic attitude' towards weapons, producing a nihilistic destructiveness. This compared adversely with the Croatian political culture of peaceful co-existence.[75]

Professor J Maric, at Belgrade University, took a different tack. Serbs, he stated, were well-intended, peaceful and did not 'denigrate other peoples'.[76] Maric contends that while

---

[72] Weine, op cit, 133–46.

[73] Kaličanin, Predrag (1994), *The Stresses of War and Sanctions*, Belgrade Institute for Mental Health.

[74] Kecmanović, Dusan (2002), *Ethnic Times: Exploring ethnonationalism in the former Yugoslavia*, Westport, CT Praeger Publishers, 147.

[75] Kecmanović, ibid.

[76] Kecmanović, Dusan (2002), *Ethnic Times: Exploring ethnonationalism in the former Yugoslavia*, Westport, CT, Praeger Publishers, 148.

they did not have high level of material wellbeing, they did not subscribe to the superficial politeness found in the West. Serbian psychiatrists, while ostensibly presenting their case in a balanced and objective fashion, were both publicising the Serbian case and seeking to justify ethnic cleansing practices in the Bosnian war. By ignoring the aggressive role of the Serbian government, these psychiatrists acted, in effect, as genocide apologists.

Milosevic signed the Dayton peace accord on December 1995, effectively shutting the door on the Bosnian Serb leadership. The accord partitioned Bosnia and Herzegovina into Serb and Muslim–Croat areas and ended the war. The political tide turned and many Bosnian Serbs held Karadzic responsible for their isolation.[77] In 1995, Karadzic was indicted by an international War Crimes Tribunal for the massacre of Muslim and Croatian civilians. He resigned in July 1996, swearing he would never stand trial. After the fall of Milosevic, he went underground in Serbia. There he remained, protected by a network of Serbian loyalists until his arrest in 2008.

Radovan Karadzic — a psychiatrist's own story[78]

> Why not? It's all strange here, nothing is normal. — *Psychiatrist Dr Ferhid Mujanovic, after Kosovo Hospital was shelled by the Serbians.*

At 15, Radovan Karadzic moved to student quarters in the city of Sarajevo, living in a multi-ethnic neighbourhood and mixing comfortably with Serbian, Croatian and Muslim neighbours. The young Karadzic was described as naïve, but

[77]

http://www.bosnet.org/archive/bosnet.w3archive/9709/msg00036.html.

[78] Weine, op cit, 106–32.

endearing. Neighbours recalled a shy farm boy wearing a grimy white pullover knitted with wool from his village.[79] Later, his striking looks—he was over six foot tall with a Byronic shock of hair—attracted attention, and he became a serial seducer of women. In 1965, Karadzic, with a high school diploma from the medical vocational school,[80] studied at the University of Sarajevo. He received his medical degree on 19 July 1971 and then qualified in psychiatry.

During this time, Karadzic had joined and left the Communist Party, became involved in student politics and dabbled in literary circles. He wrote four volumes of poetry which he recited in public, accompanied by the *gusle* (a one-stringed Serbian instrument), to indifferent response. Karadzic had no doubt about his talent as a poet, but the literary circles with whom he associated were dubious, regarding him as little more than a dabbling amateur. This did not deter him. He published several volumes of his work, receiving state-funded prizes for his efforts. He also wrote children's stories and composed Serbian folk music, which he performed on radio.[81]

Analysis of his early poetry reveals prophetic, if not apocalyptic, visions of the future.[82] In 1971, 21 years before the war, he wrote a poem called 'Let's go down to the town and kill some scum'. Another poem of that time, 'Sarajevo', speaks of the city burning in a 'blood-soaked tide'. His fourth volume, published in 1990, reveals an obsession with

---

[79] Wilkinson, Tracey (1995), 'Bosnians recall Karadzic, a neighbor turned enemy', *Los Angeles Times*, 23 July. Available at http://articles.latimes.com/1995-07-23/news/mn-27059_1_bosnian-serb. Retrieved 11 January 2012.

[80] Mezedi, I, personal communication.

[81] Kaplan, op cit

[82] Weine, op cit, 118–25.

violence, notably in 'The Morning Hand-Grenade'.[83] According to Marko Vesovic,[84] a writer who knew him from university days, 'we had considered his case hopeless as far as literature is concerned'.

Karadzic married Ljiljana Zelen — a Serbian psychiatrist-in-training from an upper-class Sarajevo family — who later practised as a psychoanalyst. They had two children. With suspicious amounts of money at his disposal, he was thought to be a police informer for KOS (the Counterintelligence Agency of the former Yugoslavia) [85] and was shunned by many.

Karadzic worked at the Djuro Djakovic Adult Education Centre. To further his skills, he had Tavistock Group Therapy training [the Tavistock in London is a highly regarded centre for education and training in different therapies.] He moved to the psychiatric clinic in Kosevo hospital, Sarajevo until 1983, spending 1980 training in psychotherapy at the Zagreb Centre for Mental Health. From 1983 till 1984 he was at the Vozdovac Health Centre in Belgrade. Karadzic continued to engage in activities that would fulfil his grandiose self-image, becoming the psychiatrist for the Sarajevo soccer team, one of the leading teams in Bosnia, and later for the Belgrade Red Star team. Despite subjecting the players to mass hypnosis,

---

[83] Dekleva, K B and Post, J M (1997), 'Genocide in Bosnia: the case of Dr. Radovan Karadzic', *Journal of the American Academy of Psychiatry and the Law*, 25, 4, 485–96.

[84]

http://www.pbs.org/wgbh/pages/frontline/shows/karadzic/interviews/vesovic.html

[85]

http://www.pbs.org/wgbh/pages/frontline/shows/karadzic/interviews/vesovic.html

the teams fared no better.[86]

Ever enterprising and needing money for investments and gambling, Karadzic sold fraudulent medical certificates and prescriptions to those who wanted to avoid military service or retire early. On 26 September 1985, he was sentenced to three years in prison and fined for fraud and embezzlement of public funds. He was charged with using a $100,000 grant meant for farmers to build his own chicken farm in nearby Palé. Karadzic spent only 11 months in prison. He later claimed that he had been a political prisoner and the experience had hardened him, but it is likely the offences were criminal, not political, and his government contacts ensured he did not serve a long sentence.[87]

He returned to psychiatric practice when political pressure to take him back was asserted on the hospital. He worked at the Vozdovac Health Centre in Belgrade in 1987 and that year he presented a paper to a psychotherapy conference analysing a poem about bizarre bodily mutilation. A much-touted book on depression never eventuated. The last record of him working in psychiatry is from February to March 1992 at the Nedjo Zec psychiatric clinic in Kosevo Hospital, Sarajevo. In his last year at the clinic, Karadzic was always accompanied by bodyguards, who caused staff and patients distress by insisting on body searches. Karadzic's availability became increasingly limited, and there were always lines of unhappy patients outside his office. His supervisor, Dr Ismet Ceric, eventually requested he take leave. After he went to Palé in 1992, he did not practise psychiatry again.

Karadzic's possible motivations and mental state

You want to take Bosnia and Herzegovina down the same highway to hell and suffering that Slovenia and Croatia are

---

[86] Kaplan, op cit

[87] Kaplan, op cit

travelling. Do not think that you will not lead Bosnia and Herzegovina into hell, and do not think that you will not perhaps lead the Muslim people into annihilation, because the Muslims cannot defend themselves if there is war — How will you prevent everyone from being killed in Bosnia and Herzegovina? — *Dr Radovan Karadzic (October 1991), demonstrating the skills acquired from years of psychotherapy training*[88]

Little is known about Karadzic's upbringing. His father would undoubtedly have stoked his nationalism, but died when Karadzic was young; his reaction to the death is unknown. His mother spoke glowingly of her son and supported his political goals once he became President.[89] We know little more of Karadzic the doctor, or why he chose psychiatry. At best he was regarded as marginally competent, indifferent to the concerns of his patients, and corrupt. Dr Ceric described his work as 'ordinary'.[90] His colleagues, regaled with assertions that he would become a famous psychiatrist or poet, said that he diagnosed everybody with masked depression, provoked psychotic patients, was always late and never completed reports.[91] When a psychopathic patient with a knife went roaming in the ward, Karadzic retreated to his room, leaving a nurse to disarm and calm him.

Inevitably questions will be raised about Karadzic's mental state. He was reported to drink to excess, spend money and

---

[88] Judah, Tim (1997), *The Serbs: History, myth and the destruction of Yugoslavia*, New York, Yale University Press, 199.

[89] http://www.tnr.com/archive/0698/062998/diarist062998.html.

[90]

http://www.pbs.org/wgbh/pages/frontline/shows/karadzic/interviews/ceric.htm.

[91] Weine, op cit, 79.

gamble heavily at casinos.[92] Dr Ceric said he had psychosomatic symptoms. In springtime and autumn he was depressed and 'a little bit, sometimes euphoric' during summer and winter. Selling medical certificates, gambling and indiscriminate spending are indicative of a grandiose and reckless nature, with strong elements of opportunism.[93] Vesovic described Karadzic as a psychopath, 'a man without a core'. We cannot exonerate his actions, yet some writers, noting his extreme pronouncements, would consider diagnoses like psychopathy, manic-depression or paranoia.[94]

Dr Ceric wrote that 'at the time there was a joke among our colleagues and our nurses that one day in the future, it's possible that Radovan would come to the clinic early in the morning and say, "Okay I'm back and I'm not guilty of nothing — or everything, everyone else is guilty...the Americans or something...so how about some tea or coffee."'[95] Warren Zimmerman, the last American ambassador to Yugoslavia, regarded him as barking mad, obsessed with violence and in need of psychiatric treatment[96].

What cannot be denied is Karadzic's capacity for gross denial, at times reaching delusional proportions. He alleged that Muslims destroyed the famous National Library, with its irreplaceable cultural treasures, because it was a Christian

---

[92] http://sca.lib.liv.ac.uk/collections/Owen/lists/owencd0.html.

[93] Dekleva and Post, op cit

[94] Robins, R (1986), 'Paranoid ideation and charismatic leadership', *Psychohistory Review*, 615–55. Redlich, Fritz (2000), *Hitler: Diagnosis of a destructive prophet*, New York, Oxford University Press, 334.

[95] http://www.pbs.org/wgbh/pages/frontline/shows/karadzic/interviews/ceric.html

[96] http://www.pbs.org/wgbh/pages/frontline/shows/karadzic/radovan/impressions.html, retrieved 21 November 2011.

building.[97] Far from Sarajevo being under siege by his forces for two years, he blustered that Muslim guns were there to prevent citizens from breaking out of the city. In the face of overwhelming evidence of murderous atrocities by Bosnian Serb forces, he continued to state that there was not one shred of evidence to support these claims and, once again, the atrocities had been carried out by Muslims against their own people.[98]

He never renounced his role as a psychiatrist, even after he assumed the Presidency of the *Republika Srpska*. One analyst stated that the level of violence of combatants was fanned by Dr Karadzic's 'psychobabble'.[99] Karadzic's group therapy training influenced his leadership style and choice of terror tactics. Allegations have been made that he witnessed and participated in torture at Bosnian Serb concentration camps.[100]

Karadzic's short reign as President of the Bosnian Serb Republic left an appalling legacy. The full extent of killing and destruction wrought by his forces during the war will never be fully known. The casualties and survivors, many now dispersed around the world as refugees, will suffer for the rest of their lives. Although many aspects of Karadzic's personality remain deeply enigmatic, he displayed an extraordinary degree of reckless opportunism in which the instincts of an extreme gambler were unchallenged by any

---

[97] Cigar, Norman (1995), *Genocide in Bosnia*, College Station Texas A&M University Press, 52.

[98] Kaplan, op cit

[99] Breo, Dennis (1993), 'Human rights II—Cherif Bassiouni condemns "psychology" of Balkan crimes', *Journal of the American Medical Association*, 270, 643–44.

[100] (1995), 'Witness from hell', *De Telegraaf* [Amsterdam], May 27, in Deklava and Post, op cit

restraint or fear of the consequences. His most enduring characteristics are his grandiose self-image, reckless and profligate nature, boundless opportunism and grotesque capacity for self-deception. If nothing else, they disqualify him as a candidate for Hannah Arendt's 'banality of evil'.

Conclusion

...of all the professions, medicine is one most likely to attract people with high personal anxieties about dying. We become doctors because our ability to cure gives us power over the death of which we are so afraid... — *Sherwin Nuland*[101]

The three facets of the medical role are sapiential, authoritarian and charismatic. Sapience, of course, comes from training and experience, while authority is not just implicit but constantly reiterated by the title 'Doctor'. The charismatic role accounts for the fact that doctors are dealing with powerful and mysterious forces. The basis for medical involvement in political abuse goes deep into the psychology of medicine and the personality of the practitioner. At its heart is an extreme grandiosity, a belief that 'treating' (in reality, extirpating) the illness affecting the nation is merely an extension of the ancient and honoured role of treating the sick patient. During the nineteenth century, the belief arose that it was only a question of degree in moving from healing the individual to healing the nation. The murder of other human beings (the emphasis being on those defined as 'the other') was, to some, merely a mental leap from the adjustment required of the doctors to detach themselves from the patients in order to treat them.

In 1937, the Serb philosopher and nationalist Vaso Cubrilovic, who had taken part in the plot to kill the Archduke Franz Ferdinand, anticipated ethnic cleansing in psychological terms. He proposed to remove Albanians from

---

[101] Nuland, Sherwin (1995), *How We Die: Reflections on life's final chapter*, 1st Vintage Edition, New York, Vintage, 258.

Serbian lands by 'the creation of a suitable psychosis', that is, to drive them away by intolerable terror. It is significant that the language used to justify racial genocide was derived from medicine in portraying the enemy in pathological terms. The concept of cleansing or disinfection, particularly since the early 1900s, was intended to facilitate the illusion that the mass murders were intended to promote 'hygiene'. This designation of the victim of eugenic or ethnic genocide as some sort of pathology infecting the society as a whole was a regular part of the process of legitimising massacre as a public health measure by using 'reverse jargon'.[102]

Turkey's Dr Nazim referred to his Armenian victims as dangerous microbes or abscesses; Hitler and his medical acolytes described Jews, *inter alia,* as parasites, a plague, lice, vermin, cancer, tumours, racial tuberculosis and gangrenous excrescences that had to be eliminated.[103] Stalin and Beria promoted the term *purge* to denote the deportation of millions of ethnic Soviet minorities to Siberia, regardless of the mortality. Japanese germ warfare referred to the population in Manchuria as 'logs', whom they used for horrifying experiments; in Rwanda, the Hutu term for Tutsis was 'cockroaches'; Albanian commanders called the Roma 'majutsis', meaning, lower than garbage.[104] Animalisation and insectification of people, as Rowan Savage shows in his essay here, is the 'simplest' form of dehumanisation, and it is that

---

[102] Blum, Stanton, Sagi and Richter, op cit

[103] Biddiss, op cit

[104] Savage, Rowan (2006), '"Vermin to be Cleared off the Face of the Earth": Perpetrator representations of genocide victims as animals', in Tatz, Colin, P Arnold and S Tatz (eds) *Genocide Perspectives III Essays on the Holocaust and other genocides*, Sydney: Brandl and Schlesinger with the Australian Institute for Holocaust and Genocide Studies, 17–53.

sense of designated enemies as other than human that allows the ideological perpetrators and their minions to justify their actions.

Why do some elements of the psychiatric profession ally themselves with genocide in this way, a way that stridently contradicts every principle of care and healing to which its practitioners are dedicated? Of all the medical sub-disciplines, psychiatry has the most direct link with shamanism, the first specialised role in hunter-gatherer society. The role of the shaman was not just healing the individual but ensuring the harmony of the tribal group by placating the gods, coping with drought or scarcity and predicting the future. In doing so, it became an elite and hereditary priestly group. This tendency continued in the post-Enlightenment decline in religion and its substitution by psychiatry and psychology.

Of all the sub-disciplines, psychiatry was the youngest and the last to achieve professional recognition. By virtue of the terrain in which it operates — the mind — psychiatry is predisposed to overdetermination, making it especially susceptible to utopian ideology or irenic fantasies. The first organiser of the profession, Pinel, driven by the spirit of the French Revolution, sought to change the environment of the patient through 'moral therapy'. Full recognition of the discipline came at the start of the twentieth century from Emil Kraepelin. There is no denying his organisational genius; this, coupled with the development of a rational system of classifying diagnoses, set the profession on track to become a medical speciality.

German psychiatry's greatest asset proved its undoing: academicians perceived themselves as scientists and saw patients as research material.[105] This was a Faustian pact of the most ominous nature — it laid the seeds of the total moral

---

[105] Engstrom, op cit

collapse of German psychiatry under the Nazis.[106] Kraepelin has to take credit for the catastrophic effect of the theory of degeneration on German psychiatry—and ultimately the lowest point in the history of medicine. More than any of his colleagues, Kraepelin had the intelligence and vision to see that degeneration was an ultimately doomed and immoral proposition. By articulating social facts into an implied threat to the collective wellbeing of the nation,[107] Kraepelin was the chief architect of the psychiatric debauchment that followed. It was no coincidence that Ernst Rüdin, his successor at Heidelberg, was the driving force behind the Nazi euthanasia program.[108] Another follower, Robert Gaupp, stated in 1938 that Kraepelin's work comprised nothing less than 'the foundation of all Nazi racial hygiene laws'.[109] English psychiatrist Michael Shepherd described Kraepelin's ideas as proto-fascistic.[110] When Kraepelin died in 1926, Hitler would have been mostly unknown to him.

Whitely states that psychiatry 'now constitutes an amorphous system of beliefs, behaviours and attitudes whose functions and doctrines are unsettlingly to those held by

---

[106] Hanauske-Abel, Hartmut (1996), 'Not a slippery slope or sudden subversion: German medicine and national socialism in 1933', *British Medical Journal*, 7 December, 313 (7070), 1453–63.

[107] Engstrom, Eric, Burgmair, W and Weber, M M (2002), 'Emil Kraepelin's 'Self-Assessment': clinical autography in historical context', *History of Psychiatry*, March, 13, 49, 89–119.

[108] Pilgrim, David (2008), 'The eugenic legacy in psychology and psychiatry', *International Journal of Social Psychiatry*, 54, 272–84.

[109] Engstrom, Eric J and Weber, M M (2007), 'Making Kraepelin history: A great instauration?', *History of Psychiatry*, 18, 3, 267–73.

[110] Shepherd, Michael (1995), 'Two faces of Emil Kraepelin', *British Journal of Psychiatry*, August, 167, 2, 174–83.

conventional religions'.[111] Its practitioners undergo years of special training to gain access to knowledge inaccessible to the public (increasingly less so in this age of the internet) allowing them special powers (enforcing treatment). Their terrain, despite constant reiteration that they are now brain-based, is 'the mind', a territory with as little definition as 'the soul' is to the public.

Canonical texts are regarded as being of unshakeable authority but lead to intense (and to the public, largely incomprehensible) disputes. Its ultimate expression, personal psychotherapy, models itself on sacramental involvement and sin confession, establishing a ritual practice akin to regular attendance at Catholic mass. Like any church, psychiatry can be broken down into diverse parts, with different competing schools squabbling over ideology but sharing the same goals and distinguishing itself from opposition, that is, non-professional or lay competitors. Like other institutions in the public relations-driven jargon-rich discourse, psychiatric colleges all have 'mission statements'.

Consider, as an example, the Royal Australian and New Zealand College of Psychiatry.[112] It takes a stand on selected and appropriate public issues, such as child abuse or detention of refugees; yet it shies away from matters that would be seen as falling directly into its bailiwick. At times it appears to take a distinctly moral or censorious approach, sometimes quite legitimately in relation to issues around stigma, for example complaining that the Jim Carey movie *Me, Myself and Irene* was offensive to mental patients. It is preoccupied with sexual misconduct by doctors (most

---

[111] Whitley, Rob (2008), 'Is psychiatry a religion?', *Journal of the Royal Society of Medicine*, December, 101, 12, 579–82.

[112] It should be stated that in this regard, the RANZCP is little different from its counterparts in the United Kingdom or United States.

recently, banning delisted psychiatrists from applying to rejoin the College), but has never issued any response to the roles of men like Karadzic and his Serbian colleagues in the Bosnian genocide.

Are psychiatrists as individuals inherently prone to human rights abuse? There is nothing to indicate that most psychiatrists involved in such activities are anything but law-abiding and exemplary citizens. In the former USSR, it would appear that the majority of Soviet psychiatrists were reluctant to participate in state-sanctioned abuse of psychiatric diagnosis and treatment, and 'wriggled out' of such roles as soon as it was politically possible. [113] [114] The German psychiatrists who led the genocide were not marginal characters, misfits or psychopaths, but some of the most prominent academics. Rüdin and Gaupp, for example, were leaders in the field. Other academics involved in wide-ranging abuses included Julius Hallervorden, director of the prestigious Kaiser–Wilhelm Institute, who collected brains of euthanasia victims for his neuro-pathological collection, and Carl Schneider, who studied victims before they were murdered and then dissected their brains. Colonel Aubrey Levin, who ran the anti-homosexual Aversion Project in the South African Defence Force, had extreme right-wing views, yet was an otherwise unremarkable personality.

Karadzic, in contrast, was an extremely dubious, if not marginal, character. His work was at best 'ordinary', his attempts to establish himself as an artist (or sporting coach) close to pathetic and he constantly cast around for a role in

---

[113] Bloch, Sidney and Reddaway, P (1997), *Psychiatric Terror*, New York Basic Books.

[114] Chodoff, Paul (2009), 'The abuse of psychiatry', in Bloch, Sidney and Green, S (eds) *Psychiatric Ethics*, 4th edition, Oxford, Oxford University Press.

which he could fulfil his grandiose fantasies. Yet Karadzic the *genocidaire* cannot be separated from Karadzic the psychiatrist. He had no hesitation in shelling his workplace, suggesting that he had internalised the slights of his colleagues and wanted revenge. He thrived on the fighting, was a constant presence at the siege of Sarajevo and used group psychology to plan tactics of terror and ethnic cleansing. That he worked as an alternative therapist when he was in hiding indicates that the genocide was perhaps just another expression, albeit one with the most terrible consequences, of the quest to become the comprehensive 'healer', feasibly an aspiration of genocidal doctors.

In its capacity for overdetermination, does psychiatry have a fatal flaw? This may well be the case. The involvement with eugenics only had consequences in Germany, but led to sterilisation of the mentally ill in countries such as Sweden (as late as 1965) and the United States particularly between the two world wars. At the highwater mark of psychoanalysis in mid-century, American psychiatrists confidently issued nostrums about disturbed youth requiring counselling to solve a range of social problems. For decades, there was suppression of acknowledging child sexual abuse on the basis of Freud's oedipal theory (it was all a fantasy), that swung round to the opposite extreme after 1980 and imprisoned innocent parents on the basis of repressed memories 'discovered' in therapy. Now we see another manifestation of this tendency towards over-zealous social activism, the removal of children from mothers (if not their imprisonment) on the basis of a pseudo-scientific and unproven theory known as Munchausen's Syndrome by Proxy.

It has to be accepted that, with the best intentions in the world, the practise of psychiatry can lend itself at intervals to a view of society that can be described, variously, as patronising, paternalistic, Manichean and all-encompassing. In this scenario, the outcome is inevitable. From the individual to the profession, there arise those who ally themselves with the state to use their skills to abuse, if not destroy, other groups of people, driven by an inexorable sense of rectitude that may, in some cases at least, overlie a surging torrent of rage that led them to the profession in the first case.

As a result of atrocities committed during the Bosnian Civil War of 1992–1995, Karadzic stands indicted as a suspected war criminal for crimes against humanity and genocide, the first doctor so indicted since the Nuremberg Doctors' Trial in 1946. These crimes include killing 68 civilians in the shelling of the Markale marketplace on 5 February 1994, the use of 248 United Nations peacekeepers as human shields, and the murder of up to 7,500 people under UN protection at Srebrenica.

In 1993, the American Psychiatric Association passed a motion condemning Karadzic for 'brutal and inhumane actions'. The condemnation was issued with 'particular offence, urgency and horror because, by membership and training, Dr Karadzic claims membership in our profession'.[115]

Psychiatrists, alongside other medical and mental health professionals, have wide reaching moral responsibility. Prominent psychiatrist Thomas Szasz made the point quite bluntly: 'It is the moral duty of psychologists and psychiatrists to safeguard the dignity and liberty of people generally, and, in particular those with whom they work. If instead they take professional advantage of the imprisoned status of incarcerated individuals or populations, they are, in my opinion, criminals.'[116]

---

[115] http://www.psych.org/Departments/EDU/Library/APAOfficialDocumentsandRelated/PositionStatements/199301.aspx

[116] Szasz, Thomas Stephen (1979), *The Theology of Medicine: The political-philosophical foundations of medical ethics*, Oxford, Oxford

Regrettably, the evidence thus far suggests that doctors, regardless of prestige, ability, qualification or training, are amongst the most willing accomplices of state abuse. They will play a leading role in perpetuating the system, support and participate in state abuse and, where circumstances permit, willingly accede to leadership of repressive regimes. What cannot be doubted is that this phenomenon is a beginning, not an end, and will undoubtedly recur in future.

We kill everybody, my dear. Some with bullets, some with words, and everybody with our deeds. We drive people into their graves, and neither see it nor feel it. — *Maxim Gorky* in *Enemies*[117]

Acknowledgements

Robert M Kaplan and Garry Walter thank Dr Nerissa Soh for her assistance with sourcing material, and Vicken Babkenian and Anabell St Vincent for their advice and encouragement.

University Press, 52.

[117] *Enemies* was first published in 1906 (an English version by Kitty Hunter-Blair and Jeremy Brooks, published 1972 by E Methuen in London).

Noughts and Crosses: The Silence of the Churches in the Holocaust Years

Colin Tatz

This essay is about the indifference, even the hostile indifference, of Christian churches to the Jewish experience in the 1930s and 1940s. Even a brief review of the attitudes and actions of the German Catholic and Protestant churches, of two Popes, of the highly-regarded theologian Dietrich Bonhoeffer and of the German Jews' responses leads to this conclusion: that there are much simpler explanations of their silences and their moral abdications than can be found in the grand theorising so often required by the humanities and social sciences.

Two factors make this is a difficult assignment. First, identifying let alone pinpointing emotions and attitudes, which is so much harder than assembling chronology and narrative. Second, finding the appropriate words to capture and comprehend church conduct during the Holocaust era. (And then beyond the *Shoah* to church silence during Burundi, Rwanda, Somalia, Guatemala, North Korea, Bangladesh, Kosovo, Bosnia, Iraq, Darfur, among other such events.)

One tries to find and understand the mechanisms, the transmission belts that 'drove' their behaviour. Greed, revenge, hate and contempt explain many acts of evil; Samaritanism, generosity, charitableness, even altruism underlie acts of goodness. A word that doesn't seem to belong in the vocabularies of good and evil is *want*. It seems innocuous enough. But *want* can mislead. To *want* something is to wish or hope for it, to yearn or pine or even crave for it; the verb implies action towards something positive and definable. *Not to want* is a much more passive notion, even a negative one. *Wanting* has the common meaning of lacking, being inadequate, disappointing, sometimes not needing, and often, being unacceptable. These are not merely normal emotions and behaviours or psychological states of being; they are also political terms and attitudes and it is in these latter senses that I look briefly at what Christians and Jews wanted, didn't want, and the nature of their wanting in relation to Jews in the Europe of the 1930s and 1940s.

Indifference is another relevant word, one that on the face of it indicates neither *want* nor *not want*. Written or spoken, it conveys a sense of neutrality, of not caring one way or the other, a shrug signifying lack of concern, lack of interest, coolness or even coldness, or simply disdain, disregard or dismissiveness. It doesn't connote strength of feeling, certainly not passion. In his lectures, Yehuda Bauer, the doyen of Holocaust historians, always talks about *hostile indifference* towards Jews in that era—a notion that embodies intense feelings of either antagonism, bitterness, unkindness, malice, callousness or spite, or all of those feelings. Joining 'hostile' to 'indifference' may well be a contradiction but that in itself is appropriate for a period of history replete with contradiction, including the inconsistency of the celebrated German Protestant theologian Bonhoeffer.

Two more terms need consideration: *worthy* and its opposite, *unworthy*. Genocide scholars sometimes, but not often, talk about worthy and unworthy victims, those who do and those who don't warrant rescue or any of the several forms of intervention. Worthy here means deserving of, meriting, justifying, warranting attention or action. The Catholic and Protestant teaching that Judaism was superseded by Christianity and was therefore obsolete is but one form of *unworthiness*. Centuries of Christian teaching of contempt for Jews is another.[1] In World War II, several Polish underground movements wouldn't give arms to Jewish

---

[1] Isaac, Jules (1964), *The Teaching of Contempt: Christian roots of anti-Semitism*, New York, Holt, Rinehart and Winston.

partisans and some local right-wing resistance movements hunted down Jews in order to kill them. That was another litmus of *unworthiness*.[2] In 1985, when he was Mayor of Darmstadt, Günther Metzger told the German Council of Sinti and Roma people that their request to be included in remembrance ceremonies to mark the liberation of the Bergen–Belsen camp 'insulted the honour' of the Holocaust by wishing to be associated with it.[3] That is as good an exemplar of *unworthiness* as we will find. [Woodcock's essay here shows just how unworthy are the Romani in Romanian society.]

The Catholic Church and the Jews

The Catholic church isn't a monolithic structure now and it wasn't so in the Holocaust years. There were hundreds of Catholic churches and thousands of church men and women: some saved Jews, others defended Jews, some betrayed Jews and some killed Jews. Father Jozef Tiso, a priest, headed a Nazi puppet state in Slovakia from where Jews were deported to Auschwitz: 'It is a Christian action to expel the Jews, because it is for the good of the people, which is thus getting rid of the pests.'[4] [See Paul O'Shea's essay in this volume.] Yet Dominican nuns, led by Sister Bertranda (Anna Borkowska), assisted and even ran guns for the famous partisan Abba

---

[2] Krakowski, Shmuel (1984), *The War of the Doomed: Jewish armed resistance in Poland, 1942–1944*, Teaneck, New Jersey, Holmes and Meier.

[3] Wiesenthal, Simon, newsletter, quoted by Hancock, Ian (1988) in his 'Uniqueness of the Victims: Gypsies, Jews and the Holocaust', *Without Prejudice: The EAFORD International Review of Racial Discrimination*, 2, 45–67.

[4] Rothkirchen, Livia (1967), 'Vatican Policy and the "Jewish Problem" in "Independent" Slovakia (1939–1945)', in Eck, Nathan and Kubovy, Aryah Leon (eds), *Yad Vashem Studies*, vol 6, Jerusalem, Yad Vashem, 50.

Kovner and his men in the Vilna (Vilnius) ghetto underground.[5]

The noticeably short Vatican document, *We Remember: A reflection on the Holocaust (The* Shoah) — released on 16 March 1998, more than 50 years after the events — was presented by Edward Idris Cardinal Cassidy to a large Sydney audience a year later.[6] Cassidy talked of 'the sons and daughters of the Church...who fostered longstanding sentiments of mistrust and hostility that the Vatican documents refer to as **anti-Judaism'**.[7] If only it had been merely mistrust and hostility. *That* Jews could have lived with, as they have done for two millennia — and longer. But they had to live with and die from things infinitely greater than mere mistrust and hostility. They, and the Catholic church, have also had to live with the reality, expressed by Christian philosopher Marcel Dubois, that 'the centuries-old Christian anti-Judaism prepared the soil for modern antisemitism and the Holocaust'.[8]

Why did people behave the way they did? The Cardinal

---

[5] Paldiel, Mordecai (2006), *Churches and the Holocaust: Unholy teaching, good Samaritans and reconciliation*, Jersey City, Ktav, 219–21.

[6] Organised by the St Thomas More Society and the New South Wales Society of Jewish Jurists and Lawyers, Wesley Institute, Sydney, 29 July 1999. The booklet — *We Remember: A reflection on the Holocaust [The* Shoah], containing the speeches of Edward Idriss Cardinal Cassidy, the Australian Governor-General Sir William Deane, Rabbi Raymond Apple and Professor Colin Tatz, was published by the sponsors. The full text of Tatz's presentation is also found in his (2003), *With Intent to Destroy: Reflecting on genocide*, London, Verso, 58–66. Some of the material in these two sections on Catholics and Popes comes from that source.

[7] *We Remember*, 9.

[8] Bacharach, Walter (2000), 'The Catholic anti-Jewish prejudice, Hitler and the Jews', in Bankier, David (ed), *Probing the Depth of German Antisemitism: German society and the persecution of Jews, 1933–1941*, New York, Berghahn Books, 418.

conceded that 'many Christians did in fact fail to give every possible assistance to those being persecuted'; he talked of people who 'failed to give the witness that might have been expected of them as Christ's followers'. The tenor of this is that, at worst, the Catholic church was merely one third of the Holocaust triangle[9] that comprises the perpetrators and victims as well as the bystanders, those who by their indifference — or even their hostile indifference — allowed it to happen. Many churches and churchmen were more than bystanders: they were accessories, accomplices, collaborators, certainly companions to both ideas and actions — and murderers. The Vatican document has several references to the church or its adherents as co-equal victims. But there is a blasphemy in equating the fate of the Jews of Europe with the fate of the Catholic church or even several hundred of its servants. (There are also curious omissions of the dead in *We Remember*: the forgetting of, among others, 220,000 Roma, as many as 5.7 million Russians prisoners of war, at least 3.5 million non-Jewish Poles, nearly 6 million Ukrainian civilians, 8.2 million Russian civilians, and tens of thousands of anti-fascists, Serbian patriots, Jehovah's Witnesses and gay men.)

There are, literally, innumerable examples of Catholic clergy, whether in Germany or among her satellite allies, who strongly supported Nazism and were, in many ways, perpetrators. Among others, Ernst Helmreich has written a major work on *The German Churches Under Hitler;*[10] Klaus Scholder has published a two-volume analysis of *The Churches*

---

[9] Most Holocaust historians use this diagramatic triangular metaphor. In my courses I use a five-sided figure which adds the beneficiaries and the denialists.

[10] Helmreich, Ernst (1979), *The German Churches Under Hitler: Background, struggle and epilogue*, Detroit, Wayne State University Press.

and the Third Reich[11] and Kevin Spicer has provided much detail in several works, especially in his more recent portrait of *Hitler's Priests*.[12] This latter book devotes some 60 pages to biographies of 138 leading 'brown priests'.

Some aspects of church involvement need brief discussion. The essential thrust of *We Remember* is that there was a 'them' and 'us' dichotomy: 'us' or 'we' were the anti-Jewish church leaders and ideology-makers who taught and preached a doctrine of contempt, now regarded as morally and ethically wrong; 'them' were an aberrant group of pagan Nazis whose roots lay outside of Catholic Christianity and who murdered in the name of blood and race. This kind of rationalisation does not become the Vatican. It echoes the German historian, Ernst Nolte, who talked about 'us' or 'we' Germans, the good people, the anti-Nazis, and the 'them' Germans, Nazis who seemingly descended from some alien spaceship in 1933 and who were vanquished by the forces of good in 1945.[13]

Some 43 per cent of Germans were Catholics, and a significant 22.7 per cent of the *Schutzstaffeln* (SS) were adherents, attendees at mass, seekers of rites and rituals. Hitler was undoubtedly a radical figure, the one who put the extermination engine into operation. But the engine, and most of the vehicle's parts, was assembled well before he came to power. His radicalism was in removing the brakes that had

---

[11] Scholder, Klaus, *The Churches and the Third Reich* (1987), vol 1: *Preliminary History and the Time of Illusions 1918–1934*, London, SCM Press Ltd; Scholder (1988), vol 2: *The Year of Disillusionment 1934: Barmen and Rome*, London, SCM Press Ltd.

[12] Spicer, Kevin (2008), *Hitler's Priests: Catholic clergy and National Socialism*, DeKalb, Northern Illinois University Press.

[13] Nolte, Ernst, 'A past that will not pass: a speech that could be written but not delivered', *Frankfurt Allgemeine Zeitung*, 6 June 1986, reproduced in several places, including *Yad Vashem Studies XIX* (1988), Jerusalem, Yad Vashem, 65–73.

always held back the Church, namely, the injunction of St Augustine in the fourth century that Jews could be and even should be demeaned, brought low, expelled, harassed, deported, reviled — but not killed.[14]

In the Weimar period in the 1920s, bishops spoke out against the glorification of race and blood, but said nothing about anti-Jewish propaganda. They did, however, talk strongly about the destructive influence of the Jews. The main proponents were men like Fathers Josef Roth, Lorenz Pieper, Magnus Gött, the Franciscan Erhard Schlund, the Jesuit Gustav Gundlach and Bishop Michael Buchberger of Regensburg.

In the post-Weimar period, Hitler had strong dialogue with the Catholic leadership, who in turn began an appreciation of the values of racial purity. Archbishop Conrad Gröber ('Conrad the Brown'), while heavily involved in winning over the German bishops to the Vatican's signing a concordat with the Reich, stated:

> Every people bears itself the responsibility for its successful existence, and the intake of entirely foreign blood will always represent a risk for a nationality that has proven its historical worth. Hence, no people may be denied the right to maintain undisturbed their previous racial stock and to enact safeguards for this purpose. The Christian religion merely demands that the means used do not offend against the moral law and natural justice.[15]

Later, he protested against the euthanasia program but not against the treatment of Jews.

---

[14] Saint Augustine (1972), *The City of God Against the Pagans*, book 18, chapter 46, translation by Henry Bettenson, Harmondsworth, Penguin Books edition.

[15] Scholder, Klaus, vol 1, 394–95.

The famous Advent sermons of 1933 by Cardinal Michael von Faulhaber have been misinterpreted: he said that he didn't object to the attempt to keep national characteristics 'pure and unadulterated' but he objected to placing loyalty to race above loyalty to the church. This was misinterpreted as Catholic condemnation of Nazi ideology. It wasn't. He was a willing defender of the Old Testament, but while the people of Israel before Christ were the vehicles of divine revelation, those who came after were but 'restless wanderers over the earth'. He was therefore 'not concerned with defending the Jews of our time' — because, he insisted, 'the Jews can help themselves'.[16] [This was said in the context of the 'failed' Nazi attempt at a Jewish economic boycott, promoted by Julius Streicher, on 1 April 1933. Beginning a few weeks earlier, in March 1933, Jews and non-Jews had met in rallies at New York's Madison Square Garden to protest at German treatment of Jews. These meetings caused Nazis to fear an American boycott of their goods, leading to this notion that Jews were not only all-powerful but also capable of looking after themselves.] Cardinal-Archbishop Adolf Bertram used a similar turn of phrase when he and Faulhaber pointed out to the Pope that there were 'immediate issues of greater importance in the long term: schools, the maintaining of Catholic associations, sterilization'.[17] Although he condemned the euthanasia program, Faulhaber never once uttered a word about the persecution and extermination of the Jews. Hitler, he was happy to say, was 'the first statesman, aside from the Holy Father, who raised his voice against bolshevism'.[18] He

---

[16] Helmreich, 276.

[17] Cornwell, John (1999), *Hitler's Pope: The secret history of Pius XII*, London, Viking, 140; see also Bacharach, Walter (2000), 'The Catholic anti-Jewish prejudice, Hitler and the Jews', in Bankier, David (ed), *Probing the Depth of German Antisemitism: German society and the persecution of Jews, 1933–1941*, New York, Berghahn Books, 417.

[18] Helmreich, 239.

admired the Führer as 'a man of peace'.

The Catholic church agreed to the Nuremberg Laws which prohibited marriages between Jews and Aryans: in short, the church agreed to an inadmissible infringement of her spiritual jurisdiction to give sacraments to a baptised Jew. While many Catholic leaders abroad condemned these Laws, Bishop Alois Hudal, head of the German church in Rome, said the Nuremberg Laws were 'essential as a measure of self-defence against the influx of foreign elements'. This 'Semitic race', he wrote, wanted to 'become the financial masters of the Eternal City'.[19] Much later, he was to assist in the escape of a dozen major war criminals, including Adolf Eichmann, three Nazi camp commandants, Franz Stangl, Gustav Wagner and Alois Brunner, and such men as Klaus Barbie, (Croatian) Ante Pavelic and Josef Mengele.[20]

A pastoral letter from the German bishops, by Faulhaber, was read on the first Sunday in January 1937. It agreed with Hitler's perception of the Bolshevik danger:

> The German Bishops consider it their duty to support the head of the German Reich by all those means which the Church has at its disposal. Co-operation in repelling this threat is a religious task.[21]

In effect, the bishops were at one with Hitler in perceiving Jews as the chief engineers, carriers and exploiters of Bolshevism. Gröber characterised Bolshevism as 'an Asiatic state despotism, in point of fact in the service of a group of

---

[19] Godwin, Peter (2004), *Hitler and the Vatican: Inside the secret archives that reveal the new story of the Nazis and the Church*, New York, Free Press, 43–46.

[20] Cornwell, 267.

[21] Lewy, Guenter (2000), *The Catholic Church and Nazi Germany*, New York, De Capo Press, 219–10.

terrorists led by Jews'.[22]

The Bishop of Limburg, Antonius Hilfrich, was an opponent of the euthanasia program. He admitted the Jewishness of Jesus 'but the Christian religion has not grown out of the nature of this people'; rather, 'it has had to make its way against this people', those guilty of the murder of God.[23] Given these sentiments from senior clergymen, Lewy says it was no wonder that the lower-ranking churchmen felt free to express not just their contempt but their hatred of Jewry.

'*Kristallnacht*', the Goebbels-orchestrated pogrom of 9 November 1938, was in so many ways the trailer for the 'Final Solution'. The late rabbi and philosopher Emil Fackenheim always said that following the destruction of the Temple in 70 CE, this was the second-most climactic event in Jewish history to that point—because that action singled out Jews simply and merely *because they were*. Apart from Provost Bernhard Lichtenberg of St Hedwig's Cathedral in Berlin, this event was not commented upon by German Catholic churchmen (in sharp contrast to the condemnation by cardinals in France, Portugal and Belgium). Lichtenberg—the blessed and beatified Catholic, the man who had been imprisoned by the Gestapo for, among several things, asking his congregants at the end of his services to pray for the Jews—lamented: 'What took place yesterday, we know; what will be tomorrow, we do not know; but what happens today, that we have witnessed; outside this church the synagogue is burning, and that is also a house of God'.[24] He was taken to Dachau, and died en route, of causes unknown.

The church in parts of Germany rejected from service and

---

[22] Lewy, Guenter (1964), 'Pius XII, the Jews and the German Catholic Church', *Commentary*, 37, 2, 25.

[23] Lewy, 'Pius XII, the Jews ...', 24–25.

[24] Lewy, *The Catholic Church*, 84.

sacraments those ordered to wear yellow armbands. They were fellow Catholics but they were Jews. The church in Germany certainly protested against the euthanasia program and the Bishop of Münster, Clemens Galen, has rightly been honoured as an heroic figure for his opposition. But, like Gröber and von Faulhaber, he never protested against Jewish treatment.[25] That was left to the lone Lichtenberg.

By the end of 1942, the German episcopate was well informed of what was happening. Colonel Kurt Gerstein had joined the SS to 'take a look into Hitler's kitchen', to see for himself what was happening to Jews: after witnessing a gassing at Belzec death camp, he tried to inform the Papal Nuncio, Cesare Orsenigo. The Monsignor refused to see him. Monsignor Wilhelm Berning, Bishop of Osnabrück, and a strong Nazi sympathiser, wrote in his notes of 5 February 1942 that 'the plan for a total elimination of the Jews clearly exists'.[26] Monsignor Conrad Gröber, Archbishop of Freiberg, told the Pope on 14 June 1942 about the *Einsatzgruppen* massacres in Russia: 'The Nazi conception of the world is characterised by the most radical anti-Semitism, going as far as the annihilation [*Vernichtung*] of Jewry, not only in its spirit but also in its members.'[27]

The German bishops made no statements about the fate of Jews in Dachau or in other camps, but expressed concern solely at the possible intrusion into the indissolubility of Christian marriages. Archbishop-Cardinal Adolf Bertram,

---

[25] Griech-Polelle, Beth (2001), 'Image of the churchman–resister: Bishop von Galen, the euthanasia project and the sermons of the summer of 1941', *Journal of Contemporary History*, 36, 1, 41–57.

[26] Phayer, Michael (2000), *The Catholic Church and the Holocaust, 1930–1945*, Bloomington, Indiana, Indiana University Press, 68.

[27] Wistrich, Robert (2001), *Hitler and the Holocaust*, London, Weidenfeld & Nicolson, 136.

President of the German Bishops' Conference and the pre-eminent Catholic cleric, and others expressed concern about Jewish converts in the camps but not about Jews in general. (Three days before the war ended, the same Bertram said a Mass in fond memory of Hitler a week after his suicide.) In all their pleas and pleadings about the right to life and liberty, none of these men, including the 'heroic' figures of von Faulhaber and von Galen, could actually utter the word 'Jew'. Opposed to the euthanasia program to the extent that it least stopped, officially — though it continued secretly until *beyond* the last day of the war — they couldn't find it within their Christianness to oppose the Jewish programs. Unlike the Belgian, French and Dutch bishops, the German bishops never spoke out when Jews were being transported from their country.[28] These were the men who ordered denial of the sacraments to Catholics who engaged in duelling or who sought cremation rather than burial — but didn't deny such rites to men who killed Jews.

Two Popes and the Jews

On 14 March 1937, Achille Ratti, Pope Pius XI, wrote the first ever encyclical in German, 12 pages addressed to the German bishops. A week later it was read from every pulpit. He declared that 'whoever exalts race or nation or the State to the highest norm and worships them like idols perverts and distorts the divine order of things... True Christianity proves itself in the love of God and in the active love of one's neighbour.' He added that 'human laws which run counter to natural laws are not obligatory in conscience'.[29] The encyclical was entitled *Mit brennender Sorge,* with serious or burning concern.

In 1938 he asked the renowned American Jesuit writer on Black–White relations, John LaFarge, to help him pen another

---

28 Helmreich, 363.

29 Cornwell, 181–83.

encyclical, *Humani Generis Unitas,* a document which some historians, including Conor Cruise O'Brien, have suggested (wrongly perhaps, but quite seriously) may have averted the Holocaust. LaFarge was assisted by Gustav Gundlach, who earlier had written an encyclopaedia article defending a 'permissible anti-Semitism'. Ethnic and racist antisemitism was 'unchristian', he wrote, but he condoned 'anti-Jewishness' as a moral and legal means of com-bating 'dangerous influences of Jewish ethnicity in the ambit of economics, politics, press, theatre, cinema, science and the arts'.[30] Unlike *Mit brennender Sorge,* it mentioned Jews and antisemitism. At paragraph 132, he wrote: 'Even those who in time of war fought bravely for their country are treated as traitors, and the children of those who laid down their lives in their country's behalf are branded as outlaws by the very fact of their of their parentage... This flagrant denial of human rights sends many thousands of helpless persons out over the face of the earth without any resources. Wandering from frontier to frontier, they are a burden to humanity and to themselves'.[31]

Even so, there was no denunciation of Nazi policies and no condemnation of anti-Jewish programs. The draft, regrettably, was still very much in traditional Catholic mould. It repeated the theological casuistry about the historic curse on Jews for their rejection of Christ, and the right to continue with conversion goals. As to the circumstances in which Jews find themselves in various countries, this gives rise 'to very different problems in the practical order' and so the church 'leaves to the powers concerned the solution to these

---

[30] Cornwell, 189.

[31] Passelecq, Georges and Suchecky, Bernard (1997), *The Hidden Encyclical of Pius XI*, New York, Harcourt Brace and Company, 246–47.

problems' in the 'truly profane spheres'.[32] The 100-page draft didn't go any further or anywhere and it was left to 1965, to the most significant *Nostra Aetate* of the Second Vatican Council, to declare a total break with the centuries of contempt.[33]

When Pius XI died in February 1939, Bernard Joseph, on behalf of the executive of the Jewish Agency, wrote to the Patriarch in Jerusalem:[34]

In common with the whole civilised community, the Jewish people mourns the loss of one of the greatest exponents of the cause of international peace and goodwill... More than once did we have occasion to be deeply grateful for the attitude which he took up against the persecution of racial minorities and in particular for the deep concern which he expressed for the fate of the persecuted Jews of Central Europe. His noble efforts on their behalf will ensure for him for all time a warm place in the memories of Jewish people wherever they live.

These are not the words that Jews will ever come to use of his successor, Eugenio Pacelli, Pope Pius XII. Not only Jews but many Catholic thinkers despaired then, and now, of this man's failure to do certain things that were within his powers to do. He failed to promulgate an explicit and direct condemnation of the war of aggression, to speak out openly against the acts of violence against Jews and others under Nazi occupation. He had full knowledge of the facts from early on, and his sin, if I may use the term, was not to use the influence he had within him. He continued to remain silent

---

[32] Passelecq and Suchesky, 256–57.

[33] There are several key works on Vatican Council II: see Cassidy, Edward Idriss Cardinal (2005), *Ecumenism and Inter-Religious Dialogue: Unitatis Redintegratio, Nostra Aetate*, New Jersey, Paulist Press.

[34] Lapide, Pinchas (1967), *Three Popes and the Jews,* New York, Hawthorn Books, 116.

despite ceaseless appeals from his own adherents, from Jews and from governments, to speak out. On 6 March 1943, Bishop Konrad von Preysing asked the Pope to help save Jews, 'the many unfortunate innocents', still in Berlin and awaiting deportation. In April 1943, he wrote to Preysing saying he wouldn't speak out, advising caution 'to avoid the greater evil (*ad maiora mala vitanda*)'.[35] What could possibly have been a greater evil? He condoned the Vichy Government's 'Jewish Statutes'. The French bishops protested, but Léon Bérard, the Vichy Ambassador to the Holy See, reported to Marshal Petain that the Vatican did not consider such laws to be in conflict with Catholic teaching.[36]

The *razzia* against the Jews of Rome began early on Saturday morning, 16 October 1943: Jews were being deported from literally under the Vatican balcony. In his capacity as Bishop of Rome, Pius XII may have ordered nuns and priests to give them shelter and sanctuary, but Paul O'Shea and others[37] have established that there is no evidence, anywhere, of such a written or spoken order. (That he didn't *stop* such rescue efforts can hardly be used as evidence of his goodness, as a few faithful have asserted.) It was not uncommon for Catholics to use the Pope or his name as a moral justification for action and what is clear is that despite lack of public leadership from the Vatican, Italians (as Italians, not necessarily as Christians) rescued 7,000 Jews and hid

---

[35] Wistrich, 149–51.

[36] Phayer, 2000, 5.

[37] O'Shea, Paul (2008), *A Cross Too Heavy: Eugenio Pacelli: Politics and the Jews of Europe 1917–1943*, Sydney, Rosenberg Publishing, reprinted by Macmillan 2011; Phayer, Michael (2007), *Pius XII, the Holocaust and the Cold War*, Bloomington, Indiana University Press; Zucotti, Susan (2000), *Under his Very Windows: the Vatican and the Holocaust in history*, New Haven CT, Yale University Press.

them. One thousand Rome Jews went to Auschwitz and only 15 returned. In O'Shea's view, of all Pacelli's actions or inactions, his absent voice on the Jews of Rome was his most abject miscalculation, his worst misjudgement. Pius, according to Yehuda Bauer, raises a moral question: who is a saintly person? His answer: 'Pius rejected possible martyrdom at German hands for defending Jews. Probst Lichtenberg in Berlin died for that reason. Who should be proclaimed a saint — Lichtenberg or Pacelli?'[38]

There is a point to all of this: everyone should welcome the church's admissions, regrets, the church's remembering and the church's call for *Teshuvah*, repentance in charity of word and deed, something Cardinal Cassidy rightly described as going well beyond apology. But there is something else that is needed following the Cardinal's promise that this document is not the last Vatican word on the subject: that remembering has to be full memory, not partial memory, not selective memory, not just of the Jews but those millions of non-Jews persecuted and murdered by the Nazis, those whom Michael Berenbaum has called a 'mosaic of victims'.[39] There was, and is, the good, the bad, the ugly, and the *wanting*. We all need to look at all of these behaviours, face them, and come to terms with what they are.

The Protestants and the Jews

Looking at or into that landscape of death one understands the search for light and for some optimism. In 1953, Israel passed the Martyrs' and Heroes' Remembrance (Yad Vashem) Law, which enabled the official recognition of Righteous Gentiles, or the 'Righteous Among the Nations' — those who risked their lives, positions or property to save Jews, *for no*

---

[38] Bauer, Yehuda (2008), 'His silence spoke volumes', *The Tablet*, London, 4 October, 8–9.

[39] Berenbaum, Michael (1990), *Mosaic of Victims: Non-Jews persecuted and murdered by the Nazis*, New York, New York University Press.

reward. To have found and honoured just on 24,333 such people to date [1 January 2012] is to have uncovered a small nugget of altruism amid a universe of unalloyed evil. When we highlight Martin Niemöller, Dietrich Bonhoeffer, Helmut Gollwitzer, Elisabeth Schmitz, Marga Meusel, Hans Ehrenberg, Karl Immer and Julius von Jan, it makes us feel better about humanity. It may even offer a sense of redemption for those who feel guilt. But this predilection to always look on the bright side of things is a strange, even perverse, form of political synecdoche: looking at a part of something to represent the whole, usually with the intent of equating the whole with the part. These men and women were certainly a part of resistance to National Socialism but nowhere near representative of Protestant Germany. Wolfgang Gerlach, whose doctoral dissertation in 1970 began both the exhumation and autopsy of German Protestant anti-semitism, has a better perspective. The title of his book on the Confessing Church–the Protestant schismatic church that opposed the attempts to Nazify the church – and the persecution of the Jews is apt enough: *And the Witnesses Were Silent*.[40]

Scholder contends that the Protestant churches laid themselves 'open to völkisch antisemitism in the 1920s …under its spell even the churches did not see and hear what was going on before their very eyes, on their doorsteps and within their walls'.[41] His conclusion is fitting, except for the bizarre dates he attributes. That brand of popular antisemitism was alive and well centuries earlier. At times it was essentially racial antisemitism at work rather than simply traditional public sentiment, as shown in the letter written by

---

[40] Gerlach, Wolfgang (2000), *And the Witnesses Were Silent*, University of Nebraska Press.

[41] Scholder, vol 1, 270.

Lutheran Pastor Reichelmann to *Der Stürmer* in 1935: 'We stand enthusiastically behind your struggle against the Jewish death watch beetles which are undermining our nation...the murderers of Our Saviour'.[42] Or we can note the sentiments of Otto Dibelius, the church's superintendent, who sermonised 'that one cannot ignore the fact that Judaism is taking a leading role in all of the destructive manifestations of modern civilisation';[43] in the wake of violence and measures against Jews in 1933, he wrote, these actions 'will be for the best of the world'.[44]

In both Catholic and Protestant responses to this *tremendum* of the twentieth century there is a curious consistency: that Nazi antisemitism was quintessentially racial (and evil) and therefore quite separate from the traditional, völkisch, religious (and permissible) variety of that phenomenon. The late doyen of historians of antisemitism, Jacob Katz, encapsulated the essential relationship:[45]

The key to the understanding of what happened in the nineteenth and twentieth centuries in Jewish–Gentile relations, including its catastrophic climax in the Holocaust is not to be found in the immediate past, but in the course of Jewish history, at least since its entanglement with the history of Christianity.

---

[42] Conway, John (1968), *The Nazi Persecution of the Churches, 1933–45*, London, Weidenfeld & Nicolson, 377.

[43] Gerlach ,Wolfgang (1996), in Wollenberg, Jorg (ed), *The German Public and the Persecution of the Jews, 1933–1945*: 'No one participated, no one knew', New Jersey, Humanities Press, 68–71.

[44] Büttner, Ursula (2000), '"The Jewish problem becomes a Christian problem": German Protestants and the Jews in the Third Reich', in Bankier, David (ed), *Probing the Depth of German Antisemitism: German Society and the Persecution of Jews, 1933–1941*, New York, Berghahn Books, 438.

[45] Bacharach, 418.

After Napoleon's defeat, and at least until 1876, all birth, death and marriage records were in the hands of the German churches, kept in parish registers. These details became crucial for the Nazi identification of Jews. The supply of such information by the churches was doubtless given as a civic duty and as an act of loyalty — but with the knowledge that there would be serious consequences (of some kind) for the individuals named.[46]

We know much of the narrative history of the German Christians and the Confessing Church. In 1933, Hitler was opposed to the pluralism of the Protestants and so he attempted a unification of the 28 Evangelical churches (including Lutheran, Reformed and United) under one Reich Bishop. This was to be a counterpart to the concordat signed by Hitler and the Vatican in 1933. The scheme had popular support, with Nazism finding favour among the *Deutsche Christen* movement. That church group wanted to include in religion what had already been put in place elsewhere — the Aryan Paragraph. Just as Jews were excluded from organisations, federations, political parties and public life, so they were to be excluded from Christian teaching. There was, above all, to be a complete disassociation from the Old Testament (unlike some of the Catholic hierarchy who sought to preserve that document).

The Paragraph meant that Jewish converts were outside the church, and it was this exclusion, not to the treatment of Jews in general, that motivated the Pastors' Evangelical League to active opposition to National Socialism, at least in religious affairs. It focused around Martin Niemöller and centred on Karl Barth's celebrated essay 'Theological Existentialism Today'. The Aryan Paragraph was seen as a

---

[46] Barnett, Victoria (1988), *For the Soul of the People: Protestant protest against Hitler*, New York, Oxford University Press, 37–38.

violation of Christian teaching: evangelical churches wanted to spread the gospel, not be constrained from doing so.

The Confessing Church resisted in several ways, including hiding some 2,000 Jews. Pastor Heinrich Grüber established an office, a Büro, in Berlin to give advice and assistance not to Jews in general but to 'Christian Jews' during the brief period of forced expulsion under Eichmann's control — until he was arrested in December 1940.[47] His efforts were rarely admired or applauded by most of the Protestant churches.

Hitler lost patience with these men and women and allowed ideologues like Alfred Rosenberg and Martin Bormann to harass them. They did. Between 1937 and 1945, 18 pastors were confined to camps; Helene Jacobs was jailed and the man she served and revered, the Jewish-born jurist, Franz Kaufmann, who ran a group that hid Jews, was shot. Niemöller was confined in Sachsenhausen and Dachau and Bonhoeffer was executed at Flossenbürg in April 1945.

In 1935, a deaconess of the Berlin church, Marga Meusel, objected to the Confessing Church's timidity. She wanted to know why the church was concerned only for itself and for its Jewish converts rather for those who were suffering most. In 1938, one Protestant voice (among the very few) was heard about 'Kristallnacht' — that of Julius von Jan, a Protestant minister in the town of Württemberg, who asked: 'who would have thought that one single crime in Paris [the Polish–Jewish youth Herschel Grynszpan shooting German diplomat Ernst vom Rath] would have resulted in so many crimes being committed in Germany?'[48]

It wasn't merely a matter of timidity but rather of silence. There were no voices about the Nuremberg Laws of 1935 that

---

[47] Conway, 223.

[48] Hockenos, Matthew (2004), *A Church Divided: German Protestants confront the Nazi past*, Bloomington, Indiana University Press, 35.

'uncitizened' the Jews of Germany. There was but von Jan's reflection on the night of 9 November 1938. There was nothing to be heard about the Judeocide as such. There was only a secret memorandum to Hitler in 1936 protesting at the campaign against the Jews, the camps and the pervasiveness of the Gestapo.[49] On 19 October 1945, the Council of the Evangelical Church admitted to the moral failure of their Christianity. The Stuttgart Declaration (or Confession) of Guilt said, in part: 'For long years we have fought in the name of Jesus Christ against the spirit that found its terrible expression in the National Socialist rule of violence; yet we accuse ourselves for not speaking out more courageously, praying more faithfully, believing more gladly, and loving more ardently'. The word 'Jew' did not appear. The word 'more' suggests that the churches did do things but could have said and done 'more'. The significant Darmstadt declaration of 1947 called for the churches to reconsider and improve their attitudes towards and beliefs in the political structures that led to Germany's disaster, but many branches refused to sign it.[50] In 1950, the synod of the Evangelical Church in Germany resolved, *inter alia*, that 'We ask all Christians to disassociate themselves from all anti-Semitism and earnestly resist it whenever it stirs again, and to encounter Jews and Jewish Christians in a brotherly spirit...'.[51]

Bonhoeffer and the Jews

This essay began as a presentation to the fourth annual Bonhoeffer Conference organised by Father Stephen Moore at

---

[49] Wistrich, 133.

[50] Fahlbusch, Erwin et al, (ed) (1999), *The Encyclopedia of Christianity*, Grand Rapids MI, Eerdmans-Brill, 775.

[51] Hockenos (2004).

Kincumber, north of Sydney, in November 2008.[52] A Christian–Jewish group met to reflect on the discipleship and legacy of Bonhoeffer, using as its title the phrase coined by biographer Stephen Haynes to assess the Bonhoeffer legacy – 'A Cautious Embrace'. Historian John Moses insisted that Bonhoeffer be recognised as 'a reluctant revolutionary', a man who had the courage to shift from Lutheran notions of Christian supercessionism to seeing church and synagogue in a reciprocal relationship, a man who was moved from passivity to strong activism against Nazi tyranny.[53] Rachel Kohn posed significant hypothetical questions about how the theologian would have or may have reacted to today's jihadist terrorism.[54] Christine Winter reminded us of the Lutheran context, pointing out that the two noted Lutheran leaders of Bayern and Württemberg, Hans Meiser and Theophil Wurm, in writing their memoirs after the war, could not bring themselves to mention Jews, even in passing.[55] (In 1926, Meiser, who was to become Bishop of Bavaria from 1933 to 1955, wrote that the 'Jewish intellect' was 'excessive and even lascivious' and was 'destroying the moral fundaments of our people'.[56] In 1938, Wurm accepted the need for the race laws but in 1943 he wrote of his distress at the fate of Jews in mixed marriages and interference 'in the sanctity of marriage'.[57])

---

[52] 'A Cautious Embrace': a Christian–Jewish conference reflecting on the discipleship and legacy of Dietrich Bonhoeffer, St Joseph's Spirituality and Education Centre, Kincumber, NSW, 28–29 November 2008.

[53] Moses, John, 'Dietrich Bonhoeffer's stand on the Jewish Question during the Third Reich', Kincumber, NSW, 28–29 November 2008.

[54] Kohn, Rachel, 'Would Bonhoeffer fight terrorism?', Kincumber, NSW, 28–29 November 2008.

[55] Winter, Christine, 'Bonhoeffer and the Jews – a Lutheran context', Kincumber, 28–29 November 2008.

[56] Büttner, 436.

[57] Conway, 264–65.

Debate at the conference was sometimes heated, always considered and ended, politely, with a consensus about caution.

There can be no doubt that Bonhoeffer would have signed the *Stuttgarter Schulderklärung* and supported the 1950 resolution. Stephen Haynes has provided an insightful analysis of the contradictions and inconsistencies in Bonhoeffer as a 'bystander, resister, victim'. And, he added, as a rescuer.[58] Bonhoeffer criticised his church for what he considered its purely churchly opposition to the dictatorship; he considered Hitler the 'AntiChrist'; he was forbidden to teach, preach and publish; he was an anti-Nazi counterspy; he helped 14 Jews (11 of them Christian converts) escape to Switzerland. But when he wrote his essay on 'The Church and the Jewish Question', he always used the highly-charged term *Judenfrage*. Most people reading that in the 1930s would have understood the text: the alien Jew who posed a problem, usually a threat, to Germany. His lifelong conviction was that the 'Jewish Question' would be solved by their conversion. John Moses has written about his 'deep-seated anti-Judaistic theology'.[59] But there was no voice from him on the euthanasia issue, or on the Laws of 1935, or on the extermination of Jews. Of the November 1938 pogrom, he did comment that 'if today the synagogues burn, tomorrow the churches, too, will be set alight'.[60] For the Kincumber

---

[58] Haynes, Stephen (2003), 'Bystander, Resister, Victim: Dietrich Bonhoeffer's Response to Nazism', in Dieter, Donald (ed), *Christian Responses to the Holocaust: Moral and ethical issues*, New York, Syracuse University Press, 99–118.

[59] Moses, John (2006), 'Dietrich Bonhoeffer's Struggle for Christian–Jewish Reconciliation', The Council of Christians and Jews, Victoria, *Gesher Journal*, item 425.

[60] Raum, Elizabeth (2003), *Dietrich Bonhoeffer: Called by God*, New

conference, I read his *Letters and Papers from Prison*.[61] While this may well be but a fragment of his writings, and not 'representative', the word 'Jews' appears only twice in 371 pages, and then only *en passant*. In sum, while Bonhoeffer may have moved quickly along a spectrum that culminated in his anti-Hitler activities, he was, to the end, a product of a long-held and deep-seated Lutheran tradition which saw Jews as a quite separate people, which demonised them and saw their conversion as their only salvation.

In all such discussion, one has to recall the writings of the profound French historian, Jules Isaac. In his influential *The Teaching of Contempt*, he began the book with a quotation from his friend Pope John XXIII: 'It is a fundamental rule of life never to distort the truth.' The opening chapter has a short headnote: 'All authorities are agreed that a true Christian cannot be an anti-Semite.'[62] However terse, these aphorisms are really not that difficult to understand. There is another from Alexander Donat, a survivor of the Warsaw Ghetto: 'A Christian who witnesses inactively a crime becomes its accomplice.'[63]

The Jews and the Jews

The *Centralverein Deutscher Staatsbürger jüdischen Glaubens* (The Central Organisation for German Citizens of the Jewish Faith) began life in 1893. This body, known as CV, spent decades fighting attacks, calumnies and libels on Jews. Most often it could only resort to Paragraph 130 of the Criminal Code, on incitement to racial violence, and then, in despair at

---

York, Continuum International Publishing Group, 109.

[61] Bonhoeffer, Dietrich (1971 edn), *Letters and Papers from Prison*, (ed) Bethge, Eberhard, London, The Folio Society.

[62] Isaac, 20–21.

[63] Donat, Alexander (1968), 'Jewish Resistance' in *Out of the Whirlwind: A reader in Holocaust literature*, New York, Doubleday & Company, 53.

courts ever finding for the Jews, turned to paragraph 166 on crimes against religion. The CV had much to worry about: the closing of German borders to Jewish immigrants in 1906; the increasingly popular writings of such vigorous antisemites as Eugen Dühring, Heinrich von Treitschke, Arthur de Gobineau and Houston Stewart Chamberlain; the rise of well over 100 institutes for the study of *rassenhygiene*; the hysteria and Jew-hating crudities of Julius Streicher; court biases against Jewish plaintiffs or criminals; the German Youth Movement (*Wandervögel*) and its many branches that banned Jews; Jews having to form their own university fraternities and *Turner-schaften*; the constant attacks on Jewish music, Jewish physics, Jewish everything. Yet by March 1933, the CV issued a statement condemning reports of Nazi atrocities against Jews as 'pure invention'. Antisemitism, it said, existed and was of grave concern, 'but it was a domestic affair'.[64]

Nearly a year later, in May 1934, Rabbi Leo Baeck met Clarence Pickett, a prominent American Quaker who was visiting Germany to see what could be done for the Jews. Since before Christ, Baeck told him, Jews had been part of Germany and the Worms synagogue had recently celebrated its 900 years of continuous existence. 'The Jews love Germany and they want to stay there'. It was a good time to be a rabbi, he said: his congregation used to number 50 or 60 but now he had to run four services every Saturday.[65]

By September 1935, the newly formed *Reichsvertretung der Juden in Deutschland* (the National Representation of Jews in Germany) declared that the Nuremberg Laws 'have come as the severest of blows for the Jews in Germany'. But 'they must create a basis on which a tolerable relationship becomes

---

[64] *New York Times*, 25 March 1933.

[65] Baker, Nicholson (2008), *Human Smoke: The beginnings of World War II, the end of civilization*, New York, Simon and Shuster, 49–50.

possible between the German and the Jewish people'.[66] In effect, they were saying that if *that* was all they had to live with, they could cope with *that*.

This is precisely what the Jewish historian and philosopher Gershom Scholem always railed against: this one-sided, unrequited love affair between Germans and Jews. In his well known essay on the myth of German–Jewish dialogue, Scholem excoriated these particular Jews for their delusions and their self-deception. They may have had a passionate love for their *Vaterland* but the *Vaterland* had never had such feelings for them. It took two to make a dialogue and the Jews, he said, 'spoke only to themselves'. For 200 years, Scholem wrote, Jews could have heard the clumping of antisemitic boots behind them;[67] Helmreich described that phenomenon as the 'cannonball of anti-Semitism [that] had started rolling down the hill many years in the past'.[68] They didn't want to see or hear.

In 1932, an esteemed American writer, Edgar Mowrer, visited Germany. After dinner with a Jewish banker who had donated money to the Nazi Party, Mowrer wondered aloud 'how the People of Israel have managed to survive so many thousands of years when they obviously have a strong suicidal urge'. The banker scoffed at Hitler's rhetoric: 'just talk', he said.[69]

Am I blaming Jews for their demise? Assuredly not. But it must have been clear to many, as it was to people like Scholem and political scientist Guenter Lewy, that German Jews had surrendered part of their souls, part of their

---

[66] *Documents on the Holocaust* (1981), Jerusalem, Yad Vashem, 84.

[67] From Cynthia Ozick's essay on Scholem, 'The Heretic', *New Yorker Magazine*, 2 September 2002.

[68] Helmreich, 364.

[69] Baker, 33.

historical experience about tenure and tolerance in foreign lands, in order to devote themselves to Germanness; and in order to do that, they even dedicated themselves to disassociating themselves totally from the allegedly coarse, loud, uncouth, Yiddish-speaking *Ostjuden*, the East Europeans Jews from neighbouring Poland.[70] But they failed to see that they had never been, nor ever would be, part of 'us Germans'. This may seem a harsh conclusion, but Scholem was hardly alone in expressing it. Ursula Büttner contends that 'for the majority of German Protestants, Jews were and always would be strangers no matter how assimilated they were'; this aversion, she concludes, extended to 'Jewish Christians', people who not only once adhered to a foreign religion but who still 'belonged to a foreign people'.[71]

Some colleagues who have heard me talk on this topic ask whether I am treading the path of Daniel Goldhagen,[72] asserting that Germany was and is somehow 'genetically' incapable of embracing cultural diversity and was always a repository or reservoir of an 'eliminationist antisemitism'. No, is the answer, but I do subscribe to the view that German Jews had an unrequited love affair with Germanness. In the late eighteenth century the philosopher Moses Mendelssohn, the father of the Jewish Enlightenment, always wanted to play chess with Gotthold Lessing, the doyen of German *kultur*. Observers of friendships such as this one would comment: what kind of a faith is it that will surrender itself in order to belong where patently they can never belong?

---

[70] Aschheim, Steven (1982), *Brothers and Strangers: The East European Jew and the German Jewish consciousness, 1800–1923*, Madison, University of Wisconsin Press.

[71] Büttner, 457–58.

[72] Goldhagen, Daniel (1996), *Hitler's Willing Executioners: Ordinary Germans and the Holocaust*, New York, Alfred E Knopf.

Seeking Explanations

Motives and causal connections in history are always retrospective and, inevitably, they are often reflective, if not speculative. But they do need serious consideration.

First, while it is clear that there were fractures, fractions and frictions within all Christian churches — on doctrine, on *Gleichshaltung* or the 'synchronisation' ordered by Hitler, on euthanasia — was their general attitude to the Nazi state one of support or mere acquiescence? The question can be asked another way: was church silence, indifference or hostile indifference towards Jews a norm to which most people conformed? Christopher Browning, among a number of Holocaust scholars, has looked hard for the 'transmission belts' that drove the Nazis and their 'sacred mission'. Fear, coercion, obedience and dehumanisation have been analysed in many texts (including this volume). Browning has found an answer, perhaps *the* answer, in his research on the 500 men in Reserve Police Battalion 101 from Hamburg and later transferred to the Lublin district of Poland.[73] When their commandant, Major Wilhelm Trapp, offered them the chance of not participating in the rounding up and shooting of women and children from the town of Jozefow in July 1942, fewer than 15 stepped forward and opted for 'other duties'. These reservists were not Nazis and not specially trained; these family-men, the *Ordinary Men* of the book title, were unfit for military service, even for the real police. After initial despair, trauma and breakdown after the first day's 'work', this group became the most proficient killers of Jews in Poland. What kept some 485 united initially, Browning concluded, was male conformity.

Second, the answer may lie in tradition which, in a sense,

---

[73] Browning, Christopher (1992), *Ordinary Men: Reserve Police Battalion 101 and the Final Solution in Poland*, New York, HarperCollins.

is really a chronicle of conformity to lore, customs, norms, values and beliefs. Churchmen of all denominations have grown up with an ingrained and indelible feature of Western intellectual history, namely, antisemitism, one facet of which is that the Jews are now *Israel carnalis* (in the flesh) and no longer *Israel verus* (the true religion). Sixteen centuries of this is, indeed, weighty tradition — and heavy conformity.

Third, there is a realisation that in many circumstances the forces of nationalism and ethnic fire transcend religious adherence and religious duties of care. Many, if not most, German Catholics were clearly Germans first and foremost. Certainly the 'brown priests' of Germany were suffused by fatherland fervour. Father Dr Phillipp Haeuser was not alone in his pursuit of Nazi ideals and, as we have seen, the more elevated and reputable bishops saw the promises and premises of National Socialism as the greater attraction. Some of the 'brown priests', Spicer wrote, had less noble motives, such as disaffection with clergydom, conflict with their superiors, and plain, naked ambition.

Fourth, could an explanation lie in the fact that these churchmen simply didn't know any better, or any more than they cared to know? There is a crucial question here and in all discussions about the role of Christianity in times of gross human violence: *what knowledge would it have taken to deflect them from their paths of support or acquiescence?* Had they had the chance to look into a viewing instrument that showed them scenes from the Implementation of the Law for the Restoration of the Professional Public Service in 1933, from the Nuremberg Laws on Reich Citizenship in 1935, from 'Kristallnacht' in 1938, the first mobile gas vans in operation at Chelmno in December 1941, or of the *Einsatzgruppen* at their 'work' in 1941 and 1942, would those images have deflected them? Now we look at the body bags and human wreckage of Vietnam, Iraq and Afghanistan and ask ourselves how we could possibly have gotten *there*. Could they not have seen

'*Kristallnacht*' as the curtain-raiser, especially after Göring had said that he would not like to have been a Jew in Germany at that time? We, the populaces, were lied to, and continue to be lied to, about many things, but the real question is what the liars knew. Did *they* know enough to suggest that they shouldn't go *there*? In a strange truth, Göring didn't lie: in 1936 he said that Germany would deal with the 'Jewish Question' *so oder so*, one way or another. These clergymen may not have known about the death camps until later in 1943, but they knew enough—enough for us to sit at the thousands of conferences, seminars and university courses since those events and be incredulous that men could make the choices and decisions that they did make in the face of what they knew.

A fifth explanation comes to mind: enough indifference, lack of feeling or passion, to demur, desist or oppose. Herein, perhaps, lies the vexed matter of worthiness, or the absence thereof. Jews, after all, not only killed Christ but they rejected his messianic descent and purpose, they desecrated the host, they allegedly killed Christian children to make *matzot* at Passover time, they were the peasant peoples' worst nightmare, the pawnbrokers and the tax collectors, they caused and spread the Black Plague, they were the urban-dwellers who seemingly turned their backs on *völkisch* blood and soil and forests, who modernised the world and who tried to make rational the celebrated cults of irrationalism, who foreswore the sacred pig so precious in German romanticism, *und so weiter*. Who, indeed, could feel *for* such people? The hostile part of it is so much clearer cut.

Finally, the matter of *want* and *not want*. In political science, social science generally, in history and philosophy, we always look for explanations in ideology, in administrative and organisational behaviour, in social physics, in procedure and mechanics, in psychological states of mind, in individual or group behaviour and, all too often, in what we call 'grand theory'. There are times when the explanations are so simple that we can't bring ourselves to believe that something so plain, so unadorned, can answer the big questions.

Much has been written about the charade that was the Evian Conference in 1938, the meeting called to deal with the crisis of German Jewry. Of the nations present, 31 offered some or other technical explanation for not taking any emigrants.[74] Australia's delegate, Lieutenant-Colonel T W White, said 'it will no doubt be appreciated also that as we have no real racial problems, we are not desirous of importing one...'[75] Only one nation, the little Dominican Republic, said it *wanted* 100,000 Jews. Wanted is perhaps misleading: what General Rafael Trujillo wanted was salvation for his sullied reputation, but in the end he took 500. Not enough has been written about the attitudes of Churchill and Roosevelt towards Jews in crisis, about their not wanting to take in a clearly imperilled people. Reams have been written about the bombing of the railway lines to Auschwitz, about the British who said they couldn't do it technically so it had to be the Americans and the Americans who couldn't do it because of this, that and the other. Martin Gilbert has analysed the many rationalisations in his *Auschwitz and the Allies* and his documentary film of that title. In the end, the answer is simple: those at the helms of the Allies *didn't want to*. More reams have been written about Pius XII and his inaction, or at least his overt inaction. Paul O'Shea has traversed all the arguments in his recent book on Eugenio Pacelli. Why was this shy and cloistered man, this complex and convoluted

---

[74] All delegates expressed sympathy for German Jewry. Golda Meir was an observer from Palestine. She said later that if all that Evian could produce was sympathy of this kind, she never wanted to hear that word for, or about, Jews ever again.

[75] Bartrop, Paul, (ed) (1995), *False Havens: The British Empire and the Holocaust,* Lanham, Maryland, University Press of America, 64–65.

man, in so many ways a good man, so voluble on the Church and so silent on the Jews? Why, when he had the chance and even when the Nazis were in some fear of what he would say in his Christmas 1942 broadcast, did he agree to mention atrocities in general but no atrocity against Jews and against Poles? The answers are complex at one level, to do with Pius' saturation in the Catholic tradition of supercessionism, of the Jews as always 'the lesser victims', where, in historian Saul Friedländer's language, 'whatever the motivations of the passivity...it always resulted from a choice in which the Jew was always less than whatever other consideration he was weighed against'.[76] At another level, the key level, the answer was simple — because he didn't want to. He wanted to confront the satanic Communist menace and he did so with vigour; he didn't want to confront the National Socialists, even though he saw them as thugs and so, quite simply, he didn't.

We need to pause for a good while to consider Friedländer's diagnosis: apart from some 24,000 Righteous Among the Nations, and less than a handful of righteous nations, the Jews were always *less than* anything else they were weighed against, always *less worthy*. For a people always considered *more than*, more manipulative, more controlling, more intellectual, more lascivious, more baleful, more destructive, their modern history has been that of a *minorité fatale*, always *less than*.

In conclusion, we need to spend more time — as scholars, as students, as people with religious beliefs or at least, with an interest in the role of religion — examining and debating omission rather than commission, not wanting, not doing. Jews particularly seek to detect and to combat *overt* antisemitism. They waste endless hours, efforts and nervous

---

[76] Freidländer, Saul (1976), 'Some aspects of the historical significance of the Holocaust', the *Jerusalem Quarterly*, 1, Fall, 36–59.

energy running down offbeat talkback radio comments, ambiguous or unflattering crossword puzzle clues, perceived or real enough pro-Arab biases in the media. Anti-Defamation League commissions conduct surveys on overt antisemitism across the continents, on Palestine Authority school syllabus materials, and write texts on ways to counteract the Iranian threats to Israel and to Jews generally. They, and other such anti-racism bodies, spend almost no time on 'omissionary' antisemitism, the kind that makes Jews 'lesser victims' or unworthy victims — or the kind that doesn't consider them at all.

THE VATICAN, THE HOLOCAUST, AND THE ARCHIVES

PAUL O'SHEA

Towards the end of his long pontificate, John Paul II gave several directives to the Archivists of the *Archivo Secreto Vaticano* (*ASV*) — the 'Secret Archives'. The first instruction was to finalise the cataloguing of the German files from the papacy of Pius XI (1922–1939) and have them ready for public inspection by 2003. The second instruction was similar. Once the files for Germany 1922–1939 were completed, the files for Germany and the Holy See during the war years under Pius XII were to be prepared for eventual inspection. On 15 February 2003 the ASV opened its doors to scholars who were then able to study the files from the period 1922–1939. At the beginning of 2012, it is still unclear as to when the war files will be ready, but Bishop Sergio Pagano, Prefect of the Archives since 1997, believes the files will not be available until at least 2014. He cites the sheer scale of documentation to be sorted and classified as the reason for the delay. Pagano was quick to add that there is no conspiracy involved — it is the simple fact that it takes a great deal of time for a staff of fewer than 30, of whom about 15 are trained archivists, to make their way through several million pages of documentation.[1] Offers from various groups, such as the Anti-Defamation League in New York, to underwrite the cost of hiring Vatican approved staff to help in the cataloguing process, have been politely and firmly declined. The Vatican also holds to the principle of releasing all the files for a papacy at one time. Since Pius XII was pope from 1939 to 1958, much of the material to be sorted is post-war and more than likely

---

[1] By comparison, the National Archives and Record Administration, the National Archive of the USA, employs some 3,000 archivists and specialists.

outside the particular interest of Holocaust historians.

If this were the only archival source that could help explore the history of the Holocaust and the role of the Catholic Church during those years, historians and students would have justifiable claim to be suspicious and possibly be excused for indulging in conspiracy theories. It is one of the simple facts that the layers of myth surrounding the *ASV* have obscured some important historical realities for many historians over the last half century. This essay explores one particular aspect of this problem.

Archives and Archives

It may seem trite to open with the assertion that many people, including more than a few scholars, are blithely unaware of the complexities surrounding the Vatican archives, but continued poor history-writing from several sources make it necessary. The most recent (in)famous use of the *ASV* was undertaken by John Cornwall during the research and writing of his 1999 book *Hitler's Pope*. Cornwall claimed in his introduction that he had access to the *ASV*, and uncovered long-buried documents that caused him to rethink his previously positive assessment of Eugenio Pacelli. To the unobservant reader, this claim sounds impressive. But it is a matter of public record that at the time of his 'discoveries', he could only have had access to files up to 1922 — long before Hitler came to the attention of the then Nuncio to Germany or to Pacelli's masters in Rome. Careful wording lends Cornwall's writing an air of professional historiography that is unjustified.[2]

---

[2] See Gumpel, Peter (1999), 'Cornwell's Cheap Shot At Pius XII' in *Crisis*, December, 19–25. There have been literally hundreds of articles written on Cornwall and his methodology. In 2009, Cornwall admitted that his 1999 book lacked some historical rigour.

At the same time, it is important to recognise the work of scholars who have made extensive use of the *ASV* material since these files were made available in 2003. Using the 1922–1939 Germany files, books, articles and essays have been written that have helped shape and nuance our understanding of the Church's varied positions, internal debates, announcements and discussions surrounding the waxing and waning of the Weimar Republic, the National Socialist ascendency and finally, the first six years of the Third Reich.[3] The sheer volume of material is enough to ensure scholars will be analysing the Catholic Church and its responses and reactions to pre-war Nazi Germany for many years. Perhaps the most significant discovery has been the layers of complex and intricate details found in the files that show the Holy See slowly feeling its way, cautiously and with major reservations, trying to find a way to live and work with the new German government; the path was, as Cardinal Pacelli remarked in 1934, 'crazy'.[4]

The work undertaken by historians has been made easier through digital technology. In 2010, *ASV* joined with German scholars, Thomas Brechenmacher and Hubert Wolf, in projects to make available the files of the Munich–Berlin Nunciature 1917–1929, and the files of the Berlin Nunciature 1933–1939. All the material is freely available with substantial

---

[3] Among the growing number include Besier, Gerhard (2007), *The Holy See and Hitler's Germany*; Fattorini, Emma (2011), *Hitler, Mussolini and the Vatican*; Godman, Peter (2004), *Hitler and the Vatican*; Sale, Giovanni (2004), *Hitler, la Santa Sede e gli Ebrei*; Wolf, Hubert (2010), *Pope and Devil*; and my own work, O'Shea (2011) *A Cross Too Heavy*. It is also important to acknowledge the important work of Emma Fattorini's earlier work (1992), *Germania e Santa Sede: Le nunziatura di Pacelli fra la Grande Guerra e la Repubblica di Weimar*, which was one of the first to make use of material from the files up to 1922.

[4] Paul O'Shea (2011), 153.

contextual historical details.[5] *ASV* provides digital copies of files upon request, making research work for students outside Rome accessible and affordable.

There are dozens of archival holdings in the Vatican State and around the city of Rome. The *ASV* is simply the most well known. Each of the nine Vatican departments, or to use the technical term, 'congregations', has its own archive. The Congregation for the Doctrine of the Faith (CDF), or as it was better known before 1965, the Holy Office or Inquisition, housed in the Palazzo del Sant'Uffizio, has been gradually opening its archives for scholarly research since 1996. In January 1998, all material up to 1903, the death of Pope Leo XIII, the first pope to open the *ASV* to historians, was made readily available. Among the files were included the stories of some of the Vatican's less flattering moments—such as the trial documents of Galileo and the documents surrounding the Edgardo Mortara affair of the 1850s.[6]

To the unwary researcher and the equally unwary reader, the possibility of operating in ignorance of what is available remains a problem. Other archival sources that are related to the Vatican are found in places such as the *Archivio di Stato di Roma* on Corso del Rinascimento which holds records for the City of Rome from 1871, including the German occupation and the roundup of the Roman Jews in October 1943. It is one of the basic tools of the historians' trade to know not only what questions to ask of the issue being investigated, but to

---

[5] See http://www.pacelli-edition.de/ and http://www.dhi-roma.it/orsenigo.html

[6] Edgardo was born and raised Jewish until the age of 6 when he was taken away by papal authorities on the grounds that a domestic servant had baptised him in an 'emergency'. See http://www.historians.org/perspectives/issues/1999/9905/9905ar c1.cfm accessed 19.01.2009.

know where and how to find resources and to be imaginative in seeking them.

For students of the Holocaust and the role the Catholic Church during the war years, there is an abundance of material readily available. Much of it has not been used well. One of the most important sources is the set of 11 volumes published by the Vatican.[7]

Actes et Documents

In the storm of anti-Pius criticism that arose after the 1963 opening of Rolf Hochhuth's play, *The Deputy*, Pope Paul VI took the extraordinary measure of commissioning four professional historians, all Jesuits, to sort and sift their way through the files of the Secretariat of State of Pius XII between 1939 and 1945. Their brief was to collate a selection of documents representative of the whole collection that would give as detailed a picture as possible of the work of the Pope and his closest collaborators, One of whom was Paul VI himself. Throughout the war years he worked in the Secretariat alongside the Secretary of State, Cardinal Luigi Maglione. Giovanni Batista Montini, the future Pope Paul, was privy to much of the confidential material that made its way to and from the Pope's desk. He was one of the last surviving eye-witnesses to the internal workings of the Vatican during the war years.

The four Jesuit historians — Pierre Blet (1918–2009, France), Angelo Martini (1913–1981, Italy), Burkhart Schneider (1917–1976, Germany), and Robert Graham (1912–1997, United States) — began their work in 1964 and published their findings as they completed each major historical and logical section. All were professional historians with significant published works in church history. It would be

---

[7] In 2010, ADSS was scanned and made available online. See http://www.vatican.va/archive/actes/index_en.htm

unprofessional to assert that there was a conspiracy operating among the four men as they selected documents for publication to 'whitewash' Pius and his war record. A cursory glance at the range of documents makes it all but impossible to accuse them of anything other than compiling a comprehensive portrait of the Vatican leadership trying to cope with the often horrific news streaming in from across Europe. When one looks at the documentation describing the plight of European Jewry, the picture assumes an even more desperate and dreadful visage.

Structure of ADSS

The Vatican Secretariat of State was not the equivalent of a foreign affairs ministry, but more akin to a combination of foreign affairs, prime minister and papal secretary. The Secretariat sent and received letters, telegrams, telephone calls, press clippings, summary tables, detailed reports, confidential personal files and notes concerning the internal life of the Church—for example, in matters of Canon Law, selection of bishops, requests for faculties (authority for bishops and heads of religious orders for the good-ordering of their dioceses, monasteries, and so on), as well as the religious life of the Church in areas like Catholic Action, the operation of charitable works, the Catholic press, schools and hospitals. The documents in ADSS reflect this.

1. The archives of the Secretary of State contain:

(a) messages and speeches of the Pope;

(b) letters exchanged between the Pope and religious and secular leaders;

(c) notes of the Secretary of State, private notes and memoranda;

(d) correspondence between the Secretary of State and nuncios, apostolic delegates and apostolic administrators;

(e) correspondence between the Secretary of State and ambassadors and ministers accredited to the Holy See.

2. ADSS has published the selected texts in the following manner:

(a) The official addresses, speeches etc of Pius XII have been published in the *Acta Apostolicae Sedis* (1939–1958) or in the collection of the Pope's speeches published after his death.[8] What is contained in ADSS are extracts relevant to a particular issue.

(b) ADSS has published some, but not many, of Pius' letters to religious and secular leaders.

(c) Memoranda of the Secretariat were composed after audiences with the Pope, meetings with ambassadors or a reflection on matters that may have required further action. These were written or typed by the Cardinal Secretary of State (up to 1944, Cardinal Luigi Maglione 1877–1944), Secretary of the Congregation of Extraordinary Ecclesiastical Affairs, Domenico Tardini, (1888–1961), the Substitute of the Secretariat of State, Giovanni Batista Montini (1897–1978).

3. The correspondence exchanged with the Holy See and its representative contains:

(a) original reports sent by nuncios et alii to the Secretariat;

(b) telegrams sent from nuncios etc to Cardinal Secretary of State and others by the department of telegrams and ciphers;

(c) drafts prepared for the nuncios;

(d) drafts of telegrams to be encoded.

ADSS has published the documents in chronological order,

---

[8] AAS, or *Acta*, as it is commonly referred to, is available online via the Vatican website. See
http://www.vatican.va/archive/aas/index_en.htm

which gives an accurate impression of the flow of information into and out of the Vatican. Each document is listed with its archive number and original form (handwritten or typed). Internal cross-referencing follows in the footnotes. The editors did not print documents available in other published collections but referred readers to the appropriate sources.

The vast majority of the documents are short reports, some as brief as one line. There are occasional detailed reports, but these are the exception. During war time, letter writing was more and more a luxury that was not indulged. Increasingly, the Vatican relied on sharp and concise communication. Lengthy reports were still sent and provide valuable information, but the time it took to reach Rome increased as the war went on, and could take as long as months when sent from Eastern Europe. This needs to be kept in mind when looking at Holocaust chronology and attempting to explain why a response sometimes took so long.

There are lacunae. Notable missing documents include most of the letters from Bishop Konrad Preysing of Berlin to Pius XII in 1943 and 1944, almost any reference to the 'brown bishop', Austrian Alois Hudal, the Riegner Report (which is mentioned but not published),[9] the Auschwitz Protocols and virtually everything appertaining to Eastern Europe except for Poland and the Baltic States. Interestingly, there are few major details missing from reports concerning the killing of the Jews. It would appear that as news of the killing process became more widely known, and a sense of moral outrage on the part of some Vatican diplomats grew, especially those in Slovakia, Croatia and Hungary, the customary cautious language was replaced by something far blunter. It could also point to a sense of frustration at what could have been

---

[9] ADSS, 8.314, 19.03.1942, Nuncio Filippo Bernardino to Cardinal Cardinal Maglione.

perceived as the Vatican's delay in responding.

The 11 volumes were published between 1965 and 1981. They include over 5,000 documents in original languages, (mostly Italian, the working language of the Vatican), many with footnotes and references to other published sources. A sentence synopsis of the text in French heads every document. Each volume has an introductory essay, also written in French, giving the main themes of the particular focus for that collection of documents as well as placing the documents within the broader context of the war. At the end of the first volume there are comprehensive appendices of the nuncios, internuncios and apostolic delegates who acted as the diplomatic representatives of the Pope across the world, giving a wealth of information on who was where and when. There is a detailed appendix of the diplomatic corps accredited to the Holy See, including the changes in personnel caused by the unpredictable nature of the war. In effect, the reader is given a considerable amount of help from the editors in order to better understand the documents.

Volumes 1, 4, 5, 7 and 11 contain documents about the Vatican and the prosecution of the war in Europe and later, the global conflict. Volumes 6, 8, 9 and 10 are devoted to the work of the Holy See and the victims of the war, including the Jews of Europe. Volume 2 contains a selection of the letters of Pius XII to the bishops of Germany. Some of the letters of the German bishops to Pius are found throughout the other volumes or in independent references. Volume 3 is divided into two parts that deal with the Vatican, Poland and the Baltic States—'the East'. There is a detailed index (in French) at the end of each volume.

Within each volume there is evidence of considerable effort made to ensure a high level of continuity between the documents. One example from Volume 1 demonstrates this. In the final days before the German invasion of Poland on 1 September 1939, the Vatican was engaged in a major diplomatic effort to avoid war and bring Germany and

Poland to the negotiating table. Cardinal Luigi Maglione, the Secretary of State, was in regular telegraphic, telephone and cable communication with the nuncios in Nand Warsaw as well as the other capitals of Europe listening and suggesting strategies to avoid a war. Throughout the documents there is a high level of *Realpolitik* about Hitler, the value of his promises and claims, and the webs of alliances between different states.

ADSS 1.153

In document 153 of 30 August 1939, Cardinal Maglione, the Secretary of State, directed Archbishop Filippo Cortesi, the Nuncio to Poland, to present to the President of Poland a proposal suggesting Poland 'return' Danzig to Germany in order to bring Hitler back to the negotiating table. Cross-referenced to this document are earlier documents that show the development of this instruction which, if left standing alone and without context, could lead to a highly negative assessment of the Holy See. The reader must also keep in mind that this 'string' of documents occurred during the last days of peace, when communication between Warsaw and Rome was free and unimpeded.

> Document 102–18 August, Cortesi to Maglione: Polish government does not know what the Holy See can do to further peace; German troops are concentrated on the Pomeranian–German border;

> Document 121–25 August, Cortesi to Maglione: the Polish government has given the secret order to mobilise all men up to 40 years of age in the border province next to East Prussia;

> Document 125–26 August, Archbishop Cesare Orsenigo, Nuncio to Germany to Maglione: Germany is prepared for war with Poland but would prefer negotiation to settle problems; but be warned German honour has been insulted and they are prepared to fight;

> Document 128–26 August, Maglione to Cortesi: Cortesi is to

let the Polish government know that if they made some concession to Germany on the question of Danzig war could be avoided;

Document 135—27 August, Cortesi to Maglione: Polish government is afraid of any concessions to Germany;

Document 136—27 August, Cortesi to Maglione: added from document 135 that Poland is concerned that any move to granting concessions would suggest that German accusations of persecution of the German minority in Poland were true and the government knows too well Hitler's method of extending territorial claims through such accusations.

The outcome of all this manoeuvering came to nought; but Maglione, Cortesi, Orsenigo, and ultimately, the Pope, believed they had to make every attempt to work for peace. Perhaps the saddest and most poignant document that follows this example is the belated acknowledgement and thanks for the Pope's efforts given by the Polish government on 14 September, written three days before the Soviet Union invaded Poland from the east and two weeks before Warsaw finally capitulated.[10] In some respects, this example is atypical of much of the material. Conditions during wartime made correspondence difficult. There were 'grades' of difficulty. Diplomatic notes, letters and telegrams usually 'got through' with a minimum of interference, regardless of Axis or Allied origins. The glaring exceptions were Poland, the Baltic States (apart from the first Soviet occupation in 1940) and German-occupied Russia and Ukraine. Some letters from bishops in Lithuania and Ukraine could take several months to reach the Vatican; but Berlin Nuncio, Cesare Orsenigo, was still sending promptly delivered communiqués to Rome until late March 1945. There is, quite simply, no universal logic as to why some parts of German occupied Poland had virtually unrestricted communication with Rome and others had very limited

---

[10] ADSS, 1.201, 14 Sept 1939, Ambassador Casimir Papée to the Secretary of State.

contact.

External cross-referencing

By the time the last volume of ADSS was published in 1981, the amount of edited and published wartime material available was staggering. It began in 1946 when the International Military Tribunal published the records of the Nuremburg Trials, providing a major source of primary material on the prosecution of the war in Europe with a particular focus on war crimes, especially the genocide of the Jews. Documents on British foreign policy 1918–1945 were published between 1949 and 1983; those of the United States had been published since 1932; and in 1957 the US Department of State published, in English, documents on German foreign policy between 1918 and 1945. Between 1953 and 2000, Italy published Volumes 6 through to 10 of *Documenti Diplomatici Italiani* which covered the Fascist era, the 1939–1943 war, and the German occupation and liberation. All of these collections contained significant references to the murder of the Jews of Europe at all stages of the genocide.

The *ASV* has continued its own research. A major documentary collection was published in 2004. The two volumes of *Inter Arma Caritas: L'Ufficio Informazioni Vaticano per I Priginionieri de Guerra istituito da Pio XII (1939–1947)* is one of the most significant works published in the area of war-relief work for prisoners of war and, despite the title, other victims of war, including Jews.[11] Over three million records are contained in the collection. It is an impressive work and one that demands attention. It was released in both

---

[11] (2004), 'Inter Arma Caritas: L'Ufficio Informazioni Vaticano per I Priginionieri de Guerra istituito da Pio XII' (1939–1947) 2 vols, Vatican City.

book and CD form.

Since my focus here is on the documentary evidence found in ADSS, it is important to note some of the more important collections of Church archives from outside Rome. Chief among the published collections are works such as Dieter Albrecht's edited collection of the formal notes exchanged between the Vatican and Reich government, published between 1965 and 1980, practically contemporary with ADSS.[12] This work has been complemented and expanded through the research work of Thomas Brechenmacher at the University of Potsdam.[13] Another companion collection which appeared between 1968 and 1985 was the work of Bernhard Stasiewski and the six volumes recording the formal proceedings of the German bishops under the Third Reich.[14] Of further contextual value are the growing number of published archival records of individual German bishops. The formidable 1975 *Akten Kardinal Michael von Faulhaber 1917–1945*, edited by Ludwig Volk, is just one example.[15] In 2002, the entire Faulhaber archive was opened to researchers through the Munich Archdiocesan Archives. Since Cardinal Faulhaber was one of Pius XII's vital communication links to Germany during the war, the material in this particular archive is of particular importance.

---

[12] Albrecht, Dieter (ed) (1965–1980), 'Der Notenwechsel zwischen dem Heiligen Stuhl und der Deutschen Reichsregierung', 3 vols, Matthias-Grünewald, Mainz.

[13] Brechenmacher, Thomas (2005), 'Pope Pius XI, Eugenio Pacelli and the Persecution of the Jews in Nazi Germany, 1933–1939: New Sources from the Vatican Archives' in *Bulletin of the German Historical Institute London*, 27.2, 17–44.

[14] Stasiewski, Bernhard (ed) (1968–1985), 'Akten Deutscher Bischöfe über die Lage der Kirche 1933–1945', 6 vols, Matthias-Grünewald-Verlag, Mainz.

[15] Volk, Ludwig (ed) (1975), 2 vols, Matthias-Grünewald-Verlag, Mainz.

A word of caution is necessary. Archives in many parts of Germany and Eastern Europe often did not survive the war or were very badly damaged. Nearly the entire archive of the Berlin Diocese and the Apostolic Nunciature was destroyed in air raids. This means that attempts to rebuild the activities of the diocese and the nunciature with regard to the 'Jewish Question' is made all the more difficult. What remains fills a few slender files.[16] Maintenance of archives under Communism was not a high priority for the Church and while a lot of work has been done to centralise and record archival evidence, there is much that remains unexamined and much that is lost.

It is collections such as these that provide material to complement and sometimes challenge ADSS. One of the criticisms levelled at ADSS is what is not found in its pages. By using other published collections to cross-reference what is not found in ADSS, a more complete record is established. ADSS Volume 2 contains Pius' letters to the German bishops but it does not contain the letters they wrote to him. By using Stasiewski, the historian is able to reconstruct some of the correspondence. This is not the most satisfactory method, but until the remaining archives are opened in 2014, it may be the only method for the foreseeable future. Other sources are the hundreds of local diocesan and congregational archives that are often willing to allow researchers access to files. The work of Susan Zuccotti in *Under His Very Windows* is a case in point.

Tracing the Holocaust

In a collection as considerable as ADSS, the historian needs to look carefully for threads across the volumes. Simply looking for key words will not suffice. A general appreciation of the history of the war is essential in order to search effectively for

---

[16] Thomas Brechenmacher to Paul O'Shea, 8 March 2009.

the less than obvious antisemitic references or details about the 'non-Aryans'. The Vatican used the political language of the day, varying according to the government or diplomat it was dealing with. Circumspection when asking for details about concentration camp prisoners from the German Foreign Office was replaced with plain speaking when discussing the same matter with the personal representative of President Roosevelt. And while it is true that the Vatican was as well-informed as either Roosevelt or Churchill, although in different ways and by different means, it is inaccurate to presume that the Pope's bureaucracy was a model of perfection — it was not. Mistakes were made; prejudices were present and confusion in reports sometimes meant the picture was obscured. But our purpose here is to point out what is present in ADSS. Interpretation of the documents is not the primary intention, even though some comment may be made.

What emerges very early in ADSS is the rapidly expanding scale of both the Vatican's attempts to help victims of the war and the requests made of the Holy See by governments and aid agencies, including Jewish communal and international groups. A statistical survey of ADSS demonstrates something of the Vatican's involvement in, and awareness of, the 'Jewish Question'. At the very least, the numbers point to an active concern to receive and transmit information, request information of governments and aid agencies as well as the internal structures of the Church across Europe and even as far afield as Shanghai where a group of refugee Polish rabbis waited while Rome attempted to broker a way for them to leave China.

Within Volumes 1, 2, 3, 4, 5, 7 and 11, the documents deal with 'conventional' war, the restrictions placed on the Church in different parts of German-occupied Europe and the constant discussions with bishops, nuncios, diplomats, heads of state and military leaders over issues that ranged from discussions over episcopal appointments to appeals to spare Rome from bombing. References to the Jews are more incidental — that they appear in 'conventional' documents illustrates the pervasive nature of Nazi antisemitism. Within these volumes there are close to 100 individual documents that mention Jews, Jewish suffering, antisemitism and German anti-Jewish atrocities. The following table sets out this information.

Table 1

Vol	Title	Documents	Specific mention of Jews
1	War Mar 1939–Aug 1940	379	4
2	Letters of Pius XII to German bishops	124	4
3.1	Poland and the Baltic Sates Feb 1939–Dec 1941	344	10
3.2	Poland and the Baltic States Jan 1942–May 1946	261	6
4	War: Jun 1940 –Jun 1941	433	8
5	War: Jul 1941–Oct 1942	511	11
7	War: Nov 1942–Dec 1943	505	7
11	War: Jan 1944–May 1945	552	6

The remaining Volumes, 6, 8, 9 and 10 deal with the victims of war. Here the number of documents that deal directly with 'non-Aryans' or 'Jews' and the events led up to and including the genocide of European Jewry are numbered in the hundreds.

Table 2

Vol	Title	Documents	Specific mention of Jews
6	Mar 1939–Dec 1940	419	154 (36%)
8	Jan 1941–Dec 1942	581	195 (33.5%)
9	Jan 1943–Dec 1943	492	205 (41.6%)
10	Jan 1944–Jul 1945	488	180 (36.8%)

Of the 5,089 documents in ADSS, 734 (14.5 per cent) relate directly to the persecution and murder of the Jews.

What were matters that concerned Jews in particular that filled the documents sent to Rome? In brief, the documents refer to almost every aspect of Jewish life under German occupation. A detailed analysis of ADSS is beyond my scope here, but a tabulated excursus into the material concerning Slovakia in 1942 when the machinery and apparatus of the 'Final Solution' were in the process of refinement gives the reader a clear idea of what information Rome received and, more importantly, what were Rome's responses. The chronology that follows is taken directly from ADSS and attempts to show, across the volumes, what was known and what was done. Where necessary I have included external references.

ADSS and the persecution of the Jews of Slovakia in 1942

The year 1942 was the turning point for the Jews of Europe. Since the outbreak of war in September 1939, the European Jews who found themselves under German domination joined the Jews of Germany and Austria as the primary victims of Nazi violence. Dispossessed, despoiled and deported, walled up in ghettos, stripped of all legal protection, persecuted at whim and exploited as expendable slave labour, the Jews lived in a terrifying and murderous isolation from the rest of humanity. No other victim group of the Nazis was as isolated and vulnerable as the Jews—but, as the documents in the

ADSS demonstrate, the isolation was not unknown, nor was the implementation of the 'Final Solution'. However, the Germans could not murder Europe's Jews without considerable co-operation from non-German sources. Centuries of Christian Jew-hatred and its more virulent mutation, racial antisemitism, meant that the Berlin 'desk killers' did not have to look far to find willing accomplices. The government of Slovakia was not slow to mimic their German overlords. And the Vatican's diplomats reported regularly, and with a high degree of accuracy, the gradual process of dispossession, deportation and disappearance of the Jews.

Slovakia was different from every other country in Europe both before and during the war. Created from the dismembered Czechoslovak republic in 1939, the right-wing government was given permission by Hitler to declare itself independent — which it certainly was not as far as Germany was concerned. Its head of state was a Catholic priest, Josef Tiso, and its governing ideology was a mix of Catholic restorationism and nationalism mixed with an adapted German-style fascism, which included a vicious hatred of Jews. The Vatican looked askance at Tiso the priest in politics, not so much the politics itself.[17] When the Slovakian parliament passed anti-Jewish laws in September 1941, the papal Chargé d'affaires, Monsignor Giuseppe Burzio, was instructed to protest.[18] Maglione summoned the Slovakian minister in Rome, Karel Sidor, and expressed his anger at the

---

[17] Cf *ADSS 4.52*, Burzio to Maglione, 21 September 1940, note 2. Tardini had been instructed on 12 November 1939 to write to Orsenigo in Berlin telling his to find a way to let Tiso know of the Vatican's displeasure at his appointment as President.

[18] *ADSS* 8.153, Burzio to Maglione 18 September 1941.

passing of the laws.[19] The protest did nothing to stop preparations for deportations that were planned for March 1942.

On 26 March 1942, the first transport of 999 Slovakian Jewish girls and women left Bratislava for Auschwitz. Since the passing of the anti-Jewish laws six months earlier, Tiso's government had progressively impoverished the Jews of Slovakia, stolen and 'Aryanised' their businesses, pushed them out of the professions and industry and effectively made them paupers. It made economic sense to deport them. Prime Minister Vojtekh Tuka offered the Germans 20,000 Jews for forced labour outside Slovakia. Adolf Eichmann accepted the offer. He needed more workers for the building projects at Birkenau and nearly all the Soviet prisoners who had slaved on the new camp had been worked to death. Tuka also offered to pay RM500 per Jew on condition that they never return to Slovakia and their property forfeited to the Slovakian state. Eichmann agreed.

Between March and June 1942, 52,000 Jews were deported — most of them to Auschwitz–Birkenau. After June, the deportations slowed largely due to the interventions made through the Vatican's representative in Bratislava, Monsignor Giuseppe Burzio, not the Slovakian bishops, many of whom remained, if not hostile to Jews, then indifferent to their fate. The Slovakian minister to the Holy See, Karel Sidor, was also under pressure from Cardinal Maglione who spoke in the Pope's name. The Holy Father wanted the trains stopped. And stopped they were for several months before resuming at a slower rate in September.

Once the Vatican view was known among the Slovak bishops, attitudes began to change slowly. A pastoral letter written in April spoke of the right of the Jews to humane treatment based on civil and natural law while at the same

---

[19] *ADSS* 8.199, Maglione to Sidor, 12 November 1941.

time berating them for killing Christ. The German minister in Bratislava, Hans Ludin, complained to Berlin that deportations were slowing because of the interference of the Church which had granted, with government approval, exemptions for at least 20,000 baptised Jews, more exemptions approved by the government for at least another 15,000 Jews, and the corruption of individual officials. For tactical reasons, Himmler and Eichmann accepted the deadlock, but only as a temporary measure. The Jews of Slovakia were slated for death in the same way that every other Jew in Europe was doomed to be murdered. Transports resumed in the autumn of 1944 in the wake of the failed partisan uprising.

The following table sets out in chronological order the documents found in ADSS that deal with Slovakia in 1942. It is important to keep in mind that the information contained in each document was as accurate a record as possible at the time and is, in itself, a valuable indicator of the different types of information available — some true and some not.

Table 3

ADSS Chronology of the Persecution of the Jews of Slovakia 1942				
Ref	Date	From	To	Details
8. 153	18 Sept 1941	Giuseppe Burzio, Chargé d'affaires, Bratislava	Cardinal Luigi Maglione, Secretary of State	Reports on introduction of Jewish Code in Slovakia with comments.
8. 173	15 Oct 1941	Giuseppe Burzio	Cardinal Maglione	Report on Slovakian bishops meeting and response to race laws. Asserts Church's right to regulate marriage, defend Catholicity

				of baptised Jews.
8. 184	27 Oct 1941	Giuseppe Burzio	Cardinal Maglione	Reports inhuman treatment of Russian POWs and Jews imprisoned in eastern Slovakia.
8. 199	12 Nov 1941	Cardinal Maglione	Karel Sidor, Slovakian Minister to the Holy See	Reports on Vatican objections to racial legislation in Slova-kia: asserts right of Church to regulate marriage including mixed marriages and rights of baptised Jews. The Holy See cannot be indifferent to this.
8. 298	09 Mar 1942	Giuseppe Burzio	Cardinal Maglione	Reports that deport-ation of Slovakian Jews to Galicia and Lublin region immi-nent. At end of report Burzio wrote: 'The deport-ation of 80,000 people to Poland at the mercy of the Germans is equiva-lent to condemning the greater part to certain death.'
8. 300	10 Mar 1942	Filippo Bernadini — Nuncio Switzer-land	Cardinal Maglione	Reports received from Caritas Switzerland and Agudas Israel indi-cate deportation of 135,000 Slovakian

				Jews to begin 23 March 1942.
8. 301	11 Mar 1942	Giuseppe Burzio	Cardinal Maglione	Reports received from Slovakian military chaplains tell of SS led [*Einsatzgruppen*] massacres of Jews in German occupied Russia.
8. 303	13 Mar 1942	Angelo Rotta, Nuncio Hungary	Cardinal Maglione	Appeal for papal intervention for Slovakian Jews threatened with expulsion to Poland with attached appeal from Jewish Community of Bratislava: 'We are condemned to destruction.'
8. 305	14 Mar 1942	Cardinal Maglione	Karel Sidor, Slovak	Informs Sidor of reports of imminent expulsion of 80,000 Jews to Galicia and Lublin region. Expresses hope that information untrue.
8. 312	19 Mar 1942	Cardinal Maglione	Filippo Bernardini	Instructions for intervention for Slovakian Jews.
8. 314	19 Mar 1942	Filippo Bernardini	Cardinal Maglione	Report on situation of Jews of Central Europe — enclosed in report was

				Riegner telegram — response made Doc 322
8. 317	20 Mar 1942	Angelo Rotta	Cardinal Maglione	Appeal for intervention for Slovakian Jews to be deported to Galicia made by Chief Rabbi of Budapest. Response made Doc 322
8. 322	24 Mar 1942	Giovanni Montini, Secretariat of State, note		Pius XII agreed to discuss the matter with Slovakian minister.
8. 324	24 Mar 1942	Giuseppe Burzio	Cardinal Maglione	Reports deportation of Slovak Jews suspended because of intervention of Holy See. However, one transport left last night — girls aged 16–25. Rumoured to be sent to Russian front as prostitutes — all 999 gassed on arrival at Auschwitz.
8. 326	25 Mar 1942	Giuseppe Burzio	Cardinal Maglione	Reports government has not abandoned plans to deport Slovak Jews as reported yesterday. First group was sent. Men and

				women – 10 000 to be deported.
8. 328	25 Mar 1942	D'Arcy Osborne, UK Minister to Holy See	Cardinal Maglione	Appeal to Holy See to intervene with Tiso in favour of 90,000 Slovak Jews, especially those in ghettos close to Polish border.
8. 332	27 Mar 1942	Cardinal Maglione	Giuseppe Burzio	Maglione asked Sidor to intervene with his government to stop deportations. Burzio instructed to appeal to Tiso as a priest.
8. 334	31 Mar 1942	Giuseppe Burzio	Cardinal Maglione	Reports deportation of Jews begun and conducted with great brutality. Government claims it is in accord with the Church. Bishop Vojtaššák urged Church authorities 'not to create problems for the government or president of the republic, for Jews were the greatest enemies of Slovakia, and things should be allowed to run their course'

8. 342	09 Apr 1942	Filippo Bernardini	Cardinal Maglione	Reports gratitude of World Jewish Congress for steps taken in favour of Slovak Jews.
8. 343	09 Apr 1942	Giuseppe Burzio	Cardinal Maglione	Reports that deportation of Slovak Jews continues; Jews fleeing to Hungary, brutal scenes.
8. 345 346	11 Apr 1942	Cardinal Maglione note		Vatican protest over deportation of Slovak Jews made to Slovak minister Karel Sidor, who attempted to justify deportations.
8. 352	17 Apr 1942	Angelo Rotta	Cardinal Maglione	Reports information on Slovak Jews relayed through Hungarian woman who has impression that Pope's intervention has had effect on Tiso. She spoke highly of Burzio who, though isolated, was man of courage.
8. 354	18 Apr 1942	Cardinal Maglione	Giuseppe Burzio	Sends account of Vatican protest to Slovak minister — 11 Apr — see 334, 346.

8. 360	27 Apr 1942	Giuseppe Burzio	Cardinal Maglione	Sends copy of the letter of Slovak bishops concerning racial laws. Baptism is only sure way for Jews to reach safety.
8. 364	01 May 1942	Angelo Rotta	Cardinal Maglione	Sends letter from Fr Pozdech in Slovakia to President of Jewish Community in Budapest appealing for world wide condemnation of persecution of Jews
8. 368	07 May 1942	Babuscio Rizzo, Counsellor of the Italian Embassy	Holy See; notes	Declaration of Slovak government concerning racial legislation – 'the definitive decision for the total resolution of the Jewish problem…baptised or not, all the Jews must be removed.'
8. 382	23 May 1942	Giuseppe Burzio	Cardinal Maglione	Reports on newly passed retroactive law to legalise deportations and stripping of citizenship of Jews.
8. 383	23 May 1942	Karel Sidor	Cardinal Maglione	Provides justification for new anti-Jewish laws in Slovakia. Laws necessary to resolve

				serious 'Jewish Quest-ion' in Slovakia. European solution is to settle Jews outside Aryan areas.
8. 389	02 Jun 1942	Rabbi Joseph Hermann Hertz, Chief Rabbi of British Empire	Cardinal Maglione	Appeals to the Holy See for Slovak Jews.
8. 400	19 Jun 1942	Cardinal Maglione	Giuseppe Burzio	Instruction to con-vey to the govern-ment that the Holy See deplores racial legislation in Slo-vakia, 'which was passed with the participation of various priests, deputies of the Parliament.'
8. 426	13 Jul 1942	Domen-ico Tardini, Secreta-riat of State; notes		Concerning Slovak Jews and frustration with Tiso.
8. 430 431	17 Jul 1942	Giuseppe Marcone, Papal Represen-tative,	Cardinal Maglione	Reports difficulty trying to obtain information regard-ing Croatian Jews. Estimates up to two

		Croatia		million Jews have been murdered.
8. 471	10 Sep 1942	Calliste Lopinot, OFM Cap	Francesco Borgon-gini Duca, Nuncio Italy	Reports that news is reaching internees in Ferramonti telling of massive deportations of Jews from Germany and France to places in Poland. Jews with family members in Slovakia, Germany, Holland and France are understandably worried.
8. 492	26 Sep 1942	Italian Embassy		Information on persecution of Jews in Slovakia; estimates 70,000 Jews deported; 16–20,000 remain because of exemptions.
8. 493	27 Sep 1942	Giovanni Montini, Secretariat of State, notes		On 26 September, Myron Taylor delivered the most graphic report of the killing of the Jews to Cardinal Maglione.
8. 496	01 Oct 1942	Giovanni Montini		Information on massacre of Jews. Record of Tittmann's audience with Pius XII – 26 Sept 1942.

8. 497	03 Oct 1942	Casimir Papée Polish Ambass-ador to Holy See; notes		News of massacres of Jews in Poland – Vilna ghetto (from 80,000 to 12,000), Warsaw Ghetto (methodical empty-ing of the ghetto) deportations to Lublin; death by asphyxiation.
7.53	14 Dec 1942	Cardinal Maglione, notes		After discussing concerns about bombing of civilian targets, D'Arcy Osborne, UK Minis-ter to Holy See asked 'But why has the Holy See not intervened against the terrible massa-cre of the Jews?'
8. 573	19 Dec 1942	Casimir Papée	Cardinal Maglione	Reports information on extermination of Jews in Poland, including reports of the 'liquidation' of the Warsaw Ghetto.
8. 575	23 Dec 1942	Rabbi Joseph Hermann Hertz, Chief Rabbi of British Empire	Pius XII	Appeals to the Pope to speak out against the murder of the Jews.
8.	28	Cardinal	Amleto	Response to 575 –

577	Dec 1942	Maglione	Cicognani -Apostolic Delegate, USA	Holy Father doing all possible.

KL Auschwitz

Another example is to trace the growing awareness of Auschwitz in ADSS. The history of Auschwitz–Birkenau demonstrates the measure of success the Germans had in cloaking the real purpose of their premier permanent killing centre from both its intended victims — the Jews of Europe — and those regarded in the Nazi *Weltanschauung* as racially equal or near enough to warrant the granting of the right to live. This did not include the racially undesirable such as Poles, Slavs or the Roma or Sinti peoples. While the number of direct references to Auschwitz/Oswiecim are relatively few, the details contained demonstrate a growing awareness of the scale of the killing process and the recognition by 1944 that Jews were sent there to die. The greater number of references occurs during the deportation of the Hungarian Jews in 1944.

The table sets out the information about Auschwitz as it was received and understood at the time. It is for the historian to contextualise the material into the broader narrative.

Table 4:

ADSS References to Auschwitz in ADSS				
Ref	*Date*	*Ref*	*To*	*Details*
3.1. 208	02 Oct 1940	Cesare Orsenigo, Nuncio to Germany	Cardinal Luigi Maglione, Secretary of State	Situation in Poland is terrible. Priests arrested and depor- ted to concentration camps. Nine Vin- centian priests in Krakow were

				arrested and sent to KL Auschwitz.[20] Two already dead.
7. 82	02 Jan 1943	Polish President Raczkie-wicz, in exile in London	Pius XII	Requests word from the Pope for Poland and in response to 'extermination of the Jews and with them many Christ-ians of the Semitic race who are sys-tematically and scientifically mur-dered.' Mentions Oswiecim (Auschwitz).
7. 93	22 Jan 1943	Orsenigo	Maglione	Situation of Church in Bohemia; priests condemned to death or imprison-ed (KL Dachau, KL Auschwitz, KL Mauthausen, Lidice, Prague.
9. 442	27 Nov 1943	Maglione	Orsenigo	Urgent request for help for Cecilia Mikołajczyk, wife of Polish Prime Minis-ter, arrested and sent to KL Oswie-cim. Thefirst time name 'Oswiecim'

---

[20] KL = *Konzentrationslager*, 'concentration camp'. This abbreviation or 'KZ' were commonly used.

				appears in document originating from the Vatican in ADSS.
10. 165	24 Apr 1944	Antonio Santin, (Bishop of Trieste)	Maglione	Situation in Trieste area: persecution of Jews; shooting of hostages; danger of partisans; meeting of bishop with different groups. Jews deported to Auschwitz.
10. 204	22 May 1944	Giuseppe Burzio, Chargé d'affairs, Slovakia	Maglione	Information on fate of Jews deported to Germany. Reference made to *Auschwitz Protocol*. Attached document, not published, may not have been protocol but a summary.
10. 263	13 Jul 1944	Casimir Papée, Polish Ambassador to the Holy See	Maglione	News on deportation of Hungarian Jews. Estimated that 400,000 Jews sent to Oswiecim (KL Auschwitz–Birkenau).
10. 279	28 Jul 1944	Filippo Bernardini, Nuncio in Switzerland	Maglione	News of deportation of Hungarian Jews of Auschwitz, and their extermination. Report based on report of Rudolf

				Vrba and *Auschwitz Protocols*.
10. 330	26 Sep 1944	Domenico Tardini, Secretariat of State	Orsenigo	Plea to prevent massacre of estimated 45,000 prisoners at KL Auschwitz of Polish, Italian and other nationalities.
10. 333	30 Sep 1944	Amleto Cicognani Apostolic Delegate to USA	Sec State	Request from delegation of rabbis and representative of Jewish Committee for prisoners in KL Auschwitz.
10. 335	02 Oct 1944	Sec State	Italian Embassy	Steps taken for prisoners in KL Auschwitz.
10. 354	13 Oct 1944	Orsenigo	Sec State	Steps taken for prisoners in KL Auschwitz and Pruszkow not successful. Pruszkow used as a KL for prisoners taken during Warsaw uprising.
10. 402	21 Nov 1944	Tardini	Giuseppe Burzio, Chargé d'affaires, Slovakia	Request for new effort for Slovak Jews being sent to Auschwitz. Asking for an appeal for Jews holding American citizenship.
10. 439	25 Jan 1945	Tardini	Orsenigo	Rumours that retreating German soldiers have

				massacred prisoners at KL Auschwitz.

This selection of documents referring to Auschwitz is consistent with the emerging awareness of the extermination camp in other contemporary sources. Disbelief at reports of industrialised killing dominated Vatican and Allied responses until the spring of 1944 when the report of Auschwitz escapees, Rudolf Vrba and Alfred Wetzler, reached Switzerland. Its publication in London and New York led to a dramatic effort to pressure the Hungarian government to stop the trains to Auschwitz. The Vatican knew of the so-called 'Auschwitz Protocols' through the Swiss Nuncio, Filippo Bernardini in July 1944, but did not receive the document until October 1944.

Conclusion

ADSS represents one of the richest and most valuable sources for historians studying the role and roles of the Catholic Church during the years of the Holocaust. It does not contain everything, but then neither does any archive have 'everything'. What the student can and will find in ADSS is a substantial selection of documents that gives a comprehensive picture of how the Vatican and its representatives across Europe, and in this particular case, Slovakia, learned, in piecemeal fashion, of the ever-increasing dangers faced by the Jews, the responses and actions taken to ameliorate conditions and attempt the nigh-impossible, namely, stop the trains. The case of Slovakia shows one set of circumstances where the representatives of the Holy See did what they could with the information that was reported to them even when the results were meagre.

References
Actes et Documents du Saint-Siège relatifs à la Seconde Guerre mondiale, 12 vols, Vatican City (1965–1981).

Friedländer, Saul (2007), *Nazi Germany and the Jews 1939 –1945: The years of extermination*, New York, Harper Collins.

Paldiel, Mordecai (2006), *Churches and the Holocaust: Unholy teaching, Good Samaritans and reconciliation*, Jersey City NJ, KTAV.

Zuccotti, Susan (2000), *Under His Very Windows: The Vatican and the Holocaust in Italy*, New Haven, Yale University Press.

THE NUREMBERG LEGACY IN THE NEW MILLENNIUM

WINTON HIGGINS

> [T]hese defendants now ask this Tribunal to say they are not guilty of planning, executing, or conspiring to commit this long list of crimes and wrongs. They stand before the record of this trial as blood-stained Gloucester stood by the body of his slain king. He begged the widow, as they beg of you: 'Say I slew them not.' And the Queen replied, 'Then say they were not slain. But dead they are...' If you were to say of these men that they are not guilty, it would be as true to say there has been no war, there are no slain, there has been no crime. — *Robert Jackson, US chief prosecutor, closing address to the International Military Tribunal, Nuremberg, 26 July, 1946*

> It is the virtue of the Nuremberg trial that it was conceived in hatred of war, and was nurtured by those starved of peace. To realise how grateful we should be for this birth, consider the alternative. — *Rebecca West*

The 1945-1946 trial of major German perpetrators before the International Military Tribunal in Nuremberg has often been called the greatest trial in history. More than the prominence the major protagonists, the principles at stake guaranteed its historical importance. For the very first time the entrenched principles of state sovereignty and raison d'état came under challenge. In Nuremberg, state functionaries faced prosecution stripped of the impunity that had hitherto attached to state crimes. And they were forced to answer for actions that had hitherto self-evidently constituted prerogatives of a sovereign state, above all starting wars and massacring their own subjects — actions now declared so felonious as to attract the ultimate penalty. Nor were the orders of state functionaries any longer able to shield perpetrators from criminal liability.

In short, the Nuremberg enterprise sought to strengthen the rule of law and to extend it beyond state borders — to contribute to an *international* rule of law — to the extent that all individuals were answerable as moral and legal agents, no matter who they were, the circumstances under which they wronged others, or where they did so. In this new dispensation, every serious, deliberate wrong must attract a public and palpable legal sanction, one imposed on the perpetrator under fair procedures, in order to inhibit like wrongs in the future and to develop a particular kind of society — *civil* society, or 'civilisation'. The Anglo-American expression of this ideal hails back to the Magna Carta of 1215, conceived as a bulwark against tyranny, and includes early expressions (the American Declaration of Independence of 1776 and that country's Bill of Rights of 1791 prominent among them) of what later came to be known as human rights.

From its inception, the International Military Tribunal (hereafter 'the tribunal' or 'the IMT') had its detractors, and like most pioneering ventures, it had manifold shortcomings and rough edges for its critics to snipe at. Conservative lawyers have objected to the trial's theory and practice, especially its readiness to try defeated enemies for uncodified crimes; while later historians have criticised the way in which the trial wrote the first draft of the history of the Third Reich, including the Holocaust. Yet the trial irrevocably changed the international moral and legal climate. Together with contemporaneous moves to establish universal human rights and outlaw genocide, it made the world less safe for perpetrators. And at the dawn of the present century it gained the sort of successor that leading Nuremberg prosecutors agitated for in their later careers — a permanent international criminal court.

But also in the current century, the Nuremberg heritage has acquired a surprising, intimate opponent to add to the more predictable rogues' gallery of perpetrators and perpetrator states that have always condemned and defied it. The new opponent is none other than the American government, which back in 1945 took the leading role in establishing the tribunal, and in subsequent years took sole responsibility for mounting important precedent-setting further trials in

Nuremberg against separate categories of German perpetrators. The current American recalcitrance towards the international rule of law, especially international criminal law, poses a considerable threat to the historical authority of the Nuremberg trial, and of course, to the efficacy of its successor, the fledgling International Criminal Court (ICC).

In these adverse circumstances we need to retrieve the original inspiration for the trial, what was thereafter achieved in Nuremberg, and the immediate circumstances and wider historical context in which the tribunal handled its remit.[1] On this basis we can give its achievements and shortcomings their due proportion, as well as appreciate the tribunal's place in a wider pattern of formative international initiatives in the crucial years immediately following World War II. Just how 'grateful' should we be, in terms of Rebecca West's epigraph,[2] and thus how resolute need we be in defending the Nuremberg legacy against its current opponents? This essay addresses these questions.

New York lawyers plan a war-crimes trial

Telford Taylor opens his magisterial account of the trial with the observation that a group of New York lawyers, all at the time US wartime federal officials, laid down the principal ideas and innovations that crystallised in the four-power

---

[1] The following account sketches the direct antecedents of the IMT only. For a wider perspective on how the issue of war crimes developed during the second world war, see Kochavi, Arieh (1998), *Prelude to Nuremberg: Allied war crimes policy and the question of punishment*, Chapel Hill & London, University of North Carolina Press.

[2] The quote comes from her 'Foreword' to Neave, Airey (1978), *Nuremberg: A personal record of the trial of major Nazi war criminals in 1945-6*, London, Hodder & Stoughton, 7.

Intergovernmental Agreement and Charter signed in London on 8 August 1945 – the charter which came to constitute and govern the tribunal.[3] They did so in the autumn and winter of 1944–1945. The then US president, Franklin Delano Roosevelt ('though we do not usually think of him as a lawyer') heads his list of the lawyers in question, which naturally also includes the most passionate, eloquent and creative of the tribunal's progenitors, Justice Robert Jackson of the Supreme Court, the immediate past US attorney-general. The others held posts in the departments of State, Treasury, and War; some also held senior ranks in the armed forces, including the Office of Strategic Services (OSS, forerunner of the CIA).[4] Henry Stimson – a distinguished member of the New York bar, prominent member of the Republican establishment, and US Secretary of State from 1929 to 1933 – led the crucial campaign to prosecute war criminals before an international tribunal based on 'at least the rudimentary aspects of the Bill of Rights, namely, notification to the accused of the charge, the right to be heard and, within limits, to call witnesses in his defense'.[5] In the upshot, the trial would fulfil these criteria.

---

[3] The group enjoyed the encouragement and assistance of the Institute of Jewish Affairs: see Marrus, Michael (2006), 'A Jewish Lobby at Nuremberg: Jacob Robinson and the Institute for Jewish Affairs', in *The Nuremberg Trials: International criminal law since 1945*, (eds) Reginbogin, Herbert and Safferling, Christoph, Munich, K G Saur.

[4] Taylor, Telford (1993), *The Anatomy of the Nuremberg Trials*, London, Bloomsbury, 4. The OSS connection has often been underestimated. Its founder and director, General William ('Wild Bill') Donovan was one of the New York lawyers in question, and the trial would open with him acting as Jackson's deputy. Those working for Donovan at the OSS included Franz Neumann, the author of the groundbreaking 1942 study of the nature of the Nazi state, *Behemoth*, and Raphael Lemkin, who gave genocide its name and contributed greatly to the 1948 UN Genocide Convention.

[5] Henry Stimson, memorandum of 9 Sept 44, quoted in Shawcross,

With military victory in sight, these lawyers were grappling with how to give effect to the Allied foreign ministers' Moscow declaration of November 1943. Most Allied decision-makers assumed that, as soon as practicable, national courts in Europe would punish war crimes committed within their jurisdictions according to the laws of the land. For that purpose, captured suspects were to be sent back to the scenes of their crimes for trial according to those laws. But what of the main criminals, those whose activities transcended national borders? According to the Moscow declaration, they would 'be punished by a joint decision of the Governments of the Allies'.[6] This declaration was one of a series of general threats issued by Allied leaders during the war to try to ameliorate the Third Reich's already notorious, large-scale atrocities.[7]

From the German military catastrophe at Stalingrad in the winter of 1942–1943, after which any informed German could infer that the war would end badly, such threats may have had some psychological impact. But they fell well short of a specific plan to punish the major war criminals. Among America's allies, the punishment of war crimes hardly loomed large, with the only other serious suggestion for giving effect to the Moscow declaration being the 'political' rather than judicial one espoused by the British government: draw up a list of principal Nazi perpetrators to be shot on capture and positive identification. This proposal also enjoyed support in the USA from, among others, the influential Treasury

---

Hartley (1995), *Life Sentence: The memoirs of Lord Shawcross*, London, Constable, 88.

[6] Quoted in Taylor, 27. In what follows I draw on Taylor's both insider and highly scholarly account of the background to the London charter (chapters 1–2), as well as on Shawcross, chapter 7.

[7] For the history of these threats and declarations, see Kochavi.

Secretary, Henry Morgenthau Jr. Only Stalin evinced any enthusiasm for a trial, and his conception thereof—based on his own infamous show trials at home, ones with only one possible outcome—fell well short of due process as defined by the US Bill of Rights.

Henry Stimson and his New York lawyers eventually overwhelmed their opponents at home and abroad through their assiduous planning and bold conception of a pioneering jurisprudence around the issues the Third Reich so starkly posed: the waging of aggressive war as such, war crimes proper, and crimes against humanity (including attempts to wipe out whole peoples, not least the Jews of Europe). As Jackson would put it in his opening address to the tribunal, in his own inimitable 'winged words':

The real complaining party at your bar is Civilization... [It] asks whether law is so laggard as to be utterly helpless to deal with crimes of this magnitude by criminals of this order of importance. It does not expect that you can make war impossible. It does expect that your juridical action will put the forms of international law, its precepts, its prohibitions and, most of all, its sanctions, on the side of peace, so that men and women of good will, in all countries, may have 'leave to live by no man's leave, underneath the law.'[8]

In particular, the architects of the coming trial had to over-come 'Civilization's' dispiriting experience during and after World War I—an experience which throws this new ambition to create an international rule of law into dramatic relief.

Back then, the law was so 'laggard' that when the Allies in May 1915 issued a joint declaration condemning the Turkish authorities' ongoing massacre (or 'genocide' in the later coinage) of the Armenians, they did so knowing that this atrocity broke no international law: under the 'Westphalian'

---

[8] Quoted in Taylor, 171–72. Jackson himself is quoting from Rudyard Kipling's 1899 poem, *The Old Issue*.

principle of national sovereignty, a nation-state could persecute and massacre its own subjects at will, just as it could start and wage wars in pursuit of state policy. All the perpetrators of the Armenian genocide, bar one officer sentenced to death by a Turkish court-martial in 1919, were amnestied under the treaty of Lausanne of 1923. At the end of the war, Germany's 12 war-crimes trials in Leipzig in 1921–1922, held under the provisions of the treaty of Versailles, ended in fiasco. The New York lawyers were all too painfully aware, as well, that attempts to extend the rule of law to international affairs after the first world war, and to establish an international court with criminal jurisdiction, 'foundered on the rocks of American opposition,' as Taylor puts it—above all America's refusal to join the League of Nations and to encourage the institutional creativity it stood for.[9]

The legal coterie around Stimson in 1944–1945 worked from first principles. It made interwar attempts to outlaw war as such the leitmotiv of the trial it sought.[10] Fundamentally evil in itself, war was also understood as the *fons et origo* of all the other evils the trial would highlight; for this reason, aggressive war (or 'crimes against peace') became the centrepiece of the trial. War created the pretexts and opportunities—as well as the veil of secrecy—for war crimes and crimes against humanity, which constituted the other two heads of German mass criminality.

But the scale of the criminality on all three counts, and the problem of what or whom to put in the dock, of how to

---

[9] Ibid, 16.

[10] Stimson himself had served as Secretary of State previously, in Herbert Hoover's administration (1929–33), and keenly supported the Kellogg–Briand pact, whereby its principal signatories, and later 44 other signatory states, renounced war as an instrument of national policy: Kochavi, 229.

spread the net wide enough, called for considerable creativity. The Allies themselves would inevitably dissolve the two main institutional perpetrators — the Third Reich and the Nazi Party — as they formally did on 8 May 1945 under the terms of the German surrender; the Allies would then exercise their own sovereignty over Germany, and no German state would remain to prosecute. Ultimately *individuals* had to be brought to book, potentially in large numbers.

Colonel Murray Bernays of the Army General Staff came up with a compelling suggestion: charge the leading Nazis with the old common-law offence of *conspiracy* to commit felony, namely, that of unleashing aggressive war; and empower the intended tribunal to declare the principal perpetrator organisations to be *criminal organisations*, thus making all their members prima facie guilty of indictable offences for the purposes of subsequent prosecutions of lower-ranking perpetrators. Importantly, this step would bring domestic atrocities committed by members of these organisations against their own compatriots within the purview of international criminal law. At the same time, Colonel William Chanler — Stimson's partner in a New York law firm, but now deputy director of US military government in Europe — assembled the argument close to Stimson's heart: international initiatives during the interwar period, , the 1928 Kellogg–Briand pact, had criminalised the waging of aggressive war, which thus now constituted 'crimes against the peace' in international law.

These suggestions, which came to be called 'the Nuremberg ideas', won Roosevelt's favour. After his death in April 1945, his successor, Harry Truman, continued to support Jackson's project along these lines, albeit without FDR's enthusiasm and specialist competence. In the last dramatic week of the war in Europe, the drama was by no means limited to that theatre of war. On 2 May 1945, Truman appointed Jackson 'representative of the United States and chief of counsel' for the purposes of bringing a war-crimes trial to fruition. The next day the British cabinet withdrew its support for the 'political solution' to the war-crimes problem, partly because Hitler, Himmler and Goebbels among others had already killed themselves, and were thus no longer available for demonstrative execution. This decision left the way open for an in-principle agreement, made that same day at a meeting of the foreign ministers of the Big Three, to hold an international trial as the Americans and Soviets had wanted. The foreign ministers were meeting in San Francisco, where the inaugural congress of the United Nations was in progress. As Jackson's son William, who would also join the US prosecution team in Nuremberg, later remarked on this historical coincidence:

> It is perhaps not commonly apprehended that the principles of Nuremberg…go hand in hand with the organization of the United Nations as the twin foundation of an international society ordered by law.[11]

'The Nuremberg ideas' were ideas whose time had come.

The devil and the detail

Before they saw the light of day in court these ideas had to be tested and honed in difficult negotiations on just how such a trial would proceed, and the procedural principles it would apply. Representatives of the four intended prosecuting and judging nations (the French had now agreed to join the venture) met in London 15 times between 26 June and 8 August 1945. This 'conference' saw a clash of three quite different conceptions of law and trial procedure.

The Americans (headed by Jackson) and the British (led by the attorney-general, Sir David Maxwell Fyfe)[12] shared the common-law tradition in which judge-made law played an

---

[11] Quoted in Taylor, 42.

[12] Later the Earl of Kilmuir, Lord Chancellor 1954–62.

obvious part in proliferating and adapting a legal system, and the adversarial trial process — including rigorous cross-examination — constituted the royal road to just (and thereby unpredictable) trial outcomes. For these two delegations, the trial was intended precisely to *set a precedent* that would extend international law. But this approach was foreign to continental traditions, in which law had purely legislative sources, including explicit codes, and trials proceeded along inquisitorial rather than adversarial lines. Heated arguments thus broke out over the proposed counts of conspiracy and crimes against peace in particular, as no existing continental code supported them. As well, the Soviet negotiators could not contemplate the possibility of acquittals, and had no taste for criminalising aggressive wars as such, only 'Hitlerite' ones.

Jackson's talents did not extend to diplomacy, and Maxwell Fyfe's own diplomatic skills were sorely tried as he chaired the meetings and mediated between Jackson on the one hand, and the French and Soviet representatives on the other. Jackson was determined to defend the whole package of ideas he had arrived with, and made no bones of his government's intention to mount the trial alone if the other powers did not accept it. He regarded Soviet participation as unhelpful in any event. The USSR had without provocation invaded both Poland and Finland in late 1939, and — according to contemporary Western intelligence, since confirmed — was responsible for the Katyn Forest massacre of between eight and eleven thousand Polish officers found buried there. And yet its representatives were deter-mined to join in the prosecution of 'Hitlerite' aggressive war, and to sheet home the Katyn massacre to the German defendants. The chief Soviet delegate, General I T Nikitchenko (an army judge advocate who would become the senior Soviet judge at the trial) clearly had his orders from home, but faced an uncompromising American negotiator who would have received a Soviet withdrawal from the project with equanimity.

Before and during these difficult negotiations in London, Jackson manifested a moral and political passion that would infect his British counterpart and affect the way both would discharge their functions at the trial itself. For his part, Jackson had on 7 June 1945, at the president's behest, published a report which clearly stated his position. It alluded to the fact that US authorities held the most significant war criminals in custody, which made it the country's 'inescapable responsibility' to deal with them in the most high-minded way possible.

> To free them without trial would mock the dead and make cynics of the living. On the other hand we could execute and otherwise punish them without a hearing. But undis-criminating executions or punishments without definite findings of guilt, fairly arrived at, would violate pledges repeatedly given, and would not sit easily on the American conscience or be remembered by our children with pride. The only other course is to determine the innocence or guilt of the accused after a hearing as dispassionate as the times and horrors we deal with will permit, and upon a record that will leave our reasons and motives clear.

Jackson's concern for 'the record' was crucial: he already feared a future denialism, which only 'a well documented history' could thwart. In Nuremberg, he would make Nazi documents, photographs and film footage the core of the American case.

> Unless we write the record of this [Nazi] movement with clarity and precision, we cannot blame the future if in days of peace it finds incredible the accusatory generalities uttered during the war. We must establish incredible events by credible evidence.[13]

Maxwell Fyfe, who would for practical purposes lead the

---

[13] Quoted in Taylor, 53–54.

British prosecution team in Nuremberg, shared the same concern, and to a large extent the same approach. As he wrote in his memoirs:

[E]very devil has his advocate. We have seen apologists for everything. It is, therefore, just as well that in respect of Nazi war crimes the apologist of the future will be confronted by the admissions of the many accused found guilty, and the mass of incriminating documents produced at the trials, whose authenticity has been established by the very men who wrote them. Both devil and advocate are faced by an unscaleable barrier of truth.[14]

The coming trial would precipitate a scramble for documentary evidence of unprecedented proportions, and the German authorities' obsessive documentation would guarantee its success.

Gradually the logic of the uneven negotiating positions in London asserted itself. The French had no concrete counter-proposals, and indeed would maintain a low profile throughout the trial. The Soviets had no reasonable counter-proposals, and were easily isolated. On 26 July the results of the British elections of 5 July were announced: Labour had won a crushing victory, and was even more enthusiastic about the American approach to the war-crimes problem than their outgoing Tory counterparts. Sir Hartley Shawcross, the new Labour attorney-general, replaced Maxwell Fyfe as the London Agreement and Charter approached fruition, though the former, now destined to become the British chief prosecutor at the trial, quickly appointed the latter as his deputy.

On 8 August the agreement was signed. The charter it endorsed embodied all the New York lawyers' principles; as well, it proved itself in the main to be a coherent and workable constitution for the tribunal and guide to its

---

[14] Kilmuir, Lord (1964), *Political Adventure: The memoirs of the Earl of Kilmuir*, London, Weidenfeld & Nicholson, 126.

procedure.[15] Its coherence rested on its special indebtedness to Anglo-American conceptions of law and judicial procedure. At the same time, it contained all the features which, then as now, stirred legal controversy, not least among legal conservatives: the element of retrospectivity in the counts dealing with conspiracy and crimes against peace (article 6), the withdrawal of individual impunity for state crimes and for following orders (articles 7 and 8), and the suggestion of 'guilt by association' in the provision for indicting organisations which, if held criminal, would lay the basis for prosecutions of individuals on the basis of membership alone (articles 9 and 10).[16] As against these claims, as Shawcross would later stress in his closing address to the tribunal, the charter's only innovation was 'to provide the long-overdue machinery to enforce already-existing law'.[17]

---

[15] Taylor, 75. His one substantive criticism concerns the charter's failure to specify grounds of defence available to defendants in subsequent trials who are charged with membership of organisations declared criminal by the IMT: loc cit.

[16] Bradley Smith presents one of the most influential legal critiques of the trial in his *Reaching Judgment at Nuremberg*, New York, Basic Books, 1977. He also argues that the Anglo-American carpet-bombing of German towns and cities (including Nuremberg itself) robbed the Allies of the moral authority to try German war criminals at all. While the bombing is today widely recognised as a war crime, it was not seen in this light around the end of the war. And since misguided military doctrines partly motivated it, and it involved heavy Allied casualties, it hardly compares with most of the crimes with which the Nuremberg defendants were charged. Its death toll of 600,000 civilians is appalling, yet amounts to a tenth of the Holocaust's, to say nothing of Nazi Germany's other prisoner of war and civilian massacres.

[17] Shawcross, 119. The term 'holocaust' was first used to describe the 1896 massacre of Armenians under Sultan Hamid II; it was not a Jewish term or a Jewish-chosen one.

As we have seen, the New York lawyers had already anticipated and argued most of these points at length, but perhaps the former's ultimate vindication lies in Rebecca West's challenge, quoted at the beginning of this essay: *consider the alternative*. Undoubtedly that alternative, bar a few summary executions, would have closely resembled the dispiriting outcomes of attempts to bring war criminals to book after the first world war, and the law would have remained 'laggard' in the face of incomparably larger crimes.

To read the charter now, together with the 18,000-word indictment based on it (signed on 18 October and served on the defendants the next day), we might be surprised to find so little made of the Jewish genocide. Its extent was known to the Nuremberg prosecutors, who led the appropriate incontrovertible evidence during the trial. But in fact Raphael Lemkin had only coined the term 'genocide' the year before it began;[18] his influence as a member of the US prosecution team led to the term finding its first official use in the Nuremberg indictment. Genocide became a distinct crime in international law only with the widespread ratification of the 1948 UN Convention on the Prevention and Punishment of the Crime of Genocide. And the concept and term 'the Holocaust' for a distinct catastrophe only became international common coin in the 1970s and 1980s.[19] The charter was signed just two months after the war in Europe ended; it reflected the then current perception that the persecution and slaughter of European Jewry merged into a pattern of breathtaking criminality which also included widespread massacres of millions of prisoners of war and non-Jewish civilians, including the Romani and other ethnic groups, throughout German-occupied Europe.

---

[18] See Lemkin, Raphael (1944), *Axis Rule in Occupied Europe*, Washington, Carnegie Endowment for International Peace.

[19] Novick, Peter (2000), *The Holocaust and Collective Memory: The American experience*, London, Bloomsbury, 19–20.

Compared to the charter, the indictment based on it was marred by haste and the inordinate number of lawyers engaged in its drafting. Its worst blemish consisted in extending the conspiracy count to all the other counts, such that some defendants were charged with devising a 'common plan' to commit war crimes and crimes against humanity as well, not crimes against the peace only as the charter envisaged. As well, the Soviets insisted on including the Katyn Forest massacre in the indictment. (In the end, they adduced no evidence for this charge, and the judges passed over it in silence.) But beyond that, even the indictment was a serviceable document which centred on four enumerated counts: conspiracy ('the common plan'), crimes against peace, war crimes proper, and crimes against humanity.

Selection of the defendants provided the least propitious feature of the trial preparation. Through bungling and miscommunication, Gustav Krupp, the aged and senile patriarch of the Krupp empire—foremost exploiter of the Reich's 4,795,000 foreign slave workers who had toiled and perished in large numbers in its war industries—was indicted instead of his son Alfried, who in fact owned and controlled the conglomerate during the war.[20] The tribunal would quickly rule the former too incapacitated to proceed against, and block his replacement with Alfried on procedural

---

[20] Major Airey Neave — a young English war hero and barrister — led the initial investigation of the Krupp concern in mid-1945 on behalf of the British War Crimes Commission. His account of it in *Nuremberg: A personal record of the trial of major Nazi war criminals in 1945-6*, London, Hodder & Stoughton, 1978, makes salutary reading about the Krupp atrocities (including its exploitation of Auschwitz inmates) and the management's compact moral indifference towards them that he encountered after the war. He later played an important part in the trial assisting the bench, including taking evidence on commission.

grounds. Thus no representative of German war industry came to sit in the dock during the trial — its greatest shortcoming.

Another mistake was indicting the radio journalist Hans Fritzsche, of the propaganda ministry, as a surrogate for the dead Joseph Goebbels, Nazi Germany's propaganda minister. The Western Allies held Otto Dietrich, Goebbels's immediate subordinate, but the Soviets insisted on charging the comparatively lowly Fritzsche as a matter of national pride: they had only one other major war criminal to contribute to the collection in the Nuremberg dock, Admiral Erich Raeder.[21] Yet another mistake was to proceed with an indictment in absentia against Martin Bormann, Hitler's official secretary and manager of Party affairs who vanished when Berlin fell on 2 May 1945, and probably died that day in the fighting while escaping Hitler's bunker.

Nonetheless, when the trial began on 20 November 1945, 21 defendants sat in the dock. They represented the Reich's political, military and organisational elite, its governors of conquered territories, and its propagandists. Notionally the SS, SA, Gestapo, Reich cabinet, and military general staff and high command also sat in the dock, indicted as criminal organisations. In front of the dock sat legal representatives for each individual and organisational defendant.

Isolation, discomfort and friction in Nuremberg

I have emphasised above the extraordinary vision and determination that American policy-makers around Henry Stimson, the Secretary of War, brought to the formulation of US policy on war crimes 1944–1945, to the London negotiations, and to the drafting of the charter that emerged from them. With Jackson leading the 1,200-strong US prosecution team (and the authority figure for the wider

---

[21] Taylor, 631. The tribunal ended up acquitting Fritzsche.

American contingent of around 1,700) in Nuremberg, that determination was, if anything, redoubled, as the world was now watching. If the trial was to set an invaluable precedent in international criminal law, it could not proceed in obscurity; it needed to present a salutary spectacle reported by hundreds of radio and newsprint correspondents, expert commentators, and a considerable number of dignitaries from around the world. The British and American prosecutors in particular were conscious of the performative dimension of the trial—they were playing to the galleries of their home publics, and after that, of international public opinion. Legal criteria would soon clash with dramatic desiderata, as we will see.

American negotiators had to fight hard to gain agreement for the choice of Nuremberg, in the American zone of occupation, as the seat of judgment. The natural choice, as the Soviets insisted, was the German capital, Berlin, in their *own zone*. As a face-saving compromise, Berlin became the 'headquarters' of the IMT, under the wing of the Allied Control Council there. The preliminary sessions of the IMT were thus held in Berlin from 9 October 1945, ending nine days later with the approval and signing of the prolix indictment, after which the actual trial was adjourned to Nuremberg. Here the occupying US Third Army could protect and resource it as trial participants in their hundreds began to arrive from the four host powers and from other parts of Germany, and correspondents flocked in from all corners of the developed world. For this purpose, the army set up a special administrative zone, the Nuremberg–Fürth enclave.

Once there, the prosecutors, judges and their staffs found themselves virtually isolated. There was little land transport in or out of Nuremberg, as the ravages of war had destroyed infrastructure, and the various occupation zones across Germany set up a maze of travel and currency restrictions. Air transport was in short supply because so many Allied pilots had already been demobilised. In any event, Allied governments were preoccupied with the more immediate issues of postwar reconstruction and had no interest in trying to influence the trial's course from afar. The Western governments in particular made no attempt to influence the proceedings or their outcome.[22]

These circumstances meant that the fate of the whole Nuremberg project now very much lay in the hands of the people on the ground. If their skill or dedication faltered, the trial could descend into chaos or farce, and a vital opportunity for the development of international law and human rights would be lost.

The physicality of Nuremberg intimately impinged on the trial participants as they struggled to remain focused, faced their dilemmas and shouldered their responsibilities.[23] Ninety per cent of the old town lay in ruins after 11 Allied heavy bombing raids on this city of elegant Romanesque and High-Gothic buildings, and toy and gingerbread factories. For 500 years it had served as the effective seat of government for the mediaeval 'first reich', the Holy Roman Empire, so Hitler chose it as the symbolic heart of his own 'thousand-year' Third Reich. The city's name attached to the notorious Nazi race laws that Hermann Göring as president of the Reichstag proclaimed there in 1935. Up to 1938 annual Party rallies and mock battles were staged on the Zeppelin Field on the city's outskirts; grandiose monumental masonry, some of it bearing the fingerprints of the architect and trial defendant Albert

---

[22] Shawcross, 122.

[23] The main prosecutorial memoir writers all comment on the confronting environment, but the best descriptions of it come from two outstanding writers who covered the trial for *The New Yorker*: Rebecca West and Janet Flanner; see West (1955), *A Train of Powder*, London, Macmillan, and Flanner (1979), *Janet Flanner's World: Uncollected writings 1932–1975*, Irving Drutman (ed), New York and London, Harcourt Brace Jovanovich, 98–145.

Speer, still stood there to bear witness to the short-lived Nazi power and glory. Allied airforce and army commanders seem to have recognised Nuremberg's symbolic status, which warranted their own special attention. The US Seventh Army overwhelmed the ferocious resistance of two *Waffen-SS* divisions to seize the city on Hitler's 56th birthday, 20 April 1945, ten days before he shot himself. Now the city had been chosen to host a new drama, the day of reckoning.

Nazi Germany had not committed resources to recovering the dead from bombsites or to providing prosthetic limbs for its own war amputees. The new arrivals in Nuremberg were assaulted not only by startling images of mass destruction, but by the stench of around 6,000 corpses rotting under the rubble, rat plagues and the sight of the limbless crawling over the rubblescape, often living in cellars and bomb shelters beneath it. For want of any other burial place, relatives of the dead placed paper lanterns and candles in the rubble of last known addresses on the anniversary days of the dead beneath.[24] Jackson would note in his opening address at the trial, as he warmed to his central theme:

> It is not necessary among the ruins of this ancient and beautiful city with untold numbers of its civilian inhabitants buried in its rubble, to argue the proposition that to start or wage an aggressive war has the moral qualities of the worst of crimes.[25]

For the thousands of new arrivals whose business was the

---

[24] West, 30.

[25] Quoted in Taylor, 171. As he notes (262), 'For Jackson, the establishment of crimes against peace as an acknowledged part of international law was the crux of the entire case. The British supported that goal.' It was also the crux of Shawcross's opening address on 3 December 1945.

trial and who passed through this devastation each day, the city itself bore mute testimony to the trial's own iron necessity.

Though most of the trial participants lived better than the local population, their everyday lives were spartan, even by immediate postwar European standards. There was nothing to buy and nowhere to buy it except flea markets and outlets for rationed food, although American troops also had access to their ubiquitous do-gooder PX stores. The makeshift cafeteria in the Palace of Justice (*Justizgebäude*) served basic army food to 1,500 people each sitting day at lunchtime, though the high-ranking could do a little better at the Grand Hotel, which the occupiers had hastily refurbished as the social centre for the trial. The trial itself ran from 20 November 1945 to 1 October 1946 to a back-breaking schedule, sitting with only short breaks from 10 am to 5 pm on weekdays, and some Saturday mornings. In all, it held 216 sitting days.

Social and cultural life was minimal for lack of time, resources and camaraderie between the national delegations. The only exceptions were a high level of working co-operation and after-hours socialising between the American and British delegations, and the French started a much appreciated nightclub in the outer suburb of Zirndorf where they, along with the British, occupied requisitioned villas. The 35 German defence lawyers, of whom 14 admitted to being Nazi Party members, found their way onto nobody's invitation list. The self-isolating Soviet delegation did not do much better.

Under all these circumstances, the trial hardly unfolded as the smooth, natural and rational process that today's peace studies and human rights idealists might see in the rear-vision mirror. It lived and breathed makeshift and conflict. Prosecutors and judges all came from diverse traditions and backgrounds, and engaged in rivalry and hostility while discharging their separate functions. These conditions coloured the internal workings of the huge American prosecution team under Jackson's irascible and highly dysfunctional management.[26] And between prosecution and defence lawyers reigned mutual incomprehension. Especially in the latter stages of the trial, the defendants themselves jostled each other in shifting struggles for influence and authority, as well as engaging in mutual blame-shifting as they presented their individual defences.

But makeshift and conflict did not weaken the trial — they were its condition of existence, its lifeblood. Anna Tsing argues that it is precisely *friction* — 'the awkward, unequal, unstable, and creative qualities of interconnection across difference' — that brings to life real-world global encounters. Friction provides the 'traction' or 'grip' that move international projects forward, while at the same time challenging the dubious universalisms that (in her idiom) give rise to dreams of the seamless evolution of a benign international order. [27] It is perhaps this sort of imaginary orderly development that the legal critics of the Nuremberg trial have always hankered after. Jackson anticipated them in his opening address:

> This Tribunal, while it is novel and experimental, is not the product of abstract speculations nor is it created to vindicate legalistic theories. This inquest represents the practical effort of four of the most mighty of nations, with the support of seven-teen more, to utilise international law to meet the

---

[26] Taylor, especially 136–42 and 182. Six days after the trial began Jackson sacked General Donovan, a major figure in the Stimson group and the prosecution team, and a steady stream of senior figures resigned in exasperation as the trial proceeded.

[27] Tsing, Anna (2005), *Friction: An ethnography of global connection*, Princeton and Oxford, Princeton University Press, 4.

greatest menace of our times — aggressive war.[28]

The trial

As indicated, the scale of the Nuremberg trial beggars comparison. Though the prosecution case was overwhelmingly documentary (including photographic and cinematographic material), it still called 33 witnesses, while the defence summoned 61. The tribunal generated its own documents, especially as it needed multiple copies of all written material in each of four languages. The English version of the daily transcripts alone fills 17,000 pages. In all, the trial produced 50 million pages of typing and 4,000 recorded discs.[29] A new professional corps, simultaneous interpreters, made its debut and constituted the nervous system of this multilingual institution.

The bench consisted of two judges from each of the four powers — a voting judge, and an alternate who sat through the proceedings in case his senior became indisposed. The judges were of varying experience and ability, and the alternates tended to be the better lawyers, or to have more judicial experience, than their seniors. Sir Geoffrey Lawrence, a lord justice of the British Court of Appeal, presided, and thus ran the court during sittings. Though perhaps 'much better known as a country squire with a good stable than as a great lawyer', in Shawcross's words,[30] Lawrence made an invaluable contribution through his unfailing courtesy and firmness. He became a popular figure among the defendants, in whose favour his procedural rulings tended to err. They were not to know that, in the common-law tradition, this is usually a bad sign that the judge senses which is the weaker party and redoubles his or her efforts to be make the probable

---

[28] Excerpted in Owen, James (2006), *Nuremberg: Evil on trial*, London, Headline Review, 34.

[29] Shawcross, 107–08.

[30] Shawcross, 100.

outcome appear fair.

The prosecution bore the burden of proof the whole way. Under the agreed division of labour between the prosecution teams, the Americans were responsible for proving the first count of the indictment (conspiracy); the British count two (crimes against peace); and the French and Soviets shared counts three and four (war crimes and crimes against humanity), with the French responsible for proving crimes committed in Western Europe and the Soviets for those committed in the east. The Americans' task here was easily the most demanding, in terms of both legal theory and evidence.

Not surprisingly, the proceedings were dominated, at least until the defence case began, by the huge American prosecution team. It would send no less than 23 of its number to the lectern to handle various aspects of their case; all of them, including their leader, tended to be indifferent or inexperienced trial advocates, though Jackson's legal vision, passion and oratory soared above the rest of the legal fraternity assembled there. The British team, though only 163 strong and thus a seventh the size of its American counterpart, deployed complementary skills. Apart from the usually absent Shawcross (who delivered only the opening and closing addresses on his team's behalf), the British sent just six seasoned barristers to the lectern throughout the trial. They were led by the veteran criminal advocate Sir David Maxwell Fyfe, who also shone as an administrator behind the scenes. As the tribunal applied Anglo-American court procedure, both these teams found themselves on home ground. The French and Soviet teams were smaller still than the British, and disadvantaged by the unfamiliar procedure.

A detailed account of the proceedings falls outside the limits of this essay and so some highlights must suffice. After the tedious reading of the indictment 'onto the record' on the first two days, Jackson opened the prosecution case with an address he later described as 'the most important talk of my life';[31] his was far from the only superlative it would attract. He began right 'on message':

The privilege of opening this first trial in history for crimes against the peace of the world imposes grave responsibility. The wrongs which we seek to condemn and punish have been so calculated, so malignant, and so devastating, that civilisation cannot tolerate their being ignored, because it cannot survive their being repeated. That four great nations, flushed with victory and stung with injury stay the hand of vengeance and voluntarily submit their captive enemies to the judgment of the law is one of the most significant tributes that Power has ever paid to reason.[32]

The speech spellbound the bench, the lawyers and the gallery. Telford Taylor, normally quick to criticise his colleagues (Jackson included), felt that 'nothing said at Nuremberg thereafter matched its force, perception and eloquence. Indeed, I know of nothing else in modern juristic literature that equally projects the controlled passion and moral intensity of many passages.'[33] Jackson's opening address thus amply fulfilled both the legal and the theatrical demands on the trial.

These contrasting demands soon collided as the American prosecutors began to lead their evidence. Proceedings quickly bogged down in the mass of captured German documents tendered, and serious logistical problems arose in making them available in multiple copies to all parties in the four languages that the tribunal used. The press and public seating emptied, and the bench became irate as 'reading documents onto the record' took up day after day. In normal proceedings, this tendering of hard documentary evidence would

---

[31] Quoted in Taylor, 172.
[32] Excerpted in Owen, 34
[33] Taylor, 167.

have constituted best practice, but in Nuremberg it threatened to defeat a major purpose of the trial.

Gradually the tribunal developed ways to handle documents more expeditiously, and the American team became more selective in the documents it tendered. It also began to introduce other forms of evidence. These included the gruesome films taken by the British when they liberated the Bergen–Belsen concentration camp, and by the Americans when they overran Buchenwald and Dachau. To the outrage of those in the dock, the American prosecutors also called high-ranking German officers who testified to the military defendants' complicity in Hitler's war planning and in atrocities against civilians.

The British prosecutors had the advantages of a more circumscribed task in establishing crimes against peace, and of a very tight organisation; they called no witnesses and accomplished their task in four days. To the surprise of most, the senior French prosecutor, François de Menthon, delivered a brilliant, impassioned opening address on 17 January 1946, one that deeply impressed his audience, even the defence lawyers. But reading it 40 years later, Taylor notes 'a jarring omission of reference to Jews and the Holocaust', despite de Menthon's identifying 'racialism' as the worst aspect of Nazism.[34] The Soviet prosecution presented powerful evidence of German atrocities in eastern Europe, including a surprise star witness — Field Marshall Friedrich Paulus, who led the German forces in the disastrous Stalingrad campaign — and a documentary film recording German atrocities in the USSR, one even more horrifying than those screened by the American prosecution.

The trial had then reached what the British alternate judge,

---

[34] Taylor, 296.

Sir Norman Birkett, described in his diary as 'in a very real sense, the critical moment of the trial' — the opening of the defence case, starting with *Reichsmarschall* Hermann Göring, commander-in-chief of the Luftwaffe, founder of the Gestapo, and Hitler's longtime intimate and heir apparent.[35] Legally speaking, this was *not* the critical moment. The prosecution case against this defendant was already formidable, and his evidence-in-chief did not seek to refute it, but rather to enter a long and fiery defence of Hitler and Nazism; it thus contained corroborating admissions. Göring never wavered from the view that a death sentence was certain, and he participated in the trial only to expose it as a sham and to speak to a resurgent German posterity which, he believed, would hail him and his ilk as heroes, exemplars and martyrs.

But Birkett was right about 'the critical moment', as he was arguably not only the best jurist in the courtroom, but also keenly aware of how the trial was unfolding as a morality play writ large. In this sense, he saw Göring fulfilling a pivotal role, as he noted in his diary:

Throughout this trial the dead Hitler has been present at every session, a dreadful, sinister, and in some respects inexplicable figure; but Göring is the man who has really dominated the proceedings, and that remarkably enough, with-out ever uttering a word in public up to the moment he went into the witness box... [I]t has been obvious that a personality of outstanding though possibly evil qualities, was seated there in the dock.[36]

In his own diary, the prison psychologist Gustave Gilbert confirms Göring's dominance among the defendants as he marshalled them to a common cause and stance. Like many others, he also notes Göring's dramatic transformation in

---

[35] Quoted in Hyde, H Montgomery (1964), *Norman Birkett: The life of Lord Birkett of Ulversten*, London, Penguin, 509.

[36] Quoted in Hyde, 510.

American captivity, from a besotted, grossly obese drug addict, to a man of normal build, great charm, forceful personality and very high intelligence.[37]

Though cross-examination was unnecessary from an evidentiary point of view, from a dramatic one it would have been unthinkable for Göring's grandstanding in his own evidence-in-chief over two and a half days to have gone unchallenged. To a packed courtroom, Jackson rose to tackle him on 18 March 1946. He immediately made elementary mistakes in his cross-examination, posing open-ended questions and challenging Göring's opinions rather than his factual assertions. The latter took the invitation to grandstand once more, humiliating Jackson in the process. Having palpably lost control of the cross-examination, Jackson became even more flustered when his ill-advised appeals to the bench to control the witness were turned down: Göring was within his rights in answering open-ended questions in extenso. He was also playing to his own gallery, his fellow defendants, with great success. Jackson never gained the upper hand, and virtually every commentator and diarist present reported the appalling effect the scene had on those present. Afterwards Jackson 'was well-nigh unhinged by the torrent of criticism', his then deputy, Telford Taylor, comments.[38] 'For a few hours, the fate of the Nuremberg Trials trembled in the balance', Maxwell Fyfe notes in his memoirs.[39]

He himself was due to cross-examine after Jackson, and suddenly had to assemble new material to recover the ground

---

[37] Gilbert, G M (1947), *Nuremberg Diary*, New York, Farrer, Strauss & Co. Gilbert (28) assessed Göring's IQ as 138.

[38] Taylor, 344.

[39] Kilmuir, 113.

Jackson had lost. After a night of frantic preparation, Maxwell Fyfe began his own duel with Göring. Transposed to the former's usual places of work, what followed would have rated as little more than a workmanlike cross-examination by an experienced advocate who was on top of his brief and held some good cards. There were no open-ended questions, only questions of factual detail, the answers to which the advocate already held in his hand; and the witness's attempts at diversionary sallies were abruptly cut off.

In this particular setting with this particular witness, however, the interchange amounted to high-order courtroom pyrotechnics. Maxwell Fyfe had his own gallery to play to — the British public — and highlighted Göring's collusion in the murder of 75 recaptured RAF officers who had escaped from *Stalag Luft III*. He pressed his increasingly cowed prey into admissions that revealed the *Reichmarschall* as a heartless warmonger and murderer, a common liar, and a disgrace to any officer corps worthy of the name. In her dispatch to *The New Yorker*, Janet Flanner reported from the press gallery:

During this vital cross-examination, Sir David's professional affability disappeared…With his excellent mind, his vast legal knowledge, and the added passion of a just inquisition, he stood behind his lectern and prosecuted the seated Göring into at least a partial state of destruction. He succeeded in doing what had not yet been done: he forced Göring to separate himself intellectually from the Nazi myth, he forced him to admit the difference between the glorified Nazi plan and the ghastly human results.[40]

---

[40] Flanner, 120. Maxwell Fyfe admitted in his memoirs (Kilmuir, 97), that Göring was 'without question the most formidable witness I have ever cross-examined'. Owen (132–70) excerpts selections of the transcript of Göring's cross-examination. In a bizarre rewriting of history, Yves Simoneau's 2000 docudrama, *Nuremberg*, attributes Maxwell Fyfe's cross-examination to a resurgent Jackson (played by Alec Baldwin).

It was now clear to lay spectators — as it had long been clear to the lawyers — that Göring's position was hopeless. He lost his grip on the other defendants, who in turn abandoned all solidarity with each other.

As the other defendants now took turns to present their individual defences, they shifted blame onto each without restraint, to the prosecution's advantage. And those who chose to step into the witness box faced the nemesis of Maxwell Fyfe, who in effect now replaced the wounded Jackson as the central figure at the prosecution tables.[41]

The judges took a month of frequent, long meetings to reach their verdicts, agree on sentences and write their judgment applying the principles expressed in the charter. In the upshot they acquitted three of the 21 defendants — Fritzsche, Schacht and von Papen. The German police would soon re-arrest them and submit them to new court proceedings, in the *Spruchkammer* of the denazification program. Each of the remaining 18 defendants was convicted on at least one count; 11 received death sentences, and seven received long custodial sentences.

After their appeals to the Control Commission in Berlin failed, the 11 condemned men kept their appointment with the US Third Army's hangman in the early hours of 16 October 1946, except for Göring who took his own life two hours earlier. The remaining defendants found their way to Spandau prison in the British zone of Berlin. International criminal law had not only made its entrance; it came armed with palpable sanctions as Jackson had called for.[42]

---

[41] Taylor, 633.

[42] Well ahead of public opinion at the time, both Jackson and Shawcross were prominent opponents of the death penalty in their respective countries. Given the scale of the criminality before the

The judges cleaned up the confusion in the indictment around the conspiracy count. The charter sought to apply this count to aggressive war only, and the tribunal now reinstated the charter's more restrictive approach. It also refused to declare the Reich cabinet and German high command to be criminal organisations, as they did not constitute 'organisations' in the strict sense (the cabinet in particular had not met since 1937), and were small enough for individual prosecutions to suffice. The Allies' denazification program would trump the tribunal's adverse verdicts against the SS, SA and Gestapo in the treatment of 'lesser' criminals in the years to come.[43]

The main Nuremberg trial in historical context

Around the time of the Nuremberg trial, the Allies conducted many other war-crimes trials in Europe along more conventional lines, the most prominent being those the British conducted in Belsen and the Americans in Dachau. More importantly, the original 'Nuremberg ideas', as expressed in the charter and the tribunal's judgment, were enshrined in international law as 'the Nuremberg principles' adopted by the UN General Assembly on 11 December 1946. For three years after the trial ended, these principles and the precedent the trial had set were applied in 11 important subsequent trials of separate categories of German perpetrators. These trials were held under purely American auspices (with Telford Taylor now chief of counsel), also in the Palace of Justice in Nuremberg.

When the cold war began in earnest in 1948, the major powers' pursuit of geopolitical interests soon closed the valuable opening for progressive international initiatives that arose at the end of World War II. As we have seen, the

Nuremberg tribunal, however, it was not a suitable forum in which to raise this issue.

[43] Taylor, 628.

protagonists of the first Nuremberg trial seized this short-lived opportunity. But they were not alone in so doing. The founders of the United Nations, and the drafters of its Universal Declaration of Human Rights (UDHR) and abovementioned Genocide Convention (both adopted by its General Assembly in December 1948) built on the Nuremberg principles, and on the precedent the trial set.

The UDHR is perhaps the clearer case in point. From the US Declaration of Independence of 1776, with its famous 'self-evident truths' about equal human dignity and rights, authoritative bodies in several countries had impotently declared and proclaimed human rights in the absence of effective sanctions for their breach. The Nuremberg trial established the first supportive sanctions against major forms of human rights transgression. With that background, the UN gave its Human Rights Commission, formidably chaired by Eleanor Roosevelt, the task of drafting a declaration of universal rights.[44] Like the trial itself, the workings of the commission and its drafting committee generated *friction* in generous proportions, as Mary Ann Glendon's account makes clear: the intensifying east-west and Arab-Jewish conflicts contributed greatly to the drafting committee's dynamism up to the UDHR's unanimous adoption by the UN General Assembly in 1948.[45] In her speech to the Assembly on that

---

[44] Reginbogin, Herbert and Safferling, Christoph (2006), *The Nuremberg Trials: International criminal law since 1945*, Munich, K G Saur, 13.

[45] Glendon, Mary Ann (2001), *A World Made New: Eleanor Roosevelt and the Universal Declaration of Human Rights*, New York, Random House. See also Winton Higgins (2012), 'Human Rights Development: Provenance, Ambit and Effect', in (eds) Dudley, Michael, Silove, Derrick and Gale, Fran, *Mental Health and Human Rights: Vision, praxis and courage*, Oxford, Oxford University Press.

occasion, Roosevelt commended the declaration for its potential to 'become the international Magna Carta of all men everywhere'.[46] Before Nuremberg, its adoption would have been an empty gesture; after 1948, the project itself would not have been politically feasible. Once this valuable platform was in place, however, the elaboration of an international rule of law could proceed under the human rights agenda during and after the cold war, albeit at a slower pace. Subsequent UN conventions against torture and slavery, and asserting the rights of women, children and refugees, among others, also build on the Nuremberg principles and the UDHR in fleshing out inter-national legal protections and responsibilities.

As we have seen, the progenitors of the Nuremberg trial highlighted the need for sanctions for breaches of international criminal law, which presupposed the existence of a court with jurisdiction over *all* potential perpetrators. As Jackson noted in his opening address at Nuremberg, in an apology for the necessity, *faute de mieux*, for victors being left to try the vanquished:

We must never forget that the record on which we judge these defendants is the record on which history will judge us tomorrow. To pass these defendants a poisoned chalice is to put it to our own lips as well.[47]

Shawcross and Taylor, among others active in the prosecution at Nuremberg, were conscious of this issue and so agitated for a permanent international criminal court to succeed the IMT.[48] Only in the 1990s did we see ad hoc war-crimes trials in the Nuremberg lineage under the aegis of the UN, ones covering atrocities, including genocide, in Rwanda and former Yugoslavia. Since then, the UN has also initiated

---

[46] Quoted in Glendon, 166
[47] Quoted in Taylor, 168.
[48] See Shawcross, 137; Taylor, 641

similar criminal proceedings in Sierra Leone and Cambodia in partner-ship with the national governments in question.

The idea of a permanent international criminal court remained alive in the UN General Assembly, and came to fruition in the 1998 Statute of Rome, which set up today's International Criminal Court in the Hague — the Nuremberg tribunal's logical and more robust successor.[49]

'The end of America'

In sum, the founding of the UN, the Nuremberg trial and the UDHR, taken together, represent a dramatic leap forward in creating an international rule of law intended to uphold rights — including the right to peace, security and individual inviolability — and to impose criminal sanctions on their breach. The country that contributed the lion's share to this remarkable mid-twentieth century development was America. Fittingly, the UN was founded in San Francisco; American officials took the lead in devising and nurturing the Nuremberg project; and the UDHR was drafted on the shores of Lake Success, New York, under the leadership of one of the country's twentieth-century national treasures, Eleanor Roosevelt. This startling achievement reversed the USA's dismal interwar record of recalcitrance towards the League of Nations and towards proposals to develop an international criminal law, complete with an international court to enforce it. The country achieved an historically unprecedented moral authority.

Unfortunately, the old interwar recalcitrance seeped back into American political culture in the latter half of the twentieth century, so weakening institutions that prominent

---

[49] Kaul, Hans-Peter, 'The International Criminal Court: Key Features and Current Challenges', in Reginbogin and Safferling eds, op cit.

Americans had nurtured in the latter half of the 1940s. The country has thus turned on its own progeny, and thereby defiled its own founding ideals of individual rights, the rule of law and due process. It certainly gives comfort to perpetrators, including those who commit genocide. When this recalcitrance reached its climax in the early 2000s — subverting peace, human rights and the rule of law both at home and abroad — it is no wonder that Naomi Wolf describes the process in a book entitled *The End of America*.[50]

Successive US administrations have refused to ratify many important ramifications of international law, including UN covenants (and optional protocols to them) setting up the UN Human Rights Committee, seeking to abolish the death penalty, discrimination against women and torture, and ones in defence of the rights of children and migrant workers. The US has broken ranks with the rest of the Western world in retaining capital punishment and reintroducing torture as a routine recourse for its military and intelligence services, and its faux-judicial military commissions in Guantánamo Bay may admit evidence extracted under torture in its planned show trials — a throwback to the pre-1770s judicial torture in Western Europe.[51] Unordinary rendition program' whereby it abducts targeted individuals from any country to be tortured

---

[50] Wolf, Naomi (2007), *The End of America*, Melbourne, Scribe, 2007.

[51] The widespread US use of torture (and its provenance in directives issued by the former defence secretary Donald Rumsfeld and attorney-general Alberto Gonzales, with the connivance of the president) was confirmed in the report of the (bipartisan) US Senate Armed Services Committee Inquiry into the Treatment of Detainees in US Custody, published on 11 December 12, 2008. As the report notes, in a memorandum of 7 February 2002, Bush arbitrarily suspended the protections of the third Geneva Convention in the treatment of supposed Al Qaida and Taliban detainees, thus rendering them rightless. See also Sands, Philippe (2008), *Torture Team: Deception, cruelty and the compromise of law*, London, Allen Lane.

in client states, such as Egypt, where this practice is a normal part of quotidian governance.

America was one of just seven countries (with China, Iraq, Israel, Libya, Qatar, and Yemen) which voted against the 1998 Treaty of Rome and the establishment of the ICC. At the last minute (31 December 2000), the Clinton administration signed it, but the incoming Bush administration refused to ratify it. Quite the contrary, it has chosen the route of outright defiance of the ICC, not least in 2002, the year the court came into existence, with the adoption of the American Service-Members' Protection Act, the express purpose of which is 'to protect United States military personnel and other elected and appointed officials of the United States government against criminal prosecution by an international court to which the United States is not a party.' The legislation, which has attracted the sobriquet 'The Hague Invasion Act', in particular authorises the President to use 'all necessary and appropriate means to bring about the release of any US or allied personnel being detained or imprisoned by, or on behalf of, or at the request of the International Criminal Court'. It also prohibits any co-operation with ICC investigations. The impunity that the Nuremberg project denied perpetrators is thus reinstated as far as American power reaches. The days when that 'power paid tribute to reason' are now long gone — to return to Robert Jackson's opening words to the Nuremberg tribunal cited above.

America and its closest allies showed their contempt for the Nuremberg legacy in their unprovoked invasion of Iraq in 2003 — the specific crime of waging aggressive war, the central issue in the Nuremberg trial, the crime for which the tribunal sentenced eight individuals to death in 1946. As Geoffrey Robertson comments, 'The Bush Administration regarded international law as a set of rules that applied to other countries.'[52] Ironically, the American and British governments invoked the Nuremberg principle on the criminality of aggressive war in justifying the first Gulf war after Iraq invaded Kuwait in August 1990.[53]

The New York lawyers around Henry Stimson would have found all too familiar the pattern whereby war (even the rhetorical and protean 'global war on terror') provides the occasion and the pretext for war crimes and crimes against humanity of the kind symbolised by the US facilities of Abu Ghraib and Guantánamo Bay. What they would have found unfamiliar, 60-odd years after the Nuremberg trial, is the reversal of roles which has left their own country the most prominent international outlaw. In 1947, Stimson himself wrote:

[I]n the judgment of Nuremberg there is affirmed the central principle of peace—that the man who makes or plans to make aggressive war is a criminal. A standard has been raised to which Americans, at least, must repair; for it is only as this standard is accepted, supported, and enforced that we can move onward to a world of law and peace.[54]

But Robert Jackson and the other Nuremberg prosecutors, who went to work each day with the stench of death in their nostrils, would have found themselves in familiar territory with the massive destruction and loss of life of the Iraq war — yet another deliberately begun and unwinnable war fought with no holds barred.

For a few hopeful months in 2008, during the US presidential election campaign, it seemed that a line might be drawn under the recalcitrant turn in American political

---

[52] Klatsky Lecture 11 November 2008, extracted in his 'He's Got the Whole World in his Hands, But Can Obama Do It Justice?', *Sydney Morning Herald*, 13 November 2008.

[53] Shawcross, 137.

[54] Quoted in Kochavi, 229–30.

culture, and an attempt would be made to restore the country's moral authority. The Democratic nominee, Barak Obama, declared his intention, for instance, to close the notorious camp at Guantánamo Bay ('a tremendous recruiting tool for al-Qaida') and end other abuses of the Bush era. As his first term as President now draws to a close, though, Guantánamo is still in business, now graced with Obama's own 2011 executive order legitimating a formal system of indefinite detention without trial.[55] The same is true of the other transgressive institutions Obama inherited from Bush— 'extraordinary rendition', 'enhanced interrogation techniques', the faux-judicial 'military commissions' that bar access to properly constituted courts, and of course 'the Hague Invasion Act'.

On 2 May 2011, Obama sent troops on a mission that had them violate the borders of an allied country, gun down Osama bin Laden in his bedroom and kneecap his wife, when these troops obviously could have been given the option to arrest their 'target' alive to face trial. Compared to some of the Nuremberg defendants who enjoyed due process, bin Laden was no more than a smalltime crook, and so it is worth recalling Robert Jackson's words quoted above that the former's proposed extra-judicial killing 'would not sit easily on the American conscience or be remembered by our children with pride'. But Jackson was writing of another America, as Wolf's thesis implies. How easily extra-judicial killing sits on the present American conscience can be gleaned from Obama's recent gloating celebration of the anniversary of bin Laden's killing, including his goading his Republican opponent in his second presidential campaign for supposedly lacking the 'ticker' to order an action like this.[56]

---

[55] The *Guardian Weekly*, 27 April 2012.

[56] The Sydney Morning Herald, 2 May 2012.

International criminal law, peace and human rights now

Without American passion, creativity and resources, the Nuremberg trial would never have taken place, and William Jackson's ideal of 'an international society ordered by law', quoted above, would have remained an impossible utopia. Miraculously, perhaps, this project has now come far and appears to be still advancing in spite of — though necessarily weakened by — outright American hostility. The ICC has now been ratified by 121 states, and has engaged with the cases of such high-profile perpetrators as the former Bosnian-Serb leader, Radovan Karadzic, Ratko Mladic and the current president of the Sudan, Omar Hassan al-Bashir. The associated human rights project has been developing for much longer, and has been greatly strengthened by the monitoring or 'watch' practices that have arisen out of the Helsinki accords of 1975.[57]

However, in betraying its own mid-twentieth century handiwork, today's America is the main brake on progress in international law, justice and human rights, and no amelioration of its regressive political culture is in sight. Were a *volte face* to come to pass, however, the Nuremberg legacy might recover its true proportion in undergirding the international society based on peace, law and rights that its American progenitors foretold.

---

[57] See Higgins, op cit.

THE WAR CRIMES CASE OF KÁROLY ZENTAI AND THE QUEST FOR HISTORICAL JUSTICE

RUTH BALINT[1]

More than 60 years after the Holocaust, attempts to bring the few remaining perpetrators of war crimes to trial are complicated by questions of memory and its relationship to the contemporary societies in which they are pursued. This is particularly evident in the case of Károly Zentai, a man wanted by Hungary since 2005 for extradition and questioning over the murder of a Jewish man in 1944. Zentai has lived in Australia since 1950, a country in which a number of perpetrators and collaborators found safe refuge after the war, and in which their presence was never sufficiently cause for any Australian concern. In Hungary, the complicity of the state in the Holocaust remains subject to historical denial, silenced by the myth of Hungarian victimhood in the war. For the historian, this case provides important insights into the historical links that evolved in the postwar period between Australia and Europe, and illustrates a wider debate about memory and history in the face of the 'perpetually remade past'.[2]

---

[1] This is an extended and updated version of my article 'The Ties That Bind: Australia, Hungary and the Case of Károly Zentai' in *Patterns of Prejudice*, vol 44, issue 2, 2010.

[2] István Rév describes the way the events, ideas and the dead of the past are in a constant process of envisioning and remaking in Hungary; he posits 1989 as a particular moment in which millions lost their past and thus their future, leaving only what was unknown: 'At that point between the lost and the not-yet-comprehended, historians, politicians, and professional and amateur self-proclaimed experts offered … to remake the world.' Rév, István (2009), *Retroactive Justice: Prehistory of post-Communism*, Stanford, Stanford University Press, 9.

Given the distance to the event in temporal and, in the case of Australia, geographical terms, the role of memory is critical to understanding the contemporary context in which the case has been received in the two countries in which, at the time of mid-2012, it is still playing out. Since the French sociologist Maurice Halbwachs, himself a victim of the Nazis, first developed the notion of collective memory in the 1920s, the subject of memory has become an ever-expanding field of intensive scholarship and debate. Halbwachs' theoretical analysis highlighted the social dimensions of remembering and the way the present works to influence what is remembered in societies, and the institutions that embody the public acts of remembering.[3] Since then, memory analysis has developed most significantly in relation to the Holocaust and World War II, in particular, the connection between historical memory and human rights. Holocaust memories, write Daniel Levy and Natan Sznaider, 'have evolved into a universal code that is now synonymous with an imperative to address past injustices (both legally as well as in commemorative terms).'[4]

Halbwachs understood the link between memory, identity and human rights that is essentially the subject of this essay. For Halbwachs, as Jay Winter reminds us, collective memory is the binding agent of civil society.[5] It is those associations and narratives about the past, shared and told by different groups of people, that tell them who they are and what they do. Memory, in particular the memory of past human rights abuses, also underpins the modern institutions of law and politics. For Levy and Sznaider, the universality of human

---

[3] Halbwachs, Maurice (1992), *On Collective Memory*, edited and translated by Lewis A Cosser, Chicago, University of Chicago Press.

[4] Levy, Daniel and Sznaider, Natan (2010), *Human Rights and Memory*, Pennsylvania, Pennsylvania State University Press, 4.

[5] Winter, Jay (2012), 'Foreword: Remembrance as a Human Right', in Assmann, Aleida and Shortt, Linda, *Memory and Political Change*, London and New York, Palgrave Macmillan, ix.

rights, a phenomenon that has emerged since the decade of World War II, 'necessitates a certain distance from the actual events that are being remembered'.[6] They build on Jan Assmann's idea of a 'cultural mnemotechnique', which Assmann defines as 'the transformation of communicative, that is, lived and witness-embodied memory into cultural, that is, institutionally shaped and sustained, memory'.[7] As the actual events of the Holocaust have begun to slip out of living memory, the iconisation of its memory is undergoing its own transformation. This essay is a contribution to understanding this transition.

The politics of memory

Since the fall of Communism, the question of 'which' past to remember, which to use in the forging of a post-Communist identity has galvanised nationalist societies in East-Central Europe. Randolph Braham believes that in Hungary the Holocaust has undergone a 'history cleansing process' since 1989, largely absolving Hungarian society and its political elites of responsibility for the destruction of two-thirds of its Jewish population. A reluctance to address the Holocaust past has been aided by a resurgence of antisemitism and the revival of the 'Jewish question', the forms of which have rehabilitated old stereotypes of the Jews as alien and unassimilable, and responsible for the evils of Communism. Preoccupation with the crimes of Communism has also been at the expense of a reckoning with the Hungarian Holocaust.[8]

---

[6] Levy and Sznaider, *Human Rights and Memory*, 15.

[7] Ibid.

[8] Tim Cole makes the point that the erection of a memorial in the late 1980s and another in the late 1990s to honour Raoul Wallenberg, the Swedish diplomat who led a massive rescue effort of Budapest's Jews in 1944 and disappeared into Soviet captivity after the war, was a political exercise designed to remember Wallenberg 'as a victim of

This has represented a major setback to the project of historical understanding. Braham writes that although the number of populist champions of antisemitism and outright Holocaust denial is quite small in post-Communist Hungary, 'the camp of those distorting and denigrating the catastrophe of the Jews is quite large', and includes many respectable public figures: 'intellectuals, members of parliament, influential governmental and party figures, and high-ranking army officers'.[9] Even in its more moderate forms, these voices of historical revisionism have tended to assert that it was the Germans who committed the atrocities with the assistance of their Hungarian fascist accomplices, the Nyilas (the Arrow Cross party), while the rest — politicians, soldiers, gendarmes and citizens — were largely bystanders, or victims themselves. This remains a majority view. Within this equation, Zentai represents one of a 'few bad apples' rather than a cog in the Hungarian genocidal machine. His trial, should it ever go ahead in Hungary, is more likely to reinforce the mythology of Hungarian innocence rather than expose the complicity of the Hungarian regime in the mass murder of Hungarian Jewry.

Australia confronts an historical revisionism of a very different kind. Unlike East-Central Europe, where the atrocities took place, Australia has always seemed very far

---

"Soviet totalitarianism" rather than as a victor against Nazi "totalitarianism"'. His disappearance at the hands of the Soviets rather than his heroic rescue of thousands of Jews was highlighted (although other memorials, in the form of plaques and statues have since ensured the memory of his rescue efforts is preserved). See Cole, Tim (2003), *Holocaust City: The making of a Jewish ghetto*, New York and London, Routledge, 236–38.

[9] Braham, Randolph (1999), 'The assault on historical memory: Hungarian nationalists and the Holocaust', *East European Quarterly*, vol 33, issue 4, Winter, 411–12.

away from this history.[10] It carries its own burdens when it comes to remembering World War II, in which the theatre of battle and its war crimes are fixed firmly in the Asia-Pacific. Yet from the moment authorities began the process of selection and recruitment for mass immigration in the Displaced Persons (DP) camps of occupied Europe in 1947, Australia became complicit in enabling those who had committed war crimes to escape retribution.[11] To do so, Australian authorities participated in their own version of historical amnesia, and except for a brief period in the 1980s, deliberately ignored or downplayed the evidence of war criminals living in refuge in Australia for the next 60 years. Instead, the popular imaginary of the postwar period of immigration has privileged a narrative of rescue of Hitler's and Stalin's victims. When evidence to the contrary emerged, as it did quite frequently in the 1950s, it was buried by a combination of disinterestedness and an unwillingness to act, on the part of the authorities: a case of 'not our problem'.[12] If he is finally forced to face a Hungarian military court and found guilty, Zentai will likely represent a minor ripple in an otherwise unblemished record of Australian postwar immigration as a story of rescue and salvation of Europe's victims. Ironically, the real victims of war and the Holocaust were regarded as the least desirable of immigrants in Australia's practice of migrant selection and recruitment in

---

[10] In the geographics of the Holocaust, Australia is classified as a bystander nation.

[11] Aarons, Mark (2001), *War Criminals Welcome: Australia, a sanctuary for war criminals since 1945*, Melbourne, Black Inc, 17, 19.

[12] Further, many of those who arrived in Australia with questionable pasts went on to gain influential positions in the political establishment. See Aarons, Mark (2001), *War Criminals Welcome*, Part Four, where he details the rise of former Nazis in the conservative Australian Liberal Party.

the Displaced Persons camps of occupied Europe.

Australia does not have a strong record when it comes to prosecuting or extraditing war criminals. Yet seven years after the initial request was made for Zentai's extradition, it is still being fought in the courts, with the (then) Minister for Home Affairs, Brendan O'Connor, appealing against a decision by the courts to quash an earlier determination to extradite Zentai. This might suggest a shift in Australian attitudes, perhaps prompted by the Holocaust's increasingly 'global' presence in recent decades. It is impossible to imagine a history of the past century without the place names that have come to describe its most cataclysmic event — Auschwitz, Treblinka, Sobibor, Belzec, Majdanek and Buchenwald. There has likely been no other event in human history as extensively documented and analysed, performed and memorialised.[13] Levy and Sznaider, speaking of the Holocaust 'memory boom', believe this has facilitated a new, global and cosmopolitan memory to aid a more moral, world-centred consciousness.[14] Others have argued that the recent cultural

---

[13] Peter Novick describes a 'retrospective construction' of the Holocaust in the United States since the 1970s which he attributes to, among other things, the need to create a consensual symbol for Jewish identity (Novick (2000), *The Holocaust in American Public Life*, 7.) His analysis has since been criticised by Lawrence Baron, who argues that in the 15 years following the end of the war, American attempts to comprehend the Jewish tragedy were expressed through scholarly analyses, first-hand survivor accounts and mass media accounts. What was different was not a lack of American memory, but a different cultural framework within which it could be understood and articulated (Baron, Lawrence (2003), 'The Holocaust and American public memory, 1945-1960', *Holocaust and Genocide Studies*, vol 17, no 1, Spring, 62-88.)

[14] Levy, Daniel and Sznaider, Natan (2002), 'Memory Unbound: The Holocaust and the formation of cosmopolitan memory', *European Journal of Social Theory*, vol 5, no 1, 88. On the other side of the coin, however, this has meant a retreat into historical meaninglessness and

obsession in the West with the Holocaust is contributing to a project of forgetting in other ways. Today, the proliferation of Holocaust imagery has not necessarily assisted with historical understanding, and evidence is that it can sometimes work against it, tending towards the trivialisation of the past, its ossification in public memory.[15] The Holocaust has become a trope for things that often have nothing to do with it, and 'Auschwitz' is now a stylised, a-historical space in which to enact generic stories of pathos, drama and even comedy. Recently, too, there has been a new shift away from the theme of Jewish suffering towards a focus on the perpetrators. We have become far more interested in the human stories of Nazis than those of the victims.[16]

To make the leap from the growth of a more universal Holocaust-centred awareness to Australia's apparent newfound willingness to pursue and uphold Zentai's extradition is pre-emptive and probably misguided. Moreover, as was made clear in statements by O'Connor to the press in 2009, Australia's decision to grant extradition

---

political conservatism. See Maier, Charles (1993), 'A Surfeit of Memory? Reflections on history, melancholy and denial', *History and Memory*, vol 5, no 2, Winter, 136–52.

[15] Huyssen, Andreas (1995), *Twilight Memories: Marking time in a culture of amnesia*, London and New York, Routledge, 255–56.

[16] In Australia, this was most vividly demonstrated in 1995 with the awarding of the nation's highest literary honours for a novel that revived classic antisemitic discourses within the imaginative sphere of the Holocaust. *The Hand That Signed the Paper* won the nation's top literary award, the Miles Franklin, as well as the Vogel Literary Award for a manuscript by a writer under 35. The author, calling herself Helen Demidenko and claiming to be of Ukrainian descent to enhance her credibility, was later discovered to be Helen Darville, of English parents. The book promoted the idea that Jews were partly responsible for the Holocaust.

rests not on establishing Zentai's guilt or innocence, but in complying with Australia's extradition laws.[17] The representation of Zentai's case in the mainstream media, meanwhile, does not support the theory that Australia has developed a more refined historical understanding of the Holocaust and the issues of justice or retribution. Rather, it resembles others in the way it is told, as the story of an old man who has led a largely blameless life in Australia pursued for some-thing that may or may not have happened a long time ago.[18] Jane Cadzow's piece, published in 2008 in the *Sydney Morning Herald*, for example, under the title 'Another time, another place', capturing Australia's sense of remove from this history, and the idea that it has nothing much to do with the here and now.[19]

What makes this case of further interest is the fact that the crime Zentai is accused of has been known to authorities for over 60 years. The Budapest People's Court issued the warrant for his arrest in 1948 when his whereabouts in Allied occupied Germany were already known. Yet neither the Allies, under whose protection Zentai lived in Germany after the war, nor the Hungarian authorities who issued the arrest warrant, made any effort to bring him back to Hungary for

---

[17] *ABC News*, Friday 13 November 2009.

[18] The only exceptions to this simplistic packaging of what is a far more complex story have been a couple of articles published recently in an Australian magazine *The Monthly*, in which Hungarian writer György Vámos reviews some of the evidence, and Mark Aarons gives a brief account of Australia's tradition of apathy when it comes to punishing those who commit war crimes overseas but make their homes here: see Vámos, György (2009), 'Murder on Arena Avenue: is Charles Zentai guilty?', and Aarons, Mark (2009), 'Hideout', *The Monthly*, no 43, March.

[19] Cadzow, Jane (2008), 'Another Time, Another Place', *Sydney Morning Herald*, 14 June.

trial. It would have been far simpler to do so.[20] When he applied for passage to Australia while in the care of the International Refugee Organisation (IRO) as a DP, the Australian migration selection team was probably ignorant of the warrant. The Wiesenthal Centre, whose request to the Hungarian authorities initiated this recent case for extradition, claims it knew nothing of Zentai's case beforehand; but there is evidence that the Balàzs family had been trying to interest both the Wiesenthal Centre and the Hungarian authorities for decades.

In 2008 I travelled to Hungary where I reviewed the original evidence that initiated the request for Zentai's extradition. In Germany I uncovered documents relating to Zentai's journey through Allied occupied Germany, and his application for migration as a DP. These reveal other aspects of the case hitherto untold, and shed light on Australia's own contribution to the European process of forgetting, whereby through the postwar practice of immigration selection and recruitment in the Displaced Persons camps the crimes of the Holocaust were revised as purely German crimes, and anti-Communists regarded far more positively than anti-fascists, or even Jews, as potential 'New Australians'.

The Holocaust in Hungary and the case of Peter Balàzs

In 1944, the Jews of Hungary, numbering some 700,000, remained the most physically intact Jewish community in Europe. Close to 64,000 Hungarian Jews had already lost their

---

[20] This doesn't appear to be an isolated case. Judit Molnár notes the case of the gendarme commander Gyözö Tölgyessy, whom the Hungarian People's Prosecution requested American authorities to extradite, but which never occurred (Molnár, Judit, 'Gendarmes Before the People's Courts', in Braham, Randolph and Chamberlin, Brewster S (2006) (eds) *The Holocaust in Hungary: Sixty years later*, Boulder, Social Science Monographs, 145).

lives; 20,000 'alien' Jews had been sent across the border into Poland and shot at Kamenets-Poldolsk, and a majority of the rest were Jewish men killed when serving in labour battalions on the Ukrainian front. A series of severe anti-Jewish laws had also been implemented, restricting basic civil and socio-economic rights.[21] But the conservative government of Miklos Kallay (9 March 1942 to 22 March 1944) had stopped short of complying with Germany's demands for the deportation of Hungarian Jewry.[22] The occupation of Hungary by Germany in March 1944 led to the implementation of the 'Final Solution' with a speed and efficiency unrivalled in other Nazi-occupied countries. Within a few short months, at a time when it was clear that the war was already lost, and when the realities of Auschwitz were public knowledge among the world's leaders, more than 437,000 Hungarian Jews were deported from the provinces to the death camps. This was only made possible with the wholehearted support of the Hungarian constitutionally appointed government of Döme Sztójay, the endorsement of the Regent of Hungary, Miklos Horthy, and with the assistance of local authorities. As Braham writes: 'With Horthy still at the helm, providing the symbol of national sovereignty, the Hungarian police, gendarmerie, and civil service collaborated with the SS in the anti-Jewish drive

---

[21] As Randolph Braham notes, the persecution and scapegoating of the Jewish population, and its enactment in legislation, was already a strong feature of Hungarian politics since 1919, with the installation of the counter-revolutionary regime of Miklos Horthy; the anti-Jewish campaign was institutionalised in 1938 with the first of the so-called anti-Jewish Acts of parliament, and legislation of major anti-Jewish laws. See Braham, Randolph 'Hungary', in Wyman, David S (ed) (1996), *The World Reacts to the Holocaust*, Baltimore and London, The John Hopkins University Press, 202–03.

[22]For a discussion of the politics of 1942 in relation to Hungarian-Jewish policy considerations, see Karsai, Laszló, 'The Fateful Year: 1942 in the reports of Hungarian diplomats', in Braham, Randolph and Chamberlin, Brewster S, (eds) *The Holocaust in Hungary*, 3–16.

with a routine and efficiency that impressed even the Germans.'[23] By 1 June, the average daily number of Hungarian Jews being deported to Auschwitz was 20,000.[24]

By the end of July, virtually the only remaining Jews surviving in Hungary were in Budapest. In the month of July, 25,000 were deported to Auschwitz, at which point the government temporarily suspended deportations. In October, the fascist Arrow Cross party, under the leadership of Ferenc Szàlasi, was installed in government in a Nazi-orchestrated coup. The Arrow Cross embarked on a reign of terror, enacting frenetic killing sprees of the remaining Jews seeking refuge in the city. Thousands were arrested and shot and dumped into the Danube, and thousands more were shot or perished during a death march of 70,000 to Austria. The Arrow Cross reign lasted until Soviet forces liberated the city on 13 February 1945; during this time, those Jews who managed to stay outside of the ghetto, using false papers and not wearing a yellow star, had a slim chance of survival. Péter Balázs, an 18-year-old boy, was among those who chose the Jewish underground.

It was during this time that Zentai, a conscripted Hungarian Royal Army officer, was stationed at the Aréna Road military barracks in Budapest in 1944. Zentai's commanding officer was Bela Máder, and his fellow officer Lajos Nagy. After the war, they were tried for the murder of Péter Balázs and found guilty, Máder in 1946, Nagy in 1947. Máder was sentenced to forced labour for life; Nagy was given the death sentence, later commuted to life

[23] Braham, Randolph (1999), 'The Assault on Historical Memory: Hungarian nationalists and the Holocaust', *East European Quarterly*, vol 33, no 4, 413.

[24] Wiesel, Elie, 'Keynote Address', in Braham, Randolph and Chamberlin, Brewster S, (eds) *The Holocaust in Hungary*, xv.

imprisonment.[25] Evidence given at these trials prompted the Hungarian authorities to charge Zentai with the same crime; by that time, he was already in Germany living as a DP. These trials were part of the wave of war crimes trials held in Hungary in the immediate postwar period; approximately 27,000 people were sentenced by the Hungarian 'people's courts' for war crimes, crimes against the state or crimes against humanity, among them a number of senior government ministers.[26] These also included local and county government officials, gendarmerie and military officers responsible for the expropriation, ghettoisation and deportation of the Jews of Hungary.

At his trial, Nagy told of how, under the orders of their commanding officer Bela Máder, Zentai went out on patrols regularly to perform identity checks and round up Jews for interrogation. According to Nagy, Zentai already knew Péter Balázs: in his statement after his arrest he told the police, 'Zentai told me that the boy and his family were old acquaintances of his'.[27] The Zentai and Balázs families were both from Budafok, a small town on the outskirts of Budapest. The Balázs family were well known in their region as Jews and for their leftist sympathies; Dezsö Balázs, Péter's father, had his legal practice there until 1942 when the family moved into Budapest. Zentai, only a few years older than Péter Balázs, was apparently his 'Levente' instructor for a time in Budafok.[28] Balázs was surviving on false identity papers, and defied a call-up order for a Jewish forced labour unit in April

[25] Both men were released in 1956; Nagy went abroad.

[26] Karsai, László (2000), 'The People's Courts and Revolutionary Justice in Hungary, 1945–46', in Deák, István, Gross, Jan Tomasz and Judt, Tony (eds) (2000), *The Politics of Retribution in Europe: World War Two and its aftermath*, Princeton, Princeton University Press, 233.

[27] Municipal Archives of Budapest, XXV.1.a, 3165/1947, People's Court Trial of Lajos Nagy.

[28] Levente was a military version of the Boy Scout movement.

1944. On 8 November, Zentai recognised the boy on a Budapest tram and arrested him for not wearing the yellow star.

What happened afterwards, according to the evidence presented at Nagy's trial, is that between the hours of 3 pm and 8 pm, Zentai and Nagy beat Balázs so badly that by 8 pm he was dying. According to Nagy's evidence, they (Zentai, Máder and himself) saw that the boy was dying, and then went to an adjoining room and began drinking. In a macabre twist, Captain Máder decided to show off their handiwork to a number of other prisoners detained that night at Aréna Road. As a number of them testified at Nagy's trial, eight of them (some say six) were taken to Captain Máder's rooms, where one by one, they were shown a man lying on the floor covered by his own overcoat. His breath rattled, and it was clear that he was dying. 'Can you hear that music?' Sándor Révner stated that Máder asked him, when it came his turn to view the dying man. 'That's the way you will go too.'[29] Each of the witnesses said they were told the same thing. The prisoners were then brought back into the room and forced to say the Hebrew prayer for the dead, 'and we said that prayer according to his instructions'.[30] The next day, all but one of them escaped. Each confirmed, as did other officers present that day, that the man lying on the floor, according to his photograph, was Péter Balázs.

I have before me the original court transcripts in which witnesses describe the brutalities they endured while they were detained at the barracks. There are various references to Zentai's regular participation in these beatings. Imre Zoltan testified that in 1944, while in Budapest as a forced labourer, he was arrested and taken to the barracks 'where at Béla

---

[29] XXV.1.a, 3165/1947, Lajos Nagy.

[30] XXV.1.a, 3165/1947, Lajos Nagy.

Máder's orders, Cadet Károly Zentai and Cadet Ferenc Érsek beat me up for hours with boxing gloves until I lost consciousness'.[31] Ervin Barinkai, another soldier at the barracks, remembered seeing Zoltan 'gravely assaulted several times, especially by Cadet Sergeant Károly Zentai'.[32] Another cadet, György Varsányi, stated that 'it was Cadet Sergeant Zentai who did the beatings, I saw that myself several times'.[33]

On the night in question, József Monori, another officer assigned to the barracks under Máder's command, reported that he heard, but did not see, the beating going on behind closed doors. He 'definitely' remembered Zentai, Nagy and Máder present. He went to bed, but was woken up at around 11 pm and told to harness a horse and carriage: 'Nagy and Zentai brought down a corpse from the office, put it on the cart, and covered it with straw…Nagy sat on the driver's seat, Zentai beside him, and I sat on the side of the cart. Nagy was driving the cart. We drove along Aréna Road…down to the Danube…There Nagy and Zentai took the corpse and dumped it in the Danube. They waited a while to see if the corpse would come up but it sank.' Monori also stated that during the journey 'Nagy and Zentai were talking about how they should not have beaten the boy so hard'.[34]

These testimonies were taken before the warrant for Zentai's arrest, which was issued on 29 April 1948. After the warrant was issued, Máder, already a condemned man, stated that Zentai 'took part in patrols as well as in beating and maltreating Jews…He and 1st Lieutenant (Nagy) were always ready to volunteer to do the atrocities.'[35] Imre Parázsló,

---

[31] XXV.1.a, 3165/1947, Lajos Nagy.

[32] XXV.1.a, 3165/1947, Lajos Nagy.

[33] XXV.1.a, 3165/1947, Lajos Nagy.

[34] XXV.1.a, 3165/1947, Lajos Nagy

[35] Municipal Archives of Budapest, XXV.1.a, 582/1946, People's

another cadet, stated that the identity checks on Jews were 'mostly carried out by 1st Lieutenant Lajos Nagy and Ensign Károly Zentai accompanied by the worst imaginable beatings...Zentai hit hardest but Nagy was not far behind. They hit the Jews with fists, boxing gloves or sticks, kicked them, and I often saw these Jews beaten to a bloody pulp coming out of the office moaning and crying. Bela Máder knew about these tortures, indeed, he gave orders to them.'[36]

Hungarian journalist György Vámos, referring to the 'unusual circumstances' of judicial practices in postwar Hungary, recently cautioned that witness testimonies relating to this case should be treated with care. He offers no detail beyond remarking that social justice, as opposed to merely criminal justice, was an important objective of the government at the time.[37] This is largely true. The people's courts were driven less by legal concerns than by the desire for retribution and, in many cases, revenge. Confusion, insufficient preparation and political bias were rife during the major political trials, of which there were 14 between 1945 and 1946. 'The historical responsibility of the Hungarian principal war criminals is beyond question', wrote historian Laszlo Karsai. 'What is questionable, however, is whether the people's courts were sufficiently equipped to establish their criminal responsibility.'[38]

Yet we must tread carefully in assessing minor trials such as those of Máder and Nagy. It is common in the West to

---

Court Trial of Máder Belá.

[36] XXV.1.a, 582/1946, Máder Belá.

[37] Vámos, György (2009), 'Murder on Arena Avenue: Is Charles Zentai Guilty?', *The Monthly*, March, 38.

[38] Karsai, László, 'The People's Courts and Revolutionary Justice in Hungary, 1945–46', in István Deák et al, (eds) *The Politics of Retribution in Europe*, 248.

dismiss all postwar trials in Hungary as Communist propaganda, but it was a little more complex than that. In the first place, the Communist Party did not entirely lead the fight against war criminals in the Hungarian courts in the immediate postwar years. The people's courts were party courts, in which representatives from across the anti-fascist political spectrum were chosen to take part. Delegates from the Bourgeois Democratic Party, the Social Democratic Party, the Communist Party, and the National Peasants Party, in addition to representatives from the right wing Independent Smallholders Party, were appointed people's judges. Later, delegates from the National Trade Union Association were also included. A professionally trained judge headed each of the courts, and a majority of votes determined a verdict. What determined the outcome of a particular trial or conviction was usually less the political sway of the parties involved in the process than the personal background and conviction of the judge. Moreover, the influence of the Communist Party only increased after 1947 in the courts, and only then did the number of trials dealing with war crimes or crimes against humanity significantly decrease.[39]

In the second place, condemning all postwar trials as 'show trials' also diminishes the contributions of the many Jewish survivors who did participate in what they saw as a way of achieving some kind of justice, and the importance of these trials at this time for gaining historical recognition. Braham writes that the 'tragedy of individual Jewish communities in Trianon Hungary was exposed in the war crimes trials held between 1945 and 1948 under the auspices of people's tribunals in Budapest and various county seats.'[40] Jews were heavily involved in the judicial process in Hungary

---

[39] Karsai, László (2009), 'Esélyten, Reménytelen és Törvénytelen', *Élet és Irodalom*, vol 48, no 33, 13 August 2004. [Translated by Professor György Novak,].

[40] Braham, Randolph, 'Hungary', 208.

after the war, a fact that is often overlooked in the anti-Communist revisionism of this history. This often took great courage: to give testimonies and to stand witness was an act of bravery for many Jewish victims of wartime atrocities. This is not to say that these trials were neutral or devoid of ideological bias; but they were often the only forum in which survivors could bear witness, and this should be taken into account when evaluating their testimonies. In trials specifically concerned with deportations or murder of Jews, the spectators at these proceedings also tended to be Jewish. Journalist Geza Losonczy was present at the joint Endre–Baky–Jaross trial, the three men most directly responsible for the Hungarian Holocaust. He expressed his disappointment in the 'complete uninterestedness and indifference that the majority of the non-Jewish public manifests towards the case'. This was 'not a trial on behalf of the Jews' but 'a trial of the Hungarian nation against its executioners'.[41]

By 1948, official memory was writing the Jewish experience out of the war altogether as the Communist rereading of history began to take shape. Fascists became, before all other things, anti-Communists, their enemies Communists, even if their victims appeared otherwise.[42] Hopes for restitution and indemnification were soon dashed in the new Communist Hungary, and any chance of rebuilding their communities was soon recognised to be futile. In all Soviet Bloc countries, despite an initial flourishing of scholarly discourse and literary publications addressing the tragedy of the Jewish genocide, as the Cold War deepened towards the end of the 1940s, discussion or acknowledgement of the uniqueness of Jewish suffering during the war largely

---

[41] Quoted in Karsai, László, 'The People's Courts and Revolutionary Justice in Hungary, 1945–46', 246.

[42] Rév, Istvan (2009), *Retroactive Justice*, 222.

disappeared and the millions of Jews killed was revised as general war losses.[43] During the Stalinist era of the 1950s, the Holocaust 'as a distinct historical phenomenon was usually downplayed, distorted or at best hardly referred to even in textbooks'.[44]

Yet, following the uprising of 1956 and the subsequent liberalisation of Communism under the Kádár regime, and due to the increasing efforts of what was a comparatively large Jewish population for an East-Central European country (80,000), there was a slight thawing of attitudes.[45] Braham has argued that this period was one of increasing liberalisation, not only in economic policy but in cultural and artistic life, and that the Holocaust became an important subject for literary, artistic and scholarly attention among Jewish and Christian intellectuals.[46] This should not be overstated; as Zsuzsanna Osvath observed, 'a few texts emerged that did not capitulate to the state-imposed ban on Jewish memory', and these 'recalled, repeated and expressed the events of the *Shoah*, bearing witness to the immensity of the trauma it created'. But the dominant trend in Hungarian literature and media throughout the 1960s, 1970s and 1980s 'either

---

[43] Braham, Randolph (1994), 'Antisemitism and the Holocaust in the Politics of East-Central Europe', *Holocaust and Genocide Studies*, vol 8, no 2, Fall, 145.

[44] Braham, Randolph, 'Hungary', 210.

[45] This was momentarily thrown off course by Israel's Six Day War, which sparked a resurgence of antisemitism and anti-Zionism that also transcended Cold War borders. For example, Henry Rousso credits the 're-awakening of Jewish memory' in France during the 1970s, in particular Holocaust memory, in large part to intellectual and anti-Zionist condemnation of Israel after the Six Day War and the resurgence of antisemitism: see Rousso, Henry (1987), *The Vichy Syndrome: History and memory in France since 1944*, translated by Arthur Goldhammer, Cambridge, Harvard University Press, 132.

[46] Braham, 'Antisemitism and the Holocaust', 148.

suppressed or portrayed the *Shoah* as having only coincidentally Jewish features'.[47] As István Rév noted, the first state-sponsored Hungarian exhibition held at Auschwitz in 1965 articulated the official stance: of the 120 panels displayed, only ten related to the fate of the almost half a million Hungarian Jews who perished there, despite the fact that around one in three Jewish victims of Auschwitz were from Hungary, and not one of the panels related to the murder of thousands of Hungarian Roma. Instead, the exhibition, like official Hungarian memory, 'fell victim to the ideological war between Communists and anti-Communist Fascists'.[48]

The end of Communism led to a resurfacing of antisemitic prejudice in the public arena, drawing in part on a deep-rooted tradition of linking Jews with Communism in the popular historical imagination, in particular the high visibility of Jews in positions of leadership in the Communist regimes of 1919 and the post-World War II era. This antisemitic mythology ignored the fact that these leaders were almost all purged from their positions during the Communist era. Yet it has recently found new expression in a post-Communist preoccupation with 'the Jewish Question', a more extreme variant of which supposes that Jews used the postwar Communist regime for 40 years as payback against the Hungarians for the suffering they experienced at the hands of the Nazis.

In the first free elections of 1990, several politicians and prominent writers and journalists exploited these mythical connections. 'References to "alien" elements controlling the

---

[47] Ozsváth, Zsuzsanna, 'Trauma and Distortion: Holocaust Fiction and the Ban on Jewish Memory', in Braham and Chamberlin, (eds) *The Holocaust in Hungary*, 339.

[48] Rév, Istvan (1999), *Retroactive Justice*, 228.

media and playing a disproportionately prominent role in academia and the professions in the capital — a clear reference to Jews — were subtly interwoven with discussions of the political and socio-economic issues troubling the post-Communist society.'[49] Since then, local anger at unemployment, economic downturns, inflation, impoverishment and government corruption has continued to find a convenient target in the Jewish population. Professor György Poszler, a member of the Hungarian Academy of Sciences, remarked on the recent turn in public discourse, in which the antisemitic voice, once tentative and sporadic, has become stronger and more frequent: 'The tone has positively degraded. It would be worth...comparing these texts with the phraseology and metaphors of the extreme right wing press of 60 years ago.'[50] As recently as April 2009, at a rally of the ultra right-wing Magdar Gárda (Hungarian Guard), there were open calls for physical violence against Jews.[51]

To some extent it would be possible to argue that the silence has deepened rather than thawed. The desire to absolve Hungarian responsibility in favour of German guilt is prevalent in government, the churches and other leading institutions. There are also those who continue to 'de-Judaise' the Holocaust, relativising Jewish loss in terms of all civilian and military losses incurred in the war.[52] For Tony Judt, Hungary is the prime illustration of the difficulty of incorporating the destruction of the Jews into historical memory in post-Communist Eastern Europe. He uses the

---

[49] Braham, 'Hungary', 214.

[50] *Anti-Semitic Discourse in Hungary in 2002–2003: Report and documentation*, Desi, Janos, Gero, Andras, Szeszler, Tibor and Varga, Laszlo (2004) (eds), Budapest, B'nai B'rith Budapest Lodge, 185.

[51] Email correspondence with Associate Professor Renata Uitz, Legal Studies, Central European University, 20 May 2009.

[52] Braham, 'Hungary', 218.

example of the immensely popular Terrorháza ('House of Terror'), the museum set up in Budapest after the fall of Communism to document the history of state violence and repression from 1944 to 1989:

> the Terrorháza's version of Hungarian history draws no distinction between the thugs of Ferenc Szalasi's Arrow Cross party, who held power there from October 1944 to April 1945, and the Communist regime that was installed after the war...The not particularly subliminal message here is that Communism and Fascism are equivalent. Except that they are not: the presentation and content of the Budapest Terrorháza makes it quite clear that, in the eyes of the museum's curators, Communism not only lasted longer but did far more harm than its neo-Nazi predecessor.[53]

Tim Cole agrees that the Terrorháza not only claims an equivalence between the victims of Fascism and Communism, but suggests that the Communist era was far more significant. The specific history of the Holocaust is subsumed within a more monolithic history that traces a story of universal Hungarian victimhood from 1944 to 1989, first at the hands of Nazi Germany and their foot soldiers, the Nyilas, and then the Communists.[54] Yet across town, another museum is competing with this historical version of the Holocaust. The Budapest Holocaust Memorial Centre was created in 2004 on the site of the former ghetto in Pest.[55] The Centre's permanent exhibition, *From Deprivation of Rights to Genocide*, is a comprehensive, state-of-the-art display of the history of the Hungarian Holocaust, and pays particular attention to the

---

[53] Judt, Tony (2005), *Postwar: A history of Europe since 1945*, New York, The Penguin Press, 827–28.

[54] Cole, *Holocaust City*, 246.

[55] There is also another small Jewish museum located in the grounds of the Dohány utca (street) synagogue.

relationship between the State and the main victims of racial persecution, namely Jews and Roma. The exhibition's time-frame begins in 1938, when the first Anti-Jewish Law was enacted. Extending the periodisation of this history in this way significantly challenges the version of history presented at the Terrorháza, which starts with the period of Arrow Cross rule in 1944, thus 'forgetting' or silencing the role played by the Hungarian state in implementing the Holocaust. Despite Cole's optimism that the short distance between the Holocaust Memorial Centre and the Terrorháza would make it possible to take in both museums in one day, the Terrorháza remains the far more popular option by locals and tourists alike.[56]

Istvan Hargittai is a professor of chemistry at Budapest Technical University and one of a few to have published in Hungarian his Holocaust experiences and the wall of silence that surrounds this history. He recalls that he and his generation grew up thinking 'it was the Germans' who were responsible for the Hungarian Holocaust. Members of the Arrow Cross were outsiders, so the theory went, unrepresentative of the Hungarian people. This myth prevails. Most Hungarians, he says, have lived since World War II as if Auschwitz never happened.[57] The crimes of the Communist regime command the sphere of public debate over retribution and justice. The question of Hungarian complicity in the crimes against a significant number of its own people in World War II has yet to be asked.

Even those who might be expected to be supportive of seeing Zentai go to trial suspect that the effect is likely to be

---

[56] Cole, *Holocaust City*, 247. Of the three or four times I visited in 2008, the Holocaust Memorial Centre was virtually empty except for myself and maybe two or three other visitors, while the House of Terror was very well patronised.

[57] Interview with Istvan Hargittai, Budapest, 4 November 2008.

detrimental to the Jewish cause. Hargittai predicts that the overwhelming image of Zentai will be that of a 'poor old man' who, if sentenced, will in all likelihood become a martyr of Jewish vengeance. Nevertheless, this does not mean, in Hargittai's view, that he shouldn't be tried. But there are others who feel that the negative impact such a trial is likely to have outweighs the argument for historical justice.[58] Many intellectuals fear that a case such as this will strengthen antisemitism, particularly at a time when the rise of the extreme right is already threatening its resurgence. The fact that the Hungarian state has never acknowledged its own role in the destruction of Hungarian Jewry further complicates the issue. Without this acknowledgment, a trial such as this could become a tool for reinforcing the idea of a 'few bad apples' and the wider mythology of ordinary Hungarians' innocence and victimhood.

Károly Zentai and the route to Australia

Hungary's demand for Zentai's extradition has its own history. In 2004, Efraim Zuroff, the director of the Jerusalem-based Wiesenthal Centre, visited Hungary to launch Operation Last Chance, which offered a reward of 10,000 euros to anyone with information leading to the arrest of war criminals. For Zuroff, such an operation was motivated by a universal obligation to the victims of the Holocaust; beyond that, Zuroff defended it as particularly significant in a country where acknowledgement of the Holocaust was still poor and where, in his view, the credibility of past trials was tainted in the popular imagination by their Communist associations.[59]

---

[58] Conversation with Lázsló Czörc, Holocaust Memorial Centre, Budapest, 20 October 2008.

[59] Zuroff, Efraim (2004), 'Nem reménytelen (Not hopeless)', *Élet és Irodalom*, 6 August.

Operation Last Chance was not welcomed by a significant number of Jewish intellectuals in Hungary. A heated exchange erupted in the pages of Hungarian journal *Élet és Irodalom* (Literature and Life) between leading Holocaust historian László Karsai and Efraim Zuroff, in which Karsai attacked the operation as a 'blood money operation', labelling it unnecessary, unhelpful and 'without a chance'.[60] According to Karsai, this strategy had no merit in the cause of historical justice:

For 10,000 euros, it occurs to someone that their dear old neighbour is possibly, very probably, an Arrow Cross (mass) murderer... Now try to imagine our 80–90 year old relative one day who is taken away by policemen, interrogated for hours, kept in remand in crowded, filthy cells perhaps for weeks or months only to be told before the court that his 95 year-old accuser is not so absolutely certain that he had seen him on the bank of the Danube in Pest, or in the brickyard at Békásmegyer in October or December 1944...I still insist that there is not much chance of finding real war criminals...and even less of having them convicted in Hungary today. On the other hand, the odds are very good for hundreds of innocent octogenarians being denounced in this country in the hope of 10,000 euro blood money.[61]

Not only would such cases be virtually impossible to prosecute so long after the event, but if anything, 'a Nazi hunting campaign with blood money in Hungary today could only result in the strengthening of anti-Semitism'. Karsai challenged Zuroff instead to look in places like Canada, the United States or Australia where most, he said, had ended up after the war. In his parting shot, he used the example of the Péter Balázs case to further illustrate his point:

On July 15, a Holocaust survivor gave me a ring. He told me

---

[60] Karsai, László (2004), 'Esélytelenek', *Élet és Irodalom*, vol 48, no 30, 23 July, translated by Professor György Novak, 2009.

[61] Karsai, László, 'Esélyten, Reménytelen és Törvénytelen'.

that he had informed the Jerusalem Centre of the name and [Australian] address of the murderer of his brother. In the last 17 years the Centre has not even found him worthy of letting him know that the case has been shelved…(this) man…made it clear that he was not interested in the 10,000 euros, but wanted to see the murderer brought to court.[62]

Although Karsai did not mention the Balázs case by name, Zentai's extradition request was expedited soon after this exchange took place.

Presumably Zentai was never a big enough fish when Simon Wiesenthal was alive and his organisation was engaged in tracking down Nazis who had committed murder and brutality on a massive scale. The Balázs files held by the Holocaust Memorial Centre in Budapest attest to the long struggle of the family to resurrect the case and bring Zentai to trial. These papers tell a story of tenacity and despair, beginning with the small advertisement Péter's father, Dezsö, placed in a Budapest paper the day after Péter's disappearance, and subsequent advertisements looking for information about his son's whereabouts. 'My son, Péter Balázs, disappeared on 8 November. High reward for anyone bringing news of him' reads one, from 1 April 1945.[63] Dezsö Balázs devoted the remaining 25 years of his life, until his death in 1970, to obtaining justice for his son's murder. His other son, Adam, inherited his father's cause. I have one letter, dated 20 November 1987 from Adam Balázs to a representative of the Wiesenthal Centre visiting in Budapest at the time, in which he includes a 1958 address for Zentai in Perth. Efraim Zuroff has since maintained that the first the Wiesenthal Centre heard of the Balázs case was in 2004, and it

---

[62] Karsai, László, 'Esélyten'.

[63] *Népszava*, 1 April 1945.

acted upon the information immediately.[64]

The story of how Zentai came to be in Australia is part of the history of Australia's first immigration program, in which tens of thousands of DPs were brought out on ships from the DP camps in Germany and Italy to Australia on its mass resettlement scheme. For many genuine refugees, Australia was 'the farthest place', far removed from the Europe of old race hatreds that had led to the concentration camps of World War II; for others, Australia was a country of last resort. Zentai's own application for refugee status, for example, lists Canada and Argentina as countries of preference for immigration. There is no mention of Australia. Contemporary observers were often struck by how comparatively easy it could be, if you were non-Jewish and 'fit', to get in to Australia when applications elsewhere had failed. Ron Maslyn Williams — on location in Germany in 1949 to make *Mike and Stefani* (1952) — wrote to his boss at the Commonwealth Film Unit, Stanley Hawes: 'As one intelligent DP put it to me "It is Australia or Siberia or starvation…Australia is the gambler's shot". Moreover, "quite literally, very many IRO officials regard Australia as a kind of modern Van Dieman's (sic) land where they can dump the people who constitute IRO's problem".'

The Australian authorities, for their part, counted physical attributes above all else as criteria for migration: one needed to be fit, preferably young and, more preferably still, fair-skinned. Until 1960, humanitarian principles did not inform motives for assisted refugee migration — pragmatism did. Australia needed to expand its labour force and its population, and the only way that the government could sell its scheme of mass migration was by assuring its public that it remained committed to the principles of a 'White Australia'

---

[64] Email correspondence from Efraim Zuroff to the author, 3 May 2009.

on which the Commonwealth was founded. Jews were especially unwelcome. Immediately after the war the government announced a humanitarian scheme to permit the arrival of concentration camp victims with Australian relatives; the scheme was met by antisemitic protest, and in response, the immigration minister Arthur Calwell introduced a quota system, in which only 25 percent of each ship carrying migrants could comprise Jews. These would be admitted only on the grounds of their potential contribution to Australia's economy, not on humanitarian grounds.[65]

As Klaus Neumann has written: 'Suitable non-British settlers were young, educated and healthy and, ideally, possessed certain racial features. Australian selection teams preferred vigorous, flaxen-haired, fair-skinned and blue-eyed young men and women from the Baltic countries who did not or could not return to the Soviet Union.' These were to resemble Australia's 'own kind' as closely as possible.[66] Beyond this, a philosophy of assimilation governed immigration policy and popular attitudes towards new arrivals. Immigrants, labelled 'New Australians', were expected to merge, quickly and quietly, into the Australian cultural and social landscape. This kind of thinking also implied, of course, that people's political pasts were as irrelevant as their cultural pasts—a slate wiped clean by the

---

[65] Australia was not alone in its pragmatic approach. Contemporary observers were struck by the commonalities that existed among the recruiting nations. Malcolm Proudfoot noted that 'in spite of all the protestations of sympathy, the pivot of national immigration policies in almost all the countries was strictly practical and closely related to domestic labour requirements.' See Proudfoot, Malcolm (1957), *European Refugees: A study in forced population movements 1939–1952*, London, Faber, 418.

[66] Neumann, Klaus (2004), *Refuge Australia: Australia's humanitarian record*, Kensington, UNSW Press, 32–33.

promise of Australian acculturation.

The Zentais ticked the right boxes: 'fit worker' is handwritten across both Károly and Rozsa's migration selection forms.[67] In March 1949, Zentai, his wife Rozsa, their two sons born after the war, and Zentai's older sister, Julia, were at Tuttlingen in southern Germany's French zone, where they were interviewed and accepted by the Australian Migration Team for resettlement in Australia. Zentai's screening card twice states that he arrived in Germany on 9 March 1949, and that he had 'fled from the Communist Party'. His wife's card indicates the same information. The accompanying resettlement card from the IRO, which establishes their status as DPs, also states that Zentai and his wife were in Budafok between 1945 and 1949, and that their son Gabor was born in Budafok, Hungary, in 1946.

Except that he wasn't, and they weren't. Documents held by the International Tracing Service (ITS) tell a different story. The ITS, located in Bad Arolsen in Germany, is a massive storage house of SS records of the death camps, yet it also holds the records created by the Allies in the DP camps. Zentai's file includes his application for refugee assistance to the IRO, and lists his places of residence from 1938 onwards: in March 1945 he was already on his way to Dietersburg, Bavaria, where he arrived, according to the information he provided, on 19 April 1945 and remained until March 1948. A document dated 14 August 1946 confirms that he, his wife, his sister and his son, Gabor, born 26 February of that year, were in Dietersburg. His son Gabor is twice recorded as having been born in Arnstorf, Bavaria. Another, dated 15 July 1947, indicates that Zentai was temporarily in Kösslarn, in the district of Griesbach, also in Bavaria.

In his application for IRO assistance, a routine statutory declaration states that Karl Zentai was 'never a member of the

---

[67] NAA: Series A12014, Item 4445592.

Arrow Cross or any political party and never committed any atrocities'. It is signed by Zentai and three witnesses, dated 12 March 1948 at the Hungarian office (Ungarisches Büro) in Pfarrkirchen. A handwritten statement by an IRO officer concludes: 'On account of credibility of the statement of the Hungarian office and the witnesses he should be found eligible for refugee status with IRO assistance. Refuses to return home for the present regime there—no political freedoms.'[68]

None of these official records hint at the warrant for his arrest issued by the Budapest People's Court in April 1948, despite the fact that his whereabouts were well known to the Hungarian authorities. The warrant even lists an address, 'the American occupation zone in Germany, where his address at present is...Furth in Pfarrkirchen district with farmer Jakob Schneiderbauer'.[69] It appears that Zentai was able to make his way safely to Tuttlingen almost one year after the warrant was issued. Was the warrant ever communicated to the Allied Occupation Forces in Germany, and if so, why was it ignored? Did Zentai know about his warrant? The answers to these questions, of course, can only be speculative. Yet the inconsistencies in the records as to his whereabouts for the four years between 1945 and 1949 seem to indicate some kind of attempt to cover his tracks. In his recent interviews with the media, Zentai has never tried to deny that he was already living under the protection of the Allied Occupation Forces in Germany from 1945. Why then did he lie about his whereabouts in 1949? I contend that his decision was strategic: rewriting those four years in this way so as to convey that he was coming from Hungary in 1949 rather than

---

[68] Zentai, Karoly, CM/1, ITS Nr 2–2647.

[69] Budapest People's Court, no 1948 Nü 3440/2, [Bálazs papers held in the Holocaust Memorial Museum, Budapest].

1945 distanced his decision to leave Hungary from the immediate aftermath of World War II, thus making it simpler to
argue that he was 'fleeing the Communists', as so many other
East Europeans were doing in the years of 1948 and 1949.

Moreover, as Zentai's case makes clear, the DP camps, and
their route to Australia, could provide avenues of escape for
those wishing to avoid retribution or exposure. It was well
known to contemporaries that a number of collaborators and
war criminals were hiding in the DP camps. G Daniel Cohen
has examined the extensive technologies of screening and
identification developed by the IRO, which took over from the
United Nations Relief and Rehabilitation Administration
(UNRRA) in 1947, to determine the authenticity of refugees
and displaced persons. It was a daunting task, but according
to IRO officials, 'of first importance in its work'.[70] Refugees
were now required to fill in numerous forms and
questionnaires, yet as Cohen explains, if there was no
apparent reason for exclusion, that is, if they seemed to fit the
story they presented, they were not required to prove their
right to be included as eligible. IRO officers received manuals
that included sample cases and historical information to guide
their decisions, and were taught how to detect untrue
statements, yet in practice their mission to cleanse the system
of ineligibles was often frustrated. Visitors reported that the
'right answers' to IRO questionnaires were circulating in the
camps; further, it was clear to IRO officials that many simply
destroyed their identity papers and made up new ones. Dates
of displacement were frequently altered during interrogations
to make their applications more plausible. Within the IRO,
Cohen quotes, it was commonly believed that 'after many
months of observation and listening, the DPs are told what to
say and know how to craft an acceptable story leading to

---

[70] Cohen, G Daniel (2012), *In War's Wake: Europe's displaced persons in
the postwar order*, Oxford and New York, Oxford University Press, 41.

eligibility'.[71]

Over one million people arrived in Australia under various immigration schemes by the end of the 1950s, and there are estimates that even in its earliest years, 4,000 to 5,000 Nazis may have found sanctuary there, most of them from East-Central Europe.[72] As Konrad Kwiet notes, during the screening process they lied about their wartime activities, usually claiming to have been subjected to 'forced labour' or 'deportation to Germany'. 'In reality', he writes, 'many of them had actively enthusiastically assisted the Nazis. Their claims concealed "police work", military and *Waffen SS* service and participation in killing operations'.[73]

This should also be viewed in the context of a broader Allied retreat from the issue of denazification and punishment of wartime activities. Zentai was in Germany at the very moment that Europe's postwar memory was being moulded, by all sides, around the notion of German guilt, in which all responsibility for the war was made to lie squarely at the feet of the Germans. This focus on Germany meant the postwar status of other countries could be resolved. Thus Austria was retrospectively declared the 'first victim' of Nazi aggression and with Austria's innocence assured, the responsibilities of other non-German nationals in Europe were similarly eradicated.[74] As the Cold War deepened, the

[71] Cohen, *In War's Wake*, 42.

[72] See Aarons, Mark and Loftus, John (1994), *The Secret War Against the Jews: How Western espionage betrayed the Jewish people*, New York, St Martin's Press.

[73] Kwiet, Konrad (2009), 'Historian's View — the War Crimes Debate Down Under', paper presented at the conference *War Crimes: Retrospectives and Prospects*, Institute of Advanced Legal Studies, University of London, 19–21 February.

[74] Judt, Tony (2009), 'The Past is Another Country: Myth and

Allies were determined to avoid alienating Austria and Germany, and this meant removing attention from the past. 'In a process that would have been unthinkable in 1945', Judt wrote, 'the identification and punishment of active Nazis in German-speaking Europe had effectively ended by 1948 and was a forgotten issue by the early fifties'.[75]

IRO policy also reflected a softening towards those who previously may have been denied eligibility as collaborators. Ideological motives for assisting enemy forces, for example, became as important as their actions during the war; in other words, if someone had voluntarily enlisted in the German army because they wanted to oppose the Soviet regime, this was reason enough for inclusion. DP claims of anti-Communist sympathies and fear of Communist persecution began to carry as much, if not more, weight than claims of Nazi persecution. 'By 1950, refugees deemed "imposters" or "security threats" in the days of UNRRA were now offered the chance to emigrate to Australia or the North American continent.'[76]

This strategic refocusing of attention away from the crimes of the past identified by Judt was enormously significant for the thousands, if not millions, whose wartime pasts were being reframed by a deliberate process of forgetting and denial, and whose identities were recast as refugees of an oppressive Communist regime. Australia's own role in this

---

Memory in Postwar Europe', in Deák, István et al, (eds), *The Politics of Retribution in Europe*, 296.

[75] Judt, Tony (2009), 'The Past is Another Country', 297. Judt's statement is a slight exaggeration; though there was a marked decline in war crimes after 1948, preliminary war crimes' proceedings conducted by West German prosecutors numbered over 9,000 between 1949 and 1959.

[76] Cohen, *In War's Wake*, 49.

history was one of passivity and equally, one of denial.[77] In the 1950s, protests by the Australian Jewish community over the migration of Nazis and their collaborators were eventually silenced by the continuing apathy and even hostility to their campaign.[78] The politics and ideology of anti-Communism coloured government rhetoric and attitudes to the evidence of Nazi war criminals and collaborators living in Australia, and governed the state's failure to act.[79] This was made explicit in the official response in 1961 to a request by the USSR for the extradition of an Estonian immigrant Ervin Viks, who was accused of murdering 12,000 Jews and Roma in the Tartu concentration camp. The Liberal government of Robert Menzies refused. In a speech defending the decision, Australian Attorney General Sir Garfield Barwick declared that against the 'utter abhorrence' felt by Australians against war crimes, 'there is the right of this nation, by receiving people into this country to enable men to turn their backs on past bitternesses and to make a new life for themselves in a happier community'. He concluded, in what has become an

---

[77] As David Dyzenhaus has so aptly commented in another racial context (South Africa), the attempt to forget is not an unconscious process: 'it requires deliberate decisions from the vantage of one who does in fact remember'. See Dyzenhaus, David (1998), *Judging the Judges, Judging Ourselves: Truth, reconciliation and the Apartheid legal order*, Oxford, Hart Publishing, 92.

[78] When the Jewish Council to Combat Fascism and Antisemitism reported the names of Nazi war criminals in Australia in the 1950s, the result was ASIO's investigation of that Council for 'Communist' activity, and not of Nazi criminals (Colin Tatz, personal communication).

[79] Fraser, David (2010), *Daviborshch's Cart: Narrating the Holocaust in Australian war crimes trials*, Lincoln and London, University of Nebraska Press, 53.

infamous phrase: 'the time has come to close the chapter'.[80]

This directive to forget in order to create 'new lives' and a 'happier community' became a prevailing ethos in the next few decades, assisted by the fact that there was no legal framework established for extradition or prosecution of suspected war criminals. This changed briefly in the late 1980s when, under the Hawke Labor government, a special inquiry was set up to investigate allegations of Nazi war criminals living here, inspired largely by the forensic investigations of journalist Mark Aarons in a series of reports for ABC radio and television, which resulted in the Menzies Report. Controversial legislation was passed in parliament enabling Australian courts to prosecute suspects for war crimes (*War Crimes Amendment Act*, 1988)[81]. Most importantly, a Special Investigation Unit (SIU) was created within the federal Attorney General's department to investigate suspected war criminals. In its five short years of operation, there were 843 investigations, three individuals charged and tried in Adelaide, with no successful conviction.[82] In 1992, the SIU was closed down, and responsibility for following up war crimes' accusations delegated to the federal police, who were either unwilling or unable to investigate them. It was, in Kwiet's words, 'a clear signal that the second chapter of the war crimes debate in Australia was closed'. During his brief tenure as chief historian for the SIU, Kwiet observed both the

---

[80] Fraser, David, *Daviborshch's Cart*, 57.

[81] This statute evoked furious opposition from senior public figures: several senators, an archbishop, the head of the RSL, and at least three noted jurists. Even the *Financial Review* believed it would 'tear apart the fabric of Australian society'. Tatz, Colin (1997) 'Genocide and the Politics of Memory' in *Genocide Perspectives I*, ed Colin Tatz, Centre for Comparative Genocide Studies, 328.

[82] See Fraser, *Daviborshch's Cart*, for an extensive discussion of the war crimes legislation in Australia and the trials of the three cases of Ivan Polyukhovich, Mikolay Berezowsky and Heinrich Wagner.

negative, 'even damning' attitude that prevailed within the legal fraternity towards war crimes' legislation and the proceedings themselves; and the frequent indifference of the Australian public. He recalls:

> In the public domain the war crimes debate had, in my view, little, if any impact on public awareness and memory... The public proceedings in Adelaide took place in front of empty galleries. Quite popular in the scant media coverage were references to the accused as 'nice neighbours' or 'old' and 'sick' pensioners. For the overwhelming majority of Australians, the news of the closure of the SIU went almost unnoticed. [83]

David Fraser has also noted that the presence of unpunished perpetrators never became part of the cultural or political dynamic of Australian national identity or Australian values.[84] Yet others have recognised that in spite of a lethargic community response to war crimes trials, these are important forums for producing cosmopolitan ideals of justice and human rights. They also affirm the role of history, in the form of evidence that 'things happened', in justice work and in the work of remembrance.

Although the legal framework was successfully developed by the SIU in the late 1980s, the resources for the investigation of people who have committed war crimes overseas have not been forthcoming and there have been no charges laid since.[85]

---

[83] Kwiet Konrad, 'Historian's View — the War Crimes Debate Down Under'.

[84] Fraser, *Daviborshch's Cart*, 310–11.

[85] It is now the case that since 2002, when Australia amended its legislation to include war crimes, crimes against humanity and genocide as criminal offences in Australian law (*Commonwealth Criminal Law*, 2002), war criminals from conflicts prior to 2002 cannot be tried in an Australian court.

The Wiesenthal Centre recently listed Australia as the 'only major country of refuge' and former diplomat Fergus Hansen, in a recent report compiled for the Lowy Institute, writes that Australia 'has inadvertently become a safe haven for war criminals'. This is certainly the impression Australia has been giving the world, and presumably its war criminals, for some time. Hansen notes that there are indications war criminals have come here from Afghanistan, Palestine, Sri Lanka, Nepal, Sierra Leone, India, Cambodia, Iran, Iraq, Chile, Lebanon, Nigeria, Bangladesh, the former Yugoslavia, possibly Rwanda and East Timor as well, among other countries.[86]

The twilight of memory and the struggle for historical justice

Zentai's appeal against his extradition to Australia's Federal Court in April 2008 failed, with Federal Court judge John Gilmour finding that there was no reason why Zentai should not be extradited to face trial. The court agreed to bail for Zentai on the grounds of ill health, and his lawyers took the case to the Minister for Home Affairs, O'Connor. This appeal failed, and Zentai was ruled fit to travel. This time Zentai's lawyers based the justification for their appeal on the argument that the offence for which Zentai is convicted did not constitute a war crime at the time it was committed. The implications of an argument such as this, although not new, are momentous, legitimising what was, in effect, a fascist regime at the time and putting forward the quite extraordinary idea that for Jews like Balázs, being beaten to death was somehow lawful. A similar argument was made during the Nuremberg Trials, in which the question of

---

[86] Hansen, Fergus (2009), 'Confronting Reality: Responding to War Criminals in Australia', *Policy Brief*, Lowy Institute for International Policy, February, 3-4.

whether the 24 German leaders[87] should have to answer for actions rendered illegal after the fact — ex-post-facto — was put forward by the defence. The prosecuting lawyers never conceded this point, arguing that the charges were grounded in international law and what they called a common law of nations. Such an argument suggested that the accused had no idea they were acting illegally, an argument without merit in the minds of contemporary observers: murder is murder. The legality of the charge of war crimes was upheld at Nuremberg, and it is commendable that Federal Court judge John Gilmour resisted such logic today.

His lawyers successfully appealed the decision, taking it back to the Federal Court. In July 2010, Justice Neil McKerracher ruled that the Government had made an 'error of law' in agreeing to extradite him, and that the crime for which Zentai was charged was not an extraditable offence under the *Extradition Act*. Zentai returned home, but in 2011 the Federal Government returned to the High Court for another appeal, seeking a ruling on what constitutes a war crime. It is thought that such a ruling will have a significant impact on Australia's extradition regime.

Zentai has clearly led an exemplary life in Australia. He is the embodiment of the multicultural ideal, a man who worked, brought up a family here and settled quietly into the suburban landscape. It is not easy to watch a frail elderly man being hauled in front of the courts to face trial. He might, despite all the evidence, be innocent. There are powerful incentives to simply turn our collective back on this story and let the old man be. But are we also prepared to accept a statute of limitations on war crimes or crimes against

---

[87] Initially 24 men were indicted, three were missing — Ley suicided, Borman disappeared, and Krupp (Sr) was deemed too infirm to stand trial.

humanity? Is there a time when it is too late for justice? 'That the past slips into the oblivion of forgetting does not change its moral nature', writes Booth. 'The passage of time may dull our recollection of events, but it does not erase the (morally weighty) fact of their having happened nor the wrong involved in them.'[88]

Mnemonic struggles over past wars and injustices have become common sites of battle over the legacies of the past in contemporary politics and law. How far the practice of retribution and punishment can generate reconciliation and acknowledgement is recognisably limited. Punishment, writes Jeffrey Olick, 'cannot be the ultimate measure of how a society has "dealt" with its past'. This was one of the lessons of Nuremberg, which despite its importance in forcing a certain truth to be told and for establishing moral and legal precedents had its costs as well, 'providing an alibi for an expertly equivocating population eager to lay the blame on a narrow "clique"'.[89] As Booth writes, the trial of a perpetrator inevitably looks to individual accountability in its proceedings. 'In regimes where there was a gray area of collaboration and passive acquiescence or even support, that creates a very narrow focus...The co-responsibility of a people and state does not readily fit into the horizon of a courtroom proceeding, which looks for bloody hands that no one except the direct perpetrators will have.'[90]

The question remains: will Zentai's extradition and trial promote the cause of historical justice? Or will it, rather, reinforce the dominant mythology of a 'few bad apples'? What is most fascinating, and disturbing, are the ways in

---

[88] Booth, W James (2006), *Communities of Memory, On witness, identity and justice*, Ithaca and London, Cornell University Press, 160.

[89] Olick, Jeffrey K (2007), *The Politics of Regret: On collective memory and historical responsibility*, New York and London, Routledge, 151.

[90] Booth, W James (2006), *Communities of Memory*, 135–36

which an affair of memory of this kind is able to be appropriated and subsumed by the dominant historical narrative, reinforcing rather than challenging historical myths. The danger is that what Zentai's case reveals about the past will be rewritten by the language of contemporary prejudices rather than illuminate those of history.

Andreas Huyssen has described our time as the twilight of . memory. 'Twilight', he writes, 'is that moment of the day that foreshadows the night of forgetting, but that seems to slow time itself, an in-between state in which the last light of the day may still play out its ultimate marvels. It is memory's privileged time.'[91] As did Levi, Huyssen believes the struggle for memory is also a struggle for history. When we think of the Holocaust today, we often imagine our present time in terms of it being 'too late' for justice. But perhaps today, despite the risk of what I have outlined above, in this brief twilight of Holocaust time when victims and perpetrators are gradually leaving our world behind, we should be ensuring that these cases are told and not forgotten. Justice, not memory, is the antonym of forgetting, writes Booth. 'In other words, the imperative to remember is not the leaden voice of what has gone before, but rather it is the call of justice insisting on the irreversibility and persistence of what has been done, its claims on us which are neither diminished nor augmented by the extra-moral passing of time, and which call on us to bear these injustices in mind.'[92] History's purpose is to give meaning to the present even as it seeks knowledge of the past; justice, or the attempt at it, however flawed and incomplete, belongs squarely within the historical project of understanding. A 1987 cartoon by Ben Sargent about the

---

[91] Huyssen, Andreas (1995), *Twilight Memories: Marking time in a culture of amnesia*, London and New York, Routledge, 3.

[92] Booth, W James, *Communities of Memory*, 159–60.

Klaus Barbie trial in France remains pertinent: 'It's been more than forty years', a younger man remarks. 'Why are we hunting down a bunch of pathetic old men just to prosecute them for...er...uh...well, you know...uh...whatever that stuff was they did...?' The older man replies: 'That's precisely why.'[93]

As Huyssen writes, 'the inner temporality and the politics of Holocaust memory, however, even where it speaks of the past, must be directed towards the future. The future will not judge us for forgetting but for remembering all too well and still not acting in accordance with those memories'.[94] Zentai's case is not just about Zentai. The important question of a regime and a country that enabled, indeed encouraged, the murder of thousands of Jews like Péter Balázs, and a country that then gave murderers refuge and even prosperity is still to be addressed. It is about the legacy of both countries in the denial and silencing of a 'memory of offence', and a responsibility towards our present and their future.

---

[93] Quoted in Sodi, Risa (1989), 'The Memory of Justice: Primo Levi and Auschwitz', *Holocaust and Genocide Studies*, vol 4, no 1, 101.

[94] Huyssen, *Twilight Memories*, 260.

CHILDREN AND GENOCIDE

PANAYIOTIS DIAMADIS

This essay examines the evolution, since antiquity, of the forcible transfer of children by dominant groups at the expense of subordinate groups. It traces the development of the intentions, motivations and justifications behind this practice. Deliberate, systematic mass abduction and forced assimilation have enabled the exploitation of children as working slaves, as sexual chattels, as deft or supple skilled workers, and as 'substitute' progeny. This study highlights aspects of the phenomenon across societies and generations. It is designed to provide a broad background to the defining of the forcible transfer of children as an act of genocide, an act deemed criminal in international law since 1948.

The United Nations *Convention on the Punishment and Prevention of the Crime of Genocide*[1] identifies five acts that can constitute the crime, any *one* of which when conducted 'with intent to destroy, in whole or in part, a national, ethnical, racial or religious group', constitutes genocide. The first four acts[2] are linked by the common element of the physical extermination of, or physical harm to, human life. Article II(e) stands out because while it still involves a systematic attack on the group's essential foundations, it does not involve the actual extinction or attempted destruction of biological life.

---

[1] Adopted by the General Assembly by Resolution 260 (III) on 9 December 1948.

[2] Article II(a) — 'killing'; (b) 'causing bodily or mental harm'; (c) 'deliberately inflicting on the [victim] group conditions of life calculated to bring about its physical destruction'; (d) 'imposing measures intended to prevent births' — have the common element of involving the physical destruction of human life.

How then does the forcible transfer of children[3] achieve a perpetrator's aim of destroying a targeted group? Where did the drafters of the *Genocide Convention* (including the Polish jurist Raphael Lemkin) find cause to include this behaviour as a criminal act in the legal definition of genocide? An examination of a series of case studies across history may provide some answers.

While child removal by governmental entities has taken place since antiquity, it is only in the last century that these acts have been deemed genocidal. Specific cases show that a defining element has been the intent of the perpetrators to destroy their chosen victim groups — in whole or in part — through the removal of their young and 'processing' them into a new culture or belief system. This was usually, but not always, carried out in addition to the more typical methods employed in the physical destruction of targeted groups. Nazi Germany, for example, removed and 'Germanised' some 200,000 Polish, Russian, Ukrainian and other European children, but systematically murdered 1.1 million Jewish children.

Enslavement and voluntary assimilation

The employment of means of killing *en masse* as 'solutions' to

---

[3] As the definition of childhood differs between societies and cultures, for the purposes of this essay the phrases 'children and teenagers', 'the young' or 'youth' are used for persons below the age of adulthood. During the Armenian Genocide, for example, the United States Consul in Trapezounta (Trebizond/modern Trabzon), Oscar S Heizer, made the following note in one of his reports: 'Girls up to 15 years of age inclusive, and boys to 10 years of age inclusive are accepted; those over these ages are compelled to go with their parents', Report to US Ambassador to Constantinople Henry Morgenthau, 7 July 1915. The Ottoman Turkish authorities employed these ages to identify 'children', whereas most Western societies define the individual's 18th birthday as marking the age of maturity, regardless of gender.

social, political and economic problems have been recorded since earliest history. Thus, *The Iliad* by Homer, the Old Testament, and the archives of the Assyrian and Neo-Babylonian Empires contain the earliest accounts of targeted mass murder. These events also typically involved the wholesale transfer of captive children and teenagers for use as manual, skilled, domestic, and sexual slaves.

These situations differ from their later counterparts in the nature of the perpetrators' *intent*. The victors did not enslave tens of thousands of children and youth to destroy their opponents as distinct groups. Their defeat on the field of battle and subsequent destruction of their military capabilities were the aims of the victorious kings and generals who ordered the forced transfers of the underage persons. Forcible transfer of the young was most often a byproduct of the subjugation of the vanquished.

The rise of Islam and the Arab Empire from the mid-600s CE brought a major shift in attitude towards the enslavement of humans and transfer of youth. The Prophet Mohammed forbade free-born Muslims being made slaves.[4] Yet the economic requirements of the Caliphate demanded the continuation of the slave trade. The dilemma was resolved by sourcing slaves from among the non-Muslim peoples of sub-Saharan Africa and Europe. These new slaves were, in time, converted to Mohammed's faith, ensuring that these children would be able to live their lives as free and equal citizens. Thus victim group children were actively and passively encouraged to abandon their original identities and assimilate into the dominant group. The practice became state policy

[4] Lofkrantz, Jennifer (2011), 'Protecting freeborn Muslims: The Sokoto Caliphate's attempts to prevent enslavement and its acceptance of the strategy of ransoming', *Slavery and Abolition*, vol 32, February, 109–27.

and resulted in a substantial increase in the numbers of the dominant group at the expense of the subjugated.

Over centuries, the subject groups would cease to exist as they could no longer reproduce themselves and sustain their ethnicity and culture. An illustrative example is the indigenous Assyrian population of Mesopotamia (modern southeast Turkey and northern Iraq). In the period of 13 centuries since the Islamic conquest of their homeland, the Assyrians have changed from being the largest group in their homeland to a minority so small it is clinging to its very existence.

Lemkin and his *Genocide Convention* drafting colleagues had these practices in mind when they included the act of forcible transfer of children in their genocide definition. In the opening paragraph of the chapter on 'Genocide' in his 1944 work, *Axis Rule in Occupied Europe*, Lemkin states that the term *genocide* 'is intended rather to signify a co-ordinated plan of different actions aiming at the destruction of the essential foundations of life of national groups, with the aim of annihilating the groups themselves'.[5] Albeit a long-term method, child removal was seen as a serious contribution to the eventual annihilation or decimation of a group.

Devshirme

The Islamic Arab Empire's system of recruiting administrators and fighters from amongst non-Muslim slaves and prisoners of war was adapted by the Ottoman Turkish Empire. Founded in 1299 by Sultan Uthman I,[6] it was under his successor, Orkhan,[7] that a revolutionary tax was

---

[5] Lemkin, Raphael (1944), *Axis Rule in Europe: Laws of occupation, analysis of government, proposals for redress*, Washington DC, Carnegie Endowment for International Peace, 80.

[6] Reigned 1299–1326.

[7] Reigned 1326–1359.

introduced, the *devshirme*.[8] Payment was made in the form of children, collected from the empire's Christian subjects alone.

Under Sultan Murad II,[9] the *devshirme* became regulated. Ottoman soldiers and army doctors would tour rural areas of the Empire to draft recruits from among children aged six to 16. According to historian Artak Shakaryan, this range was so wide because the physical appearance of the child was more important than his or her actual age. 'A *devshirme* child had to be healthy, not too tall or too short and not too fat or too thin.'[10] Children who were collected and brought to Constantinople (today's Istanbul) would be shown to *devshirme* specialists. Based primarily on their physical characteristics, but also on verbal tests, these 'experts' would suggest in which realm the removed children would be suitable. The most attractive and intelligent were sent to the palace; others were absorbed by Jannisary Corps (military musketeer units); the rest were sold as slaves. Available sources allow us to approximate that 60 per cent of the children would be enslaved, 30 percent would become Janissaries, and only 10 percent would go to the palace. Until the mid-1600s, those who went to the court of the Sultan dominated the imperial government. They were totally reliant on the Sultan for their wealth and power, but their sons, as free-born Muslims, could not inherit their positions.[11]

As Bat Ye'or wrote in *The Decline of Eastern Christianity*

---

[8] It may be loosely translated as 'child-gathering'.

[9] Reigned 1421–1451.

[10] Suciyan, Talin (2007), 'Study sheds light on Ottoman Blood Tax' (interview with Artak Shakaryan), *Armenian Reporter*, 2 June, http://www.armenianreporteronline.com/generating/pdf/jun02-2007/A0602.pdf

[11] Ibid.

under Islam, the offspring of '*dhimmis*'[12] were regarded as a reservoir of slaves for economic or political purposes. In 1836, for example, Sultan Mahmud II (Adli) ordered the dispatch of Armenian children and teenagers aged eight to 15 years from Sevasteia (modern Sivas) and other Anatolian towns to the imperial capital where they were put to work at the spinning mill, royal shipyard, to manufacture ship sails and produce iron in the foundries. Payment consisted of bread and clothing. Avedis Perperean, writing in 1871, recorded that:

> this order is renewed year after year and they collect hundreds of Armenian children from every town, depriving them of their parents and their homeland, and during this thirty-day march in bare feet and rags, take them to Constantinople. Several die of cold and want on the way and later through the tyranny of their masters, while others convert to Islam, hoping thus to obtain their freedom.[13]

The *devshirme* met the need for personnel in the empire — at the expense of their Christian subjects. Generations of future leaders and potential opponents were systematically removed by the Ottoman state. The *devshirme* served different needs of the rising imperial power. First, it gave the Ottoman Turks a legitimate solution to their 'problem' of how to deal with thousands of prisoners of war captured from various Christian rival states. Second, it provided the (until recently) nomadic Turkic tribes with the knowledge of administration required to maintain an empire. Third, and arguably the most important asset, it provided the Ottoman Turkish state with a means of population control.

When the Turkic tribes first invaded Anatolia in 1061, they were a small, powerful, warrior elite. They had subjected a large non-Muslim population through force of arms while still

---

[12] Non-Muslim monotheistic subjects of Islamic states.

[13] Ye'or, Bat (1996), *The Decline of Eastern Christianity under Islam*, New York, Associated University Presses, 113.

a small minority. The system of the *devshirme* permitted the new rulers to methodically enfeeble their non-Muslim subject populations by forcibly removing a portion of their children at regular intervals. Over the lifetime of the Ottoman Empire (almost six centuries), the *devshirme* played a major role in reversing the demographic face of Anatolia. During this period, the territory went from being almost exclusively Christian in population in the 1000s, to having an Islamic majority by the 1800s. While the intent of the Ottoman Court may not have been intentionally genocidal in the Convention's sense, the effect of policies and practices such as the *devshirme* was definitely genocidal.

Colonial contexts

Just as their European rivals did, from the mid-1000s the Seljuk and Ottoman Sultans dominated peoples and lands other than their own. The Turkish Sultans looked to their Islamic religion for explanation and justification of how they came to dominate the Near East. In a similar way, the European colonisers looked initially to religion for explanations of their world views. The Renaissance and the subsequent Scientific Revolution meant that theological justification did not satisfy as it once did. Science was looked to as a means of providing more rational analyses. One result of this fusion of theology and science was the movement that came to be known as 'scientific racism' — which may be defined as 'the attempt to develop biological solutions for social problems', typically building upon theological foundations. According to Robert Proctor, it 'was an explanatory program, but it was also a political program, designed to reinforce certain power relations as natural and inevitable'.[14] In the words of social philosopher David Hume

---

[14] Proctor, Robert (1998), *Racial Hygiene: Medicine under the Nazis*, Cambridge, Harvard University Press, 13.

(regarded as the father of the social sciences):

I am apt to suspect the Negroes to be naturally inferior to the Whites. There scarcely ever was a civilised nation of that complexion, nor even any individual, eminent either in action or in speculation. No ingenious manufacture among them, no arts, no sciences.[15]

The emergence of this school of thought from the 1800s rapidly brought an impact on the indigenous peoples of a number of territories colonised by European powers and by the British Empire in particular. Unlike their continental European rivals, which preferred to maintain social and familial barriers between conquerors and conquered, the British instituted the assimilation of the indigenous peoples of a number of the territories they colonised — Australia, New Zealand, Canada, the United States as the most prominent examples.

An outcome of the social revolution brought about by the explosion of scientific knowledge of the 1800s was the incorporation of the 'racial' element to existing religious prejudices. This 'scientific racism' was particularly applied to indigenous peoples in British colonies and dominions as highlighted by the forcible transfer and accompanying assimilation of indigenous youth. 'Scientific' justification was provided by academics, theological justification from clergymen, and bureaucratic 'social' justification for the abduction of children and teenagers from hearth and home, ostensibly 'for their own good'.

Western eugenicists in the early 1900s were aware of the Janissary phenomenon. As recorded by Henry Morgenthau, converts, voluntary and forced,

strengthen the Empire as the Janissaries had strengthened it

---

[15] Hume, David (1826/2004), *The Philosophical Works of David Hume*, Boston, Adamant Media Corporation.

formerly. These Armenian girls represent a high type of womanhood and the Young Turks, in their crude, intuitive way, recognised that the mingling of their blood with the Turkish population would exert a eugenic influence upon the whole.[16]

A similar principle was at work in colonial Canada, America, Australia and New Zealand—not so much for the improvement of the British 'bloodline' by absorbing the indigenous peoples but as a way of eliminating a threat to the colonists' designs for their new lands. In these plans, non-Europeans were assigned subservient roles, if they were permitted to retain a distinct identity at all.

The Canadian residential school system, for example, consisted of a number of institutions for indigenous children, operated since the 1800s by churches of various denominations (about 60 per cent Roman Catholic, and 30 per cent Protestant). They were funded under the *Indian Act* by Indian and Northern Affairs Canada, a branch of the federal government. The schools' purpose was 'to take the Indian out of the Queen's Red Children' according to the *Gradual Civilization Act* (1857) under which the system was implemented.[17] Students were often forcibly removed from their homes, parents, and communities. Most had no contact with their families for up to ten months at a time because of the distance from home. Often, they did not have contact with their families for years at a time. The locations of the schools were planned deliberately to ensure a 'proper distance' from the reserves. They were required to stay in residences on school premises, often walled or fortified in some manner.

---

[16] Morgenthau, Henry (2004), *Ambassador Morgenthau's Story*, Whitefish, Montana, Kessinger Publishing, 182.

[17] 'Ottawa, United Church must pay for abuse', *The Globe and Mail*, 21 October 2005.

Students were prohibited from speaking indigenous languages, so that English or French would be successfully learned and their own languages forgotten. They were subject to often unreasonably severe corporal punishment for speaking other languages or practising non-Christian faiths. The process of phasing out these institutions began in the 1970s and the last one did not close its doors until 1996.[18]

Australia's practice of forcible child removal was assuredly the most thorough in the colonial context. Europeans had been visiting various parts of the Australian coast from the 1600s. The invasion and colonisation of the continent was undertaken by the British from 1788. Europeans rapidly spread out from the harbour now known as Sydney, colonising the country within 14 decades. The fierce resistance of the indigenous people was no match for the technological superiority of the European colonists. By 1860, the Parliament of the Colony of South Australia had been presented with a report declaring that the country's indigenous inhabitants were doomed to extinction.[19] A few years later (1873), the English writer Anthony Trollope wrote that the 'doom' of the Australian Aborigines 'is to be exterminated, fragments of them only remain'.[20]

In *The Australian Race*, E M Carr stated that 'the White race seems destined, not to absorb, but to exterminate the Blacks of

---

[18] See Wertz, Jay (2008), *The Native American Experience*, London, Andre Deutsch, 42.

[19] The Report of the Select Committee of the Legislative Council upon the Aborigines Together with Minutes of Evidence and Appendix, South Australian Parliamentary Papers, 1860, vol 3, no 165, as cited in Kimber, Richard (1997), 'Genocide or Not? The Situation in Central Australia' in *Genocide Perspectives I*, Colin Tatz (ed), Sydney, Centre for Comparative Genocide Studies, 34.

[20] Tatz, Colin (1997), 'Genocide and the Politics of Memory', *Genocide Perspectives I*, Sydney, Centre for Comparative Genocide Studies, 315.

Australia'.[21] The question of the dominant Europeans 'absorbing' the minority indigenous population largely grew out of the emergence of a new 'mixed race' population in Australia. Since the earliest days of British colonisation, European men had been taking Aboriginal women as sexual partners. As late as the 1890s, evidence was being presented to colonial parliamentary inquiries that the abduction and rape of Aboriginal women was common.[22] The result of these (typically involuntary) unions was the population of 'mixed race' children. 'Full-blood' indigenous Australians were deemed to be a 'dying race' and therefore of little consequence; these 'mixed race' youngsters were deemed to be a threat to the dream of an Australia that was 'white' and British.

Morgan Blum states that the solution hit upon for this 'Aboriginal problem' in newly-independent Australia was through biological absorption.[23] In brief, Aboriginal children were to be removed from their families, educated in state and private institutions as livestock and agricultural labourers or domestic servants, and severed from all contact with their native people and culture. Such removals, or 'retentions' of Aboriginal children, began as systematic policy in colony Victoria as early as 1839. The Colonial Secretary of New South Wales stated during a debate in that state's parliament on the

---

[21] Carr, E M (1886), *The Australian Race*, Melbourne, Government Printer, vol 1, 100–06, cited in Kimber, 41.

[22] Willshire, W H (1896), *The Land of the Dawning*, and evidence presented to the Select Committee on the Aborigines Bill (1897) in Reynolds, Henry (1972), *Aborigines and Settlers: The Australian experience*, Melbourne, Cassell Australia, 28–32.

[23] Blum, Morgan (2006), 'Forced child removal in Western Australia' in Tatz, C and S (eds) (2006), *Genocide Perspectives III*, Sydney, Australian Institute for Holocaust and Genocide Studies, 115–39.

Aborigines Protection Amendment Bill on 27 January 1915:

> The Aboriginals will soon become a negligible quantity and the young people will merge into the present civilisation and become worthy citizens... It is not a question of stealing the children but saving them. The moral status of these Aboriginals is very different from that of white people.[24]

Although Social Darwinist ideology held that the Aboriginal 'race' would sooner or later die out, it was decided that the process was to be hastened by 'breeding them out'. From 1839, the colony of Victoria began removing Aboriginal children from their families. In 1909, C F Gale, Chief Protector of Aborigines in the state of Western Australia, reported the view of one of his inspectors on taking children from their mothers: 'no matter how frantic her momentary grief might be at this time, they soon forget their offspring'.[25] Years later, in 1937, a federal–state government conference on Native Welfare adopted a resolution that stated, in part, that 'the destiny of the natives of aboriginal origin, but not of the full blood, lies in their ultimate absorption by the people of the Commonwealth, and it therefore recommends that all efforts be directed to that end.'[26]

Those removed have come to be called the *Stolen Generations*, a term coined by historian Peter Read in 1981.

---

[24] The Hansard was cited by Premier of New South Wales, R J Carr, during his address on 'Stolen Aboriginal Children', 18 June 1997, http://www.parliament.nsw.gov.au/prod/parlment/hansart.nsf/V 3Key/LA19970618005

[25] *Report of the Chief Protector of Aborigines* (1909), West Australian Parliament Votes and Proceedings, vol 2, 2 as cited in Tatz, Colin (1997), 'Genocide and the Politics of Memory' in *Genocide Perspectives I*, Sydney, Centre for Comparative Genocide Studies, 315.

[26] *Human Rights and Equal Opportunity Commission Australia – A national overview*, December 2007, http://www.hreoc.gov.au/education/bth/download/history/bth_ note_taking_3r.pdf

Political scientist Robert Manne suggests that 'approximately 20,000 to 25,000' were removed between 1910 and 1970, based on the Australian Bureau of Statistics report of 1994.[27] The figure may be substantially higher as the report noted that formal records of removals were very poorly kept, and many records 'went missing' when inquiries began. Although very few children of full Aboriginal descent were removed, 'half-castes' — the children of 'mixed descent' — were the most targeted. Estimates were given that between 10 and 30 per cent of all Aboriginal children born during the period were removed by state and federal authorities.

As young men formally educated in the early 1900s, Lemkin and his colleagues would have been exposed to eugenicist teachings during their secondary and tertiary educations. Such Social Darwinism as practised in Australia was the predominant ideology in the Western world. Therefore, the forcible transfers of indigenous children and teenagers in Oceania and North America into state-run institutions during the lifetimes of Lemkin and his colleagues provided them with an immediacy of experience. That was significant to their later work on codifying genocide and the relationship of children to this crime.

The Hellenic, Armenian and Assyrian genocides

Samantha Power, writing in *'A Problem from Hell': America and the age of genocide*, highlights the impact that knowledge of the Armenian Genocide had on Lemkin from his student days at the University of Lvov (modern Lvyv, Ukraine).[28] In his

---

[27] Manne, Robert (2010), 'Comment: Keith Windschuttle', *The Monthly* http://www.themonthly.com.au/nation-reviewed-robert-manne-comment-keith-windschuttle-2256 accessed 13 May 2012.

[28] Power, Samantha (2003), *'A Problem from Hell': America and the age of genocide*, London, Flamingo, 17–20.

unpublished essay, 'Nature of Genocide', Lemkin compared the treatment of the Moriscos[29] with the deportation marches of the Armenians. His conclusion was that 'techniques of physical genocide have repeated themselves through history'.[30] Attacks on the family unit constitute biological methods of genocide. Lemkin specifically cited the Ottoman Turkish Empire as another recurring theme in the history of genocide: 'The children can be taken away from a given group for the purpose of educating them within the framework of another human group, racial, religious, national or ethnical'.[31]

Robert Kempner, responsible for preparing the cases against the leading Nazis at Nuremberg, had earlier written a legal paper on the Armenian genocide.[32] The forcible transfer of Christian Hellene, Armenian and Assyrian children by the Ottoman state, its auxiliaries and successors was 'an integral part of the Hellenic, Armenian and Assyrian genocides (1914–1924) and a key historical precedent to the inclusion of the forcible transfer of children as an act of genocide.'

Amid the (till then) unprecedented civilian death toll of the triple genocide that wracked Anatolia for a decade, the forcible transfer of tens of thousands of children and teenagers is an oft overlooked aspect of the deliberate destruction of the indigenous peoples of Anatolia.[33] Taner

---

[29] See *The Revolt of the Moriscos*
http://www.historylearningsite.co.uk/moriscos.htm

[30] Docker, John (2008), *The Origins of Violence: Religion, history and genocide*, North Melbourne, Pluto Press, 12.

[31] Ibid, 13.

[32] Hosfield, Rolf (2005), 'The Armenian Massacre and Its Avengers. The ramifications of the assassination of Talaat Pasha in Berlin', *Internationale Politik*, vol 6, Fall.

[33] Bjornlund, Matthias (2009),'A fate worse than dying': sexual violence during the Armenian Genocide' in Herzog, Dagmar (ed), *Brutality and Desire: War and sexuality in Europe's twentieth century*,

Akçam and others have recognised that the pre-World War I pogrom against the Hellenes in eastern Thrace and western Anatolia constituted a dress rehearsal for the Armenian Genocide. The Danish Consul in Smyrne (modern Izmir) reported in March 1914 that the provincial *valis* (governors-general) had conducted tours of inspection of coastal settlements. They advised the local Muslim leaders to force the Hellenic population out, first by economic boycotts; and when that did not have the desired effect, by violent persecution.[34]

The favoured method of killing came to be known as the 'white death' by the Hellene deportees. It was so named because it did not involve the shedding of blood. The victims were simply marched across Anatolia, without provisions, until they dropped by the wayside of hunger, dehydration, infection, disease or exposure. Many of those who made it to the final destination — the desert of northern Syria — were butchered.[35] En route, thousands of women and children were forcibly removed from the caravans of death by the Ottoman guards, by Kurdish tribesmen or by Bedouin nomads. As recorded by League of Nations reports, 'young women and girls were kept for the harems; with few exceptions, they

London, Palgrave Macmillan, 35.

[34] Bjornlund, Matthias, cited above (footnote 33), 31.

[35] Danish missionary Karen Jeppe, described one scene she came across on her travels around Anatolia during the genocides: 'Starving Armenian women and children throwing themselves on the body of a dead donkey, tearing it to pieces and devouring it; Turkish children worrying [harassing] little Armenians till they died in the road; exhausted people falling on all fours and crawling along — still driven — till they also died among the other dead people who strewed the roads; and at last a long train of women and girls naked driven on and on', *Manchester Guardian*, 8 October 1926.

were violated as soon as captured'.[36] Cities like Harput and Mezreh became centres of the trade in Armenian, Hellene and Assyrian slaves,

where the most desirable females, first and foremost women of wealthy families, were searched for by local Muslims and checked by doctors for diseases etc. If a woman refused to follow her new 'owner', she was detained by the local authorities until she accepted a life in slavery.[37]

The Christian captives were forcibly Islamised, renamed and assimilated into the households of their captors, either as wives or servants. As time went on, the native Armenian, Hellenic or Assyrian tongues of these victims came to be forgotten. Although the older ones retained some memory of their lives before the genocide, the younger ones came to forget that they were ever Christian.[38]

One of the first individuals to attempt a rescue effort was Karen Jeppe. While she was able to affect a few individuals during the War years, the sheer scale of the problem was overwhelming. Not until the conclusion of the war and the occupation of large parts of the Ottoman Empire by the Allied powers were large numbers of Armenian, Hellene and Assyrian women released from captivity.[39]

---

[36] Records of 8th Assembly, Minutes of 5th Committee, 51 ff.

[37] Bjornlund, 23.

[38] In keeping with local tribal customs, and in order to discourage escape attempts, the perpetrators would often brand their captives with tattoos on their faces or necks. When incised into the skins of Anatolian Christian women, these markings represented a new communal as well as personal belonging.

[39] According to a League of Nations report titled 'The Rescue of Deported Women and Children', in 1921 no less than 90,819 Armenian orphans had been reclaimed from Turkey, Syria, Cyprus, Egypt, Armenia and Georgia. Macartney, C A (1930), *Refugees: The work of the League*, League of Nations Union, London,

Elif Shafak's novel, *The Bastard of Istanbul*,[40] deals with the complexity of the consequences of the forcible removal and subsequent forced Islamisation, of Christian children by Muslim soldiers and irregulars, three generations after the initial events. The novel's key episode unfolds in this way:

> ...a horde of bandits arrived, searching and plundering the houses. They stopped and ransacked every Turkish and Kurdish village in the region. It didn't take them long to find out that there was a little Armenian girl there... They had heard about the orders to deliver all Armenian orphans below the age of twelve to the orphanages around the country... Like all of the children there she was dressed in a white robe and a buttonless, black coat. There were both boys and girls. The boys were circumcised and all the children were renamed. So was Shushan. Everyone called her Shermin now. She was also given a surname: 626.[41]

While *The Bastard of Istanbul* is fiction, there are substantial threads of fact running through it. This extract refers, in effect, to a renewal of the *devshirme*. The orphanage Shushan was removed to remains nameless in the novel. One of these centres was at Aintoura in Ottoman Syria.[42] The school became home to 800 orphans, 30 soldiers who guarded the compound and a staff of 10 Lebanese. The boys were circumcised and given Islamic names beginning with the first letter of their Armenian names: Haroutiun Najarian became Hamid Nazim, Boghos Merdanian became Bekim Mohammed, Sarkis Sarafian became Safwad Suleyman.

Pelican Press.

[40] Shafak, Elif (2008), *The Bastard of Istanbul*, London, Penguin.

[41] Ibid, 242.

[42] The former French school at Aintoura is near Zouk, in the Keserwan district of Lebanon, about a half hour drive north of Beirut.

Partly due to director Nebih Bey's incompetence, poor sanitary conditions, disease and malnutrition prevailed, many children died, attracting the attention of the central government. Aintoura was visited by Cemal Pasha,[43] who upon arrival dismissed Nebih and appointed Halide Hanum[44] as principal of the orphanage. This aspect of the Aintoura story was recorded in a photograph caption in *The Lions of Marash*.[45] Cemal also brought 400 new orphans between the ages of three and 15 years. They were accompanied by 15 young women from powerful Turkish families, part of the 40-strong team whose task was to Islamise and Turkify the Christian Armenian orphans. While Lebanon was wracked by famine, livestock and grain were available at Aintoura in abundance. Education was only in Turkish. The older orphans were taught various trades, like shoemaking and carpentry. The *mullah* called the children to prayer five times a day. Every night the school band would play 'Long live Cemal Pasha'.

---

[43] Commander of the Syrian-based Fourth Turkish Army, and the junior member of the triumvirate that ruled the Ottoman Empire between 1913 and 1918. From Pasha, Cemal (1922), *Memoirs of a Turkish Statesman 1913–1919*, New York, George H Doran Company, http://archive.org/details/memoriesofturkis00cemarich

[44] Halide Edib Hanum (later known as Halide Edib Adivar, 1884–1964) was a famous Turkish feminist, author and nationalist. She was assisted by five Lebanese nuns from the Sacred Heart Order, who were made responsible for sanitation and nutrition. Besides Aintoura, Halide Hanum was also responsible for the Sisters of Nazareth school in Beirut, until its closure in 1917. Halide had the final say on everything, aiming to develop the ideal Turkish nationalist educational institution, a model for the new Turkey that was to come after the successful conclusion of the war.

[45] *The Lions of Marash* was written by Stanley E Kerr, President of the American University of Beirut. In this volume, Kerr recorded his personal experiences working with the Near East Relief organisation between 1919 and 1922.

The Ottoman Army abandoned Lebanon in early 1918, with French forces moving in. The orphanage at Aintoura was in chaos, the 470 boys and 200 girls abandoned. The Catholic clerics approached Bayard Dodge, an officer of the American University of Beirut, for assistance; shipments of food began to arrive through the American Red Cross. With order restored, the process of reversing the Turkification process began, by encouraging the use of the orphans' Armenian names.[46]

Largely through the efforts of the relief workers throughout the Ottoman Empire, the events unfolding were made known across the world almost immediately. For example, the story of one of the abducted children, Aurora Mardiganian, was made into a film in 1918, *Ravished Armenia*. Under the title *Auction of Souls*, it was screened throughout the British Empire, with *The Herald* newspaper in Melbourne advertising screenings in February 1920.[47]

The primary source of evidence on the involvement of the Turkish state in the forcible transfer of Christian young into

---

[46] The American Red Cross appointed Mr Crawford as principal, brought in Armenian teachers who delivered education in Armenian and English. In its final months, the Near East Relief organisation took over. In autumn 1919, the male orphans were sent to Aleppo, Syria, and the females to the Armenian orphanage in the village of Ghazir, Lebanon. In 1993, the school directors decided to build an extension in the rear of the complex. When the ground was disturbed, the workers came across human remains. These bones were all that remained of the estimated 300 Armenian orphans who died during the time Aintoura was run by the Ottoman state. The remains were gathered and given a Christian burial in the cemetery belonging to the Aintoura priests. *Aztag*, Armenian Daily, Lebanon, February 2006.

[47] *Auction of Souls* (advertisement), *The Herald*, Melbourne, 25 February 1920.

Muslim households comes from the Extraordinary Courts Martial, instituted by the new Turkish Government in March 1919 to try officials from the *Ittihad ve Terakke i Cemayeti*. A Turkish commentator, writing in a Turkish-language newspaper in Constantinople the following month, described these as 'the most important trial[s] in the six hundred year history of the Ottoman Empire'.[48] The trials, held in major centres across Anatolia in 1919 and 1920, were recorded in the official Ottoman government gazette, *Takvim-i Vekayi*. The Courts Martial recorded that the systematic distribution and abuse of Armenian females and boys was practised at the highest levels of Turkish society. For example, the chief police officer of Trapezounta (Trebizond/modern Trabzon), a man named Nuri, brought young Christian girls to Constantinople as gifts from the Governor-General to members of the *Ittihad*'s central Committee.

With knowledge of these events spread by the international media and by charitable organisations such as Near East Relief, it is fairly certain that Lemkin and his colleagues would have been moved by this exposure to include the forcible transfer of children in the United Nations' *Convention* a mere two decades later.

The Republican phase 1919–1924

These child removals were by no means limited to the Ottoman period. The practice continued with barely a pause as Kemal's Republican forces assumed control across Anatolia. A specific clause was inserted in the peace Treaty of Sevres (1920), binding the Turkish authorities 'to allow and give all assistance to a League of Nations Commission to make enquiries and liberate the remaining victims'. Mustafa Kemal's revolution against the Ottoman Sultan prevented ratification and implementation of the treaty's provisions.

---

[48] Tatz, Colin (1997), *Genocide Perspectives I*, Sydney, Centre for Comparative Genocide Studies, Macquarie University, 321.

Relief workers in the Middle East estimated that by 1921 there remained an estimated 12,000 captive Christian women and children (predominantly Armenian) even in the areas occupied by the Allies (mainly among the Arabs of Syria). In addition, there were some 70,000 captives amongst the Muslim inhabitants in the interior of Anatolia, in areas beyond the reach of the Allied forces and of western relief workers. In 1922, Jeppe — by now a League of Nations Commissary — reported that there were approximately 6,000 Christian women and children held in Muslim households in the French zone[49,] and at least 30,000 in the district accessible from Aleppo, including some hundreds in Aleppo itself. The French refused permission to send a rescue mission among the Arab tribes 'on the ground that this would only produce a fresh outburst of anti-foreign fanaticism', and even in Aleppo the women could not be rescued for fear of disturbances.[50]

These abductions of Christian children were not restricted to females. Vasileios Anastasiades was born in the Kaesareia (Kayseri) district of Kappadokia but grew up in the town of Ak Dagh Maden, Pontos. His family was deported in 1916. After World War I, Anastasiades was reunited with the surviving members of his family, only to be exiled again in 1920 'when the Turks hit Pelemet, attacking the French'. The men were separated from the women. The children were assembled as a separate group and sent to Zonguldagh on the Black Sea coast of north-west Anatolia:

> Next to us was a camp for Hellene prisoners of war, all but one of whom died as slave labourers. The sole survivor was Demetrios Pairahtaroglou. The soldiers gave us some of their

---

[49] The Cilicia region of modern Turkey, as well as modern Syria and Lebanon.

[50] See Macartney, C A (1930), *Refugees: The work of the League*, League of Nations Union, London, Pelican Press.

333

meagre food rations, so that we would not starve to death. When the Red Cross was notified about us and came looking for us, the Turks would move us around by night. One Christian prisoner, who was serving as a guard, told the Red Cross where we were hidden, on condition that they free him also. That is how 150 children were saved. I came to Hellas in 1924.[51]

Despoina Ioannou's story illustrates the use of forcibly removed Christian children and teenagers as slave labour during Kemal's time in power. Ioannou was born in Palaia Phokaia (modern Eski Foca), a small city north of Smyrne on Anatolia's Aegean coast. In September 1922, she was deported on foot, first to Kediz, then to Menemene. There, the male deportees were separated from the females. Ioannou escaped, only to be recaptured and returned to Phokaia. After convincing the Turkish authorities that she was someone else, Ioannou was sent on another march, this time to Ankara. There she was assigned to serve a French family as a domestic servant. Ioannou revealed her true identity when a letter arrived seeking news of her whereabouts. With the help of the French family she served, Ioannou was reunited with the surviving members of her family in Piraeus.[52]

Reverberations

Within a decade, the physical indigenous Christian presence had been virtually extinguished. By 1925, what remained was — on the surface at least — a 'purely' Turkish Muslim population. In recent years, this image has begun to metamorphose. The exploration of their own genealogies is leading large numbers of people in Turkey to 'discover' Armenians and/or Hellenes and/or Assyrians in their own

---

[51] Anastasiades, Vasileios. Extract translated by Panayiotis Diamadis.

[52] Horbos, Nikolaos (1988), *Palaia Phokaia — Mikras Asias* [Old Phokaia — Asia Minor] Thessalonike: Ekdoseis Gramma, 215–16. Extract translated by Panayiotis Diamadis.

immediate ancestry. The rediscovery of this cultural diversity in Anatolia is also making itself felt through the literature produced by authors who identify themselves as Turkish. Writers like Elif Shafak and Fethiye Çetin are a prime illustration.

Representative of the more factual strand of this movement is Çetin's *Anneannem*.[53] After the deportation of the men of her village by the military police in 1915, some of the women take their children and find refuge in a nearby village. Amongst them were 10-year-old Heranush, with her mother Isquhi, brother Horen and sister. The second village met the same fate as the first: the men were killed and the women and children banished and forced on a death march towards the Syrian desert. Heranush survived the march. She was forced out of the caravan and her mother's arms by Hüseyin, a corporal of the military police. He took Heranush into his house, gave her a new name, Seher, and an Islamic up-bringing. He treated her well, considered her his daughter, but his wife Esma treated her as a house slave, especially after Hüseyin died young. Horen also survived in this way.

Heranush's mother also survived the death march, eventually reaching Aleppo. After the war, her husband returned from the United States to seek out the family he had left behind years before. He found his wife and together they tried to find their kidnapped children. Working through intermediaries they found both Heranush and Horen. They succeeded in recovering Horen. By this time, Heranush had married and even though at first her husband agreed to visit

---

[53] *My Grandmother* was first published in Turkish in November 2004. Geerdink, Fréderike, 'Lawyer and writer Fethiye Çetin: 'My identity has never been purely Turkish', Saturday 20 May 2006, 14–27, http://www.journalistinturkey.com/stories/human-rights/fresh-air_22/

the family in Syria, he changed his mind as he feared losing his wife and children. Heranush remained Seher. Only when she had passed the age of 90 and felt the end of her life approaching, did she confide in her granddaughter. *Anneannem* was the result, published four years after Heranoush passed away.

The fate of the indigenous Christian Armenian, Hellenic and Assyrian populations of Anatolia and eastern Thrace (modern Turkey) remains a subject of extreme sensitivity within Turkey's borders. This is so not only for the Turkish state, but for large sections of the populace. According to Taner Akçam, the modern Turkish state has a 'very strong moral responsibility in relation to the Armenian, Hellenic and Assyrian genocides'. As he argues in *A Shameful Act*, there are a number of factors that form a continuity between the three genocides and the foundation of the Republic of Turkey. The political group which organised the genocides was the same party which organised the Turkish movement against the British and French occupation of parts of Anatolia. 'An important number of party members who committed crimes against the Armenians were also very active' in the movement led by Mustafa Kemal Ataturk.[54] In an interview with the *Los Angeles Examiner*,[55] Kemal laid responsibility for the Armenian, Hellenic and Assyrian genocides squarely at the feet of the *Ittihad*'s triumvirate of Talaat, Enver and Cemal: 'the former Young Turkey Party, who should have been made [to] account for the lives of our Christian subjects who were ruthlessly driven en masse, from their homes and massacred...'

---

[54] Wilson, Conrad (2006), 'University professor talks about his book on Armenian Genocide', *Minnesota Daily*, 14 November, http://www.mndaily.com/2009/02/22/university-professor-talks-about-his-book-armenian-genocide

[55] *Los Angeles Examiner*, 1 August 1926, 1.

Eastern Europe under the Swastika

The granite wall of the Exhibition Hall of the United States' Holocaust Museum in Washington DC is engraved in block letters with a statement attributed to Adolf Hitler: 'Who after all is today speaking of the destruction of the Armenians?'[56] The role of the Armenian, Hellenic and Assyrian genocides as precursors of the *Shoah* was clearly elaborated by Lemkin and others. A lesser known aspect of the devastation visited upon Poland by the Nazis was their forcible transfer and systematic 'Germanisation' of Christian Polish (and other Baltic) children. By virtue of their faith, Jewish children were destined for the death camps. Losing many relatives in the *Shoah*, Lemkin was intimately familiar with the developments regarding children and teenagers in his homeland. In Chapter Nine *of Axis Rule in Europe*, Lemkin discussed the Nazi colonisation of western Poland, a policy to which the forced assimilation of selected Polish children was crucial.[57]

On 25 November 1939, *Reichsfuhrer-SS* Heinrich Himmler was presented with a special report.[58] Given the multi-national nature of the existing population, the report pointed out, '[t]he necessity arises for a ruthless decimation of the Polish population and, as a matter of course, the expulsion of all Jews and persons of Polish–Jewish blood'. In similar ways to the fears of the Ottoman Turks regarding their subject Christian populations, the Nazis were afraid that if left alone the Polish inhabitants of the annexed territories would come

---

[56] Hitler reportedly made this statement to the summit which began the physical extermination of European Jewry, held at a villa on Wannsee on the outskirts of Berlin on 20 January 1941.

[57] Lemkin, 82–83.

[58] The report was officially titled 'The issue of treatment of population in former Polish territories from racial-political view'.

to outnumber the Germans.[59]

Over the following months, special directives were drafted considering the mass forced removal of Polish children that was being prepared. These directives were formulated into one document[60] on 15 May 1940. In December of that year, Himmler's office[61] issued a publication stressing the 'essential' nature of this 'chief national task': 'it is an absolute *national political necessity* to comb out those of German blood in the Incorporated Eastern Territories, and later also in the General Government and to return the lost German blood to its own German people.'[62] In the plans for the creation of the Thousand Year Reich, 'Germanisation' of 'racially desirable' people was as important in determining the future of the German nation as military victories against the Allies. As Himmler was once quoted as saying, 'What the nations offer in the way of good blood of our type, we will take, if

---

[59] Trials of War Criminals before the Nuremberg Military Tribunals Under Control Council Law no 10, Nuremberg, October 1946–April 1949 (15 vols, Washington DC, Government Printing Office, 1949–1953), V, 91 in Lukas, Richard C (2001), *Did the Children Cry? Hitler's war against Jewish and Polish children, 1939–1945*, New York, Hippocrene Books,
http://www.projectinposterum.org/docs/lucas2.htm

[60] The report was officially titled *Einige Gedanken ueber die Behandlung der Fremdenvoelker im Osten* (*A few thoughts about treatment of alien people in the East*) cited in Milton, Sybil (1997), 'Non-Jewish Children in the Camps', Multimedia Learning Center Online (Annual 5, chapter 2), The Simon Wiesenthal Center,
http://motlc.wiesenthal.com/site/pp.asp?c=gvKVLcMVIuG&b=395115

[61] Issued in his role as *Reichskomissar für die Festigung deutschen Volkstums* (Reich Commissioner for the Strengthening of German Folkdom).

[62] Stackelberg, Roderick and Winkle, Sally A (2007), *The Nazi Germany Sourcebook: An anthology of texts*, New York, Routledge, 271.

necessary by kidnapping their children and raising them here with us'.[63] Just as was the case in the Ottoman Empire and Republican Turkey, Nazi ideology regularly took a back seat to practicality when it suited them. The first SS ruler of the Government General, Hans Frank, once stated that,

> When we see a blue-eyed child we are surprised that she is speaking Polish...if we were to bring up this child in a German spirit, she will grow up as a beautiful German girl. I admit that in Poland one can find German racial traits among the people and with caring and development will give us Germans in the course of time a possibility to destroy this part of the General Government.[64]

On the orders of SS Gruppenführer Ulrich Greifelt,[65] six to 12-year-olds 'recognised as worthy blood bearers for the Deutschtum' were forcibly transferred to Nazi boarding schools, while younger children would be farmed out to German families by the Lebensborn program.[66]

Himmler delivered a speech on the issue of the forcible transfers of children from eastern Europe at Bad Schahen on 14 October 1943:

> I think that it is our duty to take their children with us, to remove them from their environment, if necessary by robbing

---

[63] US Counsel, Nazi Conspiracy and Aggression, IV, 559–60.

[64] Pilichowski, Zbrodnie Hitlerowskie, 18, cited in Lukas, Richard C (2001), Did the Children Cry? Hitler's war against Jewish and Polish children, 1939–1945, New York: Hippocrene Books, http://www.projectinposterum.org/docs/lucas3.htm

[65] The Chief of the Headquarters of the Reich Commissioner for the Consolidation of German Nationhood.

[66] Anordung Nr 67/I, 19 February 1942, Z/Ot,1056, 282V, in AGKBZHP cited in Lukas Richard C (2001), http://www.projectinposterum.org/docs/lucas3.htm

or stealing them... Either we win over any good blood that we can use for ourselves and give it a place in our people or...we destroy this blood.[67] [68]

Children with suitable 'Aryan' characteristics were arbitrarily removed from orphanages or abducted from parents, grandparents and guardians. Children from unmarried Polish women working as forced labourers in the Reich met the same fate, as did many Polish teenagers who were working as forced labourers.[69] The members of the Nazi Welfare Organisation (NSV), nicknamed the 'Brown Sisters' (because of their uniforms), played a major role in this systematic forced transfer of children and teenagers. NSV Youth operatives were in action throughout occupied eastern Europe. Using treats such as sweets and bread as lures, the Brown Sisters would seek information on families from unsuspecting children. Armed with this information, the NSV operatives would proceed to the local genealogical records. If the compiled data promised 'racially desirable' results, the child would vanish into the *Lebensborn* program.[70]

Even the concentration camps were scoured for candidates for 'Germanisation'. Each selected young inmate was placed in quarantine prior to deportation to the Reich. Polish inmate physicians did their utmost to rescue the youngsters by

---

[67] Partial translation of Document L-70 Prosecution Exhibit 384 — Extracts from a speech by the Reich Leader SS Himmler at Bad Schchen on 14 October 1943, 989,
http://www.mazal.org/archive/nmt/04a/NMT04-T0989.htm

[68] NO-2218, Pros Ex 447.

[69] Hrabar, Hitlerowski Rabunek, 50ff, Wnuk, Dzieci Polskie Oskarzaja, 7–8 cited in Lukas, Richard C (2001),
http://www.projectinposterum.org/docs/lucas3.htm

[70] Henry, Clarissa and Hillel, Marc (1975), *Children of the SS*, translated by Eric Mosbacher, London, Hutchinson and Co, 155–57 cited in Lukas, Richard C (2001),
http://www.projectinposterum.org/docs/lucas3.htm

creative diagnoses of various illnesses. Unlike most of those who went into the *Lebensborn* program, many of the children who returned from quarantine did not survive the war.[71]

The *SS Race and Resettlement Office*[72] established branch offices throughout occupied eastern Europe for the screening and classification of suitably 'Aryan-looking' Poles and others. Classification came in three groups: (a) children with desirable racial characteristics were dispatched to designated centres for further examination; the 'fortunate' ones went on to the homes of Nazi Party loyalists or to *Lebensborn* ('Well of Life') residences for 'Germanisation'; the unfortunate ones were murdered in Majdanek and Auschwitz; (b) 'racially' less desirable Poles who could contribute economically were sent to the Reich as forced laborers in the Reich; (c) Poles deemed worthless were deported to Auschwitz and almost certain death.[73]

In a number of *Kindererziehungslager* (child camps) around Poland, preselected children would go through a battery of tests aiming at determining their suitability to 'Germanisation'. Nazi 'racial theoreticians' had developed a checklist of 62 points to assess the candidate's 'racial suitability'. As with most Nazi 'race theory', physical traits were of supreme importance: arms, legs and heads were carefully measured; even the size of a girl's pelvis and a boy's

---

[71] International Auschwitz Committee, Nazi Medicine, III, 223–24 cite in Lukas, Richard C (2001),
http://www.projectinposterum.org/docs/lucas3.htm

[72] SS Rasse-und-Siedlungs-Hauptamt (RuSHA).

[73] Duraczynski, *Wojna i Okupacja* [War and Occupation], 393–96 in Lukas, Richard C (2001),
http://www.projectinposterum.org/docs/lucas3.htm

penis were considered important for reproductive purposes.[74] The object of the tests was not to establish the German descent of the candidate, but rather to assess their physical and mental qualities.

While the process had the veneer of science, it was completely arbitrary, relying heavily on the whim of the medical examiner. For example, 13-year-old Wojciech Wysocki was described as 'Eastern Nordic'. His calm, candid appearance made him 'very promising' for 'Germanisation'. However, if candidates displayed 'negative' character traits — a resistance to 'Germanisation' — they were removed from the program, which usually meant dispatch to a death camp and a cardiac phenol injection.[75]

The Reich authorities were under no delusions that the forcible transfer of Polish and other eastern European children could be justified by any lawful principles. As with much else that they did, they did their utmost to conceal this crime from international and domestic public opinion. The majority of written directives were classified top secret or confidential. In no Nazi document does the term 'Germanisation of Polish children' appear. The most favoured phrase was *Wiedereindeutschung* ('re-Germanisation').

It has been estimated by Tadeusz Piotrowski that only between 10 and 15 per cent of the Polish children and teenagers forcibly removed returned home after the defeat of the Nazi state.[76] As one Polish survivor of the process

---

[74] Lukas, Richard C,
http://www.projectinposterum.org/docs/lucas3.htm
[75] Ibid.

[76] Piotrowski, Tadeusz (1998), *Poland's Holocaust: Ethnic strife, collaboration with occupying forces and genocide in the Second Republic 1918–1947*, 298–99 n73 cited in Paul, Mark 'NEIGHBOURS on the Eve of the Holocaust: Polish-Jewish Relations in Soviet-Occupied Eastern Poland, 1939–1941' Toronto: PEFINA Press 2008, 22,

informed another youngster at a DP camp after the war: 'We used to be Germans. But we are Poles now. In a few weeks you will get to like it too.'[77]

According to official Polish estimates, about 200,000 children and teenagers were forcibly removed by the Nazis.[78] The Nazis went to great lengths to conceal the origin of the children who ended up in the *Lebensborn* program and kept few concrete statistics on the abductions. Available figures allow scholars to draw some conclusions about the numbers of forcibly transferred eastern European children and teenagers.[79] Dr Isabel Heinemann estimated that at least 20,000 Polish children had been kidnapped, as well as a similar number of children from the Soviet Union and a further 10,000 from western and south-eastern Europe,[80] a total of approximately 50,000 children and teenagers. Dr Susanne Urban, head of historical research at the International Tracing Service in Bad Arolsen in Germany is still dealing with cases of 'Germanisation' and finding the families and origins of victims of those abducted.

In his testimony at one trial at Nuremburg dealing with

---

http://www.glaukopis.pl/pdf/czytelnia/NeighboursEveOfTheHol ocaust.pdf accessed 13 May 2012.

[77] Quotations from Returning Europe's Kidnapped Children, (Exhibit 27), History of Child Welfare, in PAG-4/4.2; Box 81, UN-RRA/UNA as cited in Lukas, Richard C, http://www.projectinposterum.org/docs/lucas3.htm

[78] Moses, A Dirk (ed) (2004), *Genocide and Settler Society: Frontier violence and stolen indigenous children in Australian history*, New York, Berghahn Books, 260.

[79] Gumkowkski, Janusz and Leszczynski, Kazimierz (1961), *Poland under Nazi Occupation*, Warsaw, Polonia Publishing House cited in http://www.dac.neu.edu/holocaust/Hitlers_Plans.htm

[80] Moses, A Dirk (2004), cited above, 260.

the mass transfer of non-German children to the Reich, Louis Lavitan[81] stated that 'a few less than 10,000 children have been located by us, and have either been repatriated or are in stages of repatriation'. Of these, his office had 'complete evidence on exactly 340 as having been in the hands of *Lebensborn* at one time or another'.[82]

Hellenic Civil War

The transfers of youth during the Hellenic Civil War of 1946–1949 added a new dimension to this crime. Thousands of youngsters from across mainland Hellas were taken from their homes and sent across the country's northern frontiers in the later stages of this fratricidal conflict. This case was unique until that time as the primary motivation was ideological and the perpetrators were not the dominant group but a minority within the Hellenic state.

Beginning within months of the conclusion of World War II, the civil war was a result of the efforts of the Communist Party of Hellas (KKE) to secure the country for the Soviet bloc in the aftermath of Germany's defeat. The West responded with massive Anglo–American support for the Royal Hellenic Government. Beginning in early 1948, when it was becoming clear that they would be defeated, the Communist guerrillas began systematically removing their young from villages in areas they controlled. Initially, they were sent to the Communist areas along Hellas' northern frontier. From there, they were scattered across the Eastern Bloc, as far as Soviet Central Asia.[83]

---

[81] Director for the US Zone of the IRO [International Refugee Organisation], Tracing, Child Search Branch.

[82] http://www.mazal.org/archive/nmt/04a/NMT04-T0989.htm

[83] The General Inspector of the Child Gathering was KKE loyalist Georgios Manoukas. He returned to Hellas in 1961 after denouncing his actions and those of his former party.

A protest note from the government in Athens stated that more than 7,000 children from 59 rebel-controlled villages had been 'conscripted' and sent over the country's northern borders.[84] [85] With the cessation of hostilities, the Royalist government proclaimed that 29 January 1950 would be marked as a national day of mourning for the removed children.[86] An investigation by the United Nations' Special Committee on the Balkans (UNSCOB) 'verified the mass deportation of Greek children'[87] and found that the total number of persons under 15 years removed behind the Iron Curtain came to 28,296.[88] [89]

This event is perhaps unique in genocide and war crimes history as the primary motivation for the removals was neither for the purpose of religious conversion nor for reasons

---

[84] (AAP) 'Rebels take Children — Greek Protest', *Sydney Morning Herald*, 5 March 1949, 3.

[85] Citing a rebel radio station broadcast, the London staff correspondent of the *Sydney Morning Herald* reported on 13 March 1948 that 4,500 children had been removed into Russian satellite countries', 'Greek children seized from parents', *Sydney Morning Herald*, 13 March 1948, 3.

[86] (AAP) 'Greek Day of Mourning', *Sydney Morning Herald*, 24 December 1949, 3.

[87] *Report of the United Nations' Special Committee on the Balkans*, General Assembly Official Records, Fourth Session Supplement, no 8 (A/935), 21.

[88] Diamadis, Panayiotis et al (1995), *A Child's Grief: A nation's lament*, Sydney, Stentor Press, 33.

[89] It estimated that by January 1950 they had been distributed around the Eastern Bloc as follows: Albania (2,000), Czechoslovakia (2,235), Bulgaria (2,660), Hungary and Poland (3,000 each), Romania (3,801), and Yugoslavia (11,600). General Assembly Official Record: Fifth Session, Supplement II (A/1307).

of 'racial purity' — it was openly ideological. The majority of the removed children were not assimilated into other groups but encouraged to retain their Hellenic identities. The victim and the perpetrator groups were members of the same ethno-cultural entity; they were all Hellenes, divided solely by politics.

The rhetoric of the Cold War era overshadows much of the literature surrounding the event. For instance, as Karl Rankin claimed:

the [United States'] embassy believes that Markos' abduction of Greek children...is a major psychological blunder which we should exploit by [the] widest possible publication in [the] US and abroad...it can be turned into useful anti-Communist propaganda.[90]

According to the rebels who conducted the mass transfer campaign, the Hellene young were sent to the Eastern Bloc states for humanitarian reasons; to safeguard them from the onslaught of the 'monarcho–fascist' Royal Greek Army. In a radiogram sent on 30 January 1948, the rebel command in northern Hellas demanded that the Belgrade-based KKE Central Committee 'put the question of helping small children, who suffer famine and other misfortunes, in the Free Greek territory'.[91] In early March 1948, the Communist military leader, Markos Vaphiades, called for the 'evacuation' of 80,000 youths from villages under rebel control in western Macedonia. The Communist authorities in Budapest declared that Hungary welcomed the young Hellenes 'in response to the appeal of the People's Councils of Free Greece'.[92]

---

[90] Wittner, Lawrence (1982), *American Intervention in Greece 1943–1949*, New York, Columbia University Press, 162.

[91] Milan, Ristovic (2000), *Long Journey Home: The Greek refugees*, Thessalonike, Institute for Balkan Studies, 1.

[92] Jones, Howard (1989), *'A New Kind of War': America's global strategy and the Truman Doctrine in Greece*, New York, Oxford University

The Hellenic Liaison Service to the United Nations declared that the removed children were destined for 're-education', converting the young Hellenes to 'Communist ideology' and ultimately take Hellas into the Soviet bloc.[93] Although the United Nations Special Commission on the Balkans (UNSCOB) was denied access behind the Iron Curtain, individual Western investigators visited some of the centres hosting removed Hellene children in Bulgaria. They all reported a pattern of ideological indoctrination that matched the accusations of the Royalist government in Athens.[94]

While there was certainly an element of altruism behind the removals, there are a number of effects that support ideology as the ultimate motivating factor. Their education in the Warsaw Pact states was typical of the Communist regimes of that time. In two resolutions (17 November 1948 and 18 November 1949), the United Nations General Assembly called on the governments 'hosting' Hellenic children to return them to their families.[95] Nor was this the only influential body to

---

Press, 143.

[93] UN General Assembly, Official Records, UNSCOB Report A/574, 3 session, Supplement 8, 1948, 18; Annex 2, 29, 31 in Jones, Howard (1985),'The Diplomacy of Restraint', *Journal of Modern Greek Studies*, May, 70.

[94] Matthews, Kenneth (1972), *Memories of a Mountain War – Greece 1944–1949*, London, Longmans, 177, 180–82.

[95] Extracts from 'Resolution adopted by the General Assembly of the United Nations' during its Fourth Session. Threats to the political independence and territorial integrity of Greece – 288 (IV) (18 November 1949). Noting the report submitted by the International Committee of the Red Cross and the League of the Red Cross Societies on the question of the repatriation of Greek children, and expressing warm appreciation of the efforts made by the two International Red Cross organisations to facilitate the

make such an appeal. In a letter to his vice-president, Albert Barkley, United States' President Harry Truman stated that his administration 'has exerted and will continue to exert every feasible effort to encourage the repatriation of these children'. The US House of Representatives expressed its support for this outcome in House Resolution 514 of 22 March 1950,[96] while Senate followed suit with Resolution 212, adopted on 13 September 1950.[97]

According to media reports, the Communist governments had 'agreed to return any children called by petition of their parents'. By the end of 1949, the Hellenic Red Cross had forwarded 8,000 petitions but none of the children had returned.[98] By 1952, only 684 removed children had been returned to their families; by 1963, some 4,000 had returned home (including a number of children born in Communist states to children and teenagers who themselves had been removed). The assertion that the motive behind the removals was purely humanitarian is undermined by the exploitation of the removals as a means of psychological warfare against the Hellenic state, refusal to repatriate children as requested by their families and by the rebels' employment of some of

---

implementation of General Assembly resolution 193 (III) C, noting that the Greek children have not as yet been returned to their homes … 2. Urges all the Members of the United Nations and other States harbouring the Greek children to make all necessary arrangements, in consultation and co-operation with the international Red Cross organisations, for the early return to their homes of the children with the aforementioned resolution,
http://www.un.org/documents/ga/res/4/ares4.htm

[96] Woolley, John T and Peters, Gerhard *The American Presidency Project* (begun in 1999), Santa Barbara CA, University of California (hosted) Gerhard Peters (database)
http://www.presidency.ucsb.edu/ws/?pid=13766

[97] Ibid.

[98] 'Refugees: Innocents' Day', *Time*, 9 January 1950, 11.

the elder teenagers as fighters in the final battles of the civil war.

As noted by one member of the United Nations observation teams, Kenneth Spencer, the key factor in determining the question of how many of the 28,296 Hellenic children were removed voluntarily and how many by force was the status of the parents. As he noted in his article — 'Greek Children' in *The New Statesman and Nation* — in pro-rebel villages parents decided for themselves whether to send their children away; in 'hostile villages', there was 'little doubt that the approach was different and a process of virtual conscription enforced'.[99] Milan Ristovic estimated that even in anti-government strongholds along the Albanian and Yugoslav frontiers, 'the percentage of the forcibly removed "voluntary refugees" was extremely high, so that in the towns they amounted to up to 29 per cent of the population in 1948–1949'.[100]

This is an illustration of the methods used by the rebels in 'hostile' villages. Phourka is a mountain settlement nestled next to the Albanian border in the Konitsa district of the Epiros region of north-west Hellas. UNSCOB members recorded Mrs Sophia Makri's statement: when the mothers of the village heard of the rebel plan to 'evacuate' all children under 14 to the Communist countries, they hid their children rather than give them up. When the 21 mothers of the village refused to divulge the location of their children, the women were taken to an isolated spot away from the village and tortured:

---

[99] Spencer, Kenneth (1950), 'Greek Children', *The New Statesman and Nation*, 39, 31–32.

[100] Ristovic, Milan (2000), *A Long Journey Home: Greek refugee children in Yugoslavia 1948–1960*, Thessaloniki, Institute for Balkan Studies, 1.

They hung us from pine trees. They burned our feet with coals. They beat us. When we fainted they revived us with cold water from the spring. Fourteen of us died up there but we did not tell. When the Greek army entered our village they found the dead living, for out of the earth came our children.[101]

Kallirhoe Gouloumi, from the village of Gorgopotamos, also in Epirus, had a less bloody but no less traumatic story:

They were in our village for a year. First they took our animals, then our food, then our children. I had three. They did not even let me say goodbye. They said they were no longer my children but their children.

Kleoniki Kyprou, from the village of Monopilo in the Kastoria district of western Macedonia, reported: 'First they hanged the priest, then they cut off his mother's hands, and then they ordered us to follow them. What could we do?' In Albania her 8-year-old girl and 5-year-old boy were taken from her and a rifle was thrust into her hands. Tapping the weapon, the rebel *kapetanios* said: 'This is your husband, this your child'. Kleoniki was forced into the battle of Vitsi. She deserted and got back to her village — without her children.[102]

Many fathers (in some cases both parents) of removed children had migrated abroad before the outbreak of World War II. This was a common phenomenon amongst economic migrants in the inter-war period. The head of the household would migrate then bring out his immediate family as his financial circumstances improved.[103] Some of the forcibly

---

[101] 'Greek Australians seek abducted children', *Sydney Morning Herald*, 12 January 1950, 2.

[102] 'Refugees: Innocent's Day', *Time*, 9 January 1950, 11, http://www.time.com/time/magazine/article/0,9171,811653,00.html

[103] The reunion of removed children with their parents in Australia was even raised in the British House of Lords. (Hansard, House of

removed children and teenagers returned home in the 1950s and 1960s, either in Hellas or in the Diaspora. The majority were not so fortunate. A handful who became involved in activities deemed to be 'anti-Hellenic' by the state remained barred from entering their country of their birth.

The forcible transfer of children from Hellas to the Eastern Bloc states may or may not constitute a case of genocide. There is no evidence that the Communist leadership of the rebel forces responsible for the removals intended to destroy any particular group, in whole or in part. Whether their acts constitute crimes of war depends on the ideological viewpoint of the observer. Given the involvement of the United Nations in these events, it is highly probable that Lemkin and his drafting colleagues were influenced by them in their decision to include such removals as an act of genocide.

Reflections

How does forcibly transferring children achieve the perpetrator's aim of destroying a targeted group, considering that it does not involve actual killing? What is it that caused the drafter of the *Genocide Convention* (including Raphael Lemkin) to include these actions as criminal in the legal definition of genocide?

As evidenced by the contents of Lemkin's [until recently] unpublished papers, genocide in colonial contexts

---

Lords Debate, 28 June 1950, vol 167 cc 1129–31). The children of 24 such families were located in Yugoslavia. ('Greek families will get back lost children', *Sydney Morning Herald*, 4 May 1950, 11). More removed children were located across six Eastern Bloc states. ('50 Greek children expected to join parents soon', *Sydney Morning Herald*, 6 May 1950, 5). With the active intervention of the Australian government and the Australian Council for International Social Service, 62 removed children were flown here on specially chartered flights from Belgrade in October and November 1950.

preoccupied the eminent jurist. On two unpublished pages titled 'Revised Outline for Genocide Cases', Lemkin recorded religious fanaticism, military conquest, political crisis and factors weakening the victim group as 'conditions leading to genocide'. In the same documents, the 'separation of families' is a 'biological method and technique of genocide'; 'forceful conversion' is listed as a 'cultural' method of destruction.[104]

As elaborated here, motivations of perpetrators for child transfer vary. What remains a constant is the intent to destroy family and broader group solidarity by removing members of the next generation of these family and group units. Perpetrators set out to inflict trauma and humiliation by forcibly transferring the most vulnerable members of the group targeted for destruction or disappearance of their ethnicity. In this way, they try to undermine the morale and the ability of that group to resist. By abducting the young and forcibly assimilating them into the dominant group, the targeted minority is denied the opportunity to procreate and therefore to replace themselves. Through the forced impregnation of females from the targeted group, the genocidairés seek to exert a eugenic influence upon the entire population under their control, affecting demographic change to suit their designs.

Ara Sarafian has established that there are four categories of Armenians assimilated by force during the holocaust that engulfed the indigenous Christian peoples of Anatolia. Group A includes those who converted to religion and/or national identity 'voluntarily'. Group B— the individuals who were selected and assimilated by individuals. Group C includes those who were distributed to members and agencies of the dominant group by agencies of the state. Group D enlisted

---

[104] Docker, John (2004), 'Raphael Lemkin's History of Genocide and Colonialism', paper given at the United States' Holocaust Memorial Museum, 26 February, 7–8.

government-operated orphanages in the forced transfer of children and teenagers. As shown in this essay, these categories apply well beyond the bounds of Sarafian's particular case study. Yet we have to concede that while we assume that the five acts of genocide in the *Convention* are motivated by malevolence or evil, it is the *intent*, not the *motive*, that matters. Nowhere does the *Convention* indicate that the intent must be of bad faith, and so the 'excuse' of 'good intent' does not arise. In the Australian case, as with the Hellenic children, it matters not that the intent was to be for the children's benefit. What matters is whether they were forcibly removed. They were.

THE HOLOCAUST AND ROMANI ROMANIANS: DEPORTATION AND RESISTANCE

SHANNON WOODCOCK[1]

At the border *(of Transnistria)* the train stopped. They let us go to the market with the guards. Some Romanians there told us, 'Brothers, you are being sent there for extermination!' — *Irimia Gheorghe, Romani survivor*

There were two camps. Țigani *(Roma)* were on one side, and Jews on the other. We watched them dying, they watched us dying. So many were shot. When they saw a Jew — Bang! Shot! When they saw a Țigan — Bang! Shot. — *Calin Petre, Romani survivor*

In World War II, the Romanian government deported Romanian Jews and Roma to the [artificial] geographical region named Transnistria as racial, political and social threats to the Romanian nation. Bounded by the Dniester and Bug rivers in what is now Ukraine, Transnistria was administered by the Romanian government at Hitler's behest for the period of its existence between summer 1941 and January 1944. This was a territorial incentive for Romania's military role in advancing the Nazi front into Russia in 1941. Under the orders of Ion Antonescu, the antisemitic right-wing prime minister of Romania and ally of the Third Reich, approximately 150,000 Romanian Jews and 26,000 Romanian Roma were deported to Transnistria in 1941 and 1942.[2] There,

---

[1] This essay is a modified and expanded version of an article that appeared in *Interstitio, East European Review of Historical Anthropology*, the Free International University, Republic of Moldova, 2009.

[2] This is the standard figure agreed upon by the first rudimentary counts of names listed as deported in convoys and on trains in 1942. This number does not take into account the thousands of people recorded as re-deportations and staggered deportations that

both Jewish and Romani deportees were forced to labour and left to starve and freeze in a haphazard constellation of ill-administered ghettos and camps. Approximately 90,000 of the deported Jews and 6,000 Romani Romanians survived to return to Romania in 1944 behind the Russian front.[3]

Just as Jews were deported in groups according to Romanian designations of class and geographical location, Roma were deported in two distinct groups in 1942. The first were Roma identified as 'nomadic Țigani', and the second as 'convicted and dangerous...sedentary nomads'. The first group of 'nomads' were Roma of various ethnic sub-groups (Caldarari, Fierari) who often owned property in villages to which they returned in winter, and who travelled as an agricultural labour force in the summer. The second group comprised individuals with prison records (overwhelmingly for petty crimes, with incarceration periods of less than six months), and included single mothers (as 'morally dangerous'), the families and children of people without an income, and people whom the police deported without noting a justification.

The Romanian deportations of Roma as pejoratively-

---

continued until late 1944.

[3] The survival rate was much lower for Romani deportees, who were also arrested and used as forced labour as they re-entered Romanian territory, according to Ordin Circular no 150.263, 19 April 1944. ANIC Fond Inspector General of the Gendarmeria (Inspectoratul General al Jandarmeriei, henceforth IGJ), dosar 86/1944 f75, f89, f220. It is important to note that Transnistria, including the cities of Odessa and Tiraspol, had a local Jewish population of approximately 300,000 who were massacred by both Romanian and German *Einsatzgruppen D* soldiers in 1941 and 1942. Total Jewish deaths in Transnistria 1941–1944 are approximated as 260,000. Local Romani communities are not mentioned in surveys of the period outside of the deportations from Romania, though they certainly existed.

named Țigani is an event in the broader context of anti-Țigan racism as a catalyst for Romanian identity. Understanding the long history of anti-Romani persecution that informed the actions of the Romanian government, police and public in 1942, destabilises continuing assumptions that Roma were rightfully deported as criminals, somehow a social group separate from racialised categories. This blinkered approach to history has thus far ensured that the Romani experience of the Holocaust years is largely unexamined and widely considered 'unknowable'. This essay traces how local police decided who to deport to Transnistria, what happened to deportees in Transnistria, and the ways that Romani Romanians resisted exile and death in the Transnistrian *lagar*.[4] The final section documents Romani resistance to the genocide in Transnistria and thus explodes the pervasive assumption of many historians that Roma did not leave a written trace in the archives of the Holocaust. In fact, Romani people who were for the most part unable to read and write, found people to transcribe their letters for them, and they understood the bureaucratic hierarchy and where to direct their petitions. The Romanian archives hold hundreds of letters written by Romani deportees to various Romanian government officials, providing narratives of deportation and the horrific conditions in Transnistria as well as engaging with the racist discursive frameworks of persecution.

A short history of the problem: making Romanians by persecuting Țigani

The history of anti-Romani persecution in Romanian society must be read in the context of almost 500 years of institutionalised slavery. Between 1385 and 1856, every Romani person who entered the principalities of Wallachia or Moldova was considered a slave of the state. The state could

---

[4] Note the words *lagar* and ghetto were used by Romanian police and bureaucrats to describe the Transnistrian prisons.

retain slaves for their own use, or sell them to *boiers* (private landowners) or monasteries. Slaves were called *sclavi*, *robi*, or Țigani.[5] Other ethnic groups were also slaves, as with a small percentage of Tartars, but these groups were freed by the end of the 15th century. Only Roma remained slaves.[6] The term 'Țigan' came to conflate the legal and social position of slaves with ethnic Roma. To be a slave was to be considered ethnically and racially (culturally and biologically) Țigan. There was no such thing as a free Țigan, or a free Rom.

Țigani slaves were vital to the Romanian economy, working the trades of their traditional family groups. The Fierari were metalsmiths, making tools and equipment for farming. Lautari musicians played at village fairs, weddings, and for those who could afford them. The Ursari entertained with their tamed bears, and other Roma worked as horse trainers and traders, gold panners and goldsmiths, traders of small items, as domestic workers and as cleaners. As with slavery elsewhere, Țigani were controlled by a detailed legal and social system; the Țigan as slave was created and scaffolded within an entire system of stereotypes to justify violent enslavement. Elite and subaltern Romanians discursively constructed the Țigan other as lazy and stupid, yet vindictive and cunning; as requiring forced labour and close supervision in all respects.[7]

---

[5] The word 'Țigan' (plural Țigani) derives from the word 'Tsiganoi' which was widely used in the Byzantine period to name Romani populations that moved west with the Ottoman forces. Roma have consistently identified themselves thus as an ethnic group, and there are a heterogeneous dynamic community of groups within that umbrella term.

[6] Achim, Viorel (1998), *Țiganii în istoria României*, Bucharest, Editura Enciclopedia, 33.

[7] For a detailed study of the binding stereotypical discourses of

The pervasive institutional and social stereotyping of the Ţigan as the lowest social group and requiring enslavement, *especially* as they played a vital economic role in society, placated ethnic Romanian peasants. Landowners (when talking to the peasants) and peasants (when talking of themselves) articulated themselves as moral, obedient, and attached to the land — in contrast to the Ţigani who would supposedly roam the land and refuse to work at all if they weren't enslaved. In the 1848 Romanian nationalist movement, Mihail Kogalniceanu and other nationalists discursively relied on the manumission (or *dezrobirea*, literally the 'unslaving') of Ţigani as the means to produce a united ethnic Romanian nation, to be civilised and worthy of independence in the eyes of modern Europe. Romanian historian George Potra wrote in 1939 that 'the idea and fact (of *dezrobirea*) was welcomed by foreigners, from whom we asked for the recognition of certain rights'.[8] The lack of forethought or afterthought regarding what would happen to Romani individuals after slavery is evidence that uncivilised Ţigani slaves provided an object upon which the ethnic Romanian nation could cut its humanitarian teeth.

The actual steps taken in the process of *dezrobirea* were legislative, and these laws dealt with the issue of how much compensation would be paid to owners, including monasteries. There were no government measures, in terms of legislation or social policy, that addressed the supposed change in status of more than 250,000 people.[9] Ţigani

slavery and the interplay of this system with slave resistance, see Hartman, Saidiya V (1997), *Scenes of Subjection: Terror, slavery, and self-making in nineteenth century America*, New York, Oxford University Press.

[8] Potra, George (1939), *Contibuţiuni la Istoricul Ţiganilor din România*, Bucharest, in the edition republished by Cartea Veche (2001), Bucharest, 111.

[9] The figure of 250,000 is the calculation of Achim, op cit, 98, but

continued to be called Ţigani, but were no longer considered of primary state concern after the final law of *dezrobirea* in 1856. When a *boier*'s slaves became free men and women, they no longer had the right to live on his property, resulting in large numbers of homeless Roma. Many emigrated and travelled in search of places to stop and work for a living, and these Roma were easily identified by appearance, occupation and landlessness as Ţigani. Many made agreements with their former owners to continue living on that land in their employ; these people continued to be called Ţigani, despite their legal status as free men. By World War I, the Ţigani were no longer considered slaves to be privately owned, but Romani peoples continued to exist socially as Ţigani without owners, the internal ethnicised 'others' who required constant policing within the nation.

In 1918, the Treaty of Trianon granted Romania the former Hapsburg territory of Transylvania, more than doubling Romania's area and population. The increase in urban populations of non-Romanians, as well as an overall increase in non-Romanian populations, spurred two decades of Romanian ethno-nationalist policy.[10] The predominant anxieties of the Romanian state and population in the

---

Kogalniceanu himself estimated that there were at least 600,000 Ţigani slaves in (1837), *Esquise sur l'histoire, les moeurs et la langue des cigains, connus en France sous le nom de Bohémiens*, Berlin, Librarie de B Behr, Oberwaldstrasse. See also Petcuţ, Petre (2008), 'Le lendemain de l'esclavage. Les mesures de l'Etat pour la sédentarisation de Roms' in *Anuarul Centrului de Studii Rome* 1/2008, Bucharest, Editura Universiţăţii din Bucureşti, 23–40. For a fuller discussion on this theme see Woodcock, Shannon 'The Ţigani Other as Catalyst for the Creation of Modern Romania' in the same volume, 41–72.

[10] See Livezeanu, Irina (1995), *Cultural Politics in Greater Romania: Regionalism, nation building and ethnic struggle 1918–1930*, London, Cornell University Press.

interwar period were pinned to the spectres of Jewish urban control, Hungarian irredentism in newly gained Transylvania, and Bolshevism in the East. Romani Romanians were increasingly policed in their socio-economic position as the inferior, marginalised ethnic minority by Romanian state bureaucracy.[11] From the Romanian perspective, Ţigani were considered radically other *to*, but inextricably *of*, the Romanian people.[12]

The Romanian fascist movement known as the Legion of the Archangel Michael (later, the Iron Guard), gained strength in the 1930s through physical threats and popular appeal. Racist and antisemitic at heart, the Legionary movement articulated a Romanian nationalism that moved beyond socially pervasive ethno-nationalism to racialise Romanian identity in eugenic discourses on national hygiene resonant with National Socialist ideology.[13] Newspaper articles and 'scientific' studies conducted by academics at the Central Institute for Statistics described the Romanian nation as a

---

[11] Romanian Romani communities responded to the new ethno-national tensions by forming their own trade unions stressing the modernisation of Romani communities as part of the Romanian nation. They focused on literacy and the unionisation of traditional skills, stressed that they were not a political group, but considered themselves part of Romanian society of ethnicity Rom or Ţigan. See Williams, Susan (2007), 'The 'Civilised Trap' of Modernity and Romanian Roma, 1918–1934', in *Anthropology of East Europe Review*, vol 25 no 2, Fall, 12–27.

[12] The 1930 census of Romania concluded that there were 208,700 Ţigani in the country (*Institutul Central de Statistica* (1930), Bucharest), a gross under-representation by comparison with all other estimates.

[13] Romanian fascism, however, is vastly different to National Socialism. See Deletant, Dennis (2006), *Hitler's Forgotten Ally: Ion Antonescu and his regime, Romania 1940–1944*, New York, Palgrave Macmillan.

racial body threatened primarily by Jews and Țigani. An article entitled 'Race and National Destiny' in *Cuvântul*, the Legion's semi-official newspaper, on 16 January 1941 ranted that 'the decline of the Romanian people is due to the infiltration into our ethnic group of elements of inferior races, the crossing of the ancient Getic–Roman blood with Phanariot and gipsy (*sic*) blood, and, of late, with Jewish blood.'[14] Sabin Manuilă, director of the Central Institute for Statistics, referred to 'the Țigani problem' as 'the most important and acute racial problem in Romania',[15] and suggested in a 1941 memo to Antonescu that 'unilateral transfer' of these populations — to send them outside Romanian borders — was the solution.[16]

Antonescu walked his own line of institutionalised antisemitic and anti-Romani persecution after purging the Legion in January 1941, and in the following years as an ally of Germany with attendant pressure to follow Nazi racial

---

[14] 'Race and National Destiny' in *Cuvântul* XVII (new series) no 91, Thursday 16 January 1941 in Petculescu, Constantin and Florian, Alexandru (eds) *The Killing Idea: The dimensions of the Legionary ideology*, Bucharest, Noua Alternativa, 359 as cited in Giurescu, Dinu C (2000), *Romania in the Second World War 1939–1945*, East European Monographs, Boulder Distributed by Columbia University Press, 66. Please note the translator's use of 'gipsy' from *Țigani*, a common and grammatically incorrect slippage of the Romani subject to the realm of the fantasmatic uncapitalised 'Other' in Western discourse across the centuries.

[15] Cited in Deletant, Dennis, op cit, 189 and referenced to Bucur, Maria (2002), *Eugenics and modernization in interwar Romania*, Pittsburgh, University of Pittsburgh Press, 147.

[16] See Achim, Viorel (2001), 'The Romanian Population Exchange Project Elaborated by Sabin Manuilă in October 1941,' *Annali dell'Instituto storico italo-germanico in Trento*, 28, 593–617.

policies.[17] It is possible to say that Antonescu's racial policies were in line with Nazi genocidal racial policies, although he proved more canny in considering the economic and political effects of deportations of Jews to Transnistria at crucial moments in the war, halting fresh and large-scale deportations of Jews and Roma in 1943 rather than pursuing a 'final solution' as in German-administered territory. Romanian pre-war anti-Romani racism—inherent, reproduced and policed in the naming and marginalisation of Romanian citizens deemed to be 'Țigani'—was thus fully racialised in the fascist decade of Legionary popularity. It was this racially identified group that was targeted for deportation and destruction in the Holocaust alongside Romanian Jews. Antonescu's intent to destroy certain perceived parts of the Romani community (as *Țigani*) through their deportation, forced labour, and murder in Transnistria, was implemented by members of the Romanian government, military, and the military police, the gendarmerie.[18]

Deportation to Transnistria

Marshall Ion Antonescu issued two decrees in May 1942; first, for the census of all 'nomadic' and 'sedentary' Țigani, and second, for the deportation of 'all nomadic Țigani'. The specific order to deport 'nomadic Țigani' read:

In line with the general order to remove all parasitical and disorderly elements, Marshall Ion Antonescu orders—

---

[17] See Deletant, Dennis, op cit, for a detailed analysis of Antonescu in relation to Hitler.

[18] We can understand the persecution of Roma as Țigani by remembering that Jews (*Evreii*) were persecuted and identified as the pejorative and stereotype-laden name *Jidani* (usually translated as 'kike' in English). It is striking to think that while scholars wouldn't dare to refer to Jews by the pejorative names the perpetrators called them, Roma and Sinti are still commonly referred to as *Zigeuner*, *Cigany*, *Țigani* and Gypsies by non-Romani scholars.

through this act—that all groups of nomadic Ţigani from the whole country be sent to Transnistria. These measures are to be executed through local organs of the gendarmerie, so that no group of Ţigani and no police can know the final scope of the order. The removal will be implemented by the legions of the gendarmerie. These orders are to be executed immediately. For other categories of Ţigani the orders will be given in good time.[19]

The frame for the decree refers to the removal of 'parasitical' elements from Romanian society, in line with racialised discourse of the time. Important is the intentional withholding of information about what awaited deportees in Transnistria, although local police documents continually referred to 'evacuating' deportees to the *lagar* (prison) in Transnistria.[20] From the archival evidence, it can be concluded that Romanian gendarmes across the country easily understood who was meant by the category 'nomadic Ţigani'. Without confusion, gendarmes identified and deported groups of Caldarari, Fierari and other Romani family units who were beginning their summer work season of travel. These groups often owned property and animals in villages where their families had lived for generations, and travelled on established routes between markets and fairs with their trades in the summer. Their property was nationalised in many cases, and simply taken over or stolen by Romanian inhabitants in other cases.[21] On 1 June 1942, 11,441 people

[19] ANIC Folder IRJ, dosar 258, f4. 1942, end of May, Order from the President of the Council of Ministers, the Military Cabinet, to the General Inspectorate of the Gendarmerie

[20] The verb 'evacuation' and the noun *lagar* were also used for Jewish deportees.

[21] Through Law Nr 315, 30 January 1942. Order to apply this law to the property of deported Ţigani sent to all regions on 4 September 1942. ANIC fond IGJ, dosar 126/1942 f10–11. Each case can be

identified as 'nomadic Ţigani' were assembled across Romania and marched on foot under armed guard to Transnistria.[22] The quotation that opens this essay is from a survivor of this forced march to Transnistria.

The decree for the census of 'non-nomadic Ţigani' in May 1942 specified that gendarmes were to deport 'sedentary nomads (especially those who, being non-nomadic, are convicts, recidivists, or have no means of existence or precise occupation from which to live honestly through work, and thus constitute a burden and a danger to public order').[23]

The lists of non-nomadic Roma sent back to the Council of Ministers were short. Most gendarmerie branches simply wrote 'we don't have any Ţigani like this here'. Indeed, while 'nomadic' Ţigani were recognisable by their wagons and sometimes their dress, the concept of 'non-nomadic' Ţigani did not reference a pre-existing group that could be easily defined and deported. The Council of Ministers ordered the General Inspectorate of Gendarmerie to resolve the lacklustre performances of its regional offices, and on 25 July another telegram was sent to all branches ordering another census of 'all sedentary Ţigani who have had prior convictions, are recidivists, or live without a means of existence'.[24] Gendarmerie who still reported they had no such people in their jurisdiction were ordered by telephone again on 4

---

verified by checking property registries in regional archives. Many of the soldiers who returned from the front to find their families deported as Ţigani also found that local Romanians now owned their property.

[22] The figure is from the government count of nomadic Ţigani who entered Transnistria as a result of these marches. ANIC fond IGJ, dosar 126/1942, f20–205, 203

[23] 17 May 1942, ANIC, fond Inspectorate Regional de Jandarmi, dosar 258, f–6v,

[24] ANIC, fond DGP, dosar 188/1942, f4–48v.

August, and finally, on 15 August 1942 the General Inspectorate of the Gendarmerie telephoned every regional branch with the order to return the censuses of 'convicted, *dangerous*, etc Ţigani' on 16 August.[25] This change of categorical shorthand to qualify 'sedentary nomads' as 'dangerous' indicates a discursive shift in cadence to one of threat rather than 'burden' or 'disorder', in line with the radical racial rhetoric pervasive in policy of 1942.

This series of requests for longer lists of non-nomadic Ţigani prompted intense activity and confusion on the ground. It wasn't simply a matter of deporting everyone of Romani ethnicity, or occupation, or colour of skin, though all of these things could signify 'Ţigan'. There were clearly dark-skinned Romani Romanians who were, by their behaviour, in no way Ţigani. Similarly, there were non-Romani Romanians who were disparagingly referred to as 'Ţigani' because of their renowned laziness, dirtiness, and generally uncouth, 'un-Romanian' lifestyle—but these Romanians could not be deported as Ţigani because they were racially not capable of *being* Ţigani. Individual groups of gendarmes discussed amongst themselves how to identify people to fit the category set for deportation.

In the first place, gendarmes usually trawled prison release lists for anyone they knew as Ţigan who had been convicted of a crime. Although the ethnicity of convicts was not usually recorded, gendarmes were working in their own local communities and knew which families were considered Ţigan. In the lists they compiled of the sedentary/non-nomadic Ţigani, the column beside the names of all the family members to be deported was entitled 'observation' or 'motive for deportation'. The vast majority of those with previous convictions before the law had been in prison for just a few

---

[25] ANIC, fond Direcţia Generală a Poliţiei, dosar 188/1942, f211.

months, or had been fined for petty theft.[26] One deportee in Cernauți was listed for deportation because he had been 'active in a communist organisation'.[27]

In the city of Buzau, gendarmes explored the 'Țigani area' around the local market place, and included people who had untidy houses and courtyards for deportation.[28] In Botosani, the local gendarmes added 155 people to the list of individuals 'to be deported because they don't have certain means of existence...they go from Țigan to Țigan to work, then spend all they earn on food and drink'.[29] Similarly, in the city of Roman, the column listing motives for deportation include descriptions like 'he sits in the pub all day'.[30] In Rimnicu Sarat, the chief of the gendarmes in the village, Ilie Ionescu, had a particular obsession with deporting Țigan women who lived with men without being legally married. In response to the pleas of a father of a deported woman, he wrote that she could not return to Romania because 'she had lived as a concubine with different men, floating between the most dubious of them'.[31] In Timişoara, the Commander of Timiş–Torontal gendarmerie, Major I Peschir, argued for 'cleansing the Romanian race of Țigani', which mirrors the discourses of racial hygiene prevalent in Hungarian, Romanian and German literature available in Timişoara of the

---

[26] There are clear patterns in the police files I have seen of over-representation of Romani Romanians in sentences for theft in the 1930s.

[27] USHMM (United States Holocaust Memorial Museum) IGJ dosar/Reel 23, 408.

[28] Prefectura Judetul Buzau, dosar Nr 26/1942 'Privitor pe Țigani nomazi' file 39, 6 May 1942.

[29] USHMM, IGJ dosar/Reel 23, 353 Legiunea Botoşani, Inspectoratul Jandarmerie Iaşi.

[30] USHMM, IGJ dosar/Reel 23, 389.

[31] USHMM, IGJ dosar 86/1942, 1148/9.

time.[32]

The titles gendarmes gave to the lists of non-nomadic Țigani also indicate the different ways that local gendarmes articulated who they were to deport. In Storojinet, gendarmes made a list of 'dubious sedentary Țigani'.[33] In Lapușna, 690 people were listed in the category 'Țigani to be evacuated from the categories of the dubious, convicted, thieves, pickpockets and those who occupy themselves with stealing from which they win their existence'.[34] On this list of people to be deported are women who read palms, beggars, and the families of people with prior convictions for anything at all.

In one of the Bucharest gendarmerie, the census of non-nomadic Țigani was entitled 'stable Țigani who have been convicted of crimes, are recidivist, etc' but the list was primarily constituted by 'war invalids, children, concubines, workers, lautari, flower sellers, vagabonds, and even a small shop owner'.[35] The list of another Bucharest gendarmerie used 'dubious occupation' as a category in the column for motive of deportation.[36] Many Bucharest gendarmes simply left the 'observation/motive for deportation' column blank, or wrote 'no occupation'. Yet in these very documents from Bucharest, the column listing property is often filled with at least a cow or sheep, and regularly with houses. Considering that these individuals had not been convicted of any crimes — on the contrary, they lived a sedentary lifestyle in houses with a few

---

[32] Inspectorate Jandarm Timis-Torontal, dosar 27, 1942, 1.

[33] USHMM IGJ Reel 23, dosar 290/1942, 417.

[34] USHMM IGJ Reel 23, dosar 290/1942 ,447.

[35] USHMM IGJ Reel 23, dosar 290/1942, 'Prefectura Poliției Capitalei', 471-74.

[36] USHMM IGJ Reel 23, dosar 290/1942, 490. Legiune Jandarmerie Vlasca, Inspectoratul Jand. Bucuresti.

animals in the suburbs of Bucharest—they could not fit technically in the category of 'dubious occupation'. This is until we consider, of course, that simply being interpellated as Ţigan made the semblance of a respectable Romanian lifestyle an unacceptable parody of racial and social organisation, powered by the anxiety of Romanian ethno-national identity that the Ţigani 'other' be recognisable as such.

When the regional gendarmerie branches returned their revised and lengthened lists to the General Inspectorate of Gendarmerie, they included letters explaining the revised numbers. The gendarmes of Dolj added 1,227 people to the list, and explained that the first list had been 'superficial' and limited by time.[37] Commander Gh Tofan of the Vaslui gendarmerie wrote that they 'weren't conscientious enough on the first census'.[38] Others presented their orders to increase the lists as their own acknowledgement of how this is useful for Romanian society — for example, Commander Cristescu in Valcea wrote that he had 'put (on the list) people who are predisposed to commit all kinds of infractions, having decided that this is the moment to rid ourselves of these insubordinates of public order and security'.[39] Needless to say, only ethnic Roma thus suspected were listed and deported; no other ethnic groups of 'insubordinates' were targeted, thus proving again that deportees were targeted as an ethnic—not a 'social'—group. In Ialomita, an extra 308 people were added to the original 159, all in the category of 'people who own no property, have no occupation and are living off dishonest work'.[40]

The ad hoc development of the very concept of non-

---

[37] USHMM IGJ Reel 23, 98 and IGJ Reel 23, 240, amongst many others.

[38] 7 August 1942 USHMM IGJ Reel 23, 392.

[39] 5 August 1942 USHMM IGJ Reel 23, 207.

[40] USHMM IGJ Reel 23, 240.

nomadic Țigani to be deported shows that the category did
not simply refer to a recognisable and pre-identified group.
The terms on which such a category were to be applied, on
the contrary, were developed in regional variations when
local gendarmes responded to simple pressure; they invoked
and applied historically developed and contextualised
stereotypes of what it meant to be Țigan.

Between 12 and 20 September 1942, 13,176 Romani Romanians were deported to Transnistria on overcrowded trains as
sedentary Țigani.[41] Reports written by the gendarmes in
charge of taking Romani from their homes and putting them
on trains to Transnistria, recorded the deportees physically
resisting deportation. Like Jews, Romani deportees were not
only heavily guarded, but lied to and told they would be
given property in Transnistria in order to gain a degree of
compliance of the victims in their deportation. In multiple
cases this led to mass panic and officials in Bucharest sent
orders that police were to stop spreading such false rumours.

Resistance to genocide in Transnistria

Roma, as with Jews, crossed the Dniester river under armed
guard with constant beatings and searches. In Transnistria,
Roma were settled in a variety of camps — some entirely in the
open surrounded by armed guard, some on the collective
farms of the Ukrainian state, and others in the houses of
evacuated local peasants. Romani camps were primarily in
the regions of Oceakov (Alexandru camp), Berezovka and
Balta. As Ioanid has pointed out, 'the Gypsies (sic) suffered
the same fate as the Jews; they died either by execution or

---

[41] The numbers are certainly more than this in total, considering
continuing arrivals and those who were not on the deportation lists
or counted (later acknowledged in police and government
correspondence). ANIC fond IGJ, dosar 126/1942, f204–05, 203.

because of the cold or hunger'.[42] Having had their wealth, wagons and means of making a living confiscated, Roma were then at the mercy of the horrific winter of 1942, the resulting starvation and typhus epidemics, a total lack of Romanian administrative provision for Roma, and the cruelty of Romanian and German armed forces.[43] While the Romanian government maintained dialogue with the various international Jewish associations, which in turn secured the delivery of some financial and aid assistance for Jewish deportees, Romani Romanians had no such international assistance. Roma were not considered a factor in international relations during the war.[44]

---

[42] Ioanid, Radu (2008) in the chapter 'The Deportation, Persecution, and Extermination of the Gypsies' in his book *The Holocaust in Romania*, United States Holocaust Memorial Museum, Washington DC. While this sentence appears in the online edition of the text available at http://www.romanianjewish.org (last accessed 12 September 2008), it does not appear in the print edition.

[43] For more details of the conditions in Transnistria for Romani deportees, see Ioanid, ibid, Achim, Viorel (2004), *The Roma in Romanian History*, Budapest, New York, Central European University Press, and Michelle Kelso's groundbreaking documentary film *Hidden Sorrows: The Persecution of Romanian Gypsies in WWII* (available from the author, contact michellekelso@yahoo.com).

[44] For more on Jewish experiences of Transnistria see Carp, Matatias (1994), *Holocaust in Romania 1940–1944*, Budapest, Primor Publishing; Braham, Randolph L (ed) (1997), *The Destruction of Romanian and Ukrainian Jews During the Antonescu Era*, Boston, East European Monographs no CDLCXXXIII; Ancel, Jean (ed) (1986), *Documents Concerning the Fate of Romanian Jewry During the Holocaust Jerusalem*, the Beate Klarsfeld Foundation; Iancu, Carol (2001), *Shoah în România: Evreii în timpul regimului Antonescu 1940–1944*, Editura Polirom, Iaşi; Butnaru, I C (1992), *The Silent Holocaust: Romania and its Jews*, New York, Greenwood Press; Institutul Român de Istorie Recentă (2004), *Holocaustul evreilor români: Din mărturiile supravieţuitorilor*, Iaşi, Editura Polirom.

The following extract from an anonymously authored 'State of Affairs' report dated 5 December 1942 provides one example of the recorded situation of one part of the Romani deportees:

> During the time that they have spent in the barracks in Aleksandrodar, the Ṭigani have lived in indescribable misery. They weren't sufficiently fed. They were given 400 grams of bread for the ones that were capable of working and 200 grams each for the elderly and the children. They were also given few potatoes and, very rarely, salty fish, and all these in very small quantities. Due to the malnutrition, some of the Ṭigani — and these make up the majority — have lost so much weight that they have turned into living skeletons. On a daily basis — especially in the last period — ten to 15 Ṭigani died. They were full of parasites. They were not paid any medical visits and they did not have any medicine. They were naked...and they didn't have any underwear or clothing. There are women whose bodies...were [completely] naked in the true sense of the word. They had not been given any soap since arriving; this is why they haven't washed themselves or the single shirt that they own.
>
> In general, the situation of the Ṭigani is terrible and almost inconceivable. Due to the misery, they have turned into shadows and are almost savage. This condition is due to the bad accommodations and nutrition as well as the cold. Because of hunger...they have scared the Ukrainians with their thefts. If there had been some Ṭigani in the country who were stealing...out of mere habit, here even a Ṭigan who used to be honest would begin stealing, because the hunger led him to commit this shameful act.
>
> Due to maltreatment, by 25 November, 309 Ṭigani had died. Roma bodies were found on the Otchakov Aleksandrodar road. They died of famine and cold.[45]

---

[45] State of Affairs report from Oceacov region 5 December 1942, ANIC fond IGJ, dosar 130.1942, vol 1, f128–31. This English

In this situation of chaos, lack of provisions, and widespread death in the community, many Romani developed complicated strategies for escape. Deportees such as Ion Stancu wrote long complaints detailing the misery and injustice to Bucharest and many built networks with Romanian soldiers to create an underground trade in counterfeit travel permits. Like some Jewish deportees, Roma found ways of making business, trading, and stealing to procure food for their starving and sick families. Evidence of this resistance, on individual and group scale, can be found throughout the Romanian archives. Deported and persecuted Țigani also engaged bureaucratically with the Romanian government to contest and refute the 'status' by which they had been deported. Romani petitions for repatriation submitted to the Ministry of Internal Affairs were forwarded with clarification requests to the regional police in the complainant's village, who conducted their own investigation and replied to the Ministry. Only the miniscule number of individuals who had requests for repatriation approved and had left before January 1943 made it home before the borders were closed to all Țigani seeking return to Romania for fear of typhus epidemics. Roma imprisoned in Transnistria, however, continued petitioning the authorities throughout the war. This paper trail thus documents the active resistance of deportees and the gamut of localised Romanian reactions to and interpellations of Romani ethnicity in wartime Romania.

I focus on 'bureaucratic' resistance here to highlight the wealth of written sources concerning Romani Romanians and the Holocaust. Roma accessed scribes to write their petitions and submitted them to local gendarmerie offices, regional

---

translation is taken from the chapter 'The Deportation of the Roma and their Treatment in Transnistria' in (2004) *The report of the International Commission on the Holocaust in Romania*. This report was compiled by a board of historians at the request of Ion Iliescu then President of Romania, overseen by Elie Wiesel.

town halls, and directly to the Ministry of Internal Affairs and the General Inspectorate of the Gendarmerie in Bucharest. Requests were made by the heads of deported families (especially of nomadic Roma, in December 1942), by soldiers who returned on leave from the front to discover their families had been deported, and by extended family members who endeavoured to bring back their deported family members. Deportees and their family members dictated petitions to scribes, and thus provide narrative constructions of the deportations and interrogations of discursive interpellations of the victims as Țigani rather than Romanian citizens of Romani ethnicity. Many petitioners travelled without or with falsified permits between Bucharest (Ministry of Internal Affairs, General Inspectorate of Gendarmerie) and their home village, and some even travelled clandestinely to Transnistria on multiple occasions to check on their family, then returned to continue petitioning for their return. For escaped deportees, the extra element in the fight was to avoid arrest while 'lingering' outside official buildings trying to speak to clerks about the case. Briefly, avoiding arrest for travelling and simply being in Romania without permission required in itself a high level of discursive agility and physical mobility. Many of these escapee petitioners were arrested and re-deported to Transnistria at least once, and most often with a group of other Roma rounded up by local authorities.

Let us examine a few examples of how these requests for repatriation can be read in order to raise new questions and provide new voices in what I term the bureaucratic resistance of Romani Romanians imprisoned in Transnistria. First, look at the following returned soldier's narrative of realising his family were deported to Transnistria.

9 January 1943

Domnul Prefect,

The undersigned soldier Tudor Mamai, Reg. 21, Infantry, Bucharest, respectfully brings the following to your attention:

I fought at the front for 18 months, and in Stalingrad, in which time I had no kind of vacation. This month I was granted leave for 25 days and I returned home to my family in Comuna Balatești, Jud. Ilfov. When I got home I entered the courtyard and met a stranger who asked me what I was looking for in his house at this late hour. On my own property I asked him what he was looking for in my house. Later I found that my family had been sent to Transnistria, Comuna Bogdanovca, because we are Țigani.

At present I am serving with Reg. 21 Infantry which is at the front in Stalingrad, but I have a permission of leave for 25 days, please give a permission to return for my family, composed of my wife, Anica Mamai, and the child Ion Mamai. My true father Constantin Mamai, my mother Florea Mamai, my uncle Nicolae Raducanu, my brother in law Gheorghe Steian, my brother Dinu Ion Mamai, and my uncle Tanase Costea, and Steian Nicolae, the brother of my wife, Petre Medin my brother in law, and my uncle Dinu Lean. I am decorated with the Military Virtue *(medal)*.

With profound respect, Tudor Marin.[46]

This narrative of a soldier coming home to find his family deported was common. The use of the term Țigan as a simple unproblematised identity term, as we see in this letter, is actually quite rare, reflecting the fact that it was written before the news that Romani Romanians were being deported as Țigani reached even the front lines of Romanian regiments. In Tudor Marin's narrative, being a Romanian Țigan in no way excluded the right to own property, and the letter reminds us that Romani Romanians identified as Țigani were not excused or prevented from fighting in the Romanian army.

The variety of discourses that petitioners use to refute and nuance the interpellation of their families as Țigani are also indisputable evidence that Romani individuals and communities did engage with the power structures in which

---

[46] USHMM IGJ dosar 59, 1942, 1056.

they were named and persecuted.[47] Many argued for repatriation by invoking multiple discourses of national identity, familial love, and legal concepts of justice as tied to nation and state. Many petitioners also tried to work within the definition of Țigan which they perceived to have been given by the government to claim their family were mistaken for nomadic or non-nomadic Țigani, in various ways.

In one letter, Vasile and Teca Covaci from Comuna Acmariu in Judet Alba, requested the return of their four children.[48] They stated:

> We are Roma, and thus legally married and these are all our legitimate children. We are not nomadic Roma, we are Fierari, with property and a household and we move for work, to earn a living. At the time they were taken we were at work and the children were mistakenly taken with the other Roma. We hope that you understand our pain as parents remaining without our children, and give permission for them to return.

---

[47] This seems obvious, but in the fields of both Holocaust studies and Romani studies in general, inaccurate stereotypes of Romani relationships to events of politics and history are often used to excuse poor research by non-Romani scholars. For example, the fact that illiteracy was higher amongst Romani interwar communities than non-Romani, and also the fact that due to various factors Romani culture is more an oral tradition than written, does not mean that Romani voices in and about history cannot be read in archival sources. Subaltern and post-colonial studies have demonstrated this. Oral histories also need to be recognised in more formats than the singular controlled interview standard of most Holocaust survivor testimonies being recorded by the United States Holocaust Memorial Museum, Yad Vashem and the Shoah Foundation. An example of more fitting oral history methods might be allowing survivors and their families to talk in groups in order for familiar discursive patterns of shared narration to be documented.

[48] 27 January 1943 USHMM IGJ dosar 59, 1942, 1096

The petitioners here refer to themselves as Roma, and stress that their familial structure is the same as Romanians (marriage, legitimacy). They also stake a claim for the validity of their lifestyle as property owners who travel for work, yet it is their replacement of the term 'nomadic Ţigani' with 'nomadic Roma' that tethers their self-identified ethnic identity to that of the pejorative Ţigani 'Other' to be deported. This discursive attempt to replace the government's category with the Romani category of Fierari, a respectable traditional trade-based identity, serves to incorporate the group of self-identifying Fierari into the gendarmerie's definition of nomadic Ţigani. In fact, after much paperwork and investigation between various regions, the gendarmerie found that this entire family had been deported to Transnistria, and the father (Vasile Covaci) had escaped, returned to his home town to make the petition, and continued to live on the run. A search warrant was released for his arrest and he was redeported to Transnistria in April 1943.

This is a petition from a sedentary war veteran:

Ion D Paun 13 February, 1943.

Dear Minister,

The undersigned Ion D Paun, invalid of the war, resident in Com. Miloseşti Jud. Ialomita, respectfully brings the following:

On the 15th of September 1942, my family were coming home from agricultural work in Comuna Tandarei, and were stopped on the road by gendarmes and included in the convoy of nomadic Ţigani, and deported to Com. Cavaliopca, Jud. Oceacov, Transnistria.

This was a mistake, because my family are not nomads, but have lived in Jud. Ialomita for generations, working as useful and established tradesmen. On the other hand, I cannot work anymore due to injuries from the war, thus please repatriate them, as a passionate people caught up in a momentary mistake, without any cases against them, and known as having only acted for good in society.

Thanking you, and receive please my respect and trust for this consideration.

Ion D Paun[49]

Ion D Paun doesn't refute the categorisation of his relatives as Țigani, but as nomadic Țigani, and by claiming that they were returning from agricultural work he refutes the stereotype that Țigani don't work the land as do ideal Romanian peasants. The location of his family on land and property over generations is supplemented by his self-presentation as a good Romanian veteran of World War I. The intent to destroy all Țigani of particular groups is made clear in the subsequent decision of the General Inspectorate of Gendarmerie, that because this family did travel in the summer for agricultural work they were correctly deported as nomads, and because this man is unable to work and thus guilty of avoiding deportation, he was also to be deported to Transnistria.[50]

Cases written by sedentary small business-owning Romani Romanians in large cities often mobilised more strident nationalist discourses to request repatriation. Dumitru Marin typed his own request letters and petitioned multiple times over the period of the war. The following excerpt from the much longer letters he sent to the Minister of Internal Affairs highlights the stereotypical symptoms of 'Țigani' that he refuted in those deported, such as criminality, lack of loyalty to the Romanian nation, and nomadism. In addition, he reminds the government that Țigan Romanians (sic) fought for Romania in the Great War, thus claiming an ethnicity within the Romanian national community called Țigan.

Dear Minister,

My relatives are serious people, honest, workers and home owners,

---

[49] USHMM IGJ dosar 59, 1942, 905.

[50] USHMM IGJ dosar 59, 1942, 903

not one has any criminal records against them…In this family there were people in whose veins flowed the coagulated blood of the holy greater Romania.

Even though I am of Ţigan origin, I have lived my whole life a Romanian life, and we identified with the obligations and aspirations of the Romanian people *(neam)*. No blame, no reproach, against any one of these banished from their property and their beloved country can justify their deportation to a foreign land. I ask you respectfully with all my soul to remember that in the Great War there were Ţigan soldiers of Ţigan origin and you have seen with how much generosity they gave their blood for our country — because they do not have any other.[51]

The Romanian government had decreed on paper that all veterans of World War I, and soldiers and families of active soldiers or potential conscripts for World War II, were to be exempt from deportation. In practice, this decree was never seriously considered. The government investigation found that half of Dumitru Marin's family had not even been included on any census or deportation list—another of the uncountable number of Romani Romanian families deported to their deaths in Transnistrian ghettos without evidence other than these petitions. They were not given permission to return to Romania.

Rafaila Raveca wrote her petition in February 1943 and was clearly aware of the government decree to not deport the families of soldiers currently serving:

The undersigned Rafaila Raveca, living in Posaga de Jos in Jud. Cluj Turda, unmarried with 3 children, brings it to your attention with honour that my daughter Maria, married to Nuţ Emil, all living in this commune, was taken away together with the 4 year old child and deported to Transnistria because we are of ethnic origin Ţigani. In this case, the fact her husband, Nuţ Emil, is a mobilized soldier currently fighting at the front in Reg. 85 Infantry, Comp. 3A wasn't

---

[51] Dumitru Marin, 29 December 1942, USHMM IGJ dosar 59, 1942, 899.

considered. They were illegally deported...without any
consideration of the injustice this is for those fighting for the rights of
the People, and of the country.[52]

The following petition by a soldier home on leave from
active service doesn't mention ethnicity in terms of Romani or
Țigan identity, but petitions from the premise that the local
police chief abused his personal authority in order to deport
his family:

February 6, 1943

Dear Minister of the Interior

The undersigned Munteanu Petre, commercial trader from Comuna
Caushani Jud. Tighina, currently a soldier in Regiment 3 Border
patrol Cernauti, Comp. V-a Caușani, respectfully puts the following
complaint:

Due to the work of enemies, my parents Simion Munteanu and
Sofiea Munteanu, my brothers Ilie and Gavril Munteannu, and also
my sister Olga, married to Berdaga Haralambie, all stable residents
owning land and property and living for decades in Comuna
Caușani, Jud. Tighina, were rounded up by the Chief of Post in this
comuna and taken to Comuna Sustacova, Jud. Oceacov to the state
company there.

Soon the fatherland will send me to fight for the integrity of its
borders. It causes me pain to do this thankfully when I know my
parents, without any guilt and under the holy cross of justice, were
sent to suffer there with foreigners.

I ask you, Minister, to conduct an investigation to ascertain that my
parents were sedentary people and good citizens and that the Chief
of Police in our comuna expelled my relatives to this far away part of

---

[52] Rafaila Raveca Jud. Cluj Turda, February 1943. USHMM IGJ dosar
59, 1942 Doc 1030. The local gendarmerie replied that the daughter of
the complainant was deported because she 'refused any work she
was offered by the locals and was only interested in living by
begging and stealing from their gardens'. USHMM IGJ dosar 59,
1942, Doc 1028.

Transnistria as an abuse of his power. After this research please give permission for my parents and brothers to be free to return to the comuna where they have lived for decades and where they were born. Please find the certificates from the Mayor's office attached, I send my respect,

Petre Munteanu. [53]

The Chief of the Section of the Cauşani gendarmerie replied on a small piece of paper with two sentences stating that this family no longer owned property in the village, and that they were musicians who worked by going from place to place, and thus were nomadic Ţigani. This reply, as with the others, provides the historian with insight into how the factors of local property development and fluid government categories for 'Ţigani' intertwined. The reply of the Chief does not specify what property the family had owned before they were deported, and all deported persons' properties were nationalised or bought by bystander Romanians. The paperwork remains today in regional archives of the municipal administration. The Chief's designation of the Munteanu family as musicians — who obviously need to work by travelling to functions, including public fairs — as nomadic Ţigani, illustrates that even socially integrated and vital community service providers were deported in many cases as nomadic Ţigani, primarily because they were perceived as ethnic 'Others' to the Romanian decision-makers.

Conclusion

The repatriation requests of Romanian Romani deportees to Transnistria as Ţigani highlight the need for critical attention to how categories describing potential victims of genocide are formed, disseminated, rearticulated, and enacted. The ways that Romanian officials named and deported 'Ţigani' between 1942 and 1945 need to be approached in their historical context of more than 500 years of intense discursive

---

[53] USHMM IGJ dosar 59, 1942, Doc 1163

construction of the Țigan as enslaved and inferior other against which an ideal ethno-national Romanian identity was articulated. Antonescu's order to deport the non-nomadic Țigani is a way for us to look at how individuals and authorities in different regions decided how to identify non-nomadic Țigani from amongst Romanian Romani communities. Categorisations using words like 'dubious', 'dangerous', and 'immoral' tell us a lot about the stereotypical construction of these others which, in times of non extreme stress, were implicit and articulated in much more subtle ways. The requests for repatriation are valuable evidence of how some Romani Romanians engaged with and refuted these discursive constructions in a myriad of dynamic ways in order to survive. While the majority of those deported to Transnistria died of starvation and disease in barren ghettoes, those who did survive not only continue to tell their stories of endured atrocity, but are supported by a wealth of traditional historical sources that evidence their contemporaneous struggles for recognition and survival.

AUSTRALIAN RESPONSES TO THE ARMENIAN GENOCIDE, 1915–1930

VICKEN BABKENIAN

In December 1915, Charles E W Bean, the Australian war correspondent in Gallipoli, reported that 'the Turks as the world knows' are endeavouring 'to wipe out the Armenian nation'.[1] Bean had observed an event which would later be widely recognised as the first major genocide of the twentieth century.[2] At the time, every major newspaper in Australia regularly covered the genocide — the *Sydney Morning Herald* alone published more than 50 articles on the event in 1915. Headings like 'Armenians Butchered', 'Million Armenians Massacred' and 'More Armenians Massacred — girls sold in open market' were common and indicated the tone of the articles at that time.[3] Emerging from a world-wide movement to save the survivors of the Turkish onslaught, a relief fund was established in Australia in late 1915 and it continued for more than a decade.

While the Australian citizenry was learning about the fate of the Armenians through the media, Australian and New Zealand (ANZAC) prisoners of war captured by the Ottoman Turks were witnessing first hand the unfolding of the murderous events. Yet, despite the strong connection between

---

[1] Bean, Charles E W (1915), 'Germany's Al — the Turkish method', *Mercury*, 21 December, 6.

[2] See international affirmation of the Armenian genocide, http://www.armenian-genocide.org/affirmation.html accessed 24 August 2011.

[3] Kateb, Vahe G (2003), 'Australian press coverage of the Armenian genocide 1915–1923', MA thesis, University of Wollongong, 265–67, at http://ro.uow.edu.au/theses/215 accessed 24 August 2011.

Australia's Gallipoli experience and the Armenian genocide, Robert Manne has poignantly observed that 'not one Australian historian has devoted more than a passing page or paragraph to the relationship, or even the mere coincidence, of the two events'.[4] Consequently, the Armenian death toll has no role in Australia's collective memory of Gallipoli, only a memory and a noble story about that bloodied venue as the birthplace of a nation. This essay helps redress that omission by focusing on the role Australians played in what is certainly the nation's first major international humanitarian relief effort.

The Armenian Genocide

'The Armenian Question' emerged as an issue in international politics towards the end of the nineteenth century. The Ottoman Empire, which had ruled the largest portion of historic Armenia since the sixteenth century, had declined to the point where western diplomats came to call it 'the sick man of Europe'. The Armenians experienced increased political repression, religious persecution and heavy taxation. Following the Ottoman Empire defeat in the Russo–Turkish war of 1878, the European powers pressed the Ottomans to carry out reforms in the Armenian-inhabited regions of the Empire.[5] Abdul Hamid II, the sultan of the theocratic Ottoman Empire, was defiant. Between 1894 and 1896, a series of massacres were carried out against the Armenians, greatly shocking and alarming the western world. According to Dr Johannes Lepsius, a German missionary who witnessed and investigated the massacres, at least 100,000 Armenians were

---

[4] Manne, Robert (2007), 'A Turkish Tale', *The Monthly*, February, 20.

[5] Walker, Christopher J (1990), *Armenia: The survival of a nation*, London, Routledge, 114.

killed and another 500,000 made destitute.[6] Winston Churchill and several American writers and journalists were openly using the word 'holocaust' to describe these events.[7]

In July 1908, a group of secularist revolutionaries known as the 'Young Turks' launched a coup and within days they removed the autocratic powers of Sultan Abdul Hamid, making him a constitutional monarch. In March 1909, the Sultan mounted a counter-coup. Initially successful, he was ultimately deposed by the Young Turks. During this turbulent period, another large-scale massacre of Armenians was launched in the Adana province of southern Turkey, one in which approximately 20,000 Armenians perished.[8] After a series of military defeats and the loss of Ottoman territory in the Balkans to its former Christian subjects in 1912–1913, the Young Turks decided to follow a strategy of aggressive, narrowly ethnic Turkish political and linguistic nationalism. Fearing that the Armenian provinces would also be lost with the intervention of foreign powers, the Young Turks began to regard Armenians with increased suspicion.[9]

In October 1914, the Ottoman Empire — after much debate and dithering — entered World War I on the side of Germany. After a series of Ottoman military setbacks by the Russians, the Young Turks accused the Armenians of conspiring with the Russian forces to ensure an Ottoman defeat. The legend of 'Armenian treachery' gave the government the pretext to

---

[6] Lepsius, Johannes (1897), *Armenia and Europe: An indictment*, London, Hodder and Stoughton, 18.

[7] Tatz, Colin (2003), *With Intent to Destroy: Reflecting on genocide*, London, Verso, 18, 186.

[8] Akçam, Taner (2006), *A Shameful Act*, New York, Henry Holt and Co, 69.

[9] Nezim, Seker (2007), 'Demographic Engineering in the Late Ottoman Empire and the Armenians', *Middle Eastern Studies*, vol 43, no 3, May, 462.

sanction measures designed to remove all traces of the Armenian population from the Empire. Triggered by what many scholars argue was the impending landing by the Anglo–French forces on the Gallipoli peninsula, the Young Turk government arrested some 250 Armenian intellectuals in the capital, Constantinople (now Istanbul), on 24 April 1915.[10] This marked the beginning of what Henry Morgenthau, the United States ambassador to the Ottoman Empire in 1915, described as a 'campaign of Race extermination'.[11]

Soon afterwards, the Minister of the Interior of the Ottoman Empire, Talaat Pasha, ordered the deportation of Armenians throughout Ottoman Turkey. Their properties were seized and the deportees given insufficient provisions to sustain life. Forced to march through hostile terrain, tens of thousands died from starvation and disease. There was no security and columns of people were set upon, robbed, raped, abducted or killed by paramilitaries, by Kurdish brigands, released prisoners and gendarmes under the control of party officials or local governors. The Armenians had, as Geoffrey Robertson QC observes, 'been deliberately ordered to suffer "conditions of life calculated to bring about their destruction in whole or in part"'.[12] During the death marches, tens of thousands of Armenian women and children were abducted and were forcibly converted to Islam as a price for their lives.[13]

---

[10] *The Monthly*, February 2007, 21.

[11] Internal Affairs of Turkey 1910–1929, General Records of the Department of State, Document, no 867.4016/76, Cable Record Group 59, US National Archives, Washington DC.

[12] Robertson, Geoffrey QC, *Was There an Armenian Genocide?*, London, Doughty Street Chambers, 2009, 5.

[13] Akçam, Taner, 183.

385

Anzac prisoners of war as witnesses

Among the plethora of foreign eyewitnesses to the Genocide were the Anzac prisoners of war taken by the Turks. They include prisoners captured at Gallipoli, the Sinai, Mesopotamia and the submariners who penetrated the Dardanelles in 1915.[14] Perhaps the most well-known Australian prisoner in Turkey was Captain (later Sir) Thomas White, a pilot for the Australian Flying Corps, and in later years a cabinet minister in the Menzies government. White was captured by the Ottoman army in November 1915 while on a mission to cut telegraph wires near Baghdad. He had his first encounter with the Armenian massacres when he reached a 'mainly Armenian town' called Tel Armen in northern Mesopotamia. He noticed that only a very few Armenian women and children had remained, 'the males being conspicuously absent'. After climbing a little rise, he found 'thirty-six newly-made graves which spoke eloquently of what had become of the Armenian men'. He noticed a little girl who had been watching him from a side street and looked pleadingly towards him. Powerless to help her, White was 'horrified at the Turk's handiwork, learning later that these massacres had been simultaneous and to order throughout the entire country'.[15]

In addition to the demographic change brought about by the forced deportation of Armenians and other Ottoman Christians, the policy had served another useful purpose for the Ottomans. The homes, churches and monasteries the Armenians were forced to abandon became the prison camps

[14] See Diamadis, Panayiotis (2007), 'Precious and Honoured Guests of the Ottoman Empire', *Genocide Perspectives II*, Blackheath, Brandl and Schlesinger.

[15] White, Thomas W (1928), *Guests of the Unspeakable: The odyssey of an Australian airman – being a record of captivity and escape in Turkey*, London, John Hamilton Ltd, 122.

where many Australian and other Allied prisoners were held captive. Lieutenant Leslie H Luscombe of the 14th Battalion AIF was taken prisoner at Gallipoli on Hill 971 in August 1915. While being transported to the centuries-old Sourp Asdvadzadzin (Holy Mother of God) Armenian monastery in Ankara, he witnessed 'a sad and depressing sight' at the station in Eskisehir, a railway junction town in western Turkey:

> On the opposite side of the platform another train was standing. It was composed of a number of empty two-tier steel sheep trucks. On the platform a considerable number of Armenian women and children were huddled together. As our train pulled into the platform, Turkish soldiers armed with whips were driving the women and children into the sheep trucks. It was evidently intended to transport them to some distant concentration camp... All the Armenian men that could be rounded up were liquidated.[16]

Another prisoner was Able-Seaman John H Wheat, a crew member of the Australian submarine 'AE2', which was captured shortly after penetrating the Dardanelles in April 1915. He was taken to the Sourp Asdvadzadzin Armenian church at Afyon Karahissar, a town in western Turkey. Before the war, the Armenians comprised about one-third of the town's 30,000 inhabitants. Wheat observed that 'all the Armenians' had been 'driven from the town' before his arrival. Another prisoner interned at Afyon, George Handsley of the 2nd Australian Light Horse Unit, describes how the town 'had been the scene of a horrible massacre' before his arrival, adding that 'blood stains' were 'still there, and were quite plain on the wall of our quarantine prison room'.[17]

---

[16] Luscombe, Leslie H (1970), *The Story of Harold Earl: Australian*, Brisbane, W R Smith & Paterson, 52–53.

[17] Foster Joseph R, *Two and a Half Years Prisoner of War in Turkey*,

John Halpin, of the 12th Light Horse Regiment, captured in the Sinai, described his 'new-found home' at Afyon:

We live in an atmosphere of desecration — the desecration of the House of Christ, and His martyred children of Armenia. This was their structure, is now their resting place. By day the blood-bespattered walls cry out to us, imagination magnifies the shrieks of massacre by night. Within the narrow churchyard, their bones lie underfoot.[18]

Curious to know what had happened to the Armenians, Halpin caught the attention of a Turkish officer named Abu Makarish, passing him a few para's for information. Makarish related to Halpin how he had 'killed Armenians' sweeping his hands 'across his throat from ear to ear, in a sequence of significance' about eight times. Makarish gestured again in 'a sequence of significance...Women...screaming, childish victims of his ravishments'.[19]

The Armenian relief movement

The relief movement to save Armenian survivors began in the United States in 1915. It was sparked by a telegram sent by the United States ambassador, Henry Morgenthau, to the Secretary of State in Washington on 6 September 1915. Morgenthau reported that the 'destruction of the Armenian race' was 'progressing rapidly' and he proposed the formation of a relief fund in the United States to 'provide means to save some of the Armenians' who had survived.[20] In response to his appeal, an emergency meeting was held in

---

Series no A1336, Acc no A1336/1, at www.naa.gov.au accessed 10 September 2011.

[18] Halpin, John (1934), *Blood in the Mists*, Sydney, Macquarie Head Press, 216

[19] Ibid.

[20] Internal Affairs of Turkey 1910–1929, General Records of the Department of State, Document no 867.4016/117, Cable Record Group 59, US National Archives, Washington DC.

New York on 16 September 1915 by a group of civic, business and religious leaders. They formed the American Committee for Armenian and Syrian Relief (ACASR), with headquarters in New York. Steps were taken immediately to organise volunteer committees in every state in the nation to maximise the Fund's outreach to the American people. The ACASR was eventually incorporated by an Act of Congress in August 1919 and renamed Near East Relief (NER). Within a decade, the organisation had successfully raised over $110 million and rescued more than a million Armenians, Greeks and Assyrians from certain death. This figure included over 130,000 children who were housed, fed and educated in more than 200 orphanages.[21] The American Red Cross was also involved in sending relief supplies to the Near East and by 1918 they had appropriated about $US1.8 million for Armenian relief.

Britain soon followed America's lead and in October 1915 the Lord Mayor of London, Charles Johnson, inaugurated the Armenian Refugees (Lord Mayor's) Fund at Mansion House, London. In British cathedrals and churches it became the practice to designate a Sunday in February as 'Armenia Sunday', and to give the proceeds of the collections to Armenian relief. By the end of World War I, British charities had raised tens of thousands of pounds for the Armenian refugees.[22]

Australia's role in the relief effort

The fate of the Armenians aroused the sympathy of many Australians. In December 1915, Miss M E Searle, honourable

---

[21] See Barton, James (1930), *Story of Near East Relief: 1915–1930*, New York, MacMillan & Co.

[22] Nassibian, Akaby (1985), *Britain and the Armenian Question: 1915–1923*, London, Croom Helm, 63.

secretary of the newly-formed Armenian Relief Fund, made an appeal by letter to the editor of the Melbourne *Argus*. Searle stated that the Young Turks were bent on 'exterminating the Armenians' and had made 'appalling progress' towards this goal. She urged fellow Australians to follow the American lead and to 'spare something for these most pitiful of all'.[23]

The Fund had emerged from a large wartime Australian culture of relief movements for various countries, such as the Belgian Relief Committee, Serbian Relief Committee and Polish Relief Committee. Searle's efforts helped raise a modest £300 until her work was taken over by the Friends of Armenia organisation in early 1917. The organisation was formed in Melbourne by three prominent citizens: Dr Alexander Leeper, Master of Trinity College in the University of Melbourne, William H Edgar MLC, and Pastor James E Thomas, President of the Council of Churches of Victoria.[24] In February 1917, a public meeting was held in the Assembly Hall, Collins Street, Melbourne, by the Friends of Armenia committee, chaired by William H Edgar. The stated purpose of the meeting was to awaken 'fresh interest in the cause' of the Armenians. A motion was put forward by members of the committee calling for

the attention of the public to the urgent needs...of the remnant of Armenia. We are convinced that their claims for help are so strong that the whole civilised world should co-operate forthwith to save them. We trust that the government of Australia and the community at large will take up their cause, so that, where possible, protection and help may be given, and that liberal supplies of money may be received.[25]

---

[23] Babkenian, Vicken (2010), 'An SOS from Beyond Gallipoli: Victoria and the Armenian Relief Movement', *Victorian Historical Journal*, vol 81, no 2, 257.

[24] Ibid, 257.

[25] Ibid, 258.

In response to requests made by the Friends of Armenia committee, the Lord Mayor of Melbourne, Sir David V Hennessy, convened a meeting with the Council of Churches of Victoria in March 1917. He suggested that 'the various Churches should set apart a Sunday for special collections in aid of the suffering Armenians'. They agreed to designate 22 April 1917 as 'Armenia Sunday', a day for intercessions and collections for the starving Armenians. The Lord Mayor proclaimed:

> I gladly accede to the request made to me by several prominent citizens of Melbourne, and by the Victorian Friends of Armenia Committee, to open a fund for the relief of the remnant of Armenia. Many of these poor people are dying through starvation in Mesopotamia and Arabian Deserts, whilst others who are returning to Armenia are in urgent need of help and the re-establishment of their desolated homes.[26]

This initiative by the Lord Mayor, supported by the Church leaders in Victoria, became the first major grassroots drive for destitute Armenians. The appeal was a great success; the Melbourne *Age* reported that over £2,000 had been collected. A ladies subcommittee was formed and some bales of goods were made up for transport to Armenia at the earliest opportunity. Unfortunately, the lack of shipping facilities prevented their dispatch.[27]

The Commonwealth Button Fund (CBF), an organising body which co-ordinated and sponsored the fundraising activities of other funds, produced a badge to help with the Armenian relief campaign in November 1917.[28] It featured a

---

[26] 'Appeal for Distressed Armenia', *Argus*, Melbourne, 21 April 1917, 16.

[27] 'Help for Armenia — Over £3000 raised', *Age*, 5 December 1917, 9.

[28] Print for Badge: Servia Syria Armenia, National Archives of

coloured illustration of a Middle Eastern scene, with date palms, a white town with minarets and three Arabs on camel against yellow sand and a blue sky. The words 'Servia Syria Armenia' were printed in red across the sand. During the war these badges were sold in trams, buses, at railways stations and rallies to raise money for the stated cause.

Before long, the movement for Armenian relief spread across to other Australian states. In December 1918, the Lord Mayor of Sydney, James J Smith, along with many prominent businessmen and clergy, adopted a resolution put forward by Sir Thomas Anderson calling for a 'fund to be established in NSW...to save a Christian people, who are now living in abject poverty, from extinction'.[29]

In a pioneering move to increase collections, the New York based ACASR commissioned a veteran Hollywood film producer, William N Selig, in early 1919 to produce a film based on the story of Aurora Mardiganian, an Armenian girl who had survived the genocide. The Armenian relief committees in Australia received a copy of the six-reel film and eagerly used it as an effective fundraising tool. On 28 February 1920, the Union Theatres Ltd under the auspices of the Sydney and Melbourne Armenian relief committees, presented a premiere at the Princess Theatre in Spring Street, Melbourne.[30]

While only one reel of the film has survived, a book entitled *The of Souls: The Story of Aurora Mardiganian* first published in 1918, provides the screenplay. It opens in an Anatolian village on Easter Morning 1915, where the large

---

Australia, Series no A1861, Acc no 3905, at www.naa.gov.au accessed 8 August 2011.

[29] Babkenian, Vicken (2008), 'Edith May Glanville: Champion of the Armenian Relief Fund', *Journal of the Ashfield and District Historical Society*, 8.

[30] 'Aid for Armenia', *Herald,* 28 February 1920, 6.

Mardiganian family is preparing for the forced deportation. On the road, Aurora is continuously molested and she finally apostatises in order to save her mother, but to no avail. At a certain point during the exodus, 16 girls in the caravan are 'crucified' on crude crosses — the most sensational scene in the film. Aurora is finally rescued and taken to Russia, where she embarks on a Norwegian ship for the United States.[31] It was the first movie ever made explicitly for the work of advocacy for humanitarian relief. It was described by the Melbourne *Herald* as the 'most powerful human drama of all time'.[32]

The internationalisation of the Armenian Relief movement

In May 1922, the Reverend Dr Lincoln L Wirt, an American Congregational minister and the International Commissioner of the NER, visited Australia to organise and expand Australia's relief potential. He had spent much time in the Near East and had been directly involved in the relief work. Prior to his arriving, Wirt had helped establish committees in Hawaii, Japan, China, and the Philippines.[33] The stated aim of his mission was to 'forge a chain of mercy' from one end of the world to the other.

Wirt travelled to the major capital cities in Australia where public meetings were organised. He spoke of the dire needs of

---

[31] Gates, H L (1919), *The Auction of Souls: The story of Aurora Mardiganian, the Christian girl who survived the Great Massacre*, London, Odhams Press.

[32] Babkenian, Vicken (2010), 'An SOS from Beyond Gallipoli', 'An SOS from Beyond Gallipoli: Victoria and the Armenian Relief Movement', *Victorian Historical Journal*, vol 81, no 2, 261.

[33] Babkenian, Vicken (2010), 'Cuba, China, Korea, Hawaii and the Armenian Genocide', *Armenian Weekly*, 10 November, available at http://www.armenianweekly.com/2010/11/10/cuba-china-korea-hawaii-and-the-armenian-genocide/

the Armenians and called on Australian government to provide a 'mercy ship' for goods donated by Australians to be sent directly to the areas of need. The heads of the major religious organisations, as well as prominent political and civic leaders, expressed their support. The Prime Minister of Australia, William 'Billy' Hughes, promised 'that free freight would be provided by the Commonwealth Steamers'.[34]

As a result of appeals made in Melbourne, Sydney and Adelaide during Wirt's visit, shipments of relief supplies — which included flour, tinned milk, clothing, leather and woollen material — were dispatched aboard the Commonwealth Government steamers, *Hobson's Bay* and *Parratah*. The supplies were escorted by Miss Hilda J King, the daughter of the Reverend Joseph King, formerly organising agent of the London Missionary Society in Australia.[35]

Before returning to the Near East, Wirt had succeeded in forming relief committees in every state in the Commonwealth. He expressed his delight at the result of his mission, which had far exceeded his greatest expectations: 'I have never seen anything like the generosity of the Australian people. I look upon it all as more beautiful than anything else in my life.'[36] On 16 September 1922, shortly after Wirt's departure, news of the destruction of the port city of Smyrna at the hands of the Turkish nationalists reached Australia.[37] Fire had been set to the Armenian quarter, spreading ferociously to the Greek and European quarters. Over 300,000 Armenians and Greeks fled to the quay for safety and were

---

[34] 'Starving Armenia — Public Appeal', *Sydney Morning Herald*, 9 August 1922, 12.

[35] 'Armenian Relief — flour from Victoria', *Argus*, 6 September 1922, 19.

[36] 'Armenian Relief — Victoria's first contribution', *Argus*, 5 September, 1922, 9.

[37] 'Smyrna Burning', *Argus*, 16 September 1922, 25.

later removed to Greece as refugees. The Reverend Dobson, previously an Anzac chaplain at Gallipoli, witnessed the catastrophe and was involved in providing relief to the victims of the tragedy. He later wrote a detailed report on the event, poignantly titled 'The Smyrna Holocaust'.[38]

In November 1922, with the help of Wirt, the Australian committees established an orphanage in Antilyas, Beirut, named the 'Australasian Orphanage'.[39] The orphanage initially housed some 1,700 Armenian children who had no responsible living relatives upon whom they had any moral or legal claim for support. The site was previously a paper mill and was well supplied with fresh water. It was partly surrounded by an orange grove on one side and the Mediterranean Sea on the other, which became a convenient bath house for the orphans. The motto of the orphanage was 'Hold Fast to Honour'.[40]

Letting the public know

In their drive to educate the public, the Armenian Relief committees prepared a number of pamphlets containing vivid descriptions and photographs portraying the plight of the Armenians. One of them — titled 'An SOS from Beyond Gallipoli' — included an excerpt from an 'authenticated' telegram purportedly sent by Talaat Pasha to the provincial governors in 1915 stating: 'the government has decided to complete the extermination of all Armenians resident in Turkey, without regard to whether they are women, children or invalids'.[41]

---

[38] Dobson, The Reverend Charles (1923), *The Smyrna Holocaust*, London, The Anglo–Hellenic League.

[39] 'New orphanage at Beirut', *New York Times*, 16 November 1922, 3.

[40] Babkenian, Vicken 'Edith May Glanville', 11.

[41] 'Relief of Distress: Armenia', National Archives of Australia, Series

The Australian daily newspapers provided invaluable assistance to the relief committees. From the early days in 1915, when Miss M E Searle made her first appeal until the early 1930s, the daily papers gave liberal space to news items on various phases of the relief work. The official organ newspapers and magazines of Australian religious and humanitarian organisations — such as the *Red Cross Record* and the *Australian Christian World* — gave prominent coverage to the Armenian relief appeal. The South Australian Armenian relief committee went as far as publishing a magazine titled the *Armenian*, with the intention of awakening the interest of the public towards the Armenian plight.[42]

In a bold attempt to grapple with the problem of supporting such a vast number of orphans, the South Australian committee announced in 1922 the formation of the Armenian Adoption Association, appealing for 2,000 members. Soon after, the Sydney committee developed its own way of helping the orphans with the 'Big Ten' movement. Members were requested to ask ten of their friends to subscribe 6 shillings per week for one year to be paid to the member as their 'Captain'. The money's collected were used to 'rescue, feed, clothe, and educate' a 'helpless' Armenian child for a year.[43]

Because of the strict censorship practiced by the Ottoman government during the war, visual publicity illustrating the Armenian plight was generally unavailable until after the war. Following the armistice, moving picture companies with the assistance of the NER, produced a number of

---

no A457, Acc no A457/1, at www.naa.gov.au accessed 24 August 2011.

[42] Babkenian, Vicken (2009), 'A Humanitarian Journey: The Reverend James Edwin Cresswell and the Armenian Relief Fund', *Journal of the Historical Society of South Australia*, no 37, 68.

[43] *Australian Christian World*, 30 March 1923, 16.

documentaries for educational purposes. Many of these films made their way to Australia, such as 'Alice in Hungerland' and 'Jackie in the Near East'. The latter documentary was based on the work of Jackie Coogan, a famous child movie actor in America, who was involved in helping promote the cause of the destitute Armenian and Greek children in 1924. Arguably the first 'celebrity humanitarian', Coogan successfully helped gather a shipment of over one million dollars worth of supplies donated by the children of America. As the leader of the 'children's crusade', Coogan accompanied the shipment and was given a royal welcome by the orphans when he arrived at the orphanages in the Near East.[44] Another documentary, entitled 'Uncle Australia Sees It Through', illustrating Australia's role in the relief effort, was also produced by the NER, and shown to gatherings across Australia.[45]

The Revered James Edwin Cresswell's tour of inspection

In December 1922, at a conference held in Melbourne by the interstate representatives of the relief committees, it was decided to form a national executive committee. The Reverend James E Cresswell, a Congregational minister from Adelaide, was appointed unanimously as National Secretary of the Australasian Armenian Relief Fund. Cresswell was asked by the committee to make a tour of the Near East and report on the work being carried out. In January 1923, Cresswell embarked on his mission aboard the *Hobson's Bay*. He was accompanied by Melbourne nurse, Miss G Gordon,

---

[44] Babkenian, Vicken (2011), 'Hollywood's First Celebrity Humanitarian That America Forgot', *Armenian Weekly*, 7 January, available at
http://www.armenianweekly.com/2011/01/07/hollywoods-first-celebrity-humanitarian-that-america-forgot/

[45] Babkenian Vicken, 'Edith May Glanville', 11.

who had volunteered to engage in relief work at the Australasian Orphanage. Part of their equipment was a large Australian flag to be used as a symbol of Australia's humanitarian presence overseas.[46]

Cresswell's first destination was Syria, the epicentre of the relief operations. After having disembarked at the port of Antioch, Cresswell and Miss Gordon travelled eastwards to Aleppo. It was here that they first encountered the situation of some 6,000 Armenian and Greek refugees who had recently fled persecution in Turkey. Cresswell found the refugees clad in mere rags gathered apparently from the 'rubbish heaps of years'. They had sought shelter in caves which had previously been used as slaughter houses. One of the caves was set apart as a field hospital treating patients suffering from pneumonia and tuberculosis. Another was used as a church. Cresswell recorded his observations:

The sights within these caves are beyond words. No words seem adequate to describe the misery that must be the portion of these poor people... Here were women pale and emaciated, children with swollen abdomens, the result of starvation. Again, one saw little babies pinched and pallid— further on a little one just recently born, one tiny atom among thousands of the suffering children to be seen here.[47]

Travelling in a south-westerly direction on a bleak journey through arid and barren grasslands, the pair arrived at Antilyas in February 1923, warmly received at the Australasian Orphanage. They were greeted by the directors, Mr and Mrs John H Knudsen of New Zealand, whom Cresswell described 'as the most efficient heads of orphanages' he had met.[48] Present also was Miss Hilda King

---

[46] Babkenian, Vicken, 'A Humanitarian Journey', 69.

[47] 'The Armenian', *Armenian Relief Fund Committee*, Adelaide, May, 1923, State Library of South Australia, 4–5.

[48] 'Armenian Relief—work by Australian section', *Argus,* 7 August,

who was conducting relief work amongst the orphans. Cresswell was presented with a beautiful embroidered tablecloth in appreciation on behalf of the orphanage teachers and workers. The desire was expressed that this should be used at the periodic gatherings in Australia of the national Armenian relief committee.

Cresswell toured the orphanage. He was impressed to find that in addition to receiving food and clothing, the boys had 14 different trades to choose from as a means towards their future self-support.[49] The directors were assisted by about 40 teachers and vocational leaders, as well as the same number of women known as 'mothers' who attended to the food and clothing of the children.[50] He inspected the dormitories and noticed blankets which had recently arrived from Melbourne and remarked: 'It was delightful to turn over the corners of these blankets and find the name of a well-known Australian firm, and to know that in Australia we are ministering to such dire necessity as one sees here.' He continued to see a vast array of Australian brand products being consumed 'and heard of those who spoke with no little appreciation of South Australian honey'. He witnessed the orphans, some of them quite small boys, making boots out of leather from Sydney tanneries. Further on, he visited the bakery where Australian flour was being made into tiny loaves of bread which were an essential part of the orphans' diet.[51]

Cresswell departed Antilyas in March 1923 and continued his journey to refugee camps and orphanages in Palestine,

---

1923, 13.

[49] 'Feeding the Starving — Australians in Armenia', *Argus*, 21 April 1923, 6.

[50] *Argus*, 7 August 1923, 13.

[51] *Argus*, 7 August 1923, 13.

Turkey, Southern Russia, Armenia and Greece before returning home from his tour aboard the *Makura* in August 1923.[52]

The Armenian Relief Fund and Save the Children Fund

In late 1919, Australian opera singer, feminist and peace
activist, Cecilia A John, formed a branch of the Save the
Children Fund, an organisation aimed at helping destitute
children, in Melbourne, Victoria. A co-founder of the
Women's Peace Army in 1915, John had previously worked
with the International Red Cross in Geneva and the SCF in
London.[53]

The refugee crisis in Greece reached its peak in 1923 when
the total number of refugees from Turkey swelled to about 1.4
million, becoming the greatest single refugee movement in
history to date. A relief worker observing the child refugees
remarked: 'They have forgotten how to smile...Fear is the one
emotion with which they are familiar.'[54] A large portion of the
Armenian and Greek refugees had been settled in Salonika,
the second largest city of Greece and capital of the northern
prefecture of the same name. After protracted negotiations
between Cecilia and the executive committee of the Armenian
Relief Fund of Victoria, it was resolved to merge their appeals
to one. The purpose was to render the greatest possible
assistance to the humanitarian crisis engulfing the Near East.
The co-operative association of the two funds was formally
inaugurated at a meeting of elected representatives of both,
held on 3 December 1923.[55] The name of the new joint

---

[52] Babkenian, 'A Humanitarian Journey', 72.

[53] http://adbonline.anu.edu.au/biogs/A090484b.htm, accessed 28
April 2009.

[54] Freeman, Kathleen (1965), *If Any Man Build: The history of the Save
the Children Fund*, London, Hodder and Stoughton, 32.

[55] Annual Report: Victoria (1924), *Save the Children Fund and Armenian Relief Fund*, Save the Children Archives, Melbourne, 1925, 1.

committee was the Save the Children Fund and Armenian Relief Fund (SCF & ARF).

The Armenian Relief Fund of Victoria thereby terminated its connection with the NER administration, and automatically became associated with the activities of the Save the Children Fund International Union, and the Lord Mayor of London's Armenian Fund, which were intimately related by written agreement. The Chairman of this new joint committee was Meredith Atkinson, previously the director of tutorial classes at the University of Melbourne, and Dr Leeper the Vice-Chairman. The Armenian relief committee in Adelaide followed Melbourne's move and merged with the SCF. The Sydney and Perth committees on the other hand continued their association with the NER, and the headquarters of the Australasian Armenian Relief Fund moved to George Street, Sydney, in 1924.[56]

The SCF and ARF focused their attention on the humanitarian crisis engulfing Greece and Armenia sending large consignments of food and clothing to the refugee camps. The well known Melbourne firms, Swallow and Ariell, Myer Pty Ltd, Messrs C M Read & Co, along with others generously assisted in the relief campaign. The Victorian and South Australian governments participated by allowing relief parcels donated to the SCF and ARF to be carried free of charge on their State railways.[57]

---

[56] 'Near and Far', *Sydney Morning Herald*, 11 September 1924, 5.

[57] 'Greek–Armenian Refugees', *Argus*, 22 March 1924, 37.

Australians in Greece

Australians were also at the forefront in the relief work in Greece. Lieutenant George D Treloar, an Anzac veteran from Ballarat, Melbourne, was appointed as the League of Nations' representative at Salonika responsible for the settlement of refugees in eastern Macedonia and western Thrace in 1922. Within a year, he was handling more than 108,000 refugees. For his outstanding humanitarian work, Treloar was appointed to the Order of the Saviour (gold cross) by the Greek government, and a refugee village, Thrilorion, near Komotini, Greece, was named after him.[58]

Joice NanKivell was born in Ingham, Queensland in 1887 but had spent most of her childhood on a farm in Gippsland, Victoria. After the death of her brother during World War I, her father abandoned the farm and NanKivell went to Melbourne where she reviewed books for the *Herald* and worked as secretary to Professor Leeper at the University of Melbourne. In response to the Smyrna Catastrophe, Joice along with her Gallipoli veteran husband, Sydney Loch, volunteered to conduct relief work at a Quaker-run farm school near the teeming refugee camps of Salonika. They were joined by Caroline Ethel Cooper, daughter of the deputy Surveyor-General of South Australia, who had previously worked with the Lochs during the famine in Poland in 1921.

Caroline and the Lochs set about improving conditions for the refugee villagers, who found themselves without proper water supply or any form of medical assistance. To help the villagers become self-sufficient, Joice sourced wool and cotton, had a loom built, learned about natural dyes and formed a women's weaving co-operative called Pyrgos Rugs. She designed Byzantine style rugs, two of which are now on

---

[58] http://adbonline.anu.edu.au/biogs/A120286b.htm accessed 3 May 2009.

display: one in the Powerhouse Museum in Sydney and the other in the 12th century tower that is now the Loch 'Australian' Museum in Ouranoupolis, Greece. In addition to teaching the women and children literacy and economic skills, Loch acted as an assistant medical officer. Throughout her life, Loch maintained a keen interest in humanitarian work. During World War II she helped save thousands of Polish and Jewish children from the Nazis by leading a daring escape known as 'Operation Pied Piper'. She has been awarded more medals than any other Australian woman for her heroism, her humanitarian work, and her innovative programs instituted in various refugee camps throughout Europe.[59]

Caroline remained at the Quaker Relief unit in Salonika until 1928. Before returning to Australia in 1930, she assisted the work of Miss Karen Jeppe, the commissioner for the protection of women and children in the Near East, based in Aleppo, Syria. Jeppe had been appointed by the League of Nations to reclaim the thousands of Armenian women and children who had been abducted during the Armenian Genocide and forcibly converted to Islam. While visiting the headquarters of the Armenian Relief Fund of NSW in Sydney, Caroline thanked the New South Wales committee for the generous contribution towards Karen Jeppe's work. Caroline stated that 'Miss Jeppe much appreciated the help of Australia', and that the money sent had been 'used for a soup kitchen and a clinic for the orphan children'.[60]

Australian women advocate the Armenian cause

Australian women played a prominent role in the cause of

---

[59] See de Vries, Susanna (2006), *Blue Ribbons, Bitter Bread: The life of Joice NanKivell Loch, Australia's most heroic woman*, Sydney, Pirgos Press-Tower Books.

[60] 'Near and Far', *Sydney Morning Herald*, 29 January 1930, 10.

Armenian relief both on the field and at home. Three prominent feminists of Sydney, Lady Caroline Edgeworth David, Edith May Glanville and Eleanor Mackinnon (OBE), were the driving force behind the success of the Fund in NSW. Lady David, the wife of Sir Tannatt William Edgeworth David, a renowned geologist, became the president of the New South Wales branch of the fund in 1922. Lady David along with Edith Glanville, a well known social worker and honorary secretary of the fund, spoke at public gatherings in which branches of the fund were formed in towns across New South Wales.[61] They also helped organise many fundraising events such as bazaars and fetes where needlework made by the orphans in the Near East were sold. During one of these events, Mrs Preston Stanley MLA, the first female member of the NSW Legislative Assembly, made this moving appeal on behalf of the Armenians:

When one reflects upon the moving history of that all too tragic nation...one is deeply concerned. Armenia is an honourable nation with one of the saddest histories...surely we will not be deaf to the cry of 120,000 orphans.[62]

Eleanor Mackinnon, the founder of the Junior Red Cross in 1914, was also a prominent member of the Armenian Relief Fund of New South Wales. In 1925, Eleanor was selected to represent Australia at the Sixth General Assembly of the League of Nations held at Geneva. She was invited to speak on the platform on the situation of the Armenian refugees by Fridjof Nansen, the President of the League of Nations. During her speech, Eleanor reminded the delegates that

the Armenians have lived in such a state of misery, persecution and suffering and have been subjugated to such atrocities as might well freeze our blood even to hear of them.

---

[61] 'Near and Far', *Sydney Morning Herald*, 8 May 1923, 8.

[62] 'Starving and Persecuted Armenians', *Australian Christian World*, 17 July 1925, 11.

I do not wish to harrow your feelings, but I would ask you whether we are not indebted to this people.[63]

In Victoria, prominent feminist and academic, Jessie Webb, was also an outspoken advocate on behalf of the Armenians. Jessie was chosen as Australia's alternate delegate to the Fifth General Assembly to the League of Nations held in Geneva in 1924. On her return to Australia, Webb appealed to the women of Australia 'who live in such free and happy conditions' to show 'practical sympathy with Miss Jeppe's undertaking by raising the money necessary' for the rescue of Armenian women.[64]

In addition to Hilda King, Miss G Gordon, Joice Loch and Caroline Holmes, three other Australian women are known to have conducted relief work among the Armenian refugees. Leila Priest, a nurse from Tasmania, had joined the NER after having served in the US army during the war. She was sent to Alexandropol, Armenia, in 1919 where she provided relief to over 20,000 orphans who were being cared for by the NER.[65] Another nurse, Isobel Hutton RRC, who had previously been with the AIF in Palestine, also joined the NER following the War. She was sent to Aleppo where she conducted relief work among the approximately 70,000 'wearied and frightened' Armenian refugees.[66]

In 1926, Edith Glanville was appointed as liaison officer between the League of Nations (the predecessor to the United

---

[63] 'Minutes of the League of Nations', 25 September 1925, National Library of Australia.

[64] 'Women in Harems', *Argus*, 12 March 1924, 7.

[65] 'The Armenian Atrocities — A Tasmanian Nurse's Experience', *Mercury*, 8 September 1925, 3.

[66] Teal, Helen (1921), 'Public Health Nursing in the Near East', *American Journal of Nursing*, vol 21, no 11, 1 August, 791.

Nations) and the NER organisation.[67] In the same year, Glanville embarked on a journey to the Near East in order to investigate the condition of the Armenian refugees and orphans. She reported her findings at the NER conference which met prior to the annual League of Nations Assembly meeting at Geneva.[68]

The Relief Fund wraps up

By 1928, only a core group of 500 orphans had remained at the Australasian Orphanage, and by the following summer, it was closed. The orphanage program not only provided the orphans with a home but gave them the means for self support. The Armenian relief movement continued to exist in Australia until the early 1930s, during which time a vast number of Armenians and other Ottoman Christians had been saved from starvation and disease. Thousands of Armenian women and children had also been reclaimed through the work of Karen Jeppe which was generously supported by Australians. Cresswell eloquently expressed the significance this event had for his own beloved nation:

The generosity of the people of Australia had made the name of the Commonwealth known to almost every person in and around Athens. From Jerusalem in the south, up through Syria, Greece, Turkey, and even southern Russia, there sprang up the lips...words of thankfulness for the kindness of Australia.[69]

Conclusion

Despite a strong connection between Australia's Gallipoli experience and the Armenian genocide, the latter does not form part of Australia's collective memory of Gallipoli today.

---

[67] 'The Near East: War Conditions in Syria', *Sydney Morning Herald*, 2 April 1927, 10.

[68] Ibid.

[69] 'Grateful to Australia', *Sydney Morning Herald*, 31 October 1923, 5.

Australia's response to the Armenian genocide provides an early instance of international humanitarian activism that served as a precursor to many further instances of Australian engagement in relief operations through the League of Nations and the United Nations.

The Armenian relief movement mobilised a broad spectrum of Australia's political, civic and religious leaders, with Australian women playing a prominent role. The relief campaign produced a generous response, culminating in the establishment of an Australian-run orphanage in the Near East. As a result of the global reaction to the Armenian genocide, a significant number of Armenians and other Ottoman Christians were saved from death and destitution. Through the Armenian Relief Fund, Australia became one of the leading countries in the world to help rescue the Armenians from oblivion. It was a landmark event which would see Australia enter the world stage as an international humanitarian force.

The conundrum lies in the dissonance between these two mindsets and behaviours: on the one hand, an outstanding set of achievements in humanitarian intervention for a victim community; on the other, an expungement of Armenian history at the hands of Turkey, a former enemy now embraced, almost 'loved', by modern Australia for helping the country 'find itself' as a nation, as a separate national identity rather than a sibling daughter of Mother Britain. Recent federal governments have sought to minimise criticism of these 'partners in war', to evade discussion of any of the genocidal issues involved. Given the extent to which state and federal governments supplied transport and waived charges to assist Armenian refugees, there was clearly governmental complicity in relief action. How, then, is it possible for recent governments to disassociate themselves from the events of 1915 to 1923, and beyond?

RESPONDING TO GENOCIDE IN RWANDA: LOCAL KNOWLEDGE AND COUNTER-STORIES

DAVID DENBOROUGH AND CHERYL WHITE

(in collaboration with Hodali Irakoze Pierre Claver, Jill Freedman and Gene Combs)

From April to July 1994, a genocide perpetrated against the Tutsi people in Rwanda claimed over one million human lives. It is now 18 years later and the survivors of the genocide continue to face profound hardships in relation to housing, health, education, extreme poverty, and security. The vast majority of survivors still live in great suffering and with nightmares of the traumatic past. The genocide aimed to eliminate the Tutsi, and this entailed the elimination of families — fathers, mothers, and children. After the genocide, the survivors regrouped on the basis of kinship, friendship, or just kind-heartedness of spirit. Associations fighting for victims' rights are constantly committed. Ibuka is a national organisation in Rwanda that represents survivor associations throughout the country (see Kaboyi, 2007).

Six years ago, the authors first met with Kaboyi Benoit, at that time the executive secretary of Ibuka. After initial introductions, and in response to our 'down under' accents, Benoit said 'Ah, Australia...there's a country that knows all about genocide.'

This recognition and our conversation following signalled the beginning of a partnership between Ibuka and Dulwich Centre Foundation International, an Australian-based organisation which responds to groups and communities who have experienced significant hardship. Much of our work involves cultural partnerships and building the capacity of local workers through the use of narrative practices to elicit and richly describe local knowledge. Within any community experiencing social suffering, community members will be responding to these difficulties: they will take whatever action is possible—in their own ways, based on particular skills and local knowledge—to try to address the effects of the hardships on their lives and of those they love. These initiatives may not currently be widely recognised, and they may not in themselves be enough to overcome all that is presently facing their community. But these initiatives are highly significant. They make it possible for community members to identify these initiatives, to describe them so that the skills and local knowledge implicit within them become more visible to themselves and to others, and to trace the social histories of these skills and knowledge so that the ways these are linked to local culture and tradition are understood. These initiatives can be strengthened in ways that make further action possible.

After our initial meeting, Kaboyi Benoit expressed his willingness for meetings to be held between Ibuka trauma counsellors/assistant lawyers and a range of international narrative therapists and community workers. Four such meetings have taken place. The partnership has also resulted in an interview with Kaboyi Benoit, 2007, and two publications: *Strengthening Resistance: The use of narrative practices in working with genocide survivors* (Denborough, Freedman and White, 2008) and *Working with Memory in the Shadow of Genocide: The narrative practices of Ibuka trauma counsellors* (Denborough, 2010).

This essay conveys some of the intricate, local knowledge of Ibuka counsellors/survivors in relation to:

• the continuing effects of the genocide;

• what sustains survivors as they live in the shadow of genocide;

• ways in which survivors negotiate 'living side by side' with those who have done them great harm; and

• ways of responding when survivors cannot locate the bodies of loved ones.

Significantly, we also explore how narrative practices have been used to facilitate the excavation, documentation and circulation of this local knowledge and what this is making possible.

(i) Local knowledge in relation to the continuing effects of genocide

One of the first realms of local knowledge that was articulated by the Ibuka survivors/counsellors relates to the continuing effects of the genocide. The following collective narrative document was constructed from the rescued spoken words of participants:

The effects of the genocide that took place in Rwanda in 1994 are not over. Many people still live with the effects of the extreme violence, killings, and degradation that took place here during those one hundred days. So many of our loved ones are no longer with us. We are a group of trauma counsellors and assistant lawyers who work for Ibuka — the national survivors' association in Rwanda. We work around our country to support and assist survivors of the genocide.

The people with whom we meet are often dealing with many different effects of the genocide. They may be having nightmares and be unable to sleep. They may experience powerful feelings of despair and hopelessness. Often they have profound sorrow, fears, or anger. Some may not know whether they wish to live or to die, which means they are negotiating with death. Some survivors experience severe headaches. Others have difficulty swallowing and may feel as if they are choking. Many survivors are very isolated, very alone. When you have lost so many people it is sometimes very difficult to have relationships with others again. Some women who were raped during the genocide are now HIV-positive and are living with the consequences of this.

And then there are the problems of memory. Some survivors have lost their memories and therefore have lost aspects of their past. Others have painful memories that return again and again. What is more, some survivors may feel guilty for being alive. The genocide has made them doubt that they have a right to live. These are all effects that the genocide is still having on survivors.

There are also circumstances in the present that are very difficult to deal with. Some survivors are living in the same villages as those who killed their relations and family members. There is hostility and hatred that they have to deal with every day. Many survivors are also living in severe poverty. These are continuing obstacles to dealing with the effects of the genocide.

Children and young people are also living with the effects of the killings. Even if they were not born at the time of the genocide, they are living with the effects that these events had on their parents and relatives.

These are just some of the effects of the genocide that people are living with. These are the effects which we are responding to in our work (Denborough, Freedman and White, 2008, 1-2).

The retelling of this document, which took place in a ceremonial way within our first meeting, was experienced as powerfully resonant by Ibuka counsellors who stated:

This is an important document. We would be honoured if you could send this to others, to your friends in other countries who are also dealing with difficulties. And to the United Nations!

Listening to this collective retelling enabled the Ibuka counsellors to place their initiatives, their efforts and anguishes, into a broader storyline. Such retelling enables a particular distance from the immediacy of one's own experiences, which in turn provides the possibility for renewed compassion for one's own life and the life of one's community. And through interweaving the words of many, a sense of 'communitas' (Turner, 1969, 1979) is generated. The generation and performance of this particular document can be seen as a form of 'communalisation of suffering'

(Humphrey cited in Westoby, 2009, 88) to accompany the many other collective rituals of remembrance that are held in Rwanda during the 100 days of memory each year.[1]

The effects of genocide are informed by an 'externalising' ethic (White and Epston, 1990; White, 1997). Narrative practice refuses to locate problems within people — instead, it insists that problems are placed back into the social contexts in which they were produced. And so, rather than survivors being described by professionals as 'suicidal', the description reads: 'Some may not know whether they wish to live or to die, which means they are negotiating with death.' Similarly, rather than experiences of 'survivor guilt' being located internally, the description reads: 'What is more, some survivors may feel guilty for being alive. The genocide has made them doubt that they have a right to live.'

As Kaboyi Benoit explains, the message of this document about the current effects of genocide has a wider significance:

During the genocide, the wider world largely turned its backs on us and we know that many people regret this. Perhaps if the wider world reads this document, if they realise that the effects of the genocide are continuing, they will also realise that it is possible for them to take action now to assist us in our work with survivors (personal communication, 15 November, 2007).

(ii) Local knowledge in relation to 'living in the shadow of genocide'

Narrative practice is vitally interested in what has been referred to as 'double-listening' (White, 2004) and the

---

[1] Each year in Rwanda, 100 days are set aside as a memorial period to acknowledge the 100 days of the killings that took place in 1994. Throughout this period, memorial and remembrance events are held throughout the country. To read about the ways in which Ibuka workers construct 'double-storied' remembrance events, see *Working with Memory in the Shadow of Genocide* (Denborough, 2010).

development of 'double-storied testimonies' (Denborough, 2006). It is both relevant to elicit and richly acknowledge the effects of the externalised problem — in this case the continuing effects of the genocide — and to unearth the diverse responses, initiatives and skills of survival that survivors/ counsellors are enacting as they live in the shadow of genocide. A particular method was used to ensure a 'rich description' of these survival skills.[2]

The words and stories of Ibuka counsellors were collated into a collective document entitled: 'Living in the shadow of genocide: how we respond to hard times — stories of sustenance from the workers of Ibuka.'

Included here are just five of the 15 themes that comprise

---

[2] Participants were asked to break into groups of three and consider the following questions:
• Please describe something (a particular value, belief, skill or knowledge) that gets you or your family/friends through hard times.
• Share a *story* of a time when this special value, belief, skill or knowledge has made a difference to you or to others.
• Please speak of the social history of this skill, value or belief. How did you learn this? Who did you learn it from? Or who did you learn it with?
• Is this linked in some way to any particular groups, family, communities or cultural histories of which you are a part?

Participants were asked to consider these questions in groups of three. Each person took turns to respond to the questions, to ask the questions, and to take notes of the responses. Participants were invited to try to elicit particular details, to pay attention to metaphors and word images, and to take note of rich descriptions including ways in which people included sensory descriptions in their responses. All the responses from participants were then gathered and woven into a collective document. Patrick Iregura played a critical translating role throughout this process.

this document:

— Listening and learning from the lives of others

Listening to the stories of others helps some of us get through. In our work, we hear stories from people who are carrying on their lives even though so much has happened to them. I recall listening carefully to one widow in particular who is continuing to live and care for her three children. This idea of listening to people carefully came from my mother. She would always listen to me during my childhood. Listening is also a part of Rwandan culture. We have seen people overcome very difficult problems. Their lives serve as an example that problems can be solved, that many things are possible.

— Tears and then talking

Some of us are sustained by our tears. To cry, to shed tears, to allow them to fall, can make a difference. For some of us, there is a tranquillity that comes after tears that can allow us to sleep. After sleep, we may then take time to talk to someone. One person described that, 'When I am sleeping, the tears that I have cried give me strength. When I sleep after I have cried, I am tranquil. There is no noise, only calmness. This way of sustenance came from my mother. Whenever my mother was in pain, she used to allow herself to cry. After her tears had fallen she would go and talk to her friends.' Some of us are sustained by tears and then talking.

— New ways of carrying on traditions

There is a tradition in Rwanda that we respect the parents in our families. We see them as capable of everything, and we trust the answers that they give to us. We rely on their advice. Many of us lost our parents in the genocide and so we have to find ways to continue to stay in touch with their advice. One person said, 'When I have hard times, I write. I imagine that it is my father writing to me, giving me answers. I think these answers are the appropriate ones.' Some of us are finding new ways to carry on our tradition of seeking and respecting advice from our parents.

—Recalling good memories

Sometimes good memories protect us. During the war, I was fighting on the front when we ran short of ammunition. We were left with no options. We had nowhere to flee and no supplies. It was at this time that I started to think about how my life was going to end. I remembered then that my father used to say that a true man, a real man, is strengthened by the good moments in his life. And then good memories started to come into my mind. I started to think about my girlfriend who I had left in my village. And I remembered how my father loved me so much. At this point, I stood up and told the rest of the company to pull back. We did this and even though it was through bullets and fire we made it. We found safety. Sometimes good memories protect us. And some of us learnt this from our families.

—Realising I am not the only one to have that kind of pain

The experiences we have had are so extreme that we may think we are the only ones to know this kind of pain: the pain of torture, the pain of seeing your loved ones murdered, the pain of surviving when others were killed in your place. Now, though, we realise that others also know this kind of pain. When an old woman came to see me in counselling she told me a terrible story. At first I was not sure what to do, but then an idea came into my head. I decided to talk to some other old ladies and hear what happened to them. I realised that that old woman who came to see me wasn't the only one to have that kind of pain. Once we realise this, it is then possible for people to talk together. Now, whenever I have a problem, I talk to someone else to see if I am the only one to have that kind of problem. That's how some of us sustain ourselves. We consider not only what we went through, but also what others have endured.

Other themes among the 15 included: 'Acts of prayer — talking with a strength beyond us', 'music and song', 'finding ways to rest', 'making family', 'bringing emotions and opinions out into the world', 'respecting ancestors', 'sports', 'keeping a distance', 'hard work for ourselves and for our loved ones', and 'turning to friends and seeking company'.

The generation and retelling of this document was partly a response to the Ibuka counsellors' descriptions of the 'problems of memory': 'Some survivors have lost their memories and therefore have lost aspects of their past. Others have painful memories that return again and again.' Eliciting local knowledge about what sustains survivors in the *present*, carefully excavating the *social histories* of the values and skills implicit in these practices of sustenance, and then documenting/representing/circulating this knowledge, involves travelling down alternative pathways to memory and to history. When within the document survivors speak in terms of 'this way of sustenance came from my mother' or 'some of us learnt this from our families', they are linking their actions in the present to the legacies of lost loved ones. They are travelling through time in ways that contribute to sustenance. In contexts where relationships with memory are fraught, this process seeks to work both individually and collectively to develop an alternative 'rich textual heritage' (Lowenthal in Wertsch, 2002, 62) and to provide a more 'usable past' (Wertsch, 2002, 45).

Along the way, this process of excavation, documentation and retelling can contribute to the development of a particular 'community of memory' (Bellah, Madsen, Sullivan, Swidler and Tipton, 1985, 105). Just as the earlier document represented the 'communalisation of suffering', this form of documentation represents shared memories of sustenance. As the Ibuka counsellors described:

This document can be used to advocate for survivors. And we can also use it in our work with survivors. It can assist us to notice the many different forms of resistance that we as survivors are demonstrating.

The 15 themes of the document also act as the seeds of 'counter-stories' (Nelson, 2001):

...counter-stories aim to free not only individuals but the entire group whose identity is damaged by an oppressive master narrative' (183). As Nelson (2001) describes, many counter-stories start small—'like a seed in the crack of a sidewalk, but they are capable of displacing surprising chunks of concrete as they grow' (169). The Ibuka counsellors reported that when they shared the document 'Living in the shadow of genocide...' with others during the 100 days of commemoration that take place each year in Rwanda, this sharing contributed to a decrease in the number of survivor crises.

Further, in their daily work, Ibuka counsellors elicit and co-author counter-stories with individuals and groups in highly skilful ways. They do so by using the following principles:

• Bridging the gap: listening for what survivors have endured and the effects of this;

• Bringing the current effects of the genocide out of the shadows;

• Listening for what has survived and how this has survived;

• Tracing histories of what is important to survivors;

• Making it possible for survivors to see how they are carrying forth the legacies of loved ones who have died;

• Acknowledging special skills of survival;

• Never separating healing from justice;

• Enabling survivors to make contributions to others; and

• Sharing memory: finding ways to ensure that survivors are not left alone with memories that are too hard to bear.[3]

---

[3] For more detailed descriptions of these principles, and for examples of the work of Ibuka counsellors, see Denborough (2010), *Working with Memory in the Shadow of Genocide: The narrative practices of Ibuka counsellors*, 8–9.

(iii) Local knowledge in relation to 'living side by side with those who have done us harm'

In November 2010, Ibuka counsellors spoke of the dilemma of how they can assist survivors in 'living side by side' with those who have done their families great harm. Many survivors of the genocide in Rwanda continue to live in the same villages as those who participated in the killings. Some women also live alongside those who sexually assaulted them. Eighteen years on from the genocide, even in situations in which the perpetrators served prison sentences, many have now been released and Ibuka workers report that some survivors currently live with continuing threats and hostility.

As the counsellors are survivors, it was decided to elicit and describe the skills, practices, philosophies and local knowledge that they themselves are using to respond to the complexities of 'living side by side'. In small groups, they were invited to name their particular responses, to share stories about these, and to trace the social histories or the source of their particular approaches. Individual responses were then woven into the following collective document:

Living side by side with those who have done us harm

We are survivors and we are also counsellors. So we bring together our experiences as survivors and our experiences as professionals. These are like two different worlds. When we bring these two worlds together — the world of our experiences, and the world of the trainings that we attend — we create new understandings. As we go, we even have to coin new words.

This document describes some of the skills that we as survivors use here in Rwanda as we have to live side by side with those who perpetrated the killings during the genocide.

This is very difficult. Some survivors are living in the same villages as those who killed their relations and family members. These survivors are sometimes living with continuing threats and violence to try to intimidate them not to speak of the past, not to seek justice. And when survivors

do speak up, when they do seek justice they must deal with
people's reactions. There is hostility and hatred that they have
to deal with every day. Now that the *Gacaca*[4] process is over,
witnesses who have testified are sometimes harassed and
persecuted.

So how do we as survivors respond? How do we go about
living side by side here in Rwanda? There are many different
ways. We do not all do the same thing. We have documented
here some of the skills we use. We hope this document may
be of assistance to others.

To keep a distance

Some of us try to keep a distance from those who caused our
families harm. At first, straight after the genocide, many
survivors moved to a different part of the country — especially
from rural areas into the towns. Now, with the unity and
reconciliation policies of the government this is not possible.
But even if we cannot move, if we are forced to live in the
same community, then we might still try to keep a distance

---

[4] *Gacaca* is a traditional form of dispute resolution in Rwanda that
was used to bring perpetrators of the genocide to some form of
community justice. As Rakiya Omaar (2007) explains: '[After the
genocide] it was very apparent from the outset, that given the
unprecedented level of *Gacaca*, popular participation in the killings
in Rwanda, unprecedented in world history in terms of the
percentages of people from the very old to the very young who
participated, that it was never going to be possible to achieve justice
using the formal western justice system. If there was even an attempt
to put the majority of detainees through the courts, let alone all those
yet to be arrested, then they would die of old age in the prisons
because the entire system would be overwhelmed. The formal court
system was simply not a viable option (54).' The community courts
were therefore established as a method of transitional justice,
designed to promote three imperatives (which were sometimes
competing and conflicting): justice, truth, and reconciliation. For
more information see Omaar (2007).

because this lessens the chance of a direct clash. For me, if I realise that something is going to bring me into direct contact with the person who harmed my family, I try to avoid him. I do this so that I will not lose momentum. I know that seeing him will take me back to zero. It will cost me all the efforts I have made to rebuild my life. I don't want to be stopped in my path towards a better future. I don't want to lose momentum in reconstructing my life, so I try to keep a distance. Sometimes we have to keep this distance only in our minds. Some of us act as if the perpetrators are not actually living here. I relate as if they are non-existent. This is my way of keeping a distance. I try to convince myself that they are not here. I don't give them any space in my mind. I erase them from my mind. Some of us still find ways to keep a distance.

Acts of prayer

Others of us turn to prayer. My prayers strengthen me to live alongside the perpetrators. God has often understood me in ways that provide strength. And when I feel there is no justice then I remember that it is God who judges. This gives me strength to live side by side during this lifetime. Some of us also join prayer groups. Being part of something bigger can bring a sense of peace. When I am joined with others, and feel a sense of peace, it helps me to consider forgiveness. Before the genocide almost all families were very religious. For many survivors, acts of prayer are not only a way of finding a refuge but also a way of honouring what our parents and relatives respected. Some of us turn to prayer in order to live side by side.

To rebuild a certain bond

For others, when we realise there is no way we can change this situation, we accept it and then try to be diplomatic and friendly with those who are a threat. If we are living in the same neighbourhood, we find ways to rebuild a certain bond. Often we have to make the first move. This might involve socialising or taking part in community events. If they have a family member in hospital then we might show our concern and care for that person. Some of us act as engaged citizens to try to rebuild the bonds in this country.

To focus on the positive aspects of cohabitation

Some of us try to not only remember the terrible history here but also to focus on the positive aspects of cohabitation. I look for any service I can offer. And I look for any form of integrity in the families that have caused my family harm. Even with people who have done the worst, there is always something you can build on. It is easy to find hate, but I have found that it is also possible to find one aspect from which to build a new relationship. Some of us try to focus on the positive aspects of living side by side.

To speak in a general way

Sometimes we have to express our frustrations and we have learned to do this in particular ways. During public presentations of meetings, we speak generally. If the person standing next to me is from a perpetrator family, then I will not curse his family. I will not express my outrage directly at him. I will instead curse in a general way. I will express my frustration at the whole general group of perpetrators and the harm that they have done. Some of us have learnt special skills in how we express our frustrations.

Deep breathing

The act of breathing deeply is significant to me. As soon as I come in contact with a person who will raise all the memories and who could break my heart, I step aside and I breathe deeply. In order to appease the negative emotions rising within me, in order to appease the flashbacks, I deeply breathe.

Times when survivors have a voice

There are other times and places where survivors have a voice. During the commemoration period, if a survivor has a trauma crisis then this is an opportunity to get everything off their chest, to give voice to all their frustrations. During such a crisis, survivors can say whatever it is necessary to say. Sometimes we even find people expressing their emotions by doing or recalling what they had endured during the genocide. During the commemoration period there are also events that give voice to all that we experience. These moments and these commemoration events are important. They contribute to making it possible for us to live side by side in this land.

Offering forgiveness for peace

Sometimes, particularly in the country, in small villages, when survivors notice how delicate our position is, when we are surrounded by the families of perpetrators, we may go to these families and offer them forgiveness even before they have asked for it. Life in the village depends on harmony between people so sometimes we offer this forgiveness for peace.

Seeking justice

In order to live side by side, it has been important for many of us to seek justice. Despite the difficulties and disappointments many survivors have experienced with *Gacaca*, trying to find the truth of what happened in the genocide, is also about living side by side.

Families

Sometimes, living side by side happens within families. In families where there was intermarriage and one parent has been killed by the other side of the family, what is to happen with the children? They are sometimes raised by the side of the perpetrator because no one wants them to be completely isolated from their family. In these situations, for the children, even though the family has taken part in the massacre, we must find ways to integrate these families, to live side by side.

Responsibility

One of the things that can help us to live side by side is when only one member of a family was the perpetrator but the others were innocent or did not take part in the killings. When we know this, when we remember this, it can help. Even though the family's reputation is tarnished, we acknowledge that the responsibility was only with the people who committed the acts. When we know this it can become possible to rebuild relationships with that family.

Sticking together

When we are lucky enough to have a few neighbours who are also survivors this makes the difference. If there are three of four families in the same neighbourhood then we try to help one another. We gather every once and a while and discuss the challenges we are facing. Some of us have also sought out training so we can assist others. Because we can relate to each other's difficulties, we stick together and this can make all the difference.

Working hard

As survivors, we work hard. We work hard so that we can prove to the perpetrators that they did not ruin us completely. Others did not expect us to survive or to go on and live good lives. So we work hard so that we can have a better life, so that we can thrive.

The source of these skills

What is the source of these skills, these strategies, this strength? Like a river, there are many different sources.

Necessity

For some of us, the reason why we live together is that we don't have anywhere else to go. If we did have somewhere else to go, some of us would have gone there.

Rwandan culture

We draw strength from our culture. There are traditions within Rwandan culture that train us to be tolerant and resilient and to value our relationships with others. These cultural practices encourage us to always move forwards, to look to the future. And these ways of thinking tend to bring people together. We draw on these aspects of our culture and they support us to live side by side.

Concern for our children

For some of us, it is our concern for our children that gives us strength and makes it possible to start new relationships with the families that have done us harm. My children will grow up in this country. I don't want them to be isolated here and so I have taken the initiative to start participating in the lives of the other families. The source of some of our initiatives to make peace is our concern for our children. We are taking this journey for the new living.

Government policy

Our government promotes unity and reconciliation. It tries to introduce these notions at all different levels of life in the community. This policy contributes to our efforts, our skills and our strategies.

Social interest

Here in Rwanda, we are not autonomous individuals. People are interdependent. Our economic and social interests are joined. We need each other. This knowledge is one of the sources of our efforts to live side by side.

Drawing inspiration from our loved ones

We are survivors and we draw inspiration from our lost loved ones. We use their strength to move us forward and to better our lives. We use our parents as inspiration. We continue their dreams, their ambitions, and the projects that they had for their lives.

Our lost loved ones inspire us to live a good life. For when we are living a good life it is then possible to live side by side with pride. Every day, as we live in the shadow of genocide, we draw inspiration from our lost loved ones, and keep their legacies alive.

We are survivors and we are counsellors. These are our skills of living side by side in the shadow of genocide. We have also included the sources of our skills, our strategies, and our strength. Like a river our skills have many sources. We hope our words may be of assistance to others.

The words in this document were also transformed into a song *'Vivre ensemble dans l'ambre du génocide'* (Living side by side in the shadow of genocide)[5] which was ritually performed and recorded. This song became a motif that was repeated at significant times during the week-long workshop.

The development and performance of such a document and song can serve many purposes. For instance, each time they are performed this enacts:

• An acknowledgement of the difficulty of the continuing circumstance of survivors;

• A recognition of the skills, knowledge and agency of survivors;

• A proclamation of preferred collective identity;

• An honouring of those who have been lost and the legacies that are being carried forth;

• A method of sharing knowledge between survivors;

• An invitation to other survivors to consider their own skills, knowledges that are implicit in how they are responding to 'living side by side'.

This entire process involved eliciting and richly describing particular local knowledge about 'living side by side'. This emphasis on local knowledge recognises the profoundly diverse concepts of living that individuals, groups, communities and cultures use in attempting to deal and come to terms with experiences of social harm. One aim of narrative

---

[5] The words of the document were skilfully transformed into song in French by Pierre Blanc-Sahnoun. The recording of the song features Pierre Claver Hodali Irakoze, Venant Tumukunde, Pierre Blanc-Sahnoun and Aya Okumura. The song can be heard at: www.divshare.com%2Fdownload%2F13249090-823&h=9b5de

practices is to honour and sponsor such diversity. The phrase 'living side by side' had been offered by the Ibuka workers and so this was the theme around which the response was generated. Had the Ibuka counsellors initiated conversations that privileged alternative concepts such as those of 'reconciliation' or 'forgiveness' (which are common themes in other contexts), then the document created would have richly described these alternative concepts and the social histories of these. But these were not the concepts that were put forward. Instead, narrative practices were used to elicit and then richly describe the knowledge, values, skills and philosophies implicit within the phrase 'living side by side'.[6]

We are now looking forward to sharing this document with others who are 'living side by side' with those who have done them harm. We are also interested in exploring how this sort of document could be shared and put to broader use within 'peace-building', 'justice', 'social healing' and/or 'reconciliation' projects within Rwanda and elsewhere.

(iv) Exchanging local knowledge and enabling contribution

Over the last six years, collective documents, songs and messages have been exchanged between Ibuka counsellors and Aboriginal Australian, Jewish and Native American colleagues (Denborough, Freedman and White, 2008). One of the most powerful exchanges took place in Cairns, when we played a DVD of the Ibuka document 'Living in the shadow of genocide: how we respond to hard times' to a group of Aboriginal and Torres Strait Islander counsellors who made up the 'Drop the Rock' team. Tileah Drahm-Butler sent the

---

[6] See Lederach (1995) in relation to the significance of elicitive approaches to peace-building in order to avoid cultural imposition. For rich discussions about diverse concepts of 'forgiveness', see Wiesenthal (1998). See also the special issue of the *International Journal of Narrative Therapy and Community Work* on 'The question of forgiveness' (2002, Issue no 1).

following message back to Ibuka workers:

> Hearing your words and stories about how you are going about reclaiming your lives and living with dignity makes me think of our ancestors. These are the sorts of things they would have been trying to do fifteen years on from the genocide that took place in this land. We would like to send to you our 'Drop the Rock song' in appreciation of your words and your work.

This song was embraced by the Ibuka counsellors[7].

This sort of interchange involves an exchange of local insider-knowledge between groups of genocide survivors and their descendants (see Epston, 1999, 2001). Within these exchanges, all those who are participating experience being linked with and making contributions to the lives of others (Denborough, 2008). This experience of making contributions to the lives of other survivors can be powerfully significant — particularly when these contributions are consistent with carrying on legacies from one's ancestors.

On our most recent visit, Ibuka counsellors explicitly requested that our discussions consider a complex dilemma they are often dealing in their work:

> During the *Gacaca* justice processes, some survivors had hoped that perpetrators who came forth and confessed their crimes would be able to tell us where they buried our loved

---

7 As Jill Freedman (personal communication, 20 January 2011) describes: 'We brought a number of copies of the song on CDs. We played it and talked about it and Patrick Iregura translated the lyrics, and then the Ibuka counsellors wanted to hear it again. Although most of the Rwandan counsellors don't speak English, the next day at break, you could hear people singing "Drop the rock. Drop, drop the rock..." I think this song really brought home to the workers of Ibuka that these were real people from a different place who wanted to link with them'.

ones. But some of us did not learn this and it has undermined the healing process. Now some survivors are continually asking and lamenting 'how can we find the remains of our loved ones? How can we bury them?' How can we assist these survivors who cannot find the bodies of their loved ones?

The Ibuka counsellors said they would be interested to hear from Jewish colleagues about how they have responded to similar situations. During this most recent meeting, a number of Jewish narrative practitioners were present. Prior to coming to Rwanda they had conducted their own research both personally in relation to their families, and professionally, about some of the ways in which Jewish survivors of the Holocaust had responded to 'the problems of memory'.

In response to the Ibuka counsellors request, these Jewish practitioners gathered together some of their 'local knowledge' on this issue of honouring those who have been killed when their bodies have never been found. Representing the Jewish colleagues who were present, the following knowledge was shared[8]:

Good morning. This is a very profound moment for us. We will do our best to respond to your question by sharing with you thoughts that have been gathered through a group effort. As you probably know, the majority of the six million Jews who were murdered in the Holocaust were burned and so no remains were left. In Jewish tradition, the taking care of dead ones and burying them is a profoundly sacred act. It is considered an act of genuine kindness as you have no intention of receiving back. Being unable to bury our loved ones is a devastating experience in Jewish culture. As a result, after the Holocaust, very many practices have developed in

---

[8] The Jewish narrative practitioners present included Yishai Shalif, Yael Gershoni, Jill Freedman, Ruth Pluznick, Rachel Paran, and Tali Gogol-Ostrowsy. Yishai Shalif spoke on behalf of this group.

response to this difficulty of not having the remains of our loved ones. I will share with you some of these responses.

Many Holocaust survivors place in their wills that when they die and are buried they want not only their name written on their grave, but also the names of their loved ones who have no graves. In Jewish graveyards you can see these inscriptions.

As there were whole villages and whole communities in which no one was left, in cemeteries there are also headstones which list the names of those communities — in order to commemorate whole villages from where there were no survivors.

Naming is also significant in Jewish tradition. In many ways names have become a way to commemorate those who died with no remains. Children who were born after the Holocaust have been named after family members whose remains were not found. Similarly, places of significance such as homes, universities, avenues of trees, and institutes have also been named after people and communities who died during the Holocaust.

In Israel there is a particular national day on which we remember the Holocaust. It starts with a ceremony in which six fires are lit in memory of the six million people who perished. Usually these fires are lit by survivors or their descendants.

In more religious circles, there are a range of religious practices that are conducted in memory of those ones who died. In Jewish tradition, a person who lost a loved one says a particular prayer for 12 months after the death. This prayer is called a *Kaddish*. Because so many within the Holocaust did not have anyone to say *Kaddish* for them, a particular *Kaddish* day is set aside for them. We fast during this day in the temples and we say laments and prayers during this day.

Another project involves a particular Jewish text that has six parts. These six parts act as a reminder of the six million who died in the Holocaust. Every day, thousands and thousands of Jews say parts of these prayers in remembrance of those who died.

There is another response that is highly significant. Many Jews who know they will never find the remains of their loved ones seek memories of them. To this day, 65 years since the Holocaust, there is a program on the radio in which people call up and ask listeners if anyone has particular memories of their lost loved ones.

Many people also undertake personal searches, they travel back to Europe trying to find remains of memories. Some people transform these memories into movies or books.

And just as you have here in Rwanda, there is also a project in the centre for commemoration to collect the names of those who died. Any person who knows someone who perished is asked to fill out a form with their information on it. So far they have collected three and a half million names and the process continues. On a personal note, whenever I go to this place and see the empty places set aside for those whose names have not yet been recorded I am very moved.

These are some of the ways that Jewish people have responded to the devastating experience of not being able to find the bodies of their loved ones.

A Hebrew prayer was then sung. The Ibuka counsellors spoke between themselves for a time before responding:

It was very moving to us to listen to the ways you are continuing to honour the victims of the Holocaust. It means a great deal to know that as a people, after many generations, you are able to keep the spirit of remembrance.

When you described the steps you are taking, I was reminded of all that we have been through here in Rwanda. I particularly related to the idea of having a place in the cemetery for the loved ones lost, a place of remembrance with their names and maybe a picture. I have made a personal commitment to do similarly, so that I too will be able to (visit) the cemetery and remember and feel more connected to those I have lost.

Your words reminded me of the many forms of commemoration that we undertake here during the 100 days of memory each year. For instance, every year, in honour of those who were thrown into the rivers we go to the water for memory. There are so many ways in which we share memory during those 100 days.

Thank you for your words. It is important for survivors who are not able to bury their loved ones in dignity, to find other ways to honour them. I am going to share these stories with those with whom I am working. Please tell others in the Jewish community that they are our brothers and sisters. Please tell your people that.

Some of the Jewish participants were visibly moved by this exchange to the extent that the Ibuka counsellors offered comfort and tissues. A direct descendant of survivors of the Holocaust tried to articulate the significance of this exchange:

Something has changed for me today which is difficult to put into words. Until today, the Holocaust has always been a solely 'Jewish' experience. But being here with you, I feel joined in our mutual suffering and survival. One of the things that genocide tries to do is separate peoples and having the chance to feel that our experiences could be a contribution to you gives us renewed strength. At the same time, being welcomed by you in these ways, hearing from you about the ways in which you live in the shadow of genocide, and how you live side by side with those who have done you harm, has much to teach us. I am reminded by you that we are more than 'victims' to our experiences; we can also do great social good because of what we have learned from these experiences. In this way, the suffering of those who perished 'will not be for nothing'. Taking what we learned from their experiences and using it to make changes in our own communities and the world is a way to honour the lives and deaths and suffering of those we love.

At the end of this ritual, one of the Ibuka workers invited everyone to stand and to join in memories and honouring through song.

Reflections

The words of Ibuka counsellors/survivors spoken 14 years after the genocide in Rwanda were so significant to Aboriginal Australian colleagues because it was as if these offered a glimpse as to how Aboriginal ancestors may have tried to deal with the genocide in Australia. And then the words of Jewish colleagues were so significant to Rwandan survivors because they demonstrate that 65 years after the Holocaust, future generations are continuing to honour and remember lost loved ones. These exchanges across time, across place, across culture involve the sharing of intimate local knowledge. This richly described knowledge honours the dead and the suffering, and contributes to the construction of sstories. These are stories of individual and collective identity that honour acts of resistance and sustenance, and that link these with the skills, values, commitments and philosophies of lost loved ones.

Over the last six years, Ibuka, Dulwich Centre Foundation International, and Evanston Family Therapy Center, have engaged with narrative therapy (White and Epston, 1990; Freedman and Combs, 1996; White, 2007) and collective narrative practice approaches (Denborough, 2008) in order to facilitate the excavation, documentation, performance and exchange of the local knowledge of Ibuka counsellors/ survivors.

This has included intricate insider knowledge in relation to:

• the continuing effects of the genocide,

• what sustains survivors as they live in the shadow of genocide,

• ways in which survivors negotiate 'living side by side' with those who have done them great harm, and

• ways of responding when survivors cannot locate the bodies of loved ones.

This essay has detailed this knowledge and the narrative processes that have facilitated its visibility.

Looking back, looking forwards

We began this essay with the words Kaboyi Benoit greeted us with when we first visited Rwanda: 'Ah, Australia...there's a country that knows all about genocide'. Since that first meeting, six years ago, we have consistently retold Benoit's words in our work in Australia with both non-Aboriginal and Aboriginal colleagues. His words remind us to refuse to forget the genocide that occurred in this land, Australia, and to respond in partnership to its continuing effects.

It is hoped that there will be continuing possibilities to facilitate the linking and sharing of local knowledge between survivors of genocide and their descendants in Rwanda, Australia, in Jewish communities around the world, and elsewhere.

Acknowledgements

This chapter describes work developed from a partnership between Ibuka (a national organisation in Rwanda that represents survivor associations), Dulwich Centre Foundation International and Evanston Family Therapy Center. It has been written by David Denborough and Cheryl White (Dulwich Centre Foundation International) in collaboration with Hodali Irakoze Pierre Claver (Ibuka) and Jill Freedman and Gene Combs (Evanston Family Therapy Center). The following Ibuka counsellors have contributed to the content of this paper: Bonheur Albertine, Ingabire Agathe, Kabagambe Cyrille, Umubyeyi Reginne, Mwenzikazi Francoise, Murorunkwere Julienne, Habumuremyi Epaphre, Bakansanga Appolline, Nkima Claire, Karikwera Charlotte, Mukansoro Emmilienne, Kambibi Emilienne, Niyonsaba Asterie, Umulisa Clarisse, Twahirwa Laurent, Nyiramucyo Odette, Uwamwiza Jeannette, Dusabe Jessica, Kibukayire Olive, Rugwizangoga Yvonne, Mukarubayiza Beatrice,

433

Harerimana Theophile, Umwiza Josephine, Vuguziga Paul Marie, Murebwayire Alice, Uwera Josette, Ukeye Josee, Musabyeyezu Sophie, Mukamana Adelite (The Co-ordinator of Counselors), Rutayisire Eugene, Munyaneza Francois, Dusabeyezu Alphonsine, Uwitonze Therese. Uwantege Jacqueline and Maggie Ziegler from the Kigali Genocide Memorial Center also participated at the most recent workshop referred to in this chapter. The following international colleagues have also been involved in the exchanges and meetings described here: Yishai Shalif, Ruth Pluznick, Yael Gershoni, Saviona Cramer, Barbara Wingard, Tileah Drahm-Butler, Rachel Paran, Tali Gogol-Ostrowsy, Kaethe Weingarten, Rick Maisel, Paul Browde, Jeff Zimmerman, Ron Schweitzer, Amaryll Perlesz, David Moltz, Eve Lipchik, Murray Nossel, Jonathan Morgan, Vanessa Jackson, Loree Stout, Angel Yuen, Gene Combs, Carolyn Koolmatrie, Norma Akamatsu, Manja Visschedijk, Jussey Verco, John Stillman, Anne Kathrine Løge, Pierre Blanc-Sahnoun, Linda Moxley-Haggart, Carla Abrams, Yves Bree, Julie Epp, Don Gapp, Deborah Gill, Hilda Nanning, David Newman, Aya Okumura and Russ Whitewood. Patrick Iregura has played a critical translation role throughout all the work described here. The support of Forongo Janvier, Mukamana Adelite and Muanguha Freddy has also been significant.

References

Bellah, R M, Madsen, R, Sullivan, W M, Swidler, A, and Tipton, S M (1985), *Habits of the Heart: Individualism and commitment in American life*, Berkeley CA, University of California Press.

Denborough, D (2006), 'A framework for receiving and documenting testimonies of trauma', in Denborough, D (ed), *Trauma: Narrative responses to traumatic experience*, Adelaide, Australia: Dulwich Centre Publications, 115–31. (Reprinted from (2005), *International Journal of Narrative Therapy and Community Work*, [3 and 4], 34–42).

Denborough, D (2008), *Collective Narrative Practice: Responding to individuals, groups, and communities who have experienced trauma,* Adelaide, Dulwich Centre Publications.

Denborough, D (2010), *Working with Memory in the Shadow of Genocide: The narrative practices of Ibuka trauma counsellors,* Adelaide, Dulwich Centre Foundation International.

Denborough, D, Freedman, J, and White, C (2008), *Strengthening resistance: The use of narrative practices in working with genocide survivors,* Adelaide, Dulwich Centre Foundation.

Epston, D (1999), 'Co-research: The making of an alternative knowledge, in *Narrative Therapy and Community Work: A conference collection,* Adelaide, Dulwich Centre Publications, 137–57.

Epston, D (2001), 'Anthropology, archives, co-research and narrative therapy', in Denborough, D (ed), *Family Therapy: Exploring the field's past, present and possible futures* Adelaide, Australia, Dulwich Centre Publications, 177–82.

Freedman, J, and Combs, G (1996), *Narrative Therapy: The social construction of preferred realities,* New York, W W Norton.

Kaboyi, B (2007), 'A small light as we walk this long road: The work of Ibuka', *International Journal of Narrative Therapy and Community Work,* (1), 47–50.

Lederach, J P (1995), *Preparing for Peace: Conflict transformation across cultures,* Syracuse NY, Syracuse University Press.

Nelson, L H (2001), *Damaged Identities, Narrative Repair,* Ithaca NY, Cornell University Press.

Turner, V (1969), *The Ritual Process: Structure and anti-structure,* New York, Aldine de Gruyter.

Turner, V (1979), *Process, Performance and Pilgrimage: A study in comparative symbology,* New Delhi, Concept Publishing Company.

Wertsch, J V (2002), *Voices of Collective Remembering,* Cambridge, Cambridge University Press.

Westoby, P (2009), *The Sociality of Refugee Healing: In dialogue with Southern Sudanese refugees resettling in Australia,* Champaign IL, Common Ground.

435

White, M (1997), *Narratives of Therapists' Lives*, Adelaide, Dulwich Centre Publications.

White, M (2004), 'Working with people who are suffering the consequences of multiple trauma: A narrative perspective', *International Journal of Narrative Therapy and Community Work*, (1), 45–76. Reprinted in Denborough, D (ed), (2006), *Trauma: Narrative responses to traumatic experience*, Adelaide, Dulwich Centre Publications, 25–85.

White, M (2007), *Maps of Narrative Practice*, New York NY, W W Norton.

White, M, Epston, D (1990), *Narrative Means to Therapeutic Ends*, New York, W W Norton.

Wiesenthal, S (1998), *The Sunflower: On the possibilities and limits of forgiveness*, New York, Schocken Books, Inc.

Looking Upstream: Increasing Options to Prevent Genocide

Isabelle Macgregor and Devin C Bowles

Genocide prevention scholarship focuses almost exclusively on immediate causes of genocide, those 'downstream' factors which tip an already troubled nation or region into committing atrocities. Neglected are those 'upstream' factors which trouble a nation or region in the first place. These include poverty, lack of freedom, education and health care, and environmental degradation and resource scarcity. While these are not direct causes of genocide, they contribute to them, thereby increasing the likelihood that genocide will occur. Because of the focus on interrupting the downstream causes of genocide – using measures which are implemented only when it is believed genocide is imminent – prevention analysis has generated strategies like sanctions, peacekeeping operations and prosecutions. Each of these measures has associated costs and is likely to be implemented by the international community in only a limited range of circumstances. Further, the triggers for the implementation of these measures generally involve serious discrimination and some level of violence, making it likely that even when full-blown genocide is averted, lives are nonetheless lost and tensions are raised within the society along ethnic or religious lines, increasing the long-term likelihood of genocide.

The upstream causes of genocide represent a number of prospective intervention points for prevention which have not received enough attention. These include the stimulation of the economy, the promotion of democracy, the provision of education and health care, and the protection and management of environmental resources. These measures are not new, but their role in genocide prevention has been largely unrecognised. While each upstream preventative measure is associated with implementation costs and factors making it unlikely to be implemented in certain situations, these costs and factors are different from those associated with downstream preventative measures, making the upstream measures a useful complement. By looking at both ends of the stream, genocide scholars can increase policy options for prevention, deterrence or deflection of the crime.

Major causes of genocide in the literature

To prevent genocide, we have to understand its root causes. Genocide and mass killing do not simply erupt spontaneously. They are incremental processes, building blocks, which aggregate and develop into their final form. The literature has produced diverse explanations. This essay focuses on structural causes. While precedent factors are analysed in the broader conflict-prevention literature, most scholars concentrates on the more 'last-minute' causes – those which have already been preceded by some level of violence. Few scholars trace the causes back to the contexts before the violence or repression began.

There are a number of possible genocidal catalysts. Helen Fein suggests war, challenges to the structure of domination, the threat of internal breakdown or social revolution, or economic development or recession (1984, 5). Many scholars see genocide as arising during periods of change, especially – as Mark Levene argues (2000) – when empires, even nation states, are forming or crumbling. Genocide is sometimes seen as caused by hegemonic myths, and sometimes extreme religious views, which identify the victims as being outside the perpetrator's 'sanctioned universe of obligation' (Fein 1984, 18), for example, the Nazis' 'master race' myth. Genocide can also occur when a particular group becomes the scapegoat of an anxious state – when leaders believe that a particular group is weakening the already vulnerable state (Kuper 1984, 39). Genocide can be a retributive act against a group whose members have caused pain in the past. This becomes particularly likely where one group suddenly becomes the governing class and the other the subject class (Fein 1984, 11). Kuper points out that this can occur during the 'decolonisation of a two-tier structure of domination', as in Burundi and Rwanda following the withdrawal of the Belgian colonists (Kuper 1984, 34). 'Developmental' (Fein 1984) or 'creeping genocide' (Levene 1999) are the names given to a form which Kuper simply refers to as 'genocides against indigenous peoples' (1984, 32). These 'episodes' are aimed at getting rid of obstacles blocking the path of economic exploitation.

Straus argues for a general consensus in the recent genocide literature—for example, among scholars Mark Levene, Michael Mann, Manus Midlarsky, Jacques Semelin, Benjamin Valentino and Eric Weitz—that genocide develops from a process of 'escalation and contingency'. These analysts contend that there is a degree of improvisation and that genocide does not seem to be predetermined or inevitable. Straus adds that while this 'casts further doubt on the prospects of a general theory', if genocide is not highly pre-planned, this should provide opportunities for the international community to 'shape outcomes' (2007, 492, 493). These authors agree with Fein that war was (and is) an important factor in determining when and why genocide occurs (Straus 2007, 494)—demonstrating that genocide prevention scholarship can potentially benefit from the more general conflict-prevention literature.

The conflict-prevention literature

The existing genocide literature does very little to answer the question of why some conflicts escalate into genocidal killing and others do not (Valentino et al 2004). It is therefore difficult to know how to prevent a genocide. There is, nevertheless, a significant literature on conflict-prevention and, if genocide is one of the paths down which a disintegrating, conflict-ridden state can go—as Straus puts it, as 'part of a range of possible outcomes of violence' (2007, 500)—this literature should be utilised.

The Carnegie Commission on Preventing Deadly Conflict outlines two broad strategies for conflict-prevention. *Operational prevention* involves measures in response to an immediate crisis. *Structural prevention* involves measures to keep crises from occurring in the first place, or to keep them from recurring (1997, xix). Structural prevention approaches 'not only make people better off but also inhibit the need to resort to violence' (Hamburg and Holl 1999, 368). It also involves the promotion of 'thriving states with representative government, the rule of law, robust civil societies and open economies with social safety nets' (Hamburg and Holl 1999, 368). It is this structural prevention, consisting of 'upstream' measures, which is lacking from the genocide literature. These include:

• Promoting indigenous democracy;

• Fostering equitable socio-economic development, for example, the provision of skills, knowledge, freedom and health; and

• Facilitating education on violence prevention, conflict resolution and mutual accommodation (Hamburg 2010b, 12).

Conflict-prevention requires a concerted, long-term strategy on the part of the international community, and this must encompass a wide range of developmental measures. No one element of a society can successfully be developed to the neglect of others — they must be developed in unison. As Hamburg and Holl state, 'economic growth without widespread sharing in the benefits of growth will not reduce prospects for violent conflict — and it could exacerbate tensions' (1999, 374).

The broader conflict-prevention literature presents a number of precursor events of violence that are, for the most part, not addressed. Linking with this broader field would thus provide genocide theorists with an increased number of potential upstream points of intervention.

Downstream genocide prevention strategies: an analysis and critique

Peacekeeping

The most direct form of genocide prevention discussed is peacekeeping (Woodhouse, Bruce and Dando 1998, Shawcross 2001, Krasno, Hayes and Daniel 2003, and Lebor 2006). Its directness means that it does not rely heavily on theories of genocide causation. Military force is deployed to stop violent conflict with the threat or practice of violence which, borrowing from Clausewitz, forces potential *genocidaires* to do the peacekeeper's will (1950).[1] The benefit of this option is that success in most circumstances is highly likely if the mission is adequately supported and if the primary goal of the mission is short-term genocide prevention. Unfortunately, these assumptions cannot be taken for granted because of the costs and limitations associated with such idealised intervention.

There are three main costs to outside countries deploying a peacekeeping mission: financial costs, the lives of its troops, and the commitment of its military forces. The capacity and willingness of would-be *genocidaires* to forcibly resist the intervention force dictates the size of these costs to the international community. Ideally, the intervention force has sufficient fighting capability to make the option of genocide unattractive to those who might otherwise engage in it, leading to a minimum of casualties both for the intervention force and locals. Constraining the international community's drive to deploy an overwhelming force are opportunity costs that come with military--the inability to project military force elsewhere — and financial costs. Even when an overwhelming

---

[1] 'War is thus an act of force to compel our enemy to do our will' (1950:3).

international force is deployed, refinement of asymmetrical warfare puts it at risk, as demonstrated in Iraq and Afghanistan. Further, as genocide analyst Benjamin Valentino (2006, 740) argues:

'humanitarian intervention' is nothing more than another name for war. The ends of humanitarian intervention may be different from those of traditional wars, but the means are much the same. And as human rights advocates understand better than most, war is never cheap or clean. It seldom makes anything better without making something else worse.

Arms alone rarely change hearts and minds. One important limitation of peacekeeping missions is their failure to address the causes of genocide. Depending on the specific circumstances, a genocide prevention mission might have to support efforts to strengthen the rule of law, protect the integrity and independence of the judiciary, promote honesty and accountability in law enforcement, enhance protections for vulnerable groups, reintegrate ex-combatants and strengthen civilian control mechanisms. It might also be beneficial to provide support to local human rights organisations (ICISS report 2001, 23). Technical assistance for any equitable reform of the legislative, judicial or penal system could also be given (Cockell 2002, 197).

Yet the forced marriage between military intervention and civilian development is often problematic. If military missions are to reduce capability, and civilian missions are to enhance it, then international actors must be able to distinguish and effectively target the separate people and structures to be disempowered or strengthened. This task, particularly when genocide is imminent and there is a high level of internal tension within a society, is exceptionally difficult.

There is also the risk that foreign intervention—which is seen to benefit one group over another—will exacerbate internal conflicts. These unintended consequences of humanitarian intervention are liable to bog down military and civilian missions, leading either to premature withdrawal of international forces or increased costs to the countries supporting them.

The current geopolitical situation makes large-scale peacekeeping efforts to prevent genocide unlikely in the foreseeable future, for two reasons. First, the humanitarian intervention in Libya may have made international support for intervention less likely. To intervene in accordance with international law, an international force requires the authorisation either of the government of the country in which intervention is occurring or United Nations Security Council. Yet Russia and China viewed the recent military action in Libya as exceeding that which was authorised, making similar authorisations less likely to pass in the future, as has been shown by their veto of force in the current (2011–2012) Syrian uprising. This, in turn, may limit future humanitarian intervention to countries where governments acquiesce.

Second, demand for humanitarian intervention often exceeds what the international community is willing to offer. International police, such as UN police (UNPOL), represent the low end of the continuum of force which the international community might offer. International police deployments generally have lower human, financial and opportunity costs than full-scale humanitarian interventions. Despite international demand and the acknowledgement of its importance, UNPOLs deployable capacity is lacking. There is not adequate recruitment or preparation, and timely deployment of qualified police to new missions is therefore impaired. The UN is also currently unable to adequately manage and guide their police forces (Smith et al 2007, xiv). As Durch and Berkman state, 'serious lags in police deployments have been chronic' (2006, 44). After a UN mission, it takes approximately nine months for the authorised number of police personnel to deploy. Though member states must offer police personnel to the UN, they are generally reluctant to nominate officers, as police are often needed in their own countries and states do not like parting with them (Smith et al 2007, xiv).

Many of the countries which traditionally contribute to military intervention forces will be reluctant to do so in the future. Even before the global financial crisis, there were far more potentially pre-genocidal situations than there were forces to be deployed. It has traditionally been Western, technologically-advanced democracies which engage in peacekeeping missions. The global financial crisis has wrought havoc with the economies of the United States and the European Union as a whole. At the time of writing, the military budget of the United States is being reduced, impacting its war-fighting capability. Military deployments are exceptionally expensive, for instance the post 9/11 US wars in Afghanistan, Iraq and Pakistan are thought to have cost some $4 trillion (Watson Institute for International Studies, Brown University, 2011). The financial situation of Western democracies dramatically reduces the likelihood that they will bear the costs of military engagement solely for the purpose of genocide prevention.

Additionally, many Western democracies are war-weary, having been engaged in Iraq and Afghanistan for years. Their people have little appetite to see more troops come home in coffins. Involvement in both these countries continues to stretch Western militaries, limiting their capacity to deploy forces elsewhere.

Libya provides an example. Colonel Muammar Gaddafi's government is believed to have participated in the bombing of civilian passenger Pan Am flight 103 from London to New York on 21 December 1988 (known as the 'Lockerbie bombing'). He also characterised those participating in a revolt against him as 'cockroaches', and threatened to execute all those who took up arms against him (Bellamy 2011), strongly suggesting that atrocity crimes were imminent. The opportunity to remove him from power and prevent impending atrocity crimes must surely rank highly on the list of scenarios in which Western democracies would be prepared to deploy military force in order to prevent genocide or other atrocity crimes. Yet they gambled that airstrikes and political pressure would be enough to achieve their aims, because of an unwillingness or inability to bear some or all of the three types of costs of further involvement. While Libya is now free of Gaddafi, it is unclear whether the fragmented opposition will cohere into a stable, democratic government. (The signs in mid-2012 were not hopeful, with increasing friction between tribal militias.)

In sum, humanitarian intervention is an important, last-minute tool to prevent genocide but a number of factors limit the circumstances under which it is likely to occur. The need for overwhelming force favours intervention by wealthy, technically-advanced countries and reduces the likelihood that any countries without a high level of military capability will intervene in this way. Yet these countries will have a low willingness to engage in such missions over the medium term. Intervention against potential *genocidaires* with advanced war fighting capabilities is also unlikely because of the need for military dominance. Finally, humanitarian intervention alone does little to address the causes of the genocide and can inflame underlying tensions within a society. At best, it simply decreases the intensity or extent of the violence; at worst, it increases suffering and exacerbates conflicts.

Sanctions

After a potential genocide has been detected, sanctions may prove an important preventative. Sanctions imposed on a state inhibit its ability to interact internationally, thus dissuading it from pursuing murderous policies (Doxey 1980, 9; ICISS report 2001, 29). This approach can be used in cases when general diplomatic pressure might not appear decisive enough but when the use of force is too extreme (Carter 1988, 12).

For expository purposes, sanctions can be classified as economic, diplomatic or military, though overlap between categories occurs. Economic sanctions may target the foreign assets of a country or particular leaders. Restrictions on income-generating commodities such as oil, diamonds, timber and drugs are becoming common. Restricting access to petroleum can also restrict military operations (ICISS report 2001, 30) — although they can also prove disadvantageous in situations immediately preceding genocide as they could also immobilise the victim group. 'Freezing' assets is a common sanction (Alerassool 1993, 8, 20). Diplomatic sanctions often involve restrictions on diplomatic representation, including expulsion of diplomatic staff. This is largely symbolic and limits the possibility of illicit transactions like the sale of sanctioned goods, purchase of military-related material or the movement of funds. They might also prove disadvantageous if they diminish contact with the country and thus potential influence. Such sanctions include restrictions on travel for specific leaders. One form would be suspension or expulsion of the perpetrating state from international bodies (ICISS report 2001, 30). These sanctions are not likely to be successful on their own but they create severe inconveniences for the country's politicians and bureaucrats and cannot be ignored. Military sanctions can be effective. They can involve arms embargoes or the halting of military co-operation and training programs shared with that country (ICISS report 2001, 30).

The costs of sanctions to the international community are relatively small compared to armed intervention. Most sanctions involve the cutting of ties between participating sanctioning countries and the sanctioned country or group. The cost borne by each sanctioning country is therefore relatively small, as the sanctioned target accounts for only a small proportion of its economic, diplomatic, or military activity.

Sanctions have drawbacks. Most are blunt instruments that can be applied only to countries or a small number of individuals, rather than segments of the society. This can lead to civilians suffering because of sanctions directed at their government or prevent arms sales to victims of genocide, impeding self-defence. Once in place, sanctions can be difficult to lift. Each of these unintended consequences of sanctions can make genocide more likely. Additionally, to be most effective, any kind of embargo must be implemented quickly, often requiring the co-ordination of many countries.

Sanctions work best when targeted at either a few leaders or whole countries. There has been little success in applying most sanctions to large, potentially or actually genocidal social groups. For instance, during the 1990s, Bosnian Serbs could not be directly targeted by UN sanctions. Instead, the UN applied a range of sanctions against Yugoslavia, including freezing all Yugoslav financial assets on their territory, stemming the flow of hard currency into Serbia. The goal was to decrease Serbia's ability to support the Bosnian Serbs and prompt Belgrade to urge the Bosnian Serbs to make peace (Sloan 1998, 15, 46). While the Serbian leader Slobodan Milosevic publicly appealed to the Bosnian Serbs to accept the Vance–Owen peace plan (Sloan 1998, 48–49), neither his requests nor the sanctions were enough to halt Bosnian Serb violence.

Even when implemented quickly, sanctions are often indiscriminate weapons and can, on occasion, do more harm to the civilian population than to the targeted group (ICISS report 2001, 29). If the objective is to bring about economic and social disintegration, making it physically impossible for the state to continue its actions, sanctions may lead to the unexpected suffering and death of civilians (Kuyper 1978, 10). This was demonstrated when the UN imposed sanctions on Iraq in 1990. All transhipment of oil was forbidden as well as all trade with Iraq, except in medicine and food. They did not have the desired effect, instead causing harm to the Iraqi population. The magazine *US News & World Report* claimed in its 17 May 1993 issue: 'While ordinary Iraqis have suffered fearfully under the international sanctions, smugglers and clandestine sales of Iraqi oil have kept [Saddam] Hussein and his murderous coterie of hangers-on in relative comfort' (Summers 1995, 221). As Harff states, wherever possible, 'economic sanctions should not apply to domestic goods, those whose lack would endanger the survival of the population of the culprit state...'(1984, 153).

One claim is that civilian populations may be protected by 'smart sanctions', those designed to target specific decision-making personnel. This argument dovetails with Valentino's claim that leadership is an important cause of genocide and, where leaders see advantage in genocide, they will frequently pursue it as a strategy (Valentino 2004, 4–5). These might involve targeted 'financial sanctions, travel sanctions, specific commodity boycotts, and arms embargoes' (GAPWP Programme Statement 2008–2010, 24). According to Moller, 'smart sanctions' are not always smart. For example, there has been a travel ban on Robert Mugabe preventing him from flying out of Zimbabwe. This means that it will be harder for anyone in the country to overthrow him as there is always a greater possibility of ousting an absent leader. Smart sanctions, therefore, need to be tailor-made for each situation (2008). The risk is that the international community will outsmart itself with such sanctions; while efforts to use smart sanctions are frequently made, their negative effects are normally more diffuse than intended. Economic sanctions often hurt those already most disadvantaged, as more powerful groups ensure that their relative advantage is maintained. Even when not the case, the deprivation caused by sanctions can increase tensions within a society, making genocide more likely.

If genocides tend to occur when the balance of power is tipped drastically in favour of one group over another, then arms embargoes can in some situations make genocide more likely, as they prevent the less powerful side from arming itself. Bosnia demonstrated the problems which can arise in the implementation of military sanctions. The UNs blanket arms ban in the Balkans, imposed on 25 September 1991, left the two warring factions unevenly matched: the Muslims defenceless against well-equipped Serbs (Robertson 2002, 304; Krasno et al 2003, 239; Gow 1997, 37; Ramet 1999, 211). The Bosnian government repeatedly called for the embargo to be lifted to give the state and its threatened people a chance to defend themselves, claiming that it was an illegal breach of its right to self-defence under Article 51 of the UN Charter (Gow 1997, 37, 38). Once the UN arms embargo had been applied, it was extremely hard to reach an agreement to lift it—there would have to be a vote in the Security Council; France, the UK and Russia were unwilling to lift it (Gow 1997, 38).

Speed is essential for embargoes to work. If action is not immediate, the target state will have time to anticipate and adjust to sanctions, lessening their damaging impact (Kuyper 1978, 10). It can do this through stockpiling materials, finding alternative sources, producing substitutes, stimulating and diversifying national production and imposing controls on key commodities (Kuyper 1978, 11; Doxey 1980, 106).

Because of the seeming decline of America's superpower status and the economic and military rise of developing countries like China, co-ordination between many countries is now required for effective sanctions. Yet group sanctions produce co-ordination problems. The countries involved may have different objectives. Many states, for economic or other reasons, do not apply sanctions strictly (Kuyper 1978, 10). Members of the UN, for example, generally avoid decisions about enforcement because they do not agree on culpability and are not prepared to undertake the inherent risks and costs (Doxey 1980, 81). Perhaps more importantly, governments often operate to maximise their own self-interest, rather than for any greater good. The Apartheid case in South Africa demonstrates a common situation where the self-interest of global superpowers ranked higher than their humanitarian ideals. Despite global opposition to the regime, serious international sanctions were blocked by the economic self-interests of Britain and the United States. The first mandatory UN sanctions were imposed in December 1963. They were relatively weak, simply proscribing the shipment of equipment and materials for arms manufacture. No serious measures beyond this were adopted until 1985 (Institute for International Economics 1998). Britain and the United States refused to act because of their trade interests (Danaher 1989, 131, 142, 143). This illustrates the difficulties of international co-ordination.

Punishment as a deterrent

If the prosecution and punishment of genocidal criminals acts as a deterrent to others, then it might be viewed as an early prevention strategy. To be effective, prosecution must be rapid and consistent. Clearly this has not been the case. Trials have been inconsistent and slow even when they take place. The most effective forms of trial are most likely to be international tribunals, yet these are rare in the legal realm. After the Nuremberg and Tokyo trials of the Axis leaders, there were no new international tribunals until the Security Council created the international tribunals for Rwanda (ICTR) and the former Yugoslavia (ICTY) in the 1990s (Fierke 2005, 73). While the International Criminal Court (ICC) offers some hope, it prosecutes only when the suspect's own country refuses to do so and there is no guaranteed uniformity in procedure and sentencing (Lebor 2006, 221–20).

The deterrent effect of prosecution is lessened the longer it takes to bring criminals to justice, and is negated entirely if trials fail to take place. There was a significant lack of timely punishment for the genocide in Cambodia. It is only now that a UN-backed Cambodian tribunal has become a reality. The delays in Bosnia and lack of prosecution of leaders of the Sudanese genocide would give comfort to potential genocidaires calculating the odds of prosecution.

The costs of prosecution are often too great to bear, especially for a post-genocidal state. The traditional Gacaca system implemented in Rwanda is an example. There has been a conscientious effort to prosecute all those involved in the killing and throughout the 1990s, more than 100,000 suspects were forced to wait in detention. More than 18 years after the genocide, tens of thousands still awaited trial. This has been a huge economic burden on a country which is already one of the poorest in the world (Schabas 2005, 880; Fierens 2005, 900).

There are also drawbacks to using the possible deterrence capacity of prosecution as a preventative measure. The existence of tribunals can also serve to hamper the peace process: in a country where atrocities are continuing, the prospect of a trial means that it is more difficult to induce the combatants to sign a ceasefire (Bjorn Moller interview, Danish Institute for International Studies, 29 May 2008). The arrest warrant for Sudanese President Omar Hassan al-Bashir for genocide and crimes against humanity prompted concerns for the fate of a potential political settlement in Darfur and the hybrid United Nations–African Union peacekeeping force (Thakur 2008; de Waal and Stanton 2009).

Effective deterrent prosecution is unlikely to be implemented for several reasons. First, it requires significant finances and resources both on the part of the international community and the country in question. Second, it is often not possible if genocide suspects have fled or are being protected, potentially by a different country. Third, it might not be diplomatically expedient to press charges and risk a delicate peace settlement. Prosecution can only be classified as an upstream preventative measure if trials are speedy, efficient and uniform. As this is not the case, it probably has no significant deterrent impact and should be viewed as a downstream measure.

Conclusions

The three downstream prevention measures examined require

a medium to high level of international co-operation to be implemented. Armed humanitarian intervention and sanctions require this co-operation to be achieved in a short space of time, once it is clear that genocide is likely. While there have been instances where this has occurred, an ideal policy toolbox would contain prevention measures that did not require a high level of international consensus.

Downstream measures also tend to rely on the knowledge that genocide is about to occur. This means that they are reliant on identification of pre-genocidal situations. While criteria for making such an assessment have been suggested (one of the most prominent examples is that of Fein, 1984), the prediction of genocide is hardly an exact science. Indicators may not provide sufficient detail regarding the kind, scale, time or place of these incidences. It is still not possible to predetermine the extent of the wider implications, for example, a subsequent refugee crisis (Thoolen 1992, 172–71). Beyond questions of timing and scale, there is room for doubt in any prediction of which situations might tip into genocide. Yet doubt provides countries which do not feel it is in their interests to intervene with an excuse for inaction. Even when all countries are operating with the best of intentions, the international community may not be able to bear the multiple costs of erring on the side of assuming that most or all potentially pre-genocidal situations will turn genocidal. This is particularly true for policy measures with high costs, such as armed humanitarian intervention and some forms of sanctions. Finally, if the international community hesitates until indicators of imminent genocide are recognisable, any measures implemented are likely to come too late to fully avoid death, suffering, and the hardening of ethnic and other divisions.

Upstream genocide prevention strategies: a formulation and analysis

The limitations of the downstream intervention measures discussed above call out for additional policy options, particularly those that are less costly and can be implemented unilaterally, well in advance of the genocide. Because of the problems of genocide prediction, they will need to be applied to a broad range of situations, some of which would not have become genocidal. Therefore, they should have positive outcomes beyond genocide prevention. Development aid meets all of these criteria, yet with very rare exceptions (Hamburg 2010a, Hamburg 2010b), the genocide literature pays little attention to development as a form of prevention. Development should ideally occur across a broad range of areas simultaneously, including those discussed below.

Economy and infrastructure

When poverty exists alongside ethnic or cultural divisions, mass killing can result. The provision of economic equality might thus prevent genocide. In the long term, there needs to be a general promotion of economic growth through better terms of trade. This involves allowing developing countries greater access to external markets, encouraging necessary economic and structural reform, and providing technical assistance for strengthening regulatory institutions (ICISS report 2001, 23). The World Bank launched its Operational Policy on Conflict and Development Cooperation in 2000, committing it to more vigorous action regarding countries at risk, experiencing or recovering from conflict (Cleves et al 2002, 322).

Economic development can increase risk of genocide if it occurs for just one group. Fein notes that development of unsettled land by states or multinational companies often creates conflict with the indigenous people, as profitable expansion provides the incentive to destroy indigenous people either directly or indirectly. She therefore advocates institutionalising human rights impact reports, similar to environmental impact reports, before such a project is approved (1999, 469).

Democracy and freedom

Political inequality provides fertile ground for genocide. Promotion of democratic systems and values around the world is an important preventative measure. Democracies generally provide higher levels of 'public goods' to their populations than non-democracies. To maintain office, democratic leaders must win the support of a majority of citizens. In non-democracies, leaders owe their power to a smaller, less representative group of supporters (Valentino et al 2010, 529).

Countries in which rights and participation are based on ethnicity are more likely to lead to genocidal situations than nations which base rights on common citizenship. It is important to promote integration through establishing decentralised power-sharing and forums for multi-party dialogue. It might also be necessary for a peace-building mission to provide technical assistance to reform deficient governance institutions like the judiciary, the police or the civil service. Supervising transitional elections and supporting a free press is also significant (Cockell 2002, 197; ICISS report 2001, 23).

Conflict is common in societies which lack a democratic political system capable of managing disputes peacefully through dialogue, negotiation and compromise (Save-Soderbergh and Lennartsson 2002, 359). Preventative efforts should therefore ensure that all major groups in society participate in political power, administration, the army and police. It is not just a matter of creating democracy. Majority rule can still bring about the persecution of minorities, as was seen in Rwanda and Cambodia. A preventative mission should oversee the development of checks and balances in political institutions (Stewart 2002, 127). According to Horowitz, a mitigation of conflict can be achieved through the use of political incentives to encourage inter-ethnic moderation, for example, if politicians must rely in part on the votes of members of groups other than their own in order to be elected (Horowitz 2003, 12, 14). Establishing political inclusivity is particularly difficult; nevertheless, there have been instances in which it has almost certainly prevented conflict.

The UN planning and supervision of Cambodian elections in 1993 probably prevented future violence in that country. The aim was the introduction of democracy and peace to Cambodia, a country which had undergone 22 years of civil war. The United Nations Transitional Authority in Cambodia (UNTAC) protected the electoral process and ensured civil order, while the actual electoral process was run by UN volunteers. This involved the registration of the 4.8 million prospective voters. Despite difficulties, the electoral process was a success (Shawcross 2001, 54, 55, 63). The mission repatriated over 350,000 Cambodian refugees and opened up Cambodian society to 'press freedom, pluralism and grassroots organisations independent of the state and governing party' (Fawthrop and Jarvis 2005, 107).

Legal inequality is prevalent in high risk societies. The protection of law is an essential component of genocide prevention. The rule of law 'forms the basis for the just management of relations between and among people. It also helps ensure the protection of fundamental human rights, political access through participatory governance, social accommodation of diverse groups and equitable economic opportunity' (Hamburg and Holl 1999, 375). The promotion of justice should emphasise three areas: human rights, humanitarian law, and non-violent alternatives for resolving disputes, including more flexible intrastate mechanisms for mediation, arbitration, grievance recognition and social reconciliation. These areas require constant attention through democratic processes (Hamburg and Holl 1999, 375).

Education and skills

Education may be an important component of genocide

prevention. As David Hamburg (2008, 1133) states:

Just as lifelong learning in mathematics, science, and technology is essential for the success of a modern economy, so too the teaching of pro-social behaviour across the lifespan can help to prevent immense destruction. This involves explicit information and hands-on experience with conflict resolution, violence prevention, mutual accommodation between groups, and conditions conducive to peaceful living.

It has been suggested that the education of women is a lucrative development investment in developing countries. Education increases the skills and choices of women, and of their children. Education also helps to delay marriage — partly because of an educated woman's greater chances for employment — and increase knowledge and use of family planning (Hamburg 2006, 37). Reduced population growth means that the society will place less pressure on environmental resources.

Health care

The links between health and peace have been under-explored. Furst et al state that 'an adverse public health situation may spur violent conflict, and violent conflict may favour the spread of infectious diseases'. Better understanding of this dynamic would help make critical infrastructure and public health systems 'crisis-proof' and thus reduce the occurrence of armed conflict (Furst et al 2009).

Health serves as an effective bridge to peace for several reasons. First, health is a shared interest valued throughout the world. Second, health interventions have an immediate impact of people's lives, as well as long term benefits. They inspire 'trust, confidence, and hope' in the societies in question and, in many cases, further development cannot be achieved without first reducing illness and death — for example, in African countries ravaged by AIDS. Third, health interventions are seen as largely non-ideological and thus more acceptable than some other programs (Hamburg 2006, 42). The advanced medical capabilities of Western nations place them in an excellent position to implement 'medical diplomacy' or 'health diplomacy'. Without clean drinking water and medical care, anger and frustration can grow within a society, leading to internal and regional conflict. Many of the world's current conflict zones—Sudan, Somalia, the Democratic Republic of Congo, the Palestine Authority and Sri Lanka—also 'bear disproportionate burdens of disease'. Medicine is rightly seen as a peacekeeping tool (Wexler 2009).

Beyond the direct links between health and peace, healthier populations are also more economically productive, providing a second route link peace (Hamburg 2006, 35). Health and internal stability are linked: 'healthy populations are able to work, cultivate food, and earn wages—all of which contribute to economic productivity and a functioning society' (Wexler 2009).

Environmental protection and management

The link between environmental protection and conflict-prevention is recognised by scholars and policymakers outside genocide studies (Homer-Dixon and Blitt 1998). As Hamburg and Holl assert, natural resources often lie at the heart of conflicts which have the potential for 'mass violence'. Perpetrators sometimes manipulate resource shortages for their own ends, for example, using food or water scarcity as a weapon. Conflicts can also arise over competing claims of sovereignty over certain resources such as rivers or oil. Increasingly, there is 'environmental degradation and resource depletion in areas characterised by political instability, rapid population growth, chronic economic deprivation and societal stress' (Hamburg and Holl 1999, 373). Environmental management is important if we are to prevent genocide and mass killing. Hamburg and Holl argue that more effort is needed to develop 'sustainable strategies for social and economic progress' and that this sustainability is likely to become a key principle for development (1999, 373).

In 2005, the Division of Early Warning and Assessment (DEWA), within the United Nations Environmental Programme (UNEP), developed the 'Environment and Conflict Prevention Initiative'. This initiative is designed to 'promote conflict-prevention, peace, and co-operation through environmental protection, restoration, and resources'. The environment becomes a 'pathway to co-operation' (Environmental Change and Security Program, Woodrow Wilson Center 2005). The Environment, Development and Sustainable Peace Initiative states that the protection of trans-boundary rivers in Africa is highly important. Water scarcity in Southern Africa increases potential for conflict in the 15 international river basins in that area. These rivers are also vital for socio-economic development, farming and hydroelectric power (Tanzler et al 2004, 13).

Conflicts based on environmental resources are most likely to occur in the world's poorest countries, those least able to implement sustainable development. The provision of assistance generally falls to multilateral agencies like the World Bank. This organisation is attempting to remedy the problem through distributing more than US$ 20 billion annually and acting as a trustee for the Global Environment Facility (GEF). This facility is 'designed to add environmental dimensions to projects funded for more general development purposes' (Payne 1998).

Assistance packages might be used to tie border groups in one or more countries to their shared interests in land and water development and environmental protection (Hamburg and Holl 1999, 374). Environmental protection and development can also strengthen a country's economic growth and population health.

Analysis and conclusions

One drawback to development as genocide prevention is that it is unclear which, if any, genocides were prevented. This raises challenges for scholars seeking to study this form of prevention and for political leaders seeking to justify the costs. Valentino states that while the costs of prevention in a conflict will be much less than a purely reactive intervention, these costs must be multiplied many times because these prevention measures are likely to be applied to many crises that would never have become genocidal (2006, 735). But if prevention is based on developmental aid, then benefits include not just averted genocides, but the prevention of more conventional violent conflicts, decreased social unrest, reduced population growth, increased economic development, healthier populations and more robust environmental systems. These are valuable outcomes, not just for the country or region directly impacted, but for the world community.

Upstream intervention, and particularly development, also generally avoids issues of state sovereignty—a powerful restriction on downstream prevention. How does one justify forfeiture of state sovereignty to allow sanctions, a military presence or fact-finding investigations when no atrocity has yet been commit-ted? Even without the legal questions, until atrocities are committed, the people may 'prefer their tyrants rather than see their homeland overrun' (Teson 2003, 105–06). Few countries are likely to reject a broad, well-planned aid package on the grounds that it interferes with state sovereignty, even if they resist democratic reforms.

Options to prevent genocide must include more than only downstream policies. While these can be crucial to stop deadly violence, by themselves they do not result in real peace, only a cessation of violence. A wide-ranging program of aid and development is the best means of preventing genocide in the long term. Prosperous, healthy nations with educated populations and economic and legal equality are unlikely to witness genocide. Upstream strategies for prevention therefore seem to complement the downstream strategies on which genocide literature has focused and are worthy of exploration as methods to prevent genocide.

References

Alerassool, M (1993), *Freezing Assets: The USA and the most effective economic sanction*, New York, St Martin's Press.

Bellamy A J (2011), 'Libya and the Responsibility to Protect: the exception and the norm', *Ethics and International Affairs*, vol 25; no 3, 263–69.

Carnegie Commission on Preventing Deadly Conflict (1997), *Preventing Deadly Conflict, Final Report*, New York, Carnegie Corporation.

Carter, B E (1988), *International Economic Sanctions: Improving the haphazard US legal regime*, Cambridge, Cambridge University Press.

Clausewitz, C von (1950, 1832), *On War*, Washington DC, Infantry Journal Press.

Cleves, P, Colletta, N, Sambanis, N (2002), 'Addressing Conflict: Emerging Policy at the World Bank', in Osler Hampson, F, Malone, D M (eds), *From Reaction to Conflict Prevention*, London, Lynne Rienner Publishers.

Cockell, J G (2002), 'Planning Preventive Action: Context, Strategy, and Implementation', in Osler Hampson, F, Malone, D M (eds) *From Reaction to Conflict Prevention*, London, Lynne Rienner Publishers.

Danaher, K (1989), 'The US Struggle Over Sanctions Against South Africa', in Orkin, M (ed) *Sanctions Against Apartheid*, Cape Town, David Philip Publishers.

de Waal, A, Stanton, G H (2009), 'Should President Omar al-Bashir of Sudan be Charged and Arrested by the International Criminal Court?', *Genocide Studies and Prevention*, vol 4, no 3, 329–53.

Doxey, M P (1980), *Economic Sanctions and International Enforcement*, New York, Oxford University Press.

Durch, W J, Berkman, T C (2006), *Who Should Keep the Peace? Providing security for twenty-first-century peace operations*, Washington DC, The Henry L. Stimson Centre.

Environmental Change and Security Program (2005), Woodrow Wilson Center http://www.wilsoncenter.org/index.cfm?fuseaction=topics.item&news_id=114264&topic_id=1413, accessed 18

October 2009.

Fawthrop, T, Jarvis, H (eds) (2005), *Getting Away With Genocide? Elusive justice and the Khmer Rouge Tribunal*, Sydney, UNSW Press.

Fein, H (1984), 'Scenarios of Genocide: Models of Genocide and Critical Responses', in Charny, I W (ed), *Toward the Understanding and Prevention of Genocide: Proceedings of the international conference on the Holocaust and genocide*, Boulder USA, Westview Press.

Fein, H (1992), 'Dangerous States and Endangered Peoples: Implications of Life Integrity Violations Analysis', in Rupesinghe, K, Kuroda, M (eds), *Early Warning and Conflict Resolution*, New York, St. Martin's Press.

Fein, H (1993) 'Accounting for genocide after 1945: Theories and some findings', *International Journal on Minority and Group Rights*, vol 1, no 2, 79–106.

Fierens, J, (2005), 'Gacaca Courts: Between Fantasy and Reality', *Journal of International Criminal Justice*, vol 3, no 4, 896–919.

Fierke, K M (2005), *Diplomatic Interventions: Conflict and change in a globalizing world*, Basingstoke UK, Palgrave Macmillan.

Furst, T, Raso, G, Acka, C A, Tschannen, A B, N'Goran, E K, Utzinger, J (2009), 'Dynamics of Socioeconomic Risk Factors for Neglected Tropical Diseases and Malaria in an Armed Conflict', in *PLoS Neglected Tropical Disease*. http://www.plosntds.org/article/info:doi%2F10.1371%2F journal.pntd.0000513 accessed 19 October 2009.

Global Action to Prevent War Project (GAPWP), Program Statement 2008–2010 (2007), *Preventing Armed Violence and Ending War*, http://www.globalactionpw.org/ accessed 15 June 2007.

Gow, J (1997), *Triumph of the Lack of Will: International diplomacy and the Yugoslav war*, London, Hurst & Company.

Hamburg, D A, Holl, J E (1999), 'Preventing Deadly Conflict: From global housekeeping to neighbourhood watch' in *Global Public Goods: International co-operation in the 21st*

461

century, Kaul, I, Grunberg, I, Stern, M (eds), Oxford, Oxford University Press.

Hamburg, D A (2008), 'Education to Protect Humanity' (editorial), *Science*, vol 320, no 5880, 1133.

Hamburg, D A (2010a), *Preventing Genocide: Practical steps toward early detection and effective action*, Boulder CO, Paradigm Publishers.

Hamburg, DA (2010b), 'Recent Advances in Preventing Mass Violence', *Annals of the New York Academy of Sciences, Psychiatric and Neurologic Aspects of War*, vol 1208, 10–14.

Harff, B (1984), *Genocide and Human Rights*, Graduate School of International Studies, Denver, Northwestern University.

Homer-Dixon, T and Blitt, J (eds) (1998), *Ecoviolence: Links among environment, population, and security*, Lanham, Rowman and Littlefield Publishers Inc.

Horowitz, D L (2003), 'The Cracked Foundations of the Right to Secede', *Journal of Democracy*, vol 14, no 2, 5–17.

International Commission on Intervention and State Sovereignty (ICISS) Report (2001), *The Responsibility to Protect*, Ottawa, The International Development Research Centre.

Institute for International Economics (1998) http://www.iie.com/research/topics/sanctions/southafrica.cfm accessed 2 May 2006.

International Committee of the Red Cross (ICRC) (1999) Arms availability and violations of international humanitarian law http://www.icrc.org/web/eng/siteeng0.nsf/html/57JQ3M accessed 19 October, 2009.

Krasno, J, Hayes, B C, Daniel, D C F (2003), *Leverage for Success in United Nations Peace Operations*, Westport, Praeger.

Kuper, L (1981), *Genocide: Its political uses in the twentieth century*, London, Penguin.

Kuyper, P J (1978), *The Implementation of International Sanctions*, The Netherlands, Sijthoff & Noordhoff International Publishers.

Leaning, J (2002), 'Identifying Precursors', in Rittner, C, Roth, J

K, Smith, J M (eds), *Will Genocide Ever End?*, St Paul MN, Paragon House.

Lebor, A (2006) '*Complicity with Evil*': *The United Nations in the age of modern genocide*, New Haven, Yale University Press.

Levene, M (2000), 'Why is the Twentieth Century the Century of Genocide?', *Journal of World History*, vol 11, no 2, 305–36.

Moller, Bjorn, (29 May 2008), personal communication with Isabelle Macgregor.

Payne, R (1998), 'The Limits and Promise of Environmental Conflict Prevention: The Case of the GEF', *Journal of Peace Research*, vol 35, no 3, 363–80.

Ramet, S R (1999), *Balkan Babel: The disintegration of Yugoslavia from the death of Tito to the war for Kosovo*, third edition, Oxford, Westview Press.

Robertson, G (2002), *Crimes Against Humanity: The struggle for global justice*, London, Penguin Books.

Save-Soderbergh, B, Lennartsson, I N (2002), 'Electoral Assistance and Democratization', in Osler Hampson, F, Malone, D M (eds), *From Reaction to Conflict Prevention*, London, Lynne Rienner Publishers.

Schabas, W A (1997), 'Sentencing by International Tribunals: A human rights approach' http://www.law.duke.edu/journals/djcil/articles/djcil7p461.htm accessed 2 May 2006.

Schabas, W A,(2005), 'Genocide Trials and *Gacaca* Courts', *Journal of International Criminal Justice*, vol 3, no 4, 879–95.

Shawcross, W (2001), *Deliver Us From Evil: Warlords and peacekeepers in a world of endless conflict*, London, Bloomsbury Publishing.

Sloan, E C (1998), *Bosnia and the New Collective Security*, Westport, Praeger.

Smith, J G, Holt, V K, Durch, W J (2007), *Enhancing United Nations Capacity to Support Post-Conflict Policing and Rule of Law*, Stimson Center, Report No 63, Washington DC, The Henry L Stimson Center.

Stewart, F (2002), 'Horizontal Inequalities as Source of

Conflict', in Osler Hampson, F, Malone, D M (eds), *From Reaction to Conflict Prevention*, London, Lynne Rienner Publishers.

Straus, S (2007), 'Second-generation Comparative Research on Genocide', *World Politics*, vol 59, no 3, 476–501.

Summers, H G (1995), *Persian Gulf War Almanac*, New York, Facts on File.

Tanzler, D, Dabelko, G D, Carius, A (2004), *Environmental Cooperation and Conflict Prevention at the World Summit on Sustainable Development*, Adelphi Research, Mesoamerican Center for Sustainable Development of the Dry Tropics, National University of Costa Rica, The Environmental Change and Security Project (ECSP), Woodrow Wilson International Center for Scholars.

Teson, F R (2003), 'The liberal case for humanitarian intervention', in Holzgrefe, J L, Keohane, R O (eds) (2003), *Humanitarian Intervention: Ethical, legal and political dilemmas*, Cambridge, Cambridge University Press.

Thakur, R (2008), 'Al-Bashir Arrest Controversy', *Canberra Times*, 15 July 2008 http://www.canberratimes.com.au/news/opinion/editor ial/general/albashir-arrest-controversy/810954.aspx accessed 20 August, 2008.

Thoolen, H (1992), 'Information Aspects of Humanitarian Early Warning', in Rupesinghe, K, Kuroda, M (eds), *Early Warning and Conflict Resolution*, New York, St Martin's Press.

Valentino, B, Huth, P, Balch-Lindsay, D (2004), 'Draining the Sea': Mass Killing and Guerrilla Warfare', *International Organization*, vol 58, no 2, 375–407.

Valentino, B (2006), 'The Perils of Limited Humanitarian Intervention: Lessons From the 1990s', *Wisconsin International Law Journal*, vol 24, no 3, 724–40.

Valentino, B, Huth, P K, Croco, S E (2010), 'Bear Any Burden? How Democracies Minimize the Costs of War', *The Journal of Politics*, vol 72, no 2, 528–44.

Watson Institute for International Studies, Brown University (2011), The Eisenhower 'Costs of War' Research Project,

464

http://costsofwar.org/ accessed 30 July 2011.
Weitz, E D (2003), *A Century of Genocide: Utopias of race and nation*, Princeton and Oxford, Princeton University Press.
Wexler, R (2009), 'Medical Relief: Effective diplomacy', The Diplomatic Courier: A Global Affairs Magazine www.diplomaticourier.org accessed 11 October 2009.
Woodhouse, T, Bruce, R, Dando, M (eds) (1998), *Peacekeeping and Peacemaking: Towards effective intervention in post-cold war conflicts*, London, Macmillan Press.

RIGHTEOUSNESS IN THE FACE OF EVIL

PAUL R BARTROP

Genocide scholars study human evil. By contrast, only very rarely have acts of human goodness been examined, with the singular — and crucially important — example of those who tried to save lives during the Holocaust, people recognised by Israel and many around the world as the Righteous among the Nations (*Chassidei umot ha-olam*).[1] So little work has been done in respect of goodness during genocide, other than in the Holocaust, that one might despair at the predominance of evil in the world over the relatively few chronicled acts of goodness.

Yad Vashem — the Holocaust Heroes' and Martyr's Remembrance Authority in Israel — is charged with remembering the tragic events of the Holocaust and acknowledging those non-Jews who risked their lives, property or status to save Jews. Soon after the Yad Vashem statute was passed unanimously by Israel's Knesset on 18 May 1953, it was realised that a definition of 'righteous' behaviour was needed. After much redrafting, it was decided

---

[1] On Righteous Gentiles — in an already large literature — see especially Paldiel, Mordecai (2007), *The Righteous Among the Nations: Rescuers of Jews during the Holocaust*, New York, Harper; Tec, Nechama (1987), *When Light Pierced the Darkness: Christian rescue of Jews in Nazi-Occupied Poland*, New York, Oxford University Press; Gushee, David P (2003), *Righteous Gentiles of the Holocaust: Genocide and moral obligation*, 2nd ed, St Paul MN, Paragon House; Tammeus, Bill and Cukierkorn, Rabbi Jacques (2009), *They Were Just People: Stories of rescue in Poland during the Holocaust*, Columbia MO, University of Missouri Press; Oliner, Samuel P and Oliner, Pearl M (1988), *The Altruistic Personality: Rescuers of Jews in Nazi Europe*, New York, Free Press.

that for a person to be classed as 'Righteous', several criteria must first be met, specifically, that only a Jewish party can put forward a nomination; that helping a Jewish family member or individual to convert to Christianity is impermissible; that the assistance given had to have been repeated and/or substantial; and that the assistance had to have been given without any financial gain other than reasonable expenses for rent and food. Since 1963, a commission headed by a justice of the Supreme Court has been charged with investigating and awarding the title of 'Righteous among the Nations' to those fitting the criteria.

On balance, it might be said that the main forms of help extended by the Righteous during the Holocaust fitted one of four main categories: hiding Jews in the rescuer's home or on their property; providing false papers and false identities; smuggling and assisting Jews to escape; and, through various means, rescuing Jewish children. Given the enormous risks involved in rescue efforts, it is remarkable that any of these initiatives took place. This was a time when living space, food, sanitation facilities, and medicine were at a premium, and those who hid Jews risked not only their own lives, but, crucially, those of their families. Depending on where one was located, people caught hiding Jews were, more often than not, executed – either on the spot, or later, in public as an example to others. The eminent Holocaust historian, Christopher Browning, was once asked why there were so few 'Righteous'; his reply was to ask, how come there were so many?[2] Despite the immense dangers, by the beginning of January 2012, Yad Vashem had recognised 24,355 men and women from 45 countries as 'Righteous', representing over 10,000 authenticated acts of rescue.

---

[2] Personal communication from Colin Tatz; Browning made this comment at a Macquarie University workshop in the late 1990s.

It isn't easy being a rescuer. To stand out from the crowd, to refuse to acquiesce, to not compromise one's own values in order to guarantee personal safety at the expense of others — these are extremely difficult decisions for people when exposed to extreme situations. Human behaviour during the Holocaust is the paradigmatic example of this, but there have been many other instances, both before and after the Holocaust, that also fit the paradigm. This essay is a first attempt to look at several instances of goodness in genocide beyond the Holocaust. Acts of heroism do not have to be on a grand scale to be effective, and those attempting them do not always have to put their lives on the line when confronting acts of genocidal violence. While showing that there have been *some* exceptionally brave acts on the part of *some* individuals, this brief analysis demonstrates that it is in small ways that the worst excesses of genocide can sometimes be avoided.

The nature of 'goodness'

What do we mean when we speak about goodness in the face of evil? Genocide occurs for several reasons: to eliminate a real or imagined threat, to terrorise a real or potential enemy, to acquire wealth, and in the current context, most frequently to implement a belief or an ideology (for example, racial or ethnic 'purity'). In the latter case, genocide speaks of human dreams: of how we can perfect humanity, or the society in which we live, or the community of which we are part. In attempting to reach such 'perfection', some people deem it both necessary — and even proper — to eliminate those whom they consider impeding their goal. In their view, they do so with the 'best of intentions', and for the current good and guaranteed future of their group. Their victims, on the other hand, have neither a present nor a future, other than as a group that until now has avoided their intended fate.

While this might sound 'reasonable' to some, the twentieth century witnessed dozens of acts of murderous violence. Some were the victims of this violence; others were its perpetrators, who planned, carried out, and/or presided over it. Some stood by and watched it unfold, while others took it upon themselves to try to stop it. The perpetrators were committed, for reasons clear to them, to the realisation of the dream of achieving homogeneity, a 'pure' society comprised only of others like themselves, a place representing the closest possible approximation to their 'vision' of human perfection.

Even though perpetrators of genocide saw (and see) themselves as 'noble servants' undertaking a necessary struggle, obviously their victims do not agree. Nor, for the most part, do the vast majority of bystanders, though all too often they are either immobilised by the sheer horror of what they are witnessing, or silently acquiesce in the perpetrators' actions. Practically all agree that the deeds of genocide perpetrators are violent, inhumane, and from the perspective of Western tradition at least, morally wrong. Yet it takes exceptional courage and commitment to stand against them.

Theologians and philosophers are much more concerned about the problem of evil than they are about good. From a religious perspective, some will ask, if God (or the gods) is all-loving and all-powerful, why do the wicked prosper and the righteous suffer? While an answer might be that we are too puny to recognise God's Master Plan, but that everything will nonetheless work out for the best in the long run, this is far from acceptable to many secular thinkers, who prefer to look for other reasons to explain the problem of evil.[3]

---

[3] The problem of evil in the world is a massive one that has occupied the thoughts of philosophers, theologians and dreamers (among others) for millennia. While it is clearly not possible to provide a bibliography of the subject in a single footnote, the following are useful starting points insofar as they also refer to genocide: Wolfe, Alan (2011), *Political Evil: What it is and how to combat it*, New York, Knopf; Katz, Fred E (1993), *Ordinary People and Extraordinary Evil: A*

Very few consider the opposite pole of evil, namely, good. What is a 'good' action? Is it simply the opposite of evil? If evil behaviour is a departure or aberration from the norm, can that norm be labelled as 'good'? And if a person engages in some caring or compassionate action, is that *beyond* good? Further, does it matter why he or she does it? If a person does something out of the ordinary for the betterment of humanity, by what are their actions motivated? If they feel better by their actions than they did beforehand, are they in fact *self*-interested rather than *other*-interested? In some traditions, the motive matters less than the action, and thus if by virtue of that action a victim might be spared suffering or death, then it doesn't really matter why action was taken. On the other hand, the very notion that a 'good' action is something beyond 'normal' makes one wonder whether that norm is, in fact, ethically neutral until tested. The questions mount up with each successive issue raised.[4]

Goodness during genocide

Recently one of my seminar students asked: *is there a hierarchy of righteousness when we speak about acts of goodness in genocide?* An excellent question—the more so as I had been discussing

---

report on the beguilings of evil, Albany NY, State University of New York Press; Eagleton, Terry (2010), *On Evil*, New Haven CT, Yale University Press; and Morrow, Lance (2003), *Evil: An investigation*, New York, Basic Books.

[4] An excellent discussion of the question of goodness can be found in the Introduction to Grant, Ruth W (ed) (2011), *In Search of Goodness*, Chicago, University of Chicago Press. Other discussions of human goodness can be found: Needleman, Jacob (2007), *Why Can't We Be Good?*, New York, Jeremy P Tarcher/Penguin Books; and Shermer, Michael (2004), *The Science of Good and Evil: Why people cheat, gossip, care, share, and follow the golden rule*, New York, Henry Holt. A major recent work arguing that humans have become more and more good as society has evolved is Pinker, Steven (2011), *The Better Angels of Our Nature: Why violence has declined*, New York, Viking.

the actions of those who had saved lives as well as those who had saved elements of culture and gone out of their way to raise international awareness of what they had witnessed or experienced. There can be no greater act of righteousness than the saving of an innocent human life in danger, but what can we say about other acts of selfless courage that see people put themselves in danger to save the cultural, religious or other artefacts of another people's entire identity? They, too, have an important role to play in combating genocidal evil, given that genocide often seeks to destroy all traces of a group's existence. The issue was articulated in a short story by the Yiddish writer Chaim Grade, published in English in 1954:

> Here in Paris there's an old lady, a Lithuanian. I know her well. Everybody knows that in the Vilna ghetto she saved the lives of Jews, and also hid books. The Germans sentenced her to death, but she was spared by a miracle. She's an old revolutionist, an atheist; that is to say, she doesn't believe in God.
>
> Why do you think [she] saved the lives of Jews? [She] didn't try to make anyone an atheist; on the contrary, she hid our sacred books. [She] saved the lives of Jews not from pity alone, but for [her] own sake as well. [She] wanted to prove to [herself]…that the whole world does not consist only of criminals and those who are indifferent to the misfortunes of others. [She] wanted to save [her] own faith in human beings and the lives of Jews as well.[5]

In this case, the old woman sought to reaffirm life in the face of the forces that would destroy life, of humanity in the face of those who would expunge it. The nature of the many acts in which people of good will can engage when seeking to

---

[5] Grade, Chaim (1954), 'My Quarrel with Hersh Rasseyner' in Howe, Irving and Greenberg, Eliezer (eds), *A Treasury of Yiddish Stories*, New York, Viking, 604. This short story was later the basis of a Canadian movie, *The Quarrel* (director Eli Cohen 1991).

rescue humanity is immensely varied. But these acts serve to crack the edifice of terror, provide hope for others, and work for the defeat of those whose anti-human ideologies and goals threaten to return the world to a new Dark Age.

I have retrieved here but a few of these inspirational stories which might otherwise be lost and/or unrecognised. They are 'good' actions in the midst of the horror of genocide, and show what can be done in a positive and life-affirming sense, rather than through our continuing emphasis on the worst expressions of human behaviour as witnessed through the actions of the murderers.[6]

Zoran Mandlbaum

Zoran Mandlbaum is a former president of the Jewish community in the city of Mostar, the capital of Herzegovina. He is best remembered for having rescued innumerable Bosniaks during the Bosnian War of 1992–1995, earning the title of the 'Oskar Schindler of Bosnia'.[7] Born on 9 September 1946, as a young Jewish boy growing up in post-Holocaust Yugoslavia he was all too aware of how the Nazis and their collaborators had murdered many members of his family, and was conscious of the need to take care of life in the face of atrocity.

When the war began, the Mostar Jewish community, first established in 1570, had a population of some 128 members. For one of the few occasions in the history of Western warfare, Jews were on this occasion not a target for any of the warring

---

[6] For the most part, these accounts are largely unknown to the general public, and have been drawn from Bartrop, Paul R (2012), *A Biographical Encyclopedia of Contemporary Genocide: Portraits of evil and good*, Santa Barbara CA, ABC-CLIO.

[7] Schindler was a German industrialist who saved 1,100 Jews by employing them in his hardware factory, claiming that his products were essential to the Nazi war machine.

parties, and the Jewish community was more or less ignored by the Serbs, Croats and Bosniaks. Faced with this unique circumstance, and mindful of the Holocaust experience that preceded him, Mandlbaum decided to achieve positive human out-comes rather than simply stand by.

At first he helped civilian Serbs leave Mostar for safer territory. He then began remarkable initiatives, using his position to serve as a go-between respected by all sides. This was especially valued by those being held as prisoners in notorious Croat-run concentration camps like Heliodrom and Dretelj, where conditions were harsh and inhumane, with severe overcrowding, inadequate medical and sanitary facilities, insufficient food and water, deficient ventilation, and in the summer, suffocating heat.

Mandlbaum tried to find ways to get letters, news and food to those imprisoned. At the same time, he was also active in trying to save lives and bring families together. Coming from a city whose various communities had been largely integrated, he helped reunite dozens of couples in mixed relationships within the wider community; secretly he took one or another of those separated in the divided city across the Neretva River and to their waiting partner.

His activities did not stop there. Recalling how Jews seeking to flee Nazi persecution were forced to have the letter 'J' stamped in their passports as a draconian discriminatory measure, Mandlbaum decided that this negative could be turned into a positive through the forging of false documents for Bosniaks. He arranged that their identity documents also bear the letter 'J' (in Croatian, *Jevrejin* or Jew), and thereby certify that the bearers were Jewish. With these new identities, people were able to procure official documents to enable them to leave the country (and in some cases, obtain release from the concentration camps). He issued more than 200 documents bearing a 'Jewish' identity, facilitating the holders to leave the war zone for Croatia or other countries.

Soon after war came to Mostar, local Croatian forces gained control over most of the city. The Bosniak population west of the city centre were either expelled or sent to concentration camps. Those on the eastern side of the city were confined in a kind of ghetto, and lived through daily shelling and sniper fire. Cut off from the city and deprived of food supplies and medicine, the population soon found itself in crisis. Mandlbaum used his neutrality to bring in convoys of humanitarian aid. Managing to break through the military blockade, between 1993 and 1995 the Jewish community sent over 106,000 kilograms of food through to east Mostar, and thousands of letters from outside.

Unlike most residents of Mostar, Mandlbaum had the choice of whether or not to stay. He could have found safety elsewhere. Many Jewish families emigrated to Israel, or to Canada, Germany, Britain or Sweden. Closer to home, some moved to Croatia or Serbia. By the end of the war, it was estimated that only about 30 members of the Jewish community remained in Mostar. Mandlbaum could have stayed in the city to ensure the Jews were safe. But while doing this he remained in Mostar to help some of the innocent citizens who were in danger.

His efforts were not universally appreciated. During the war he faced a number of assassination attempts, was evicted from his apartment, and had his car blown up. When asked later why he put his own life at risk, he stated that as a Jew he called upon his religious heritage for inspiration at a time when he could otherwise easily have looked the other way. He was aware of the ruling in the Talmud that states: 'He who saves a life, saves a whole world' (Mishnah Sanhedrin 4:5; Babylonian Talmud Tractate Sanhedrin 37a), and that owing to the Jews' experience in World War II, Jews had a positive role to play in the future of Mostar. He was very conscious of his duty: in the fate of Mostar's Bosniaks, he recognised the historical fate of Jews everywhere. He wanted to show that people from different backgrounds, ethnicities and religions could live together. Zoran Mandlbaum continues to live in

Mostar. His attitude today is the same as it was during the war: he did nothing special, only that which was right in the face of suffering.

Sister Rachele Fassera, CMS

Rachele Fassera is a Roman Catholic nun of the Comboni order, best known around the world for her efforts in rescuing almost all of the girls kidnapped from her school by members of the Lord's Resistance Army (LRA) in northern Uganda in October 1996. She was born in Pessina Cremonese, Italy, on 15 June 1946. At the age of 19 she gave up her job with an Italian electricity company to become a missionary. Joining the Comboni Sisters, she was posted to Uganda in 1982 where she taught biology and eventually became the deputy head-mistress of St Mary's College for Girls, a residential boarding school in Aboke, northern Uganda.

Continuous war and massive killing of innocents was taking place in this region between the guerrilla army known as the Lord's Resistance Army (LRA), led by religious fanatic Joseph Kony, and the security forces of the Ugandan army. By 1986 the region had become completely devastated, with LRA slaughter and brutality, and the destruction of villages, homes, and schools the order of the day. The LRA made the kid-napping of children a priority: about 90 per cent of LRA soldiers were children under 16, and teenage girls were routinely forced to become sex slaves and 'wives' of the rebels.

At around 2:00 am on the night of 9–10 October 1996, some 200 armed members of the LRA broke into the dormitories of St Mary's College and abducted 139 girls aged between 13 and 16. They left at about 5:00 am, taking all the girls with them. After crisis discussions with other members of the faculty and the Mother Superior, Sr Alba, Sr Rachele and a young male teacher, John Bosco, decided to follow the rebels into the bush to rescue the girls. She took all the money she could find from the school office—enough to meet a ransom demand if there was one. The road was signposted with traces left by the rebels: food remains, discarded loot, and the like.

Eventually locating them later the same day, Sr Rachele immediately entered into negotiations with the commander, Mariano Ocaya. He was not interested in money, but offered instead to surrender some—though not all—of the girls. Making the offer that 109 of the girls could go, his trade-off was that 30 had to stay. Faced with this decision, Sr Rachele begged him for the lives of *all* the girls, offering her own in exchange for their freedom. He refused. If she did not accede to his demands, she was told, the LRA men would keep all 139. Thirty of the most attractive girls, already chosen by the rebels, would have to remain, and as an added trauma Sr Rachele herself would have to convey the news. After this, she was sent away with the 109 she had rescued, while the LRA and their captives slipped back into the bush.

Returning to Aboke, Sr Rachele immediately sought all possible means of freeing the girls, and appeals were made throughout the world to find ways of achieving their release. In a direct appeal to Pope John Paul II, she secured his support, and at his Sunday Mass on 20 October 1996 the Pope publicly called for the girls' freedom. This took the case to the international media, leading to other efforts to release the girls. Over the next several years, Sr Rachele met with United Nations Secretary-General Kofi Annan, United States First Lady Hillary Rodham Clinton, South African President Nelson Mandela, Libyan President Muammar al-Gaddafi, Sudanese President Omar al-Bashir, Zimbabwean President Robert Mugabe, presidents of a number of other African nations, members of the European Parliament, and many other diplomats. In short, the Aboke abductions and Sr Rachele's dramatic actions in pursuit of the LRA kidnappers drew what was up to that point unprecedented international attention to the insurgency in northern Uganda.

Waging her struggle for many years, Sr Rachele also

sought every avenue to negotiate the release of other hostages as well as the Aboke girls, making contacts wherever possible with political, military, religious, and other organisations in the region. In June 1997, she met with LRA commanders in Juba, Sudan, who initially denied that they held the girls. After a standoff, the commanders admitted that they did have the girls, and offered to release them if the Ugandan military declared a ceasefire. The Ugandan government of President Yoweri Museveni rejected the proposal and stated that it was not responsible for anything that might happen to the girls. Constant political bickering of this sort undoubtedly set back their cause repeatedly throughout the early part of the 21st century.

Five of the 30 girls died in captivity, while over time all but two of those remaining eventually made their escape. On 14 March 2009, Catherine Ajok, the last of the abducted Aboke girls still held by the rebels, returned to Uganda with her 21-month baby, who she said was fathered by Joseph Kony.

The story of Sr Rachele Fassera's action is an outstanding example of how to live by the courage of one's convictions, even at personal risk, and then to seek a peaceful solution through negotiation and dialogue. Her efforts helped bring world attention to the LRA's practice of abducting children, and even forced the Museveni government to start direct negotiations with Sudan in an effort to obtain the Aboke girls' release.[8]

---

[8] See also De Temmerman, Els (1995), *Aboke Girls: Children abducted in Northern Uganda*, Kampala, Fountain. With regard to the Lord's Resistance Army, a useful starting place is Eichstaedt, Peter (2009), *First Kill Your Family: Child soldiers of Uganda and the Lord's Resistance Army*, Chicago, Lawrence Hill Books.

Jakob Finci

Jakob Finci, a native of Sarajevo, is a leading member of the Bosnian Jewish community. During the Bosnian War of 1992–1995, as president of *La Benevolencija*, Bosnia's Jewish cultural, educational and humanitarian society, he provided medical and relief supplies and arranged for the evacuation to safety of over 3,000 people of all backgrounds.

Originating from a family that arrived in Sarajevo in the mid-16th century after the Jews' expulsion from Spain, Finci was born on 1 October 1943, soon after his parents had been liberated from an Italian internment camp. He graduated in law from the University of Sarajevo in 1966, and became an expert in international trade law. With war looming, in 1991 he set to work to bring goodness to his city. He was among a number of those again supporting the establishment of *La Benevolencija*, a Jewish cultural, educational and humanitarian society first established as far back as January 1892 for the purpose of fostering Jewish culture and tradition, rescuing Bosnian Jewish history, assisting with educational activities, and providing humanitarian assistance and health care to those in need.[9]

As vice-president in 1991, and then president from 1993, Finci directed an organisation that became the only local body delivering humanitarian relief on a non-sectarian basis. With the conflict spreading from Slovenia to Croatia during 1991, *La Benevolencija* managed to get medicine through the front lines to a small group of elderly Jews trapped in besieged Dubrovnik. In Sarajevo, Finci and his colleagues stockpiled medicines and foodstuffs sufficient to get through the winter. When the first shots were fired in the Bosnian War in April

---

[9] The website for the reconstituted *La Benevolencija*, outlining its many contemporary activities as well as its international connections, is: http://www.benevolencija.eu.org

1992, the organisation immediately planned and carried out the first evacuation of children and the elderly. *La Benevolencija* also opened a soup kitchen, serving 300 hot meals a day, seven days a week, for anyone who arrived.

The commitment shown by Finci, Ivica Ceresnjes, the then-president of the Jewish community of Bosnia–Herzegovina, and countless volunteers, saw remarkable humanitarian work undertaken during the siege of Sarajevo. In the first two years of the siege, *La Benevolencija* opened three pharmacies and dispensed 1.6 million prescriptions; opened the city's only clinic, where multi-ethnic staff tended 25,000 patients; gave away 380 tonnes of food; served 110,000 hot meals in the soup kitchen; started a postal service that handled 100,000 letters; set up a two-way radio connection with the outside world; looked after refugees from elsewhere in Bosnia; and started a thriving Sunday school for 50 children, only 20 of whom were Jewish.

On account of *La Benevolencija's* Jewish identity, the organisation found itself in a unique position of neutrality. Finci sought, and received, clearances from all warring parties that eventually enabled nearly 3,000 people, in 11 mixed rescue convoys of Muslim, Croat and Serb families, to flee the country. Somehow, the organisation managed to obtain permission from the Bosnian government for people to leave, negotiated safe passage from the Serbs, and arranged their entry to Croatia. Finci also arranged for 'new' Jews to leave — people who arrived at *La Benevolencija* headquarters stating that they had suddenly discovered a long-lost Jewish connection in their family. Among his many activities, Finci smuggled people out on false documents, even arranging for one elderly Muslim couple to use his own late parents' identities (and papers) as a way to clear Serb roadblocks.

Arranging for food convoys was not easy. Finci and his colleagues had to negotiate with all sides, and clear a path through up to 38 different checkpoints between Sarajevo and the ingress port of Split, Croatia. Finci would himself accompany *La Benevolencija's* two trucks to Split each month to get the much-needed supplies, and soldiers on all sides respected the efforts of the Jewish welfare body.

In 1995, Finci became the first elected president of the Jewish community of Bosnia–Herzegovina. By war's end, he had become one of Bosnia's most respected public figures. The esteem in which he was held saw him as one of the founders, in 1997, of a new Interreligious Council of Bosnia and Herzegovina (IRC), which worked towards reconciliation between the three ethnic groups, seeking to achieve peace and co-existence through the building of tolerance and a civil society. In February 2000, he was also elected chairman to a national committee charged with setting up a truth and reconciliation commission.

In an ironic twist, in 2008 Finci — though ineligible to run for parliament or the presidency owing to the terms of the Dayton Peace Agreement which only allows Serbs, Croats and Bosniaks to run for public office — was appointed to represent his country when he became the ambassador of Bosnia and Herzegovina to Switzerland.

Mbaye Diagne

Mbaye Diagne was a Senegalese army officer who worked as a United Nations Military Observer (MILOB) in Rwanda before and during the 1994 genocide. One of nine children, he studied at the University of Dakar before joining the Senegalese army. In 1993 he was assigned to the United Nations Assistance Mission for Rwanda (UNAMIR) covering the implementation of the Arusha peace settlement. He was stationed at the Hôtel des Mille Collines, one of Kigali's luxury hotels and the scene of a major sustained rescue of Tutsi throughout the genocide.[10]

---

[10] This was the location of the efforts by the hotel manager, Paul

Within hours of the start of the genocide on 6 April 1994, Diagne decided that his orders not to intervene were unacceptable. The morning after the assassination of President Juvénal Habyarimana, the next in line of succession, the moderate Hutu Prime Minister he Uwilingiyimana, was herself assassinated, with her husband, by Presidential Guards. Learning of Uwilingiyimana's murder, Diagne decided to investigate by going to the scene of the crime. There he found the Prime Minister's five children hiding in the adjoining housing compound of the United Nations Development Program. After a fruitless wait for UN evacuation trucks, he put the children into his own vehicle, hid them with blankets, and returned them to the relative safety of the Mille Collines. He then faced the problem of finding a way to evacuate them, undetected, to the airport, crossing the various checkpoints established by the *Interahamwe* militias, and once there, to obtain a passage for them out of the country. He achieved this and the children were removed safely on a Canadian transport that took them to Nairobi in Kenya.

It was a reckless and risky move, but would be only the first of many occasions on which the young officer would ignore the standing orders from UN headquarters to remain neutral. As a MILOB, his job was to try to find ways to prevent conflict and report on what he had seen; it was essentially a liaison and investigation role in which he was under orders not to get involved in any way. That was not what Diagne did. In the weeks following the start of the

---

Rusesabagina, to save the lives of over 1,200 people during the genocide. His means of doing so have since attracted considerable critical attention. See Rusesabagina, Paul (2006), *An Ordinary Man: An autobiography*, New York, Viking. The movie version of Rusesabagina's experience, *Hotel Rwanda* (director Terry George, 2004) predated by two years the appearance of his autobiography.

genocide, he worked hard to save the lives of hundreds of Rwandans, charming his way past the militias, smiling, joking, sharing cigarettes with the murderers, and over and over again talking his way through the roadblocks. His solo rescue missions, nearly always at great peril to himself, attained legendary status among the UN forces in Kigali.

Diagne's strength lay in his ability to persuade others of his friendliness and comradeship. His disposition helped him gain the confidence of families, groups, and leaders to all parties in the conflict. On occasion he would have to pass through up to 23 *Interahamwe* checkpoints to get to the people he was trying to save. The *Interahamwe*, who, depending on the time of day, could be drunk or drugged, had to be convinced on each occasion that he was not harbouring Tutsi. Diagne would find Tutsi who were hiding, drive them back through the same checkpoints, and then relocate them – often in the Amahoro Stadium, from where he would then ferry them to some other place of refuge. He was forced to undertake countless missions, as he could only carry three to four (sometimes, five, though this was extremely hazardous) at a time. Once, he spent an entire day operating in precisely this fashion after he came across a group of 25 Tutsi hiding in a house in Nyamirambé, Kigali. On each occasion he bluffed his way through roadblocks. He relied on his extensive contacts among the Hutu military and militias, his ability to defuse tense situations owing to a sharp sense of humour, and, from time to time, bribery in the form of cigarettes or money. His dynamism saw him seemingly everywhere at once.

It certainly helped that in his position as a MILOB he had access to most of the city and was known widely by all sides of the conflict. But in engaging in his acts of selflessness, he was repeatedly forced to flout his standing operational orders. UNAMIR's commander, General Roméo Dallaire, was aware of what Diagne was doing, but neither stopped him nor reprimanded him. While everyone in the UN establishment seemed to know of Diagne's actions, some believed that

Dallaire would not discipline him because it was a role Dallaire himself would have preferred to be doing.[11]

On 31 May 1994, Diagne was driving alone back to UN headquarters in Kigali with a message for Dallaire from the Chief of Staff of the Rwandan Armed Forces, Augustin Bizimungu. At this time the rebel Rwandan Patriotic Front (RPF) was closing in on Kigali, and engaging in fierce fighting with the Rwandan army. A random mortar shell, fired by the RPF towards a Hutu extremist checkpoint, landed behind his jeep. Shrapnel entered the rear window and hit Diagne in the back of the head, killing him instantly.

Mbaye Diagne was universally recognised as a real-life hero of the Rwandan genocide. On learning of his death, UNAMIR Force Headquarters held a minute of silence in his honour, and a small parade took place at Kigali airport on 1 June. A devout Muslim, he was buried in Senegal with full military honours. Later, his wife and two small children accepted, on his behalf, the UMURINZI Campaign against Genocide Medal awarded by Rwanda.[12]

Vedran Smailović

Vedran Smailović, known throughout the world as 'The Cellist of Sarajevo', was an inspirational musician whose playing of Tomaso Albinoni's *Adagio in G Minor* during a crucial time in the Bosnian War brought home to the West the horror of the siege of Sarajevo in a particularly poignant

---

[11] Dallaire's views on Mbaye Diagne can be found in Dallaire, Romeo and Beardsley, Brent (2003), *Shake Hands with the Devil: The failure of humanity in Rwanda*, Toronto, Random House Canada, 400.

[12] Extensive interviews with people who knew Diagne in Rwanda have been reproduced in the on-line resources accompanying the Frontline documentary *Ghosts of Rwanda* (director Greg Barker, 2004) http://www.pbs.org/wgbh/pages/frontline/shows/ghosts

manner. Born in Sarajevo on 11 November 1956, he came from a family of musicians. As an adult, the highly talented Smailović became well known for his playing with the Sarajevo String Quartet. He also played with the Sarajevo Opera, the Sarajevo Philharmonic Orchestra, the Symphony Orchestra RTV Sarajevo, and with the National Theatre of Sarajevo.

After the outbreak of war in April 1992, Smailović was confident that the city's unity and pluralistic values would prevail over the destruction that was taking place in other parts of Yugoslavia, and that it would be impossible to destroy such strong communal harmony. This ideal kept him buoyant during the siege, and enabled him to tolerate the cold, the food, power and water shortages, and the constant mortar bombings and sniper fire from the Bosnian Serbs in the hills surrounding the city.

On 27 May 1992 this attitude changed. A long queue waited patiently on Vaso Miskin Street for bread, in front of one of the last functioning bakeries in the city, and at approximately 10:00 am a mortar shell hit the line, killing 22 people and wounding 160 more. Others died in subsequent days. Enraged by what had happened and feeling powerless, Smailović decided he would at least try to raise the world's consciousness. He would protest the senseless killing, in a very public way, through his music. For the next 22 days, in honour of each of those killed in the bombing, Smailović gave a performance of Albinoni's *Adagio* – in ruined homes, in the open, in the smouldering remains of the National Library. His approach was simple. Dressed in formal attire as he was when playing for the Sarajevo Symphony, he would seat himself on a battered camp stool to play his music. Sometimes the sounds of war would drown him out, but he continued playing.

His heroic antiwar statement drew world attention, though in the constant retelling of the story of 'The Cellist of Sarajevo' some of the detail was lost. (For example, word was conveyed that Smailović would always play at 4:00 pm, in the same place as where the mortar hit—notwithstanding that the attack took place at 10:00 am, or that Smailović varied his location so as not to get shot by sniper fire.) His protest didn't end after 22 days; indeed, he had been playing since the siege began until he left Sarajevo in December 1993, often playing for free at funerals, in graveyards and bombsites.

As his story began to circulate, Smailović became a symbol for peace in Bosnia. An English composer, David Wilde, was so moved by Smailović's defiant act that he wrote a composition for unaccompanied cello, simply called 'The Cellist of Sarajevo'. One of the world's most accomplished cellists, Yo-Yo Ma, then played this piece at the International Cello Festival in Manchester in 1994 with Smailović present. Several other creative artists, from rock bands to folk singers, have also paid tribute to Smailović.[13]

Vedran Smailović managed to leave Sarajevo in December 1993, relocating to Northern Ireland. Celebrated as a musician who defied the city's snipers, Smailović showed that the human spirit can resist as powerfully as the physical kind. He would not succumb to terror, making a statement that the forces that would destroy his city could not destroy the spirit of the people.

---

[13] A controversy arose in 2008 after use was made of a character based on Smailović in a novel by Canadian author Steven Galloway (2008), *The Cellist of Sarajevo*, Toronto, Vintage Canada. Upon learning of the novel's existence, Smailović publicly expressed his outrage over the appearance of a book that used his persona without authority, and with no possibility of financial compensation. He was incensed by the novel, which he saw as capitalising on his act. Galloway has repeatedly denied this; rather, he has asserted, he was paying tribute to Smailović through literature.

Father Vjekoslav Ćurić

Vjekoslav 'Vjeko' Ćurić was a Bosnian Croat Franciscan priest and humanitarian, best known for his role in helping to save Rwandan Tutsi threatened with annihilation during the genocide of 1994. Born in Lupoglava, Bosnia–Herzegovina on 26 April 1957, he studied in Visoko, central Bosnia, and in Sarajevo. He entered the Franciscan order, and was ordained on 21 June 1982. On 18 August 1983 he began his missionary work in Rwanda, one of the first volunteers of the Franciscan Africa Project.

It was in Rwanda, during and after the genocide of 1994, that Ćurić's service was at its most intense. Reportedly one of only two non-African Catholic priests to remain in the country throughout the genocide, his actions saved hundreds of lives. He revealed later that he had sheltered many Tutsi from the *Interahamwe* and *Impuzamugambi* militias, having secretly ferried them out of the country in the bottom of his truck. At the beginning of the genocide, he similarly saved the lives of a number of white clergy — many of them Belgian priests, monks and nuns — who were in danger. He allegedly received an order direct from the Vatican to leave the country, but refused to do so, claiming that while his flock was in danger he could not abandon them.

By 1994, Ćurić was a long-term resident of Gitarama, working to help develop his parish of Kivumu. He was well-known and liked, and when the killing got under way in April and May the local people looked to him for rescue. Ćurić remained in the country at a time when almost all expatriates were leaving. True to his ideals, he made a stand with the people of Kivumu. He threw himself into the work of providing assistance to all who could reach him, as well as helping others to escape. He continued preaching the Gospel, condemning the violence and calling for peace.

After the genocide, Ćurić continued his work in Kivumu. He helped resettle widows and re-establish their shattered lives, and set up educational projects for children. He remained impartial throughout, helping both Hutu and Tutsi rebuild their shared community, blind to the differences that had so divided them just weeks earlier. For this, he was viewed by many Hutu as a Tutsi collaborator. In 1996, he escaped an attempt on his life but still refused to leave, against the advice of many. His attitude was that he had stayed during the genocide and would not abandon his congregation now that peace had come.

On 31 January 1998, he was shot in his car, murdered in the heart of downtown Kigali. The perpetrators are not known. The Catholic Church immediately declared that he had gone to a martyr's death after devoting himself to the rescue of others for the glory of God and love of his neighbours. He was buried in Kivumu, the community he had served without interruption for 15 years, in a church which he and his congregation had built. His funeral was attended by Rwandan Prime Minister Pierre-Célestin Rwigema and other members of the government, along with a vast number of Catholic and other Christians, as well as representatives from the Jewish and Islamic communities.

Some in Rwanda refer to Ćurić as Africa's 'Oskar Schindler'. In 2005, Ćurić's story formed the backdrop of a movie about Rwanda, *Shooting Dogs* (directed by Michael Caton-Jones), released in the United States as *Beyond the Gates*. The writer of the original story, David Belton, was also the movie's producer; both he and the screenwriter, David Wolsencroft, knew Ćurić in Rwanda in 1994, as he had saved them from the militias on a number of occasions. They employed their memories of Ćurić as the inspiration for one of the film's leading characters, Father Christopher, played by the British actor John Hurt.

Inela Nogić

Inela Nogić is a Bosniak woman who achieved worldwide

fame at 17 when, during the siege of Sarajevo, she won the 1993 Miss Sarajevo beauty pageant, held in a basement to avoid sniper attacks from Bosnian Serb militias. Born into a strict Muslim family in 1976, she was a good student at school. With the outbreak of war in Bosnia in 1992 her neighbourhood became known colloquially as 'Little Hiroshima' because of the destruction that soon ravaged it, but Nogić and her friends decided to make the best of the situation by not succumbing. An attractive young woman in a city renowned for what some have termed 'Sarajevo style' — a combination of French chic and Italian flair — the pretty blonde commented to reporters during the siege that maintaining a good appearance through attention to hair and make-up was a way for young women to show those bent on their murder that youth, beauty and life could win out over the forces that would destroy them.

In 1993, Inela Nogić became the symbol of that attitude for all young Bosniak women. As the siege continued, the idea of organising a beauty pageant, 'Miss Sarajevo 1993', came from a group of young Sarajevans committed to maintaining the life of the city and showing the world that the conditions under which they were living were intolerable even though their spirit would not be broken. Inela Nogić was encouraged to enter by her mother. European aid agencies and NATO administrators, taken with the idea of a beauty pageant right under the noses of those seeking the destruction of the city, ensured that the contest, which took place on 29 May 1993, would be transmitted across the world. While inspiring, it was also sad to watch. Many of the young women participating, clearly affected by the siege and the war, appeared undernourished and sickly. At the end of the pageant, in an especially poignant moment, Nogić and the other contestants held up a banner that read 'DON'T LET THEM KILL US!'

An American journalist and film director, Bill Carter, had arrived in Sarajevo in the winter of 1993 to work with the Serious Road Trip, an aid organisation founded in London in

1991 for delivering food to orphans affected by war. In Sarajevo he shot hundreds of hours of video, including coverage of the Miss Sarajevo pageant. In later discussions in Italy with Bono, the lead singer of the rock band U2, Carter suggested a documentary based on Sarajevo's underground resistance movement. Bono reputedly jumped at the idea; not only to produce the film, but also to provide the necessary funds. The result was *Miss Sarajevo*. Subsequently broadcast across the globe, it provoked a viewer response calling for an end to the siege and the bloodshed. Later, Bono and U2, together with Brian Eno, and featuring a cameo solo by Luciano Pavarotti, used footage from the movie to create a film clip for a single of the same name. Inela Nogić was featured on the cover.[14]

Popular imagination soon created the urban legend that the winner of the Miss Sarajevo pageant had been killed by sniper fire, but it is possible to speculate that the pageant may have potentially saved Inela Nogić's life. As a result of the publicity, she met a Dutch journalist, and a year later the couple moved to the Netherlands, where they settled down and had two children. She then studied graphic design, and took up residence in Amsterdam.

In 1997, U2 was scheduled to perform in Sarajevo, the first rock band able to host a concert in the city since the end of the war. Bono contacted Nogić, then doing modelling work in France. He organised for his private plane to take her from Nice to Sarajevo where she was met by NATO military authorities. They escorted her to the concert at the Koševo Stadium along with the band members, and Bono sang *Miss Sarajevo* in her presence as U2's special guest.

---

[14] On his quest to bring news and awareness of the plight of Sarajevo to the world, see Carter, Bill (2005), *Fools Rush In: A true story of love, war, and redemption*, 2nd edition, Tuscon AZ, Schaffer Press.

Nogić was to say later that the objective of the pageant was to show that the war was about more than just men and guns, but that women had a part to play in defying the aims of the killers. In Balkan tradition—whether it is Serb, Bosniak or Croatian—the noun '*inat*' translates roughly into a notion of actions taken 'in spite of the consequences'. It embodies a spirit of defiance regardless of what might come next. Nogić's *inat* was thus symbolic of a wider defiance relating to Sarajevo's struggle to retain its humanity.

Conclusion

What can we learn from these brief descriptions? Are these men and women representative of how *all* 'good' people behave during genocide? To recall my student's question about a hierarchy of righteousness, is there not a significant difference between people who work to save lives—a beauty queen and a musician—regardless of the same environment of horror in which their actions were played out?

Many scholars have attempted to answer the question of why people engage in altruistic acts. The literature is now substantial, with much of it concluding that, at base, people are really decent, and that outbreaks of radical evil occur only under the most extreme conditions. More often than not, such literature fits into a self-help model designed to reinforce the 'you can do it' approach of that large and growing genre. (Few, on the other hand, have taken the other approach and tried to consider why people *do not* help. In 1970 two psychologists, Bibb Latané and John M Darley, wrote *The Unresponsive Bystander: Why doesn't he help?*, based on a series of human laboratory experiments they had undertaken earlier.[15]) Resistance to genocidal evil takes place for many reasons, some of which have been sketched in this essay. Why do people put themselves on the line to save others—or, in

---

[15] Latané, Bibb and Darley, John M (1970), *The Unresponsive Bystander: Why doesn't he help?*, Englewood Cliffs NJ, Prentice-Hall.

lieu of that, the culture of others? The question is as broad as it is difficult to answer. Some reasons will include religious and ethical beliefs; resistance against those occupying their country or perpetrating war crimes, crimes against humanity, and other massive human rights violations against fellow citizens; simple, human anger at the atrocities they were witnessing; and a sense of compassion for those in a worse position than themselves, regardless of ethnic, racial, religious, political, social or national circumstances.[16]

The accounts highlighted here—each different from the other, in many ways—point to one unifying fact: that people *can* make a difference, even amid dire of situations. 'Goodness' is very much a notion dependent on the opinion of the beholder, making it often impossible to define it in a universally acceptable manner. As applied to genocide, perhaps we can rest with the view of United States Supreme Court Justice Potter Stewart to describe his threshold test for pornography in *Jacobellis vs Ohio* (378 US 184, 1964): 'I know it when I see it.' Hardly scientific, it is nonetheless a starting point for further discussions relating to the positive behaviour that illuminates, however faintly, the awful darkness of genocide. Indeed, it is that very light that ensures that the act of saving humans can also be one that saves humanity—a necessary act of grace for us all, lest the world despair at its own impotence in the face of the destructive side of the inclination of mankind to perform acts of unalloyed evil.

---

[16] A recent work has appeared suggesting that others are also beginning to see a need to examine this issue of why. See Press, Eyal (2012), *Beautiful Souls: Saying no, breaking ranks, and heeding the voice of conscience in dark times*, New York: Farrar, Straus and Giroux, 2012.

THE AUTHORS

Vicken Babkenian is an independent researcher for the Australian Institute for Holocaust and Genocide Studies and honorary secretary of the Armenian Historical Society of Australia. He is the author of several key journal articles on the Armenian Relief Movement in Australia, and he curates exhibitions depicting the genocidal events and their aftermath in Turkey from 1914 to 1928.

Email: vbab124@gmail.com

Ruth Balint is currently senior lecturer in history in the School of Humanities at the University of New South Wales. She writes on transnational histories of migration, borders, refugees, documentary film, and contemporary Australian history. She is the author of *Troubled Waters: Borders, boundaries and possession in the Timor Sea*, Sydney, Allen & Unwin, 2005.

Email: r.balint@unsw.edu.au

Paul R Bartrop is Professor of History and Director of the Center for Judaic, Holocaust, and Human Rights Studies at Florida Gulf Coast University, Fort Myers, Florida. He was for many years honorary fellow at Deakin University, Melbourne, and head of the department of History at Bialik College, Melbourne. He is the author or editor of ten books.

Email: pbartrop@hotmail.com

Devin C Bowles is a doctoral student at the National Centre for Epidemiology and Population Health at the Australian National University in Canberra. He has research degrees in anthropology and psychology. His current work focuses on links between climate change, conflict, and health. Previous publication topics include Aboriginal history and colonisation, and impaired facial recognition.

Email: Devin.bowles@anu.edu.au

David Denborough works (with **Cheryl White**) as a teacher, writer/editor and a community practitioner for Dulwich Centre, an independent organisation operating out of Adelaide. His books include *Collective Narrative Practice: Responding to individuals, groups, and communities who have experienced trauma; Trauma: Narrative responses to traumatic experience;* and *Beyond the Prison: Gathering dreams of freedom.* See www.dulwichcentre.com.au

Email: dulwich@dulwichcentre.com.au

Panayiotis Diamadis co-ordinates the Genocide Studies course at the University of Technology Sydney, and teaches senior secondary history at St Ignatius' College, Riverview. He researches aspects of the Hellenic, Armenian and Assyrian Genocides (1914–1924), including Australian responses to those genocides and the experiences of Australian prisoners of war in the Ottoman Empire.

Email: pxdiamadis@riverview.nsw.edu.au

Michael Dudley AM is a psychiatrist at Prince of Wales and Sydney Children's Hospitals, lectures in psychiatry at the University of New South Wales, and has special interests in suicide prevention, refugee and Indigenous mental health. He is principal editor (with Derrick Silove and Fran Gale) of *Mental Health and Human Rights: Vision, praxis and courage,* Oxford University Press, 2012.

Email: m.dudley@unsw.edu.au

Fran Gale is a political scientist who researches and writes in the areas of social justice, marginality and human rights. She lectures in Social Work in the School of Social Sciences, University of Western Sydney. Fran is co-editor, with Michael Dudley and Derrick Silove, of *Mental Health and Human Rights: Vision, praxis and courage*, Oxford University Press, 2012.

Email: fw.gale@uws.edu.au

Winton Higgins is a visiting fellow at the Transforming Cultures Research Centre, Arts and Social Sciences, University of Technology Sydney, and a member of the board of the Australian Institute for Holocaust and Genocide Studies. He researches and publishes work in genocide studies, political theory, political economy, the history and theory of standardisation, and Buddhism.

Email: winton.higgins@uts.edu.au

Robert M Kaplan is a forensic psychiatrist-historian and an associate professor in the Graduate School of Medicine, University of Wollongong, NSW. He is a prolific author and sought-after speaker. His particular interest is psycho-biography, and his recent book, *The Exceptional Brain*, addresses the part that illness has played in the lives of many famous people from a variety of fields.

Email: rob.liaison@gmail.com

Isabelle Macgregor is a doctoral student in International Relations at the Australian National University, focusing on aspects of genocide prevention and intervention. She has a chapter forthcoming on media and genocide in *Impediments to the Prevention and Intervention of Genocide: A critical bibliographic review, volume 9*. She has also published work on Jewish voting in Australia.

Email: Isabelle.s.macgregor@gmail.com

Paul O'Shea is Dean of Mission at Rosebank College in Sydney. His life and work of Pope Pius XII, *A Cross Too Heavy* (Macmillan, 2011), analyses issues in Catholic, Jewish and modern European history. A director of the Australian Institute of Holocaust and Genocide Studies, he is a member of the NSW Council of Christians and Jews.

Email: pauldoshea@iprimus.com.au

Rowan Savage teaches in the fields of Genocide Studies, Communications, and International Studies at the University of Technology Sydney. In addition to his work within the academy, he is a regular contributor to the American-based popular music magazine, *Tiny Mix Tapes*. His research areas include genocide and dehumanisation, animal studies, Buddhism, gender and sexuality, and popular culture.

Email: rowan.g.savage@hotmail.com

Colin Tatz AO is a founding director of the Australian Institute for Holocaust and Genocide Studies, visiting fellow in Politics and International Relations at the Australian National University, and honorary visiting fellow at the Australian Institute of Aboriginal and Torres Strait Islander Studies. He teaches and publishes in comparative race politics, youth suicide, migration studies, and sports history.

Email: colintatz@gmail.com

Garry Walter AM holds the chair of Child and Adolescent Psychiatry at the University of Sydney. He is also the Clinical Director of Child and Adolescent Mental Health Services, Northern Sydney Local Health District. The long-standing editor of *Australasian Psychiatry*, he researches and writes on ethics, stigma, the psychological effects of severe trauma, mood disorders, and psychiatric treatments.

Email: gwalter@mail.usyd.edu.au

Cheryl White is a publisher, editor, teacher, training co-ordinator, conference and project initiator at the Dulwich Centre, Adelaide. Cheryl has co-edited *Conversations About Gender, Culture, Violence & Narrative Practice: Stories of hope and complexity from women of many cultures.* Cheryl and **David Denborough** have completed community assignments in Bosnia, Rwanda, Uganda, Canada, Brazil, Argentina, Chile, the Palestine Authority, Austria, Norway, South Africa and in several Australian Aboriginal communities.

Email: dulwich@dulwichcentre.com.au

Shannon Woodcock specialises in Romanian Romani history and genocide survival in Eastern Europe. She currently researches in Albania, and her next monograph is about surviving everyday life under the Communist dictatorship of Enver Hoxha. She has taught genocide studies in Australia, Albania and Macedonia. Her play about the after-effects of political executions in Albanian families has been performed in England and Australia.

Email: scrangasi@gmail.com